UP CLOSE
& PERSONAL?

SECOND EDITION

UP CLOSE & PERSONAL?

Customer Relationship Marketing @ Work

**PAUL R GAMBLE MERLIN STONE
NEIL WOODCOCK BRYAN FOSS**

IBM®

KOGAN
PAGE

London and Sterling, VA

To Jean, Luke and Annabelle
Paul

To Ofra, Maya and Talya
Merlin

To Mum, Dad and Julie
Neil

First published in Great Britain in 1999
Reprinted 2001
Second edition published in Great Britain and the United States in 2003 by Kogan Page Limited

120 Pentonville Road   22883 Quicksilver Drive
London N1 9JN   Sterling VA 20166–2012
UK   USA

British Library Cataloguing in Publication Data

A CIP record for this book is available from the British Library.

ISBN 0 7494 3831 2

Typeset by Saxon Graphics Ltd, Derby
Printed and bound by Biddles Ltd, Guildford and King's Lynn
www.biddles.co.uk

Contents

Forewords

This book opens with a quote from Ecclesiastes which tells us that there is 'no new thing under the sun' and this is certainly a true statement from a 30,000 foot level. When descending to a perspective much closer to the real world this view holds more nuances for debate, especially when taking into account the virtual realities that today's networked world offers.

Remember when Ford introduced the model-T and the consumers could get any colour car as long as it was black? There are still many lessons to be learnt from this classic marketing failure. Denying the e-business realities of today is providing your customers a black model-T – it is denying that your customers are looking for the choices that are out there today! As one leading banker put it, 'In the future, customers will need financial services . . . but they won't need banks.'

In today's world, markets and industries are defined in terms of customers rather than products. While market power is shifting to customers, industry boundaries are collapsing and modular production and marketing systems have become more important. Products will cease to be the basis for lasting differentiation. Instead, maximizing the number of transactions with the same loyal customer by offering a diverse array of products and services has become increasingly important.

The critical denominator in today's commercial world is customer relationship marketing, which, to go back to Ecclesiastics, is not a new fact; but the nuance is in the execution.

Technological innovation is sharply cutting customer interaction costs. It allows for an increasing reach into new markets without adding high incremental market entry costs. It allows for specific tailored customer marketing. It allows for increased responsiveness. It allows for companies to act global and tap into the 'profit pool' of markets that are cross-border.

This book clearly leads the way in demonstrating that in the e-business market-space with changing buying behaviours and new emerging business models no company can afford to stand still when it comes to customer relationship marketing. Generating customer loyalty has become a pervasive board-level issue.

Ginni Rometty
General Manager, Global Insurance Sector, IBM Corporation

In his book *Information Anxiety*, author Richard Saul Wurman points out that more information has been produced in the last 30 years than during the previous 5,000. For example, there are 600 million credit cards worldwide and 100 billion credit card transactions a year in the United States alone. And Web site hits are generating mountains of data. Industry experts tell us the amount of information available today is doubling every five years, and that many companies are able to keep up with and use less than 7 per cent of the information they produce.

All this has created a revolution in the worldwide business landscape. Companies of all sizes are experiencing the rise of intense international competition and the need for faster product cycles. Customers are becoming more independent, and more demanding. To remain competitive, corporations must be very well informed about their customers, employees and suppliers. Many are developing new business models and implementing cutting-edge knowledge management solutions to manage this explosive growth.

For instance, business intelligence technology, including data warehousing and data mining, is increasingly playing a key role in sorting everything out – gathering, managing, analyzing and distributing vast amounts of information in order to gain insights that drive business decisions and knowledge, which help build lasting relationships with customers.

But while this book discusses the importance of tapping into the knowledge wealth that exists in every enterprise, it also goes a step further, talking about the need for buy-in to a shared set of values. Relationships, if they are to have any meaning, are a two-way-street. Effective e-business and customer relationship management depend not only on good technology, but a willingness to listen and respond.

While IBM's recent success as an e-business company speaks for itself – we practise what we preach – we continue to hone our ability to truly hear what our customers have to say and to be responsive to their needs in a timely fashion. Working with and for IBM, the authors of this book are able to share some of what we learnt, hopefully to the benefit of companies large and small around the globe.

Ben Barnes
General Manager, Global Business Intelligence Solutions,
IBM Corporation

Acknowledgements

We would like to thank all those colleagues in universities and commercial enterprises who have influenced our ideas in writing this book. Any errors or misunderstandings we do, of course, attribute to ourselves.

The Authors

I should like to thank Mike Wallbridge of BT, for setting me on the road to what was later relabelled as customer relationship marketing; Doug Houston, formerly of BP and now of NatWest – a loyal customer; IBMers all over the world, and especially Harvey Thompson in the US, and Jonathan Miller, John Mullaly, Bryan Foss, Mark Cerasale, Richard Lowrie, Arthur Parker, Kevin Condron and Ron Hulman in the UK, and John Cutterham and Doug Morrison in Australia. All the members of my Database User Group, whose experience in managing customers has provided confirmation of much of our thinking. Colleagues at Swallow Information Systems (especially Dave Cox and Steve Quigley) for making sure that I understand that complaints are to be taken seriously! Colleagues at Berry Consulting, especially Martin Hickley, Julian Berry, David Backinsell and Barry Leventhal, for their wisdom on data. Colleagues at QCi Ltd, especially Paul Weston and David Williams, whose work on developing and marketing our Customer Management Assessment Tool has provided firm quantitative foundation for our assertions; Liz Machtynger for teaching me how to manage customers; Tony Woods, the canniest information master I have ever met. Clients and other colleagues almost too numerous to mention, but particularly Bill Savage at Norwich Union, Jon Epstein of Results R Us, Cliff Hudson of Homebase, Russell Bowman of British Airways, Janet Davies of American Express, Stephanie Penning and Nigel Armstead at SAS Institute.

Merlin Stone

1

Customer relationship marketing: one more time?

The thing that hath been, it is that which shall be; and that which is done is that which shall be done; and there is no new thing under the sun.

(Ecclesiastes 1:2)

New management paradigms have a way of going from blue sky ('what a wild idea!') to hyper expectation ('implementing these procedures and technologies will solve *all* your problems and give you a significant competitive advantage') through to disillusion ('it didn't work – I want my money back'). The importance of managing customers and being managed by customers became a real force in corporate philosophy in the mid to late 1990s. At this point, there is therefore the possibility that we could now be moving into the trough of despond and looking around for the newest management panacea. Yet there is clearly some way to go. The American Customer Satisfaction Index, an index that has tracked levels of customer satisfaction in major US industries since 1994, shows that satisfaction scores for airlines, banks, department stores, fast food restaurants, hospitals, hotels and telephone companies have actually all declined. A number of reasons can be advanced for this, especially in view of the downturn in the economic cycle in 2001 and the events of 11 September 2001. They might include cost reduction pressures, reduction of investment in human factors in favour of technology, or even the attitude of senior management, as it seeks to shape the culture, structure, systems and processes within a company. Whatever the explanation, there is important work still to be done if companies are to reap the benefits of relationship marketing and improve their customer relations.

Co-operatives of buyers and sellers can be traced back to the eighteenth century during the time of the Napoleonic wars but the earliest trading co-operative, recognizable in modern commercial terms, was set up in 1844. A group of 28 impoverished weavers founded a mutual-aid society, called the Rochdale Society of Equitable Pioneers, in England. The Rochdale Society developed a set of principles that might still have something to offer a contemporary enterprise. These related to control, treatment of members, re-investment, distribution of profits, training and development, and even strategic alliances.

Rather more recently, Berry (1983) was probably one of the first researchers to introduce the concept in its modern sense. Berry took the view that the approach to marketing, which had developed very largely over the last fifty years or so in the United States, was inappropriate in some business situations. Traditional marketing is based on the idea of the marketing mix and takes a predominantly short-term transactional approach, using the concept of exchange. By the early eighties it had become apparent that this paradigm was no longer the best framework for business-to-business marketing or even for services, where long-term relationships with customers are often critical to success.

The concept of customer relationship marketing has become one of those 'born again' marketing terms to be found on the lips of every marketing manager, most service managers, some advertising managers and even a few sales managers. It is often associated with phrases or buzzwords that seem to hype up the pace such as 'one to one marketing' or 'marketing to a segment of one'. Yet it is often not fully understood or properly implemented. This is because, in practice, it can be very hard to manage. As an ordinary person, anyone can understand intuitively what is meant by a relationship. Relationships exist when two people acknowledge each other, they kick back and relax together, they share common interests and help each other out. Can you really do that if your customer base numbers several hundred thousand or even just a few hundred?

Many modern businesses still formulate their marketing platforms based on the old ideas of transaction marketing. Marketing is something we do to our customers. We collect some information about them, we figure out what that means in terms of products and services and then we try to provide them. Periodically, we recheck our information to make sure we are on track. For many of these companies this is sufficient, but this is not customer relationship marketing. The customer does not participate in this process. There is no actual relationship in which both parties participate equally. Other companies want to move beyond one-off transactions or even repeated transactions to an interactive, two-way connection with their customer base.

WHY IS RELATIONSHIP MARKETING IMPORTANT?

In a small business or one with very few customers, it is easier to keep in touch with what your customers would like you to do. As the scale and scope of an enterprise increases, the marketing problem becomes more acute. How can you be sure that the mailshot to 100,000 people does not include one or two who complained to you only last week? What about the 10,000 people who bought your product just to try it but who will probably stay loyal to their old supplier? Is it worth worrying if we lose 5,000 customers each month if we can replace them with another 5,000? Grönroos (1990) suggested that transaction marketing was probably still the best approach to large scale consumer markets and that customer relationship marketing was at the other end of the spectrum for business to business or services.

In 1990 it was possible to choose from one of 40 different credit cards on offer in the UK. Ten years later, that number had increased to over 1,500. Now ask yourself (as a consumer of financial services) what is likely to influence your choice of service provider. Certainly there will be some objective measures to do with features and service but in fiercely competitive markets, where highly targeted niching is possible, it is probably the relationship with your supplier that swings the balance.

Customer relationship marketing is more than just a different way of combining existing marketing tools and managing them. Between 1990 and today, the world has seen enormous transformations in the extent to which organizations can deploy computing power. This technology has altered and continues to alter some markets out of all recognition.

The financial services industry is just one example but it only takes a moment to remember how the Internet, or even just TV shopping channels, have changed things. Call centre technology has developed in response to these changes. Mobile telephony, call centres, customer contact centres, IP (Internet Protocol) telephony and digital interactive television (DITV) are working away on other areas. Indeed, some writers such as Copulsky and Wolf (1990) associate customer relationship marketing very closely with the technology that is often used to support the approach. They use the term in the highly specific sense of database marketing where a range of demographic, lifestyle and purchasing behaviour data are maintained. This is then used as the basis for targeting differentiated products to selected customer groups. In turn, their response to each marketing contact is tracked and used to further refine the approach.

IS CUSTOMER RELATIONSHIP MARKETING PROFITABLE?

Big databases are expensive to develop and maintain. Organizations such as Wal-Mart have spent literally hundreds of millions of dollars on their technology. Setting aside for the moment the possible coincidence that Wal-Mart became one of the world's most successful and important retail chains over a period of not much more than a decade, was this really worthwhile?

Most marketing texts will tell you that acquiring customers is much more expensive than keeping them. Figures of between 5 times as much and 7 times as much are quoted (Kotler, 2003: 75). This is most obvious in direct marketing, where the costs of acquiring and keeping customers can be accurately quantified but it is also true in other marketing environments. Unfortunately, few management accounting systems allow all of the costs associated with acquiring new customers to be quantified, or can identify changes in the number of customers or even changes in what each customer is buying from you. Nevertheless, it is possible to illustrate the profit potential of customer relationship marketing with two simple arguments: one based on costs, the other on profits.

First, based on costs. Suppose a company loses 100 customers each week and gains 100 new ones. In one sense, therefore, it seems to maintain its position. In reality, since the cost of acquiring those new customers is higher than the cost of maintaining the existing customer base, significant profit potential is being lost. In addition, extra marketing and administrative costs are being incurred. For each new customer, the costs of welcoming and learning about those customers must be borne. All of the internal administration concerning credit checking and billing must be set up. There are also opportunity losses. Since we do not know so much about a new customer, the prospects for upselling and cross selling are reduced. It is true that the new customers might actually be of better quality but high rates of churn are sustainable only if there is a constant supply of new customers and if the (expensive) resources to determine their potential value are quickly available.

Second, based on profit. Classic marketing theory concentrates on transactions rather than relationships. This tends to give an emphasis to attracting new customers rather than retaining existing customers. Unfortunately, this is also reflected in the orientation of accounting systems, which tend to look backwards. A profit and loss statement tells a manager largely about what has already happened, from which some inferences about what is happening right now may be made. It is true that future orders may be reflected in an accounting system in the form of advance payments but these revenues should properly be accrued and credited to a future period. Thus managers are encouraged to focus on pre-sales activity and sales activity rather than on post-sales activity. Few organizations seem to differentiate between the sources of their revenue in terms of new and existing, customers and products. Reichheld and Sasser (1990) have suggested that a company can improve profits by anywhere between 25 and 85 per cent by reducing customer defections by a mere 5 per cent. However, to understand these kinds of benefits, accounting systems need to be modified to show some relationship measures. These might include lifetime value of loyal customers, share of customer's wallet (how much of their total spend in a product or service category is attracted by your company), value added through upselling (encouraging customers to buy enhanced versions or to use additional services) and cross selling (selling other products such as setting up a loan to a credit card customer).

COSTS AND BENEFITS OF CUSTOMER RELATIONSHIP MARKETING

The benefits of customer relationship marketing were neatly summarized by Day, Dean and Reynolds (1998) and are usually in one or more of these areas:

- Closer relationships with customers. Over time, the company develops links with customers through technology, knowledge, information or even social ties. Such a tie gives the company an advantage. Similarly, the more customers share information with the company about themselves, the more reluctant they are to repeat the process with a rival (Craig, 1990; Grönroos, 1990, 1993; Peppers and Rodgers, 1994).
- Improvements in customer satisfaction. There is a dialogue between the company and the customer that enables the company to ensure that customer satisfaction is maintained. The dialogue enables the company to tailor products and services very closely to (individual) customer needs and to develop new products and services to meet changing needs or even anticipate emerging needs (Clark and Payne, 1994; Palmer, 1994; Peppers and Rodgers, 1997).
- Financial benefits ensue. You gain: (1) Increased customer retention and loyalty – customers stay with you longer, buy more from you, and buy more often (increased *lifetime value*); (2) Higher customer profitability, partly because the costs of recruiting customers are reduced – indeed, they may even pay a premium for services. Apart from anything else, you have a lesser need to recruit so many if you want to do a steady volume of business. As each party learns to interact with the other, relationship costs on both sides fall. There is an increased level of sales since existing customers are usually more responsive to your marketing efforts. Improved customer retention and improved employee retention may be associated (Reichheld and Kenny, 1990; Reichheld and Sasser, 1990; Fay, 1994).

In dollars and cents, this means that your management accounts need to present new kinds of measures that will enable marketing managers to make more informed decisions based on a customer relationship marketing philosophy. Let us take retention as an illustration:

1. Obtain measures of retention. This can be presented in terms of 'churn', 'attrition' and persistence depending on whether customers rotate between suppliers (car insurance), move to other products (white goods) or simply lapse (magazine subscriptions).
2. Find out why customers are lost. Some cannot be retrieved if they have moved outside the product category or if their lifestyle has changed. Nevertheless, a proportion might have drifted away for relatively trivial reasons. For example, people only buy household

furnishings periodically. They may simply have lost touch with you since they last bought a couch.

3. Calculate the lost profit. Here is where the notion of lifetime value comes in. This is difficult, but not impossible, to estimate accurately. Suppose the average customer buys ten TVs over their lifetime at an average spend of £500. Assume the profit on each sale is 40 per cent. The total potential profit from each new customer is therefore 40 per cent of £5,000 or £2,000.

4. Now multiply that by the number of retrievable customers who are lost. If that figure were even as small as 1,000 each year, it would be worth spending up to £2 million if all of these customers could be retained, or even £1 million to retain half of them.

CUSTOMER-LED OR MARKET ORIENTED?

It is important to clarify what we mean by customer relationship marketing in terms of a marketing approach. A few years ago, a marketing book like this would have talked about a product versus a market orientation. This is a rather sterile debate nowadays but how can it be suggested that a customer-led approach is somehow wrong?

Obviously, it would be foolish to go so far as to suggest that customer-led marketing is totally mistaken. After all, a marketing concept which says that an organization's purpose is to discover wants and needs and then satisfy them more effectively and efficiently than the competition has served marketers well over many years. Nevertheless, it is very important to recognize that customer relationship marketing is meant to be market oriented and not customer oriented. In consequence, some relationship marketing ideas ('some customers can be bad for you') can be rather shocking to traditional marketers.

A customer-led business focuses primarily on existing markets. Typically, it uses tools like focus groups and customer surveys to enhance understanding of those customers and techniques like concept testing and conjoint analysis to guide the development of new products and services. Retail banking is a good example of this approach. Many retail banks have developed large customer information files from data generated by the banks' transaction systems. This sounds pretty good until you realize that can lead to a rather reactive, short-term response. Two well-known management gurus have called this 'the tyranny of the served market' (Hamel and

Prahalad, 1994) since managers tend to see the world only through the eyes of their current customers. It is suggested that the tyranny of the served market can substantially reduce a firm's ability to innovate since customers are 'notoriously lacking in foresight' and they point to the problems that arose in the disk drive industry as an example. Furthermore, traditional market research tools are often limited when it comes to developing innovative products or services. These depend on customers being able to articulate what they need and being able to help devise solutions to these problems. In particular, customer satisfaction surveys are unreliable indicators of intentions to purchase or to remain loyal.

Market-led businesses are committed to understanding both the expressed and latent needs of their customers and the capabilities and plans of their competitors. They work in a quite different information environment which is much more open and fluid. They continuously create superior customer value by sharing knowledge broadly throughout the enterprise and may integrate their knowledge base with that of some suppliers and customers. They scan the market more broadly, adopt a longer-term focus and attach much more value to generating knowledge. Based on a closer relationship and a two-way dialogue, a market-oriented company closely observes how customers actually use products and services in everyday life and thus acquire information not available by normal market research. In some cases they may even second their own staff to work with customers.

They also work closely with lead users. A lead user is not necessarily a large customer. It is a customer, or potential customer, whose needs are advanced compared to the market as a whole and who expect to benefit from a solution to those needs (Tabrizi and Walleigh, 1997). The aim, therefore, is to 'push out the boundaries of current product concepts [by putting] the most advanced technology possible into the hands of the world's most sophisticated and demanding users' (Hamel and Prahalad, p. 102). A true lead user is, therefore, a window into the future. Of course, no one can ever forecast the future with certainty, so a probe and learn approach, as used by companies such as Motorola, General Electric or Corning, is used to maintain a strong market position. Market-oriented businesses are concerned not only with the served market but also with the unserved market, which is the basis of continuing organizational renewal.

The key differences between the two approaches are well described by Slater and Narver (1998).

Table 1.1 Characteristics of customer-led versus market-oriented businesses

	Customer-Led	Market Oriented
Strategic orientation	Expressed wants	Latent needs
Adjustment style	Responsive	Proactive
Temporal focus	Short-term	Long-term
Objective	Customer satisfaction	Customer value
Learning type	Adaptive (follows trends)	Generative (new insights help it to anticipate trends)
Learning processes	Customer surveys	Customer observation
	Key account relationships	Lead user relationship
	Focus groups	Continuous experimentation and dialogue
	Concept testing	Dialogue
	Selective partnering	

(After Slater and Narver, 1998)

SO, WHAT DOES CUSTOMER RELATIONSHIP MARKETING MEAN?

Notice that the phrase 'market orientation' has been used, not 'marketing orientation'. This is because marketing may sometimes be seen as a function that belongs to only one part of the enterprise. In customer relationship marketing it is very important that the entire enterprise buys into and feels ownership of the concept.

Based on these ideas, we would suggest that the key to successful long-term strategic positioning depends on three main activities:

- innovation;
- quality;
- customer relationships.

We therefore define customer relationship marketing like this:

> Customer relationship marketing is an enterprise-wide commitment to identify your named, individual customers and create a relationship between your company and these customers so long as that relationship is mutually beneficial.

This definition, while technically a good one, is a little lacking in feeling. In marketing one of the best ways to define a concept or technique is in terms of what you want your customers to think or feel as a result of your using it, one you could even explain to customers. So for your customers, customer relationship marketing could be described like this:

We will:

- Use our best media or data to find you. We will try not to target people who won't buy from us; in other words, we will try not to waste your time or ours.
- Get to know you and keep a two-way dialogue open.
- Try to ensure that you get what you want from us, not just in the product but in every aspect of our dealings with you. This may mean that we work closely with you to develop solutions to your problems.
- Check that you are getting what we promised you.
- Ensure commitment to these values across our enterprise, that means we will co-ordinate and manage all the elements of our value chain with you in mind.
- Develop processes and procedures to enable this to work.

This is subject to:

- The revenue we get from you exceeding the costs of serving you by an acceptable amount: it has to be worthwhile for us as well as for you.

WHAT'S DIFFERENT ABOUT CUSTOMER RELATIONSHIP MARKETING?

Reading the above simple definitions of customer relationship marketing, you might wonder what all the fuss is about. Shouldn't all companies have been practising customer relationship marketing for years? The answer to this is, perhaps surprisingly, no. There are some marketing situations when transaction marketing is still appropriate. Clearly not every organization is aiming to develop a long-term relationship with its customers. However, the approach is not confined to large organizations, nor does it necessarily depend on huge investments in IT. Small businesses are often the best relationship marketers around. Nevertheless, as a business gets larger, the organization of a relationship approach requires more thought. By the time you have a couple of million customers, such as an airline, the problem of maintaining relationships can be quite tricky.

Let us have a look at two important areas of marketing, high-street retailing and consumer goods brand management, to see where relationship marketing is making an impact.

HIGH-STREET RETAILING IN THE UK

The major development of the late 1990s was that the supermarket chain Tesco overtook its main rival Sainsbury's in market share. In 1995, Tesco held 13.9 per cent of the FMCG retail market, with Sainsbury's at only 12.5 per cent. In March 1996, Sainsbury's announced its first fall in profits for more than 20 years, from £808 million to £764 million. This announcement coincided with the imminent launch of its *Reward* customer loyalty card.

In 1995 Sainsbury's ran a localized, tactical card scheme, the *Saver Card*, in about 50 stores, which it planned to extend to the whole of the UK but then abandoned the idea. At that stage, there was still disagreement amongst senior management on the issue. There were also problems with the EPOS tills as some customers wanted to use three cards, credit/debit, discount and loyalty – and this was not possible. The late and problematic launch of the *Reward* card contrasted with the success of its DIY subsidiary at the time, Homebase, which was sold to Permira in December 2000. Homebase's *Spend & Save* loyalty card, was one of the most successful retail loyalty cards, with 40 per cent of transactions at Homebase using the card. The DIY chain was the best performing part of the group, with operating profits rising 18 per cent to £36.2 million in the year to March 1996.

The *Spend & Save* card was one of Homebase's strongest marketing weapons. Together with Homebase's strong policy on merchandise selection, store location and layout, the card made life very difficult for all its competitors during a recession that saw most of its competitors under perform. This success contrasted with Sainsbury's relatively weak performance.

The difference in the two cultures was noticeable. Sainsbury's *Saver Card* was used as a tactical tool to support under-performing stores rather than for strategic customer management. Sainsbury's conservatism led it to consider Homebase's success as an interesting experiment that worked well in a rather small market sector. Homebase's highest profits were less than 5 per cent of Sainsbury's, even after the latter's had fallen. Homebase continues to do well.

Retailers differ in their views about the relationship aspects of marketing. Among the mass-market providers, Marks & Spencer and Safeway have led the way in exploring relationship marketing. The Marks & Spencer credit card could be described as the best retail loyalty device without promotional benefits. Benefiting from Marks & Spencer's refusal to take other credit cards until April 2000 and (initially) debit cards, it led to the building of a database of customers who responded well to offers, ranging from store open evenings to financial services. Managed conservatively and with careful branding, it has no doubt been partly responsible for the high regard consumers have for retailers as potential (or actual) suppliers of financial services.

Safeway, which used to be considered as 'the company that follows Sainsbury's', used its *ABC* loyalty card to break away from this perception and has concentrated on devising ways of making its card-holders feel special, including the introduction of self-scanning. Implemented conservatively, since British retailers are not usually adventurous and are particularly concerned not to complicate matters at the point of sale, *ABC* was a real hit with customers in its five years of use to June 2000. It was partly responsible for Safeway's continuing progress against larger competitors. Tracking studies showed that Safeway had achieved image leadership in several key dimensions. Like for like sales increased by more than 7 per cent and the value of the average shopping basket increased by 12 per cent (Gofton, 1996a). After June 2000 Safeway dropped the use of loyalty cards for in-store customers, offering instead price promotions. The ABC card was continued for online shoppers, whose relationship needs are more evident. Even so, rival Tesco was unconvinced, and saw new opportunities to target Safeway customers by offering personal services through its own loyalty scheme.

Tesco, as a later entrant, was sensibly determined to take the best of what other companies have done and implement it faster, using its new found position as Britain's top grocery retailer. Its *Clubcard*, with point-of-sale statementing, was followed relatively rapidly by its own credit card, *Clubcard Plus*, with its innovative added value of giving customers a relatively simple way of lending and borrowing money, attuned to Tesco's market. This device allowed customers to substitute the card for a range of other ways of saving for 'rainy days' and celebrations. With *Clubcard Plus*, customers could pay into their accounts each month by standing order and receive interests on their deposits. Half of all the *Clubcard Plus* accounts have resulted from direct mail, and 70 per cent of the first year's targets was achieved in three months (Gofton and Cobb, 1996).

Tesco's *Clubcard* manager says that when Tesco distributes money-off coupons to its database of seven million households, it does so after much planning with its suppliers. Tesco welcomes approaches from manufacturers to be included in these promotions but is not interested in offers that will cause brand switching for shoppers already buying in

Tesco. The focus is on what will work best for the loyalty programme and for Tesco (Gofton, 1996b). All this left Sainsbury's struggling to catch up. By 2001 Tesco group sales had grown to £22.7 billion with just over £1 billion profit, an increase of 12 per cent on the previous year.

BRAND MANAGEMENT

Brand management aims to build in customers' minds a set of perceptions and attitudes relating to a product or service, leading to positive buying behaviour. In order to achieve this, brand managers must know a great deal about their customers. The power of a brand is measured to some extent by its effect on buyers. When a brand is powerful, customers will either defer or refuse to purchase if the brand is unavailable. Indeed, some brands are so strong that their usage has passed into everyday speech to replace ordinary words. People talk about *Xeroxing* a document rather than copying it and *Fedexing* a package rather than posting it.

A brand comprises a number of elements, some of which are internal to the customer and some of which are external. Kapferer (1992) calls this a 'prism of identity'. The internal elements include:

- Personality – this is the main dimension in FMCG markets and is what consumers describe when asked to talk about the brand.
- Culture – the social context in which the brand is perceived, such as the engineering excellence and solidity of Germany's Mercedes or the striving for personal success of the United States' Nike.
- Self-image – what we think the brand says about us. 'I don't just ride a bike, I ride a Harley'.

The external elements include:

- Physique – the physical characteristics of the brand; what does it do?
- Reflection – the type of user the brand is aimed at. 'If I smoke these cigarettes, I will be like the Marlboro cowboy.'
- Relationship – this is an important element of a brand. After all, if people do not buy the brand repeatedly, in other words have a relationship with the brand, then it really is not working.

Direct marketing techniques have improved to the extent where several major consumer brand suppliers have developed databases of their best customers and are starting to send them incentives to buy: the beginnings of customer relationship marketing. In fact, customer relationship marketing is becoming vital to brand managers. High-street retailers have exploited their brand names very effectively so that the power of retailers' *own brands* has grown. Retailers can draw on their huge transactional databases to switch buyers of branded goods towards their own brands. FMCG companies such as Heinz, Procter and Gamble and Unilever are fighting to catch up with other industries like insurance and finance, automotive and even utilities. They are seeking to integrate the techniques of customer relationship marketing with their traditional brand-building activities. This is based on a combination of database technology, direct mail and use of the Internet. The intention is to make the relationship with the brand strong enough to offset the effects of *own label*.

PROBLEMS WITH FUNCTIONAL MARKETING

You may have noticed that marketing is traditionally organized from a functional point of view. Thus organizations tend to focus on *techniques*, such as advertising, direct mail, selling and public relations, or *tools*, such as databases, market research and advertising agencies. However, from your customers' viewpoint, all marketing actions help to create and maintain their relationship with you.

The reason why marketing is generally organized functionally is that each function uses specific technical disciplines and agencies that work closely with managers in these disciplines. If these disciplines are not managed properly then marketing as a whole is likely to be ineffective and costly.

However, this functionalization of marketing has one big disadvantage. It leads to a lack of co-ordination of all the initiatives designed to influence and manage your customers. This lack of co-ordination is exacerbated by the fact that other functions, which may not be controlled by marketing or sales, such as customer service, credit control or distribution, also have contact with your customers. In addition, third parties working on your behalf, like distributors, couriers, transport firms, debt factors or call centres, also have their own contacts, as shown in Figure 1.1.

The result is often that the customer experiences a series of disparate and often conflicting contacts with you. Sometimes this does not

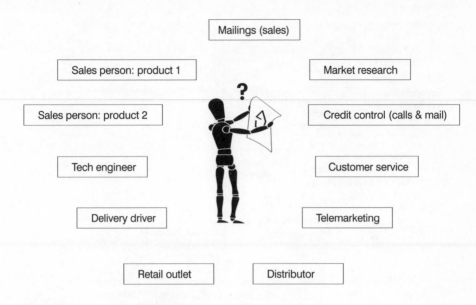

Figure 1.1 Potential customer contact points

matter. However, in an increasing number of cases, failure to manage the whole relationship leads to inconsistencies and dissatisfaction. Just imagine that you stop by your local store to complain and are promised a refund. The next day, a sales person calls to sell you the same product you just returned and then, the day after, you receive a mailshot describing you as a valued customer!

Customer relationship marketing aims to provide a framework within which all other marketing activities can be managed to win, retain and develop customers.

THE EVOLUTION OF CUSTOMER RELATIONSHIP MARKETING

The conflict between specialized marketing disciplines and customer relationship marketing can often be better understood if they are seen in a historical perspective. In many markets, you can see a cycle such as that in Figure 1.2. The cycle can be illustrated using the plain-paper photocopier market.

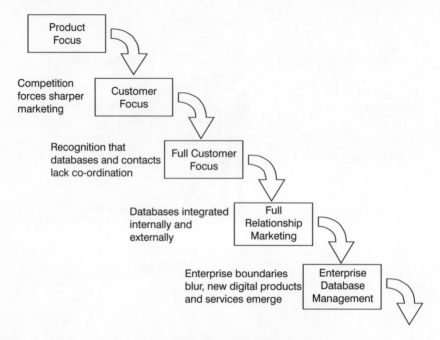

Figure 1.2 Evolutionary path to customer relationship marketing

Stage 1: Product focus

In the early stages of the cycle, the leading supplier has products or services that are significantly better than those of its competitors. Customers are happy enough to obtain them. It gains share and profitability. No matter how well other companies try to compensate for product or service weaknesses by relationship management, they will lose.

In the early period of the plain-paper photocopier market, Xerox's role was once described as 'organizing queues for the product'. The service organization found it hard to keep up with the requirements of a rapidly expanding installed base. Administration of customer accounts was not too hot, although it should have been, as customers were billed monthly (at this stage the business was rental only).

However, the customer base was expanding so fast that customer administration could barely keep up with the workload.

Stage 2: Customer focus

The high profits earned now attract competition, so several other companies begin offering a similar product or service. Competition intensifies in the areas of features and price. Companies try to maintain differentiation through the feature mix and through branding. In consumer markets, advertising expenditure increases dramatically. At this stage, Xerox still had a lead in product technology – particularly for higher volume, faster machines – but the Japanese were catching up fast. However, in order to cope with the demands of what was an exploding overall market, the Japanese were forced to use dealers to cover the market. The dealers, like Xerox, were very sales and profits oriented and were not too concerned about after-sales service and administration.

Stage 3: Full customer focus

As a result, from a technical point of view, there is little to distinguish between products. If companies have been successful in branding (as in many consumer goods markets), leaders continue to lead and to sustain their leadership by high advertising and promotional spend coupled with slight 'tweaks' to the product. Customer service now becomes very important.

Initially, customer service focuses on aspects such as product mainten-ance or customer training. Eventually it moves into the area of customer care. Here the aim is to ensure that the benefits from the product or service are delivered reliably from the first point of contact. This is not quite customer relationship marketing, since the customer may still be approached by the same organization in a different guise with an attempt to sell the same product!

For Xerox, this was the era when substantial investments were made in customer service systems and service market research. It also organized the field service operation to meet not just internal targets such as response times to calls but also targets based on what customers actually wanted. After all, the customer does not really want a fast breakdown service, what they really want is a machine that does not break down at all. Xerox therefore focused on uptime (the period for which the machine was running properly).

Although Japanese competitors were able to take a lead over Xerox in the design of smaller copiers in this phase, only Kodak and to a lesser extent IBM ever succeeded in rivalling Xerox's designs for larger copiers. For many customers, it was only Xerox's service that kept them loyal.

Stage 4: Full relationship marketing

When everyone has got their house in order in respect of product, branding and customer service, suppliers must aim to manage all aspects of their relationship with customers in a co-ordinated way. This may not be entirely feasible, especially if the customer base is very large or varied.

It is now important to recognize that diversity and to identify the different kinds of relationship that it will be possible to sustain with different types of customers. In Xerox's case, the sales force for managing sales, service and administrative relationships used account management techniques with larger customers. Smaller customers were managed using direct marketing techniques such as telephone and direct mail with as much automation as possible.

This sort of channel management strategy is representative of the general approach. Of course, it is not quite as simple as described here but the objective is good coverage of the customer base, appropriate cost control for each contact channel and use of the right skill sets at the right time.

Stage 5: Enterprise relationship management

The relationship marketing approach now has to permeate everything the enterprise does. Observing customers closely, or working directly with them to address their reprographic, data distribution and print technology needs, can show where new solutions are needed.

Once a market has become used to the benefits of customer relationship marketing, it never quite forgets the lessons. Customers will expect reasonable standards of service and relationship marketing from other suppliers of new products, even if they are not the best. As soon as competition emerges, they will also expect the best from them. So although Xerox and then Hewlett Packard established dominance in the photocopier-based laser printer market, service levels of the first few years could never be tolerated again. They had to deliver higher standards of customer service and relationship marketing than they did in the early days of photocopiers.

Before embarking on a programme to initiate or improve customer relationship marketing, it is vital for the company to identify where it stands in this cycle. This will determine what its priorities should be. In order to do this, it needs an auditing tool.

THE BASIS OF A CUSTOMER RELATIONSHIP MARKETING AUDIT

Figure 1.3 illustrates the overview that is needed to manage an enterprise-wide approach. Let us examine the elements in this model briefly.

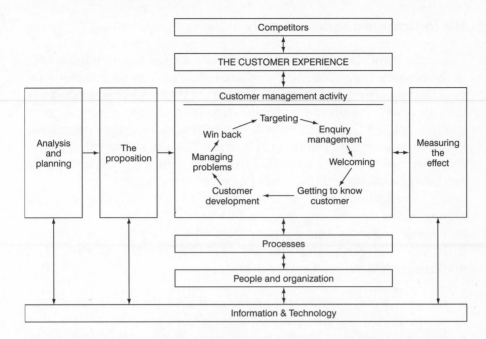

Figure 1.3 Customer relationship marketing model © QCi Assessment Ltd. Used with permission

Analysis and planning

Everything starts with understanding the behaviour, attitudes and values of different customers and customer groups. This understanding is partly derived from internal information sources such as your customer databases and partly derived from external sources such as your customer intelligence systems. This will drive more questions, which will in turn refine the research programme. Once the learning process has been started it is possible to plan for acquisition, retention and penetration of the market effectively.

The proposition

Enhanced understanding will help define the proposition to each customer group and plan the appropriate value-based activity. Having defined the proposition it should be communicated effectively to both customers and to the people who will deliver it. Not only do suppliers and intermediaries need to be informed; so do employees.

The customer management activity

These plans and objectives will then drive activities through the whole of the customer life cycle. Since we are concerned with customer relationship marketing, it is worth remembering that relationships differ as they develop. We do not treat old friends in the same way as new friends. Relationships also have different durations. Some people we know for a long time, some very briefly. The marketing relationship therefore needs to vary according to the stage in the relationship, the marketing strategy and the kind of product or service.

In the diagram, this is represented by a cycle: targeting, enquiry management, welcoming, getting to know, customer development, managing problems and winback. Not all customers move through each of these stages for the same period of time or at the same rate. The marketing approach varies at each stage:

- for prospects, as they are stimulated and then converted into customers through the enquiry management process;
- for new customers, as we make them feel welcome and get to know their relationship needs and preferred way of being managed;
- for established customers, to understand their potential for purchasing other products and services (upgrading or cross selling).

We must also ensure that we have a process, in Toyota's phrase, 'to delight customers when they are dissatisfied and win loyalty'. We also need a way of parting on good terms and winning back those customers that we would like to return.

People, processes and technology

People deliver this activity and are supported by leadership and by the enterprise structure. The enterprise structure may be real or virtual, insourced or outsourced. Crucially, all members of the enterprise must understand and accept the shared values required for customer relationship marketing. They must also possess the competencies needed to do the job and to develop these further with training.

Processes are managed within a quality system that encourages both continuous improvement and step change. Our suppliers may manage some processes for us. This may take a conventional commercial form or be based on closer relationships such as partnering or strategic alliances.

Technology supports all the above and enables the structured collection and effective processing of data to meet the fully defined business process. Information is acquired and managed in such a way as to be kept up to date.

The customer experience

Customers experience both our products and services and those of our competitors. We need to understand how these change attitudes and behaviours.

Measurement

A useful way of determining the direction of progress in each of these areas is to measure it. Developing the right metrics for some of these elements is not easy but the measurement of values, knowledge, process efficiency, profitability and customers' attitudes underpins our vision and objectives. It enables managers to judge levels of success and failure. Feeding back success and failure into the analysis refines and redefines our plans and future activity in a continuous improvement loop.

The examples from the retail and FMCG industries given earlier show that the importance of customer relationship marketing depends partly on whether an edge has already been gained by any other players in the market. If not, the potential for increased market share and profit is great.

GAINING A COMPETITIVE EDGE

The problem now is how to assess our own customer relationship marketing strategies and to measure these against the competition. To do that, some sort of measurement or audit tool is needed. The British company, QCi, has developed one such tool for evaluating a company's relative position in each of these areas. Their customer management assessment tool (CMAT) diagnostic process is based on the model in Figure 1.3. Through observation, discussion and an analysis of evidence, CMAT seeks to assess a company's customer relationship marketing capability. The CMAT software processes the results against a database of results to compare a company's progression over time. An idea of movement or progression can then be built up. It also provides a comparison of a company's relative ranking against other blue chip companies in their sector or across all sectors. This gives a score against a world-class benchmark.

The range of CMAT scores for some major organizations is shown in Table 1.2.

Table 1.2 Range of QCi's customer management assessment scores for 51 FTSE top 250 companies and multinational global corporations

Element	Mean %	Range %
Overall	34	19–66
Analysis and planning	30	10–73
The proposition	32	1–83
People and organization	40	25–70
Information and technology	40	13–94
Process management	32	7–75
Customer management activity	33	21–64
Measuring the effect	35	14–73
Customer experience	31	6–72

All the companies in the database are major corporations and most of them are household names. Since a perfect score would be 100 per cent, it is apparent that there is room for improvement almost everywhere. Notice particularly the wide range of results. None of the companies scored highly in all the areas.

The professionalism with which your customer relationship marketing is managed (designed, planned and implemented) offers scope for differentiation and competitive advantage. Positioning is an important part of this too. It supports and is supported by good customer relationship marketing. All aspects of contact with your customers must be managed and presented to them to reinforce positioning. Let us consider some of the expectations that customers might have, if they are to have a positive overall experience:

- When customers require service they expect details of their relationship with you to be available to whoever is delivering the service and to be used if relevant.
- If they are ordering a product or service they expect information they have given to you about their needs, not just recently but over the years, to be used to identify which product or service is best for them.

- If you ask them for information about their selection and use of the product at the welcome stage, they expect you to respond to their answers and acknowledge their needs.
- If they are in contact with several different members of your company's staff they expect their actions to be co-ordinated.
- They expect you to consider their needs for a relationship, not just for individual transactions within the relationship.
- If there are problems on the customer's side, such as meeting payments or service problems that are the customer's fault, they expect their past relationships with you to be taken into consideration.
- Loyal customers expect to have better relationships with you than if they were not loyal.

These are just some of the expectations your customers might have. Obviously not all your customers have all these expectations all of the time but generally some of these factors are in play at any moment. As the key to competitive marketing lies in fulfilling relevant customer expectations better than the competition, you need to take these expectations seriously. We know that customers who are satisfied with the relationship will not necessarily buy more and may even buy less if a competitor comes up with a better product or service. Nevertheless, the better the relationship you have with your customers, the more likely they are to have doubts about going to your competitors.

CUSTOMER RELATIONSHIP MARKETING AND THE PRODUCT

Of course, if your product or service does not match the customer benefits offered by the competition then nothing will protect your market share in the long run. In competitive markets, a key element in marketing is defining and bringing to the market products that meet customer needs while making the right profit for the supplier. However, usually the customer does not just buy a physical product or a tightly defined service. Customers buy a product, associated services and indeed the whole relationship with the supplier. Most customers' perceptions of the product are affected by their perceptions of other elements of the package. This is called the 'halo' effect, although in some cases 'horns' might be a better word. Hence the earlier emphasis on consistency of approach.

However, the idea of the product or service coming packaged with a variety of other elements is also a reminder not to ignore what these other elements are. Some may be under your control – such as sales documentation, packaging and telephone hotline – others less so. If you are a product manufacturer selling through retailers, the retail situation may not be under your control. So it is important to:

- Identify all elements of the package that might be perceived by your customers as important.
- Seek to optimize them, as far as possible.
- Ensure that the plan is being delivered at the point of contact with customers.

In an organization of any size this requires the management of large amounts of data. To some extent, modern relationship marketing might also be described as database marketing. The technology has certainly had an increasingly major effect on the implementation of this area of marketing.

VIRTUAL PRODUCTS AND SERVICES

Information about your customers and about the state of the relationship between them and you feature prominently in marketing. So at the centre of many companies' approaches to customer relationship marketing is the customer database. The quantity and value of information generated in business processes has risen in a series of historic steps. Initially, simple control loops exploited data arising from 'real world' production activities. These data were printed in reports or displayed on gauges to help production keep tabs on quality parameters. Other paper-based administrative control loops ensured that logistics were kept attuned to production. The 'informating' of these loops enabled the raw data to be manipulated by new and growing IT departments, where it was integrated with process control and accounting software to provide management with regularly updated performance statistics.

Next came information systems, which integrated the statistical output from the various activity focused systems to give management useful overviews of the performance of entire processes. Based on the integration of processes at managerial level by information systems, it became beneficial to shift some 'real world' activities into what might be called digital space. For example, a product design function was moved from drawing boards into a computer-aided design and manufacturing

(CAD/CAM) application. Later, networking systems permitted the CAD/CAM application to support geographically and functionally separate design teams to collaborate. Aircraft such as the Boeing 777 or the Airbus 320 and cars like the Ford Mondeo were developed by design teams working simultaneously in several countries.

With the further integration offered by client-server-based enterprise computing, employees and management are now empowered to access corporate data and key applications. At this point it is also relatively easy to allow customers secure access to parts of the system. They may be trading partners, exchanging standard business documents with the company over Electronic Data Interchange (EDI) trading networks, consultants using the company's e-mail system to enhance communications, or consumers accessing the company's World Wide Web site or bulletin boards to order products and catalogues. They may also increasingly be buying information-based products and services.

The trend to conducting activities in digital space is mainly driven by cost considerations, assisted by a continuing fall in the price of computing power and by regular advances in software functionality. To assist this trend, managers may search carefully through their business processes for gateways to digital space. A gateway is a value-adding activity, which may be informed, or existing digital information flow, which may be converted into viable services and products. This is illustrated by Figure 1.4.

Rayport and Sviolka (1995) have helped to identify gateways into this new value matrix based on two dimensions; a value chain of 'real world' activities and a generic chain along which value is added to information.

There are two ways of using the value matrix. In the first, which is suitable for companies whose information systems are not highly integrated, information arising or potentially arising from the monitoring of each 'real world' activity is examined in the light of the information value chain.

The second way is suitable for companies with highly integrated information systems. This is where advanced relationship marketing techniques pay off. Here, customer and operational databases are selectively organized and then synthesized into products according to functional concerns. Essentially what this means is that by using advanced analytical techniques such as data mining (discussed later in this book), data are reorganized according to specific customer needs. This is the so-called, 'segment of one'.

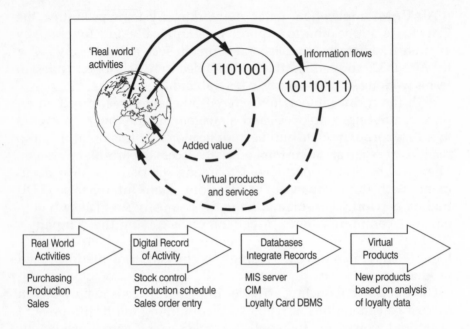

Figure 1.4 Towards a digital world

A well-known example on the Internet is provided by Amazon.Com. If you use a search engine such as Google to look something up on the Web, a link to the Amazon database will also suggest book titles on that topic area. Let us take a couple of more advanced examples.

Newspapers: In the 1970's, UK national and regional newspapers began to informate their value chains. Within a few years, control of most value-added activities had moved into digital space resulting in improved economics. Lately, over 200 newspapers around the world have set up sites on the World Wide Web, often updating news in real time. In production terms, the newspaper is now often produced by a virtual organization. Singapore's main newspaper, the *Straits Times*, is printed in Singapore but is partly copy-edited in Sydney and subcontracts graphic work to Manila. Like all newspapers, however, when you buy an issue you get the whole lot. Most people do not read newspapers from cover to cover. Thus many of the world's leading newspapers such as *The Times* of London, the *New York Times*, the *Financial Times*, *The Economist* or the *Wall Street Journal* have gone digital.

This is the gateway. Since copy and graphics are in digital form, it is already possible for you to receive daily updates of a customized newspaper, electronically delivered to your personal computer, containing only the stories in which you are interested. The way you customize your personal newspaper will give vital information to advertisers and producers of goods and services about individual customer interests and preferences.

The United Services Automobile Association: USAA is a major US direct merchandiser, using its customer database to leverage value-for-money purchases. It started as an insurer, developing information systems to help employees provide appropriate advice, products and services. The resulting information flows provided a gateway. The USAA had a huge amount of information about people, their jobs, their incomes and their reliability (in insurance terms). These were then used to support customer risk assessments and customized, individual policies. Next, USAA developed insurance products and finance packages for specific groups of customers. It now offers a wide and growing range of shopping services based on the analysis of its customer databases based on customer behaviour and their use of financing.

PERSONAL CONTACT

Does this mean that relationship marketing is all about the high-tech deployment of advanced database systems and their supporting infrastructure? Of course not. Amidst all the media hype about new technology, it is all too easy to forget that customer relationship marketing is still about people and contacts between them.

Figure 1.5 illustrates approximately the hierarchy of contact channels. Face-to-face contact in a branch or with a sales person is still enormously important, as is direct mail. Perhaps surprisingly, the use of direct mail and the use of mail as an effective, non-intrusive contact medium have grown robustly in some countries over the last decade.

Contact-channel management requires careful judgement and complete integration if it is to work effectively. For example, an initial customer contact might be made over a Web site. The customer might just e-mail for information about products or services for which a more or less instantaneous electronic acknowledgement is expected. Or, by clicking the 'call me' button, the customer is put in direct touch with a call centre. The operator in the call centre needs to know exactly what the customer has been doing on the Web site and where they have got to. They also need to know about existing relationships with

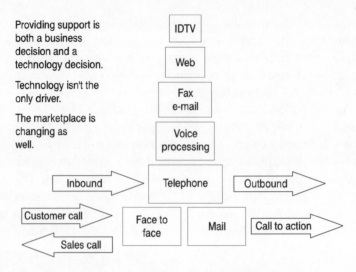

Figure 1.5 Personal contact supports other marketing technology

that customer. The follow-up to this interaction might be a personal call or a letter. In the course of this exchange, it is apparent that customer expectations about the relationship are changing as a result of the technology but, at the end of the day, people still tend to buy things from people (even if it is the imaginary Marlboro cowboy) rather than machines.

THE RELATIONSHIP-TRANSACTION-CONTACT HIERARCHY

A relationship – however long it lasts – can be broken down into a series of perceived transaction periods. These in turn can be broken down into contact episodes, of which a critical element is the service encounter or what we call 'moment of truth'.

For example, customers who buy new cars may pay two or three visits to the dealer before buying. They may have several telephone conversations with the dealer before and after the sale. They may exchange one or two letters during the transaction. They may visit the dealer after the sale to have a minor problem rectified.

Throughout this period, most customers are likely to consider themselves engaged in a relationship with the dealer. If this relationship is well managed, customers are more likely to return to the dealer for service and for a replacement car when the time comes. They may also buy a more expensive model, or buy insurance, extended warranty or finance through the dealer.

After the purchase is complete, it is therefore important that the dealer sets out to maintain the relationship. Nobody likes 'fair weather friends' and if the customer gets the impression that the dealer is only interested as long as there is a sale in prospect then they will not feel particularly loyal. In the automotive sector, this is a particular problem as the customer moves from the sales function, which is often highly effective, to the service or maintenance function. The service department often does not recognize a relationship role and, in any case, data between the two areas is rarely shared so the more highly trained sales team are not aware that the customer might have had even a minor servicing problem.

THE SERVICE ENCOUNTER OR 'MOMENT OF TRUTH'

A relationship with a customer may therefore comprise a whole series of service encounters or moments of truth, each of which shapes or influences the relationship. It does not take much imagination to guess what the effect of an indifferent response to an apparently minor fault such as a blocked windscreen washer might have on the proud owner of an expensive new car!

During each service encounter the customer may go through a range of mental states:

- Experiencing the need.
- Anxiety about how to fulfil the need, or whether it will be fulfilled at all.
- Sensitivity about whether the right choice has been made or whether to accept the way in which the service is being provided.
- Dependence or a child-like relationship to the product or service.
- Happiness or unhappiness according to the degree of success of the encounter or transaction.
- Satisfaction or resentment after the encounter is over according to the outcome.

Understanding what the customer experiences during the service encounter is vital to improving the relationship. People are much better at these sorts of judgements than machines since this is what we all do in everyday life. Tone of voice, body language, expressions of concern each make a powerful impact. The trick is to use the technology to identify moments of truth and to use a repertoire of behaviours to ensure that they are each effectively managed.

SUMMARY

Customer relationship marketing is not a panacea for all marketing ills. Nor does it necessarily imply radical change. Just as Molière's Bourgeois Gentilhomme discovered that he was 'speaking prose', so many companies are today discovering that they are managing customer relationships very well. However, there are also many companies that are not.

This introductory chapter has tried to provide an overview of customer relationship marketing and, in doing so, it has raised a number of questions:

- Have you identified those groups of customers that contribute most to your profits?
- Have you defined what different types of customer want out of a relationship with you: what will make them loyal?
- Have you set customer relationship objectives for your company?
- Do you know how loyal your key groups of customers are, from all attitudinal and behavioural points of view?
- Do you routinely measure their loyalty and the impact of your marketing, sales and service actions on that loyalty?
- Are all elements of your marketing, sales and service mix focused on delivering, maintaining and developing relationships with customers: in other words, turning the best laid plans into practice?
- Do your loyal customers feel that you reward their loyalty?
- Do all your staff, and particularly those involved in dealing with customers, understand the concept of customer loyalty and their role in maintaining and developing it? Is this understanding re-inforced by training and motivation?

We shall now try to address some of the issues that these questions raise.

2

Relationships with customers

WHO IS A CUSTOMER?

The first question to address when thinking about relationships with customers might be, 'Who is a customer?' At first sight, the answer to that question is fairly straightforward. Customers are actual or potential purchasers of products or services. A moment's thought will show that the definition must go a lot further. The choices that people make are influenced by those around them. For both consumer and business markets, therefore, a number of buying roles can be identified. These might include:

- initiator – who suggests the purchase;
- influencer – who affects choice;
- decider – who makes choices about all or part of the purchase;
- buyer – who actually purchases;
- user – who uses the product or service.

These roles might all be vested in one person or in a number of people. In a household, a child might suggest a meal item, a husband or shop-keeper might influence, the wife might decide. In a firm, the boss might initiate, colleagues might influence and a PA might make decisions, which are then implemented by a purchasing officer for users in another part of the company. The relationships that have to be established externally therefore involve a community of people who may come into contact with the supplier's organization at a number of points and in a number of ways. This is why we used the concept of 'enterprise-wide relationship management' in the previous chapter. Putting it another way, we could use the term total relationship marketing because what is needed is a shared set of values across the enterprise to the establishment of a relationship approach to marketing. This must be based on a common understanding of a model of those relationships and how to recognize what marketing actions or behaviours are appropriate at different stages.

We also distinguished previously between marketing orientation and market orientation. Narver and Slater (1990) suggested three dimensions on which a market orientation could be measured and this is used as the basis of Table 2.1.

The table shows that to develop effective customer relationship marketing, both external and internal members of the enterprise must be involved at all stages of customer contact. The example given earlier of the problems that are sometimes encountered when a customer moves from sales to after-sales is often cited. If all the contacts illustrated in Figure 1.1 are considered, it is easy to see the difficulty of developing and sustaining a total approach. When the accounts department send an invoice or statement, many companies miss the opportunity to get customer feedback. When an intermediary such as a wholesaler, logistics company or call centre is used, the style and manner of customer contact sometimes does not 'gel' with the approach that the company is trying to cultivate elsewhere.

INTERNAL CUSTOMERS

The period during which your customers consider themselves to be in a relationship with you may be quite long. Opportunities to strengthen this relationship may occur before, during and after your transactions with them.

Let us review as an example the process of booking a car in for its annual tune up. This may start with a minor contact episode, a phone conversation to book the service. During the conversation the customer has to explain what is wrong with the car and may use terms that make no real sense in technical terms: 'There is a funny rattle in second gear'.

Table 2.1 Dimensions for measuring market orientation

Customer Orientation	Interfunctional Co-ordination	Competitor Orientation
There is a commitment to customers.	Customer calls are sometimes made jointly by more than one department or division.	Sales people share competitor information.
Members of the enterprise seek to create customer value.	Information is shared across the enterprise. (This is especially important for corporate objectives. These must be clear, realistic and widely disseminated.)	There is a rapid response to competitor actions (so we must know who our competitors are).
Customer needs are understood and an effort is made to monitor changes in those needs. (Therefore, there must be good feedback loops for customer communications and satisfaction measures.)	There is a functional integration in strategy. For example, marketing and production work closely together, accounts and purchasing integrate with marketing and production.	Top managers discuss competitor strategy (which means these are identified and understood).
There is an objective to provide constant customer satisfaction (so there must be a continuing process for developing relationships with customers).	All functions seek to contribute to customer value.	Opportunities are targeted for competitive advantage (therefore, we have to understand the source of competitive advantage).
The after-sales service recognizes that the sale does not end with the purchase.	Resources are shared between business units.	Organizational structures need to be sufficiently flexible to encourage a creative and multi-disciplinary task orientation to pre-empting future possible competitor actions.

While the car is in the garage, the customer may be worried all day about whether the car will be ready in time, whether all faults will be rectified and what the cost will be. Therefore, when the customer collects the car and pays the bill, another critical point in the relationship is reached. So, your customers' relationship requirements will usually vary according to what *they* consider to be the significance of each transaction. In this example of car service, before booking in the car, the customer may want a list of service items, costs and available dates. The customers may require brisk and efficient service but want to feel that they are being understood ('funny rattle'?). When presented with the bill, it might be useful to show the customer the worn part that was replaced to help explain why an expense was so high. A follow up call to ensure that the 'funny rattle' was fixed probably would not hurt the relationship either.

Several people are involved in building this relationship: the receptionist, the service desk personnel, the service manager, the fitter, the cashier and maybe even the sales person who sold the car. The role of a range of employees is important not just in terms of service quality but also in terms of building customer relationships. Sometimes this is overlooked when an enterprise concentrates its customer relationship training simply on those people who are considered to be front line, customer-contact personnel. Schlesinger and Heskett (1991) have described this as the service/profit chain but from our point of view we would tend to regard it as the relationship/profit chain as shown in Figure 2.1.

Regarding members of the organization as internal customers is based on the assumption that satisfying the needs of internal customers improves the capability for satisfying the needs of external customers. Internal market orientation can therefore be fundamental to successful

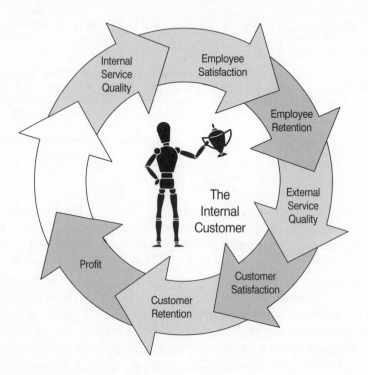

Figure 2.1 The relationship/profit chain

external market orientation. There are three main objectives to this internal marketing (after Grönroos, 1985):

- Overall – to ensure that all members of the organization are motivated to be conscious of customer needs and are committed to high standards of customer care.
- Tactical – to ensure that all staff understand what is involved in maintaining customer relationships and the importance of doing so.
- Strategic – to create an awareness of the long-term competitive position that the company is trying to achieve so that everyone buys into the customer relationship marketing mindset. This means that marketing and sales campaigns are fully explained to everyone in the organization so that they can understand what is needed and how they can best contribute towards it.

Clearly, issues such as organizational fit, the creation of an organizational culture and personal growth and development are of great importance here. These are within the province mainly of line managers but must be supported by HRM and training areas. There are also important policy issues to do with exploiting tacit knowledge (expertise) and empowerment that we shall touch on later. However, if the right kind of climate can be created, members of the organization become more confident that they can use their skills and knowledge in a satisfying and creative way. This creates good relationships between employees and consequently between employees and customers.

If we go back briefly to some of the seminal work on service quality by Zeithaml, Berry and Parasuranam (1988), we can see how successful relationship marketing depends on the presence of a number of internal marketing elements:

- **Teamwork** – management attitudes and real evidence of a belief in what the organization is trying to do (ie not just words) produce employees who are involved with and committed to the organization and its objectives.
- **Employee job fit** – recruitment must concentrate on organizational fit and job fit. If the right person with potential ability is recruited, management must ensure that training and development are available when needed.
- **Technology job fit** – the right tools for the job. Relationship marketing can work very effectively in small organizations but tends to be hungry for expensive IT resources in larger companies.

- **Perceived control** – employees must perceive that they have the flexibility to deal with customers in the right way, in line with policy. High rates of staff turnover are common in call centres and studies have found that staff departures are often associated with stress. This is not because employees find the volume of calls to be too high or because they are unhappy to deal with customer complaints. The stress is often due to the fact that inappropriate performance measures do not allow them enough time to make a cross sale or to resolve a problem.
- **Supervisory style** – this should take into account personal predisposition (how the employee likes to do the job), organizational fit (how this will affect other employees) and customer outcomes (does it get the right result?).
- **Avoidance of role conflict** – do not say one thing and do another. For example, the company says that it wants to encourage a dialogue with customers but then stifles or ignores customer feedback.
- **Avoidance of role ambiguity** – very simply, employees should understand what they are supposed to do and how this will be evaluated or appraised. If a complaining customer is a professional complainer who uses small problems as an excuse for not paying his or her bills (what we describe in chapter 11 as a bad customer) then contact staff should be confident in being tough without fear of being reprimanded.

THE SUPPLIER AS CUSTOMER

Economists have a habit of expressing the desirability of a product or service in terms of the word 'demand'. They write about the 'demand' for a product or service and use phrases like the price elasticity of demand. In English, this word carries a rather strident connotation like an instruction or a command. Marketers tend to use a more evocative term, 'market response function'. In other words, investigating and establishing the sort of response or reaction there is to a particular market offer. After all, if the individual consumer is a customer for your company's products or services then, by the same token, the company is equally a customer for the consumer's money. From this point of view, both parties are equal and, as in any good relationship, where both parties feel that what is being shared provides the sought-after benefits that each is seeking, the relationship will be sustained and will grow. Relationship marketing is often based on taking the consumer into the enterprise in a very open way so that the consumer can maximize the value that they obtain. Of course, this has some very important advantages from the company's point of view since it binds the customer to the organization much more closely.

It follows that if the consumer, or indeed the business customer, has this kind of extensive access to the enterprise, they will come into direct contact with your suppliers from time to time. It is also apparent that if the enterprise is committed to relationship marketing then its suppliers must have a good understanding of their role in the value chain for making this work.

The relationship with suppliers also needs to be considered carefully. Very close links in terms of alliances or partnerships are often very useful when a dynamic, fluid response to changing market conditions is needed. However, this can carry dangers in a competitive sense. Some of your partners may turn out to be not dolphins that help you on your way but sharks that eat up your customer base.

While there is widespread recognition of the importance of fostering long-term relationships with suitable suppliers, and some understanding of what is required to develop a networked marketing strategy, some further research is needed into the best way of managing these links. (See, for example, Matthyssens and Van den Bulte, 1994.)

Supplier relationships and supplier strategies need to be incorporated into the overall customer relationship marketing approach. As with employees, successful long-term relationships with suppliers will enhance the competitive stance of the company as a whole.

LEVELS OF RELATIONSHIP

The idea of the level of relationship your customers expect must be expressed more concisely if you are to base policy on it. Sales people talk about three levels of negotiation in dealing with customers and this is not a bad basis for the initial relationship marketing framework policy. These are based on three Ws:

- **Wish** – for salespeople, this is the price they would like to obtain. In policy terms, it could be described as the ideal relationship that we would like to achieve.
- **Will** – ideals are often hard to attain and something less has to be accepted on an everyday basis. The 'will accept' position has to be

clearly described in terms of what is and is not acceptable so that it can be understood by members of the enterprise. For example, the wish position might be that customers regard our company as a preferred supplier for all major purchases on the basis of a close working relationship. The will position might be that at least 50 per cent of purchases are placed with our organization.

- **Walk away** – these are relationships that we will not accept and this level of negotiation is linked to an idea that we discuss later. Not all customers are good customers and we need definitions of what we mean by a bad customer if we are to compete effectively. Ideally, we would like to pass these customers on to our competitors. They might be customers who have many small transactions that produce little or no profit or customers who complain a lot.

Customers will share these categories, even though they may not express them in the same way. In most cases, customers have an idea about the desired relationship and the minimum acceptable. They also have very clear ideas about what they will not accept. In terms of service quality, it is likely that if perceived relationships contrast with actual levels too starkly then customer satisfaction is likely to be reduced.

Perceptions about contacts often vary significantly from actual attributes and may be subject to a halo effect. As in personal experience, the better a customer's relationship with you, the more positive their perception of each contact. For example, loyal customers may believe that they are in contact more frequently with you than they actually are, perhaps because you are at the forefront of their thinking and may have a more positive view of each contact.

As in personal relationships, excessive or over effusive contacts may not be effective. The best example of this is the over-attentive relationship, contact which is too frequent or which gives or asks for too much information. In telemarketing, if a customer calls the response-handling centre and is answered immediately after the first ring, customers may have no time to collect their thoughts. If, coupled with this, the operator is too quick and aggressive with the opening dialogue, customers may feel threatened. Similarly, a constant flow of sales contacts, calls and mail shots may well deter some customers. In the financial services sector, some companies allow new customers a 'contact holiday' after they have purchased their first product before attempting to cross-sell or upsell other products.

It is useful to consider this in terms of a relationship threshold. Relationship standards that fall outside a certain range, above or below what is acceptable, may be strongly criticized. Performance within the threshold may be regarded as normal and acceptable. McCann (1999) has proposed the idea of a customer continuum from low to high 'lock-in'. Using a relationship-based approach for customers who want a purely transactional approach will waste both money and time. However, failing to develop the relationship with customers who require one leaves you open to the competition.

FIXING THE RELATIONSHIP THRESHOLD

Experience

Several factors influence the way in which customers develop their requirements and perceptions. The most important of these is experience, either with you or on the basis of contact with a 'benchmark' company. All suppliers of products and services are in some sense in competition with each other when it comes to relationship marketing. In this sense, a 'benchmark' company providing quite different products or services might be responsible for developing expectations elsewhere. For example, the returns policy of Marks & Spencer, the efficiency of Direct Line Insurance or the service levels of Kwik Fit exhaust centres can encourage customers to believe that all companies should work to these standards. Since customers compare and form expectations that are transferred across different suppliers of products and services, it is important to monitor the 'best of the rest' to determine where the competitive standard might lie.

In a competitive environment, customers who stay in relationships with particular suppliers do so because the total package they receive from the supplier – product, service, price, credit, relationship marketing and so forth – is right for them. There is no room for complacency. Customers of low-price suppliers may have reconciled themselves into accepting indifferent relationship standards because of low prices. However, if a competitor emerges that can match the low prices with higher standards of relationship marketing, customer requirements may change. Budget airlines provide a good example. No-frills airlines such as Ryanair, easyJet or Buzz use standard equipment, minimal service levels and fly into secondary airports to keep fares low. When a major international airline such as British Airways entered the market with its former subsidiary, Go, some budget airlines were obliged to offer 'budget business-class fares' and higher service levels to compete.

Word of mouth

Customer referrals are an important influence in buyer decisions. The proportion of referral business is a measure of satisfaction levels. This is why it is sometimes worth putting dissatisfied customers into an intensive-care relationship to avoid losing them or making special efforts to recover lost customers. Such retrieved customers can become powerful advocates, from whom recommendations can be particularly effective.

The force of recommendation is as powerful in business-to-business markets as in consumer markets. Information about relationships may be communicated within the buying centre – the group of staff who make or influence the buying decision – and to other buying centres. In buying centres that are making significant, high-risk decisions, it is particularly important for buyers to appear knowledgeable. Oral recommendations are sometimes given special status in these circumstances.

Time

A perceived scarcity of time can make customers want shorter interactions with suppliers. This can also make your customers worry about the differences between what they want to achieve and what they actually achieve in their relationship with you.

If your customers feel they are short of time, concise communications may be an important relationship proposition. However, this may be culturally dependent. In some cultures, the importance of a decision is a function of the time taken to make it. Only unimportant decisions can be made quickly. This would be true in many parts of the Middle East, the Far East, Africa and South America. It is also possible that customers will want to spend more time on purchases that they perceive as having high involvement or to which they attach great importance (high risk).

CONSUMER BUYING MODELS

Buyer behaviour models are covered in all good general marketing texts. We shall not reproduce that material in detail here. The general form of the model is illustrated in Figure 2.2.

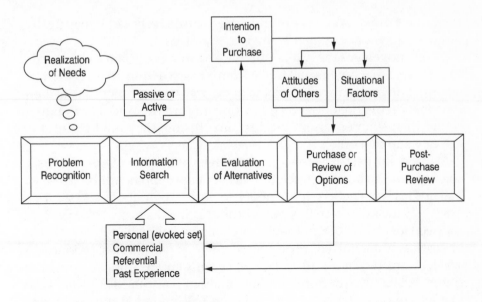

Figure 2.2 A general buyer behaviour model

Problem recognition

Problem recognition or the need to buy may emerge in two ways. Sometimes the buyer may become aware of internally felt needs. Alternatively, the buyer may be presented with buying solutions and then develops a 'matching' problem. Although developing solutions before recognizing problems may sound rather odd, it is a common form of problem solving and many decision makers will not address problems to which they have not first identified a solution. Many researchers on decision making have commented on this phenomenon (for example, Mintzberg, Raisinghani and Théoret, 1976). For example, a man sees a powerful motorbike in a showroom and suddenly discovers a need for rapid, economical travel through rush-hour traffic. Or a competitor upgrades their data warehouse, which causes the company to re-evaluate its data storage and processing capability very urgently. Understanding this sequence is an important aspect of selling.

Search for information

People are disposed to use information in different ways. Not everyone is an analytical decision maker, nor are all problems amenable to analysis. Some have to be addressed intuitively or heuristically. Strategic decisions commonly fall into this area.

As the movement towards a purchase or an act of purchase proceeds, it is possible that buyers will move from a passive to an active search for information and may reduce some of their normal defences to the daily information overload to which most people are exposed. For example, rather than skim or ignore product advertising, they might read it or actively search it out.

At this point, past experience becomes relevant. The evoked set refers to solutions to the buying problem that seem appropriate to the decision-maker. This is not necessarily confined to purchases of goods and services. They may include alternative ways of addressing the need. You can avoid the need for buying the motorbike by changing your job. Where products or services are involved, previous experiences with similar products or services are recalled and can be very influential. Information from commercial sources or from recommendations is also used. It is very hard to model the way in which all these factors will interact in any one buying decision as a wide range of forces can be present. A trusted or powerful source of information such as advice from a close friend or an instruction from a senior manager might have more impact than, say, an advertisement but each situation has to be judged contextually.

Evaluation

Most writers on decision making devote a lot of space to evaluation or choice. In practice, most decision making is designed to reduce the complexity of choice in various ways. This is especially true as a decision progresses up organizations where, very often, by the time the decision has reached a senior decision maker, many alternatives have been filtered out.

At a personal level, it is easily possible to demonstrate that a richer choice (a bigger problem space) represents a much harder decision environment than a smaller problem space. It is much harder to make a choice from a full box of chocolates than one in which only one or two pieces remain. At both a personal and a professional level, therefore, both decision makers and vendors conspire to simplify or bias the choice. This is where relationships can prove very powerful. A good relationship, whether real or perceived, between the consumer and the supplier can help the buyer rationalize choice at this stage.

Quite how any one person will respond to particular options is somewhat beyond prediction. Some customers rely more on personal advice than on information provided by suppliers. The outcome of the evaluation may also vary depending on personality, past experience and the way different suppliers provide information. Psychologists have spent many years trying to establish linkages between intentions to behave and actual behaviour without being able to develop a reliable predictive tool. Personal attitudes to the intended behaviour, the attitudes of 'significant others' and situational factors can all influence final outcomes.

In practical terms, the marketer must develop at least a working hypothesis as to how customers evaluate different suppliers, products and services. This is the link between relationship marketing and financial success. If the relationship is important to customer choice then the commercial justification for investing in creating and managing the relationship is less difficult to produce.

Purchase or a review of options

An act of purchase is clearly the best outcome from a commercial point of view but influencing the buying process positively is also valuable. Consumers do not always purchase when they go through a buying cycle but if the interaction between your organization and the consumer has influenced their attitudes positively in your favour, something important has still been achieved. Most advertising and promotion models are predicated on this basis. People do not leap off their chairs when they see an advertisement or meet a sales person but they do change their evoked set and modify their attitudes.

Post-purchase review

After the decision, your customer re-evaluates it in the light of any new information, for example information about product performance. The key message here is not to stop selling after the customer has purchased. This is absolutely fundamental to developing the customer relationship. At the very least, thank them for placing the order and keep in touch to assure satisfaction.

In some post-purchase situations, customers experience cognitive dissonance, ie they feel unhappy about what they now know. They may experience doubt, even anxiety, if the product did not come up to expectations. These customers may look for information that supports their original decision, a confirmation that they made the right choice. They may focus on the 'good deal' they got in an attempt to convince themselves that they made the right decision. They may even ignore, avoid or distort incoming information that is inconsistent with what they want to believe. 'I know this pen broke after a couple of days but it was cheap and I needed something to write with at the time.' Relationship marketing after the sale can help your customers justify the decision they made, even if there are problems after the sale.

DISTORTING THE BUYING DECISION IN YOUR FAVOUR

Branding and customer loyalty

When it comes to the purchase, brands are very important. Brands take a number of forms. These can include line brands (a group of similar products such as cosmetics), umbrella brands (such as Birds Eye or Virgin), company, family or source brands (such as Sony, Ford or Cadbury) or banner brands. Banner brands might encompass designer labels (Armani), licensed names (Disney) or retailers' brands (such as Sam from Wal-Mart or St Michael from Marks & Spencer). If the customer has a strong relationship with the brand, they can be inclined to purchase in that direction more easily. A strong brand, developed over a long period, gives the relationship a strong platform. Without it, the relationship almost has to start from scratch with every transaction. IT people used to have a saying that 'nobody got fired for buying IBM'. This meant that the reputation of IBM products and their relationship with business buyers was so powerful that most buyers thought that it would be widely shared throughout the organization. It was therefore a safe purchase, not open to challenge.

Customer loyalty and branding are closely connected. Highly visible and positive branding cannot exist without customer loyalty and customer loyalty depends, in the long run, on the relationship. If you manage relationships with your customers well, they will tend to be loyal. This will provide the opportunity for branding to get to work. Branding requires strong imprinting of images about the product in consumers' minds. These ideas will be positive if customers have frequent, good experiences in buying.

The key manifestation of disloyalty is when a customer switches suppliers or brands. Sometimes this occurs when your customers decide they need a change, not because of any problem with what they are buying from you or how you manage the relationship. People sometimes seek variety for its own sake. Trying to understand the basis of brand switching is one of the most important issues in marketing. While it cannot be avoided, good relationship marketing can encourage lost customers to return. Switches due to big price differences can be hard to prevent through relationship marketing but even here, good customers will often pay a premium for a brand or for a relationship. Some companies emphasize this in their advertising. For example, Kellogg's advertisements tell buyers that if it does not say Kellogg's on the box, it is not Kellogg's. In other words, they do not manufacture for own label. Buyers must therefore decide whether to accept a substitute or whether to possibly accept a premium price or to shop elsewhere in order to obtain the brand.

Losing customers due to problems with the quality of products or services, or due to poor relationship marketing, should be regarded as careless and unnecessary. There is no need to argue the case for quality but even the most serious of companies can have problems from time to time. This is why it is important to keep communication channels open. Loyal customers will not switch quickly but if they think nobody is listening, eventually they will be lost. Relationship marketing is based on encouraging feedback (not complaints) at every possible contact point. It is also vital to ensure that complaints, if they do arise, are dealt with quickly and positively. After all, it is more likely to be your more loyal customers who will take the trouble to complain.

High-involvement and low-involvement decisions

The rather elaborate process illustrated in Figure 2.2 is clearly not appropriate for day-to-day decision making. Not many people are inclined to go through that entire process when they buy a loaf of bread or decide whether to catch the train or the bus to work. Indeed, the general tendency is for purchasers to routinize buying in order to simplify daily life. Even choosing between brands for FMCG or groceries is something we process with very little effort.

For many purchases, perhaps even the majority, there is little imme-diate involvement by the consumer. For the marketer, purchase moti-vation is already understood and sometimes there is little that needs to be understood. Basic products may be purchased for functional reasons and carry little symbolic meaning. Their unit price is low, whichever brand is selected. The risk a customer takes by making the wrong choice of supplier or product is low because economic, psychological and social commitment to the product is low. These are low-involvement products. However, this is not to suggest that buying behaviours are not at work or that brands are failing to influence, it is simply that we need to make these purchase decisions quickly and are able to do so.

Customers sometimes feel that there is a high psychological and social risk of making the wrong choice. This applies particularly when the item to be purchased carries high symbolic value, affects the way we think about ourselves (our so-called self-concept) or affects our membership of social groups. These may be social groups to which we actually belong or those to which we would like to belong. Many products fall into this category. For example, clothes, cigarettes, alcohol, cars, books, home furnishings, club memberships and even schools or universities. Some low-price, frequently purchased products or services fall into this category too, such as pens or newspapers. These are high-involvement products and services. These are particularly important for relationship marketing. Good relationship marketing in high-involvement situations greatly reinforces customer loyalty. The alternative is customer disloyalty and strong word of mouth condemnation.

TYPES OF BUYING BEHAVIOUR

These two dimensions, branding and involvement, suggest four possible patterns of buyer behaviour, as shown in Table 2.2 (Assael, 1987).

Habitual

These are the everyday routine decisions that were mentioned earlier. Here, there is relatively low differentiation between brands and little sense of personal involvement. An example might be salt or petrol. The aim of the marketer for these kinds of products is to involve the consumer more intensively. In food products, this might be done by introducing issues of health and safety (salt with added vitamins?). In non-food products the aim is to increase the emotional stakes (this petrol protects and looks after your expensive car engine).

Table 2.2 Types of buying behaviour

	High Involvement	**Low Involvement**
Strong Branding	Complex	Variety seeking
Weak Branding	Dissonance reducing	Habitual

Variety

Here, there is strong branding but relatively low involvement such as confectionery, beer or jeans. In this case the brand leader seeks to exploit the situation by maximizing availability and purchase quantity (multiple packs). The relationship with the brand is emphasized in advertising.

Dissonance reducing

Sometimes there is high involvement with the purchase but little perceived difference between brands. Upper-end consumer electronics such as TVs or other infrequently purchased items such as carpets, furniture and perfume fall into this category. The relationship with the consumer is very important for this type of product since the marketing aim is to supply the feel-good factor, before and after purchase. Dissonance refers to two or more conflicting inner beliefs. In this case, the beliefs might be that, on the one hand I make rational choices, on the other I cannot see a sensible basis for choosing and must therefore act intuitively. Making the consumer feel good about the choice reduces dissonance by providing a rationalization for choice.

Complex

This type of purchase requires a full evaluation (a high degree of cognitive effort) and is very involving. The purchase of a car, an expensive computer or a designer suit or dress might fall into this group. Since brand differentiation is strong, the relationship has to be directed both at the end-user and at channel intermediaries such as the in-store sales force.

BUSINESS-TO-BUSINESS BUYING MODELS

It is, of course, in the area of business-to-business that customer relationship marketing first became recognized as a new and important marketing approach. There are many differences between business-to-business and consumer markets but we have described some aspects of consumer buying first for one important reason. The same people are involved. Business buyers are also consumers and however they might be affected at work, they are still subject to the same kinds of human responses.

Business markets differ from consumer markets in a number of ways. There are generally fewer buyers (which facilitates the development of closer relationships) and they tend to buy in quantity. The relationship between buyer and supplier can be very close indeed. Not only might they be linked electronically so that an EDI system allows buyers to call off products directly from the supplier's computer systems but they may also be linked operationally. A large buyer may demand certain performance criteria from its suppliers. For example, a large super-market chain may require a supplier of tuna to certify that the fish were caught using methods that did not threaten dolphins or it may demand certain standards or finishes for products. Sometimes buyers may partner with their suppliers. Some Japanese car companies have sent their own engineers to help improve the performance of their suppliers. They have also integrated supplier computer systems into their production systems using a technique known as 'synchronous automation'. This is an advance on 'just in time' (JIT) methods and co-ordinates supplier production lines with those of the buyer.

Business buyers may also be more geographically concentrated than end-users. Demand from such buyers is also more amenable to prediction. Business buying patterns reflect overall market trends. It may also be less price elastic than consumer markets.

On the purchasing side, it might be expected that a more professional approach to purchasing would be used. Whether this is also more rational is open to speculation. Certainly it is possible to identify some formalized procedures in professional purchasing but business buyers may be as susceptible to emotion as anyone else. After all, their professional livelihood is at stake and if they make a mistake this could have career consequences. They may be extra cautious and might do this by seeking to minimize perceived risk by strengthening brand preference or more established suppliers. They may also want to curry favour with the boss. Note too that they also have personal feelings and are going to be influenced by their perceptions of relationships with suppliers.

More people are involved in business buying, so some additional buying roles can be identified:

- **approvers** – people who authorize proposed actions in policy terms;
- **gatekeepers** – people who have the power to prevent or facilitate access to the decision makers such as receptionists, phone operators or purchasing agents;
- **consultants** – for products that are perceived to be very complex, technical advisers may be brought in to provide external professional advice.

The actual purchasing activity may also vary in character from consumer markets. There may be fewer intermediaries in the marketing channel with an increased inclination to buy direct from the main supplier of a product or service. There may also be an expectation of reciprocity. If a paper manufacturer makes a contract with a logistics company for distribution, it may expect the haulage company to take its paper supplies from one of its customers. In large-scale manufacturing, local sourcing or technology transfer might be important. In defence sales, for example, local component supplies and training are often central to securing a sale. This may also be true when supplying manufacturing plants or major facilities such as docks.

Service levels, reliability and delivery may also assume greater importance as may implementation. Business buyers may sometimes be interested in total solutions rather than just contributions to a process. For example, cash flow management may be of greater interest than a piece of accounts-receivable software (although tenders for software may be issued). The relationship with the buyer may thus be much more crucial to understanding what might be needed and in what form it might be supplied.

We might therefore see an approach such as that in Table 2.3 (de Chernatony & MacDonald, 1992) rather than that shown in Table 2.2.

Table 2.3 Business buying behaviour

	High Risk	Low Risk
High Complexity Product or Service	Long purchase procedure, many people involved	Technical specialists dominate
Low Complexity Product or Service	Formal purchasing personnel dominate with heavy finance involvement	Routine purchase decision, standard procedures

BUYING SITUATIONS

Business buyers might be a lot 'busier' than consumers when making buying decisions. They probably make more of them in terms of both value and frequency. Just like consumers, therefore, they need ways of separating the routine from the non-routine. Robinson, Faris and Wind (1967) described what they called a 'buy grid' to describe these different situations:

- **Straight re-buy** – a reorder without any modification, often handled routinely. If you are already supplying to a particular customer, your key relationship marketing objective is to facilitate reordering. There are also opportunities to explore cross-selling (what else they can buy) and upselling (enhanced versions of the product or service). If you are not on the current supplier list your objective is to initiate a relationship and encourage the buyer to sample the product.
- **Modified re-buy** – where the customer seeks to change supplier, or some other aspect of the purchase, but wants the same general kind of product or service. Modified re-buys often provide the greatest test of the quality of relationship marketing. Your customer is considering whether to switch products or services and may switch away from you if you mismanage the relationship with them.
- **New task** – the customer has no experience of the product or service type. This is where the full effects of Table 2.3 are experienced. The customer will generally use a lot of information, may take technical advice, may even set up a purchasing committee and may seek re-assurance from friends or colleagues. The marketing task is to make the sale and establish a relationship at the same time, not an easy thing to do. If you push too hard to make the sale, your later relationship with customers may be poor because they may have been sold the wrong product or service.

CUSTOMER RELATIONSHIP MARKETING AND THE SALES PROCESS

The sales process is illustrated in Figure 2.3. Everyone who might possibly buy the product or service is referred to as a suspect. Notice that this does not include everyone in the population! Given the importance of community and influences on the buying process, it is important to avoid targeting the marketing and sales effort at people who would not or could not buy. This may cause irritation. People who do not have children are unlikely to buy nappies (diapers). Dead people do not buy very much. Targeting accurately also saves a great

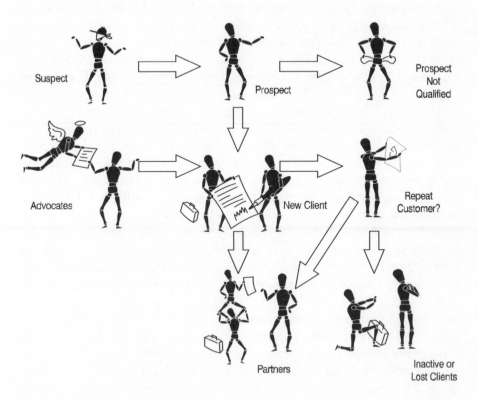

Figure 2.3 The customer development process

deal of money. It is not unknown for deceased persons to receive direct mail; it is not unknown for that mail to contain a letter that starts with the phrase, 'Dear Deceased'. (Cleaning up databases is discussed later in the book and poses quite a few problems.)

A suspect becomes a prospect as the relationship develops. These are people who may have a strong interest in buying the product. At this point, the supplier is interested in 'qualifying' prospects, that is, separating those who genuinely may purchase from those who cannot for the time being. A shortage of funds is an obvious way of disqualifying a prospect but there are other possibilities. The prospect may have just signed a long-term contract with a competitor or there may be an incompatibility in operating procedures or IT systems. Disqualified prospects may in some cases be added to the database and may form part of our relationship-building activities. After all, start up companies can one day become very large.

Some prospects are converted into first-time clients. Relationships with other clients may prove helpful during this process as prospects may well ask existing clients for advice or references. A positive, broad pattern of relationships with others in the buying process can also help.

As soon as a new client is obtained, the relationship-building process must start in earnest. This can be very influential in determining whether the client becomes a repeat customer or is lost. The relationship also affects how profitable that client becomes as the opportunities for adding value to the client's own business become clearer with learning. Just as people get closer together as a relationship develops, suppliers get closer to consumers or business clients. While this may not be a true partnership, an effective, mutually profitable relationship represents a strong, continuing marketing position. In Chapter 8, we describe the basis of the techniques used to sustain and develop the relationship that we call transparent marketing. Clients may have extensive access to the supplier enterprise and are able to develop solutions to their buying needs jointly with the supplier. Strategically, this represents a major competitive advantage. Partners also constitute advocates to other possible prospects.

Lost customers may fall into two categories. There are those customers that we lost because we did not want them. They have turned out to be bad customers and we have actively chosen to lose them. However, in many cases, there are customers that are lost either because of some failure in our product or service or some breakdown in our relationship. These we need to try to regain.

Clearly, in the customer development process, considerable investment in resources, time, money and people is being made to enhance and build loyalty. We shall discuss loyalty grids later but, for the time being, in terms of judging the amount of effort that might be justified for different types of customer, five levels of relationship building can be identified:

- **Basic** – a sales person simply sells the product.
- **Reactive** – a sale is made and the customer is encouraged to provide feedback about satisfaction and needs.
- **Account management** – the search for feedback is increased. The sales person calls the customer and actively solicits information about whether the product or service is satisfactory. Some response is made to requests for improvements or enhancements. Additional attention is paid to orders and deliveries.

- **Proactive** – the customer has privileged access to new products and additional time is spent with the customer to determine how the product or service is used. A search is made for new ways to add value to what the client does.
- **Partnering** – the supplier seeks to act as the point of first contact for a range of customer needs. The supplier works continuously with the customer to help the customer perform better. Communications to the customer are characterized by the use of the word 'we'. Product features are added to enhance the customer's performance and there may even be some integration of forward planning and strategic positioning.

SUMMARY

- Do you understand how your buyers make purchase decisions?
- Do you know who influences those decisions and how they do so?
- Do you think about the internal customers? Do you monitor employee job satisfaction and consider how this affects the way your company builds relationships with external customers?
- Do your people-policies foster team working and how do you respond to requests for better tools and training? Can you link this to relationship building?
- Do you have clear definitions of the levels of relationship that you are trying to achieve?
- What are the key differences between end consumers and business buyers for your product or service? Are you selling a high- or a low-involvement product? How complex is it? What impact does this have on your market relationship strategy?
- Are all your customer contact people trained to understand their role in building and managing relationships with customers?

3

Buy-in, policies and plans

BUY-IN TOP TO BOTTOM

Clearly, relationship marketing is part of the overall strategic process but we shall not look at corporate planning and the formation of strategies in detail. The processes by which organizations agree a vision, select strategies to pursue it and develop organizational forms and structures to implement those strategies is complex. Most good texts on corporate strategy discuss them thoroughly. We will, however, broadly review the issues involved and examine some of the more detailed implications for relationship marketing in strategic terms.

Persuading managers in most organizations of the importance of a close relationship with customers may be a case of preaching to the converted. Probably the majority of organizations – large, small, profit or not for profit – would recognize the value of close links. Quite often, however, organization structures, processes, procedures and operational necessities can bring customers into conflict with suppliers at many different levels. It is easy to think of incidents where this has happened. For example, an important, loyal customer has a supply crisis and no one feels obliged to do something exceptional to help. At an even sillier level, the customer is punished by trivial rules: 'I'm sorry, we are doing end-of-month closing and we cannot deal with your account query until next week'. Here, lip service is being paid to a relationship approach by some managers while, in practice, their everyday behaviour sends a quite different message. Consider, for instance, some of the symptoms of a lack of commitment to full customer relationship marketing:

- Many individual relationship management decisions have to be referred to senior managers.
- There are long lead times for yes/no decisions.
- Systems do not empower staff to deal flexibly with customer needs.
- Work pressures prevent staff from completing tasks so that external customers go to the end of the queue while internal customers and suppliers are prioritized.
- Staff do not have access to good quality information (accurate, up-to-date, relevant) so they do not know what to tell your customers.
- Motivation, appraisal and other people management systems pay inadequate attention to success in dealing with customers.
- Complaint rates are rising.
- Customer contact staff show signs of reduced motivation (higher rates of absence, sickness, accidents, increased quality control failures or falling productivity).
- Permanent customer loss rates or customer churn is increasing.

The essence of competitive relationship marketing lies in an enterprise-wide approach that touches on every aspect of customer-facing activity. A bored or indifferent junior clerk who happens to have a vital role in collecting and recording accurate customer data can do as much harm as a senior manager who loses sight of where competitive advantage really lies.

STRATEGY AS FIT AND STRATEGY AS STRETCH

STRATEGY AS FIT

Management writers have been pondering the question of which structure best suits different organizations for many years. Early approaches tended to be based on a model of organizations as if they were machines. The basic example with which most people are familiar is scientific management. More recent ideas like management by objectives (MBO) actually use the same sort of notions but many early writers took the same general line. However, it soon became clear that it was not possible to be so prescriptive in practice. Nor was it possible to identify a recipe for the right organizational form. Indeed, it was not even possible to identify a form that was always successful for a particular industry or market. By the 1950s and 1960s, therefore, researchers took to measuring some aspects of organizations such as their levels of hierarchy, their degree of formalization or even their production and service methods and attempted to relate this to performance. Again, varying results were produced but no consistent answers.

Eventually, by the mid-1980s, researchers recognized what many managers had probably known all along: there is no 'one best way' to set up and manage an organization. There was no single set of factors that could be correlated with success. At this point, contingency theory became popular. Contingency theory took the line that the success of an organization depends on a number of factors. Primarily these included:

- the environment (especially the market);
- organizational size (big organizations present different problems to small ones);
- technology;
- the history of the organization (which affects its culture and the way its members think about themselves);
- the expectations of employees and customers.

Unfortunately, it is quite difficult to develop working models that will guide managerial judgement if the underlying premise is, 'it all depends'. This therefore gave rise to what might be called the configuration approach to strategy.

The configuration approach aims to describe typical or archetypal organizational systems that might maximize chances of survival (and successful achievement of objectives). Basically, the approach recognizes that there is no one best way to set up and manage an organization. It argues that, if there is a careful analysis of predicted external environment and predicted position within that environment, it is possible to derive an effective organizational form. What we think is going to happen and how we think we stand in relation to those future events is then compared to our present position. Subsequently, a strategy is devised that will hopefully maximize our chances of success.

Other important aspects of the organization are then dropped into place to support this direction. The most well-known concept of the configuration strategy is that proposed by Waterman, Peters and Phillips (1980). They suggested that the success or otherwise of an organization depends on seven elements, each of which is inter-connected. These are strategy, structure, systems, style, staff, skills and superordinate goals (or shared values). Each of these seven S's is inter-dependent, each of them has to be consistent with the others and they must all fit together.

Writers such as Miller (1986) looked at this idea and concluded that success flows from designing an organization based on a fairly limited number of archetypes. He argued that there are only a limited number of constellations that are feasible in any environment and companies that follow these survive because they are better adapted. For example, most large organizations operate in stable, concentrated industries with high entry barriers whereas organic 'adhocracies' are to be found in industries with high rates of innovation and embryonic growth industries. An 'adhocracy' is an organization with a constantly changing form, literally an improvised arrangement that suits the here and now. Organizations are driven towards one of a small number of configurations to achieve internal harmony and consistency. Thus an administrative bureaucracy can only flourish in a stable environment where its formalized procedures enable it to establish highly efficient routines based on standard operating procedures. Miller also took the view that organizations tend to change in either a careful evolutionary manner or suddenly, in one strategic bound. This idea is important to the theory because only by one of these two methods is the organ-ization able to maintain its internal consistency. Piecemeal change just will not work.

STRATEGY AS STRETCH

Unfortunately, neither does this theory. In the late 1990s it is possible to observe examples of large administrative bureaucracies that work in quite different ways and yet are completely successful. For example, Microsoft is highly innovative and GE is highly traditional. Indeed, Miller himself had recognized this by 1990 when he wrote a book entitled, *The Icarus Paradox: How excellent organizations can bring about their own downfall*. However, it was Hamel and Prahalad (1994) that really tore apart this idea of fitting sets of strategic components together like pieces of a giant jigsaw puzzle. In answer to the question, 'Why do great companies fail?' they came up with two main answers:

Inability to escape the past

- Companies become mesmerized by their own success and there is no gap between performance and expectations. Thus they eschew change.
- They substitute resources for creativity simply because they have lots of them. Failure follows an absence of adaptation.

Inability to invent the future

- They have optimized their business systems and are unable to invent new rules when some force for change (like technology) requires different ways of doing business.
- There is a leadership failure because they mistake the momentum of success for progress.

To illustrate their point Hamel and Prahalad offered two lists of companies similar to this one:

• RCA;	• Sony;
• CBS;	• CNN;
• Upjohn;	• Glaxo;
• Pan Am;	• Air France;
• Sears;	• Wal-Mart;
• Firestone.	• Bridgestone.

Now they asked the question, 'If you were an investor in, say, 1980, where would you have put your money?' In each case, the 'obvious' answer was the companies on the left. Each of these firms was rich, successful, technologically advanced; each had a fine reputation and plenty of money. Twenty years later, you would have wished you had gone for the column on the right. In varying degrees, each of the firms on the left lost its leadership position to the firms on the right. Perhaps it is hard to spot the technology trends that reversed the position of RCA (inventor of colour TV) and Sony. Yet something different clearly happened to Air France, which was able to post a substantial profit in 2001/02 when most industry peers suffered large losses. What could have happened?

Hamel and Prahalad put forward the idea that the answer lies not so much in graphs and matrices that carefully balance bits and pieces of an organization like parts of a giant machine, but in the extent to which top management have a consistent vision of the future. To test strategic integrity they propose that you give each senior manager a piece of paper and ask them each to write down an answer to the question, 'How will the future of your industry be different?' Do not define future and do not define industry. Give them a week or so and then compare the answers. Are they thinking next year or next decade? Are they seeing extensions of current markets, products or services or are they seeing something totally new. How competitively unique are their answers? Do your eyes open in surprise or close in boredom?

Their point was that organizations that concentrate on 'fit' are guaranteed to atrophy and stagnate. Too cosy a fit, too tight a fit means that your organization is perfectly equipped for exactly what it does now. Perfect if the world does not change but, of course, the world is changing all the time. Thus some sort of bridge is needed between strategy as a grand design and strategy as a repositioning exercise that copes with a whole new agenda. Wal-Mart was successful because it changed the rules of the game. Sears had a major advantage in the late 1970s. It owned a chain of stores across the United States and had a strong reputation to back this physical presence. There seemed to be a major entry barrier to new competition, an investment in assets that was more or less unassailable. So Wal-Mart did not assail it. They decided that they were not in the retail business but in the logistics and distribution business. They did not compete on the basis of retail space but on the basis of very fast, competitive responses to consumer demand and they used IT to do it. Suddenly, Sears' strength became its weakness. To deal with this sort of challenge, an organization is needed that is responsive to rapid change. Strategy as stretch recognizes the paradox that while leadership cannot be planned for entirely, neither does it happen in the absence of clearly articulated and shared vision.

This is why ideas such as business process re-engineering became important. How do you manage a large organization, or even a small one, that may have to reinvent itself from time to time? Bartlett and Ghoshal considered this question (1995) and decided that the seven Ss concept was basically a power-oriented model by which managers devised strategies and then enforced the implementation of these strategies through structure and procedures. However, they recognized that this failed to engage the unique knowledge, skills and capabilities of each member in an enterprise. For an organization of any size, no amount of command and control will ensure that all participants act in the organization's best interests each time they face a decision.

Instead, it is necessary to use communication to create a shared sense of values. They cited a number of chief executives such as Goran Lindahl of ABB or Roger Enrico of PepsiCo who were seeking to achieve a different kind of control through internalized behaviours. Their idea was that shared values result in a common commitment to a shared purpose. This ensures that, where possible, enterprise participants will seek to leverage their own expertise to best advantage. So, we abandon the seven Ss and discover the three Ps:

- **People** – the fundamental source of any competitive advantage.
- **Purpose** – a shared vision of the future and where we want to go.
- **Process** – elements of the enterprise that produce outcomes. We may or may not own all these processes and we may share some of them with our customers.

This brings us back to relationship marketing. To be successful, it is necessary for most members of the organization to buy into a shared philosophy. In this case, we need buy-in at all levels in order to build long-term relationships with customers. We need everyone to see how that might affect what they do in relation to customers and we need an understanding of a shared sense of direction or purpose so that the organization adapts dynamically in a consistent way. Thus we have a fluid enterprise rather than an administrative bureaucracy or even an adhocracy.

TRANSFORMING THE ORGANIZATION

Based on ideas put forward by Dichter, Gagnon and Alexander (1993) of the McKinsey Consulting Group, Figure 3.1 illustrates the steps that must be taken to develop a customer relationship marketing philosophy:

- Performance in terms of, say, higher profits, increased customer satisfaction levels, higher retention rates or proportion of revenues derived from new products or services has to be the aim. Improvements in performance must be quantified for two reasons. First, actions and resource decisions have to be prioritized. The link between the new culture and visionary performance is the basis of prioritization. Second, unless there is a clear measure of performance, it is difficult for other parts of the enterprise to determine what they need to do in their own roles.

Figure 3.1 Six natural change laws

- Strategy still matters simply because transformation on its own is unable to overcome structural disadvantage. In essence, you have to have the right products, service and infrastructure to compete. Thus, if the wrong technology, outmoded assets or minimal customer-added value products burden the enterprise then strategic, structural changes are needed immediately.

- Teams are vital because organizational reorientation requires complete shared commitment, to the vision, to the process of change and to the people with whom you are working. This is not only in terms of the need for integration between parts of the enterprise but also because, while changing and responding, the firm has to continue to work and generate funds.

- A new way of assessing the contribution that each person makes is needed. In an organization with a traditional, rigid hierarchy, promotion often goes to those who follow the rules and stick by the book. People who challenge the rules by offering new solutions to problems are sometimes regarded suspiciously. These attitudes have to be replaced by valuing results related to the new vision. Process redesign must create a shared sense of the values that are trying to be achieved. Thus, an empowered workforce must incorporate these changes in its everyday activities with customers. In particular, leadership behaviour must be consistent with these ideas. The hard part here is that the new approach involves some loss of power at the top of the organization. Therefore, senior management must be prepared to delegate decision making.

- Change is an evolutionary process, a learning process and it may not always lead where you expect. This also means that management must not seek to retain power by planning fully in advance. Direction setting should be confined to making preliminary statements like, 'We must achieve a significant and profitable reduction in customer attrition', a top down view. Bottom up might then augment the idea with a solution: '. . . by calling important customers shortly after they receive a delivery'.
- It is much better to provide focus by choosing a few key objectives first. The focus may then be redefined, as necessary, once measurable improvements are achieved.

THREE FORCES FOR TRANSFORMATION

The transformation triangle shown in Figure 3.2 illustrates the forces that bring about the desired changes. At the heart of the exercise is the performance improvement being sought. The performance improvement is achieved by adjusting the organization in a fluid, responsive way to changing needs. These adjustments might be in terms of products and services, the location or nature of processes or in partnering with suppliers or customers. For example, a retailer might offer to dispose of an old appliance when delivering a new one, send an automatic reminder when servicing is due or even pass on details of the sale to a local service agent.

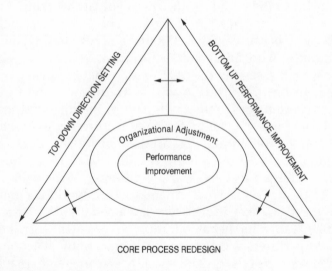

Figure 3.2 Transformation triangle

The mechanisms that enable the organization to adjust are shown on the outside of the diagram. Obviously, some coherence is still needed and this is provided by top down planning which maintains the perspective of the overall vision. Here we are concerned with leadership functions rather than management. Management support comes in the form of the bottom up activities shown on the left of the diagram. Their activities aim to translate the goals and vision into measurable performance targets and into ways of achieving those targets. Underpinning each of these are the organizational processes. For many enterprises, a full customer relationship marketing approach will require core process redesign in order to achieve a more effective strategic posture. Figure 3.3 is an expansion of the first diagram and breaks each dimension into its main elements.

It is often useful to test these ideas in terms of previous transformation efforts that the organization may have attempted, especially if they were unsuccessful. This will help to highlight the importance of taking all these factors into account and of managing the relationships between them. Change is the product and not the sum of these forces.

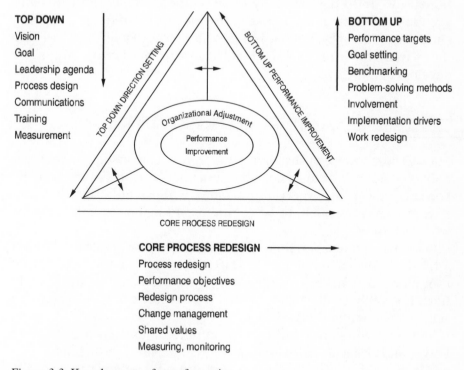

Figure 3.3 Key elements of transformation

TOP DOWN LEADERSHIP

The firm's leadership must set the direction for change by providing a recognized, clear need for change from the outset. Essentially, this means making people uncomfortable with the way things are at the moment and encouraging them to recognize why the organization must alter. It is very easy to underestimate how comfortable everyone can be with the way we do things now. The leadership agenda must be established and nurtured. A powerful group of senior line managers should develop a vision for the organization that can be quickly communicated and understood. The vision must then be spread and communicated by every possible communication channel at every opportunity. This means that the vision should be crisp, clear and easily understood. If you find yourself still talking about the vision twenty minutes after you started then it is still not sharp enough.

Precise, clearly defined goals must be established. Too fuzzy a vision will help foster resistance and delay. There is no reason, however, why the initial directions established should not be refined by responses from below. Indeed, it is usually better if they are. Once the leadership agenda is identified, the implications for process redesign, training and measurement become clearer in policy terms. Table 3.1 shows how the parameters for customer relationship marketing might be developed.

GAINING COMMITMENT TO RELATIONSHIP MARKETING

There is little chance of sustaining delivery of relationship marketing if only one or a few of the leadership functions in Table 3.1 are fulfilled. For this reason, it is very important for the whole organization, however large or small, to be committed to managing relationships with customers.

In a small organization there are fewer chances for great variations in attitude between members of staff. Therefore, if the boss is not committed to managing relationships with customers, this attitude will transfer quickly to other staff. There will be a close connection between staff behaviour and success.

In a large company, staff may be more remote from the centre of power and the scope for variation is greater. Staff can maintain standards of relationship marketing that are not underwritten by the

Table 3.1 Leadership issues for new relationship marketing strategies

Leadership Function	Intention	Dangers
Vision	A future based on enterprise-wide customer relationship marketing.	No buy-in. Traditional marketing approaches are regarded as satisfactory.
Goal	Competitive advantage and survival.	Goals based on short-term measures.
Communication	Every possible means of communication is used that are two-way, systematic and responsive.	One-off messages, individual newsletters or memos on an impromptu basis are considered sufficient.
Leadership Agenda	360-degree feedback, internal and external dialogue.	Talk the talk but do not walk the walk. Power is retained at the top and individual initiatives are 'approved' at each stage.
Process Redesign	Processes defined in terms of the customers' value added needs.	Processes defined in terms of technology, capability or cost.
Training	Emphasis on cultural change and organizational fit.	Skills- or function-based training.
Measurement	Performance measures couched in terms of the new vision, eg customer loyalty measures, lifetime value.	Performance measures still related to the past, volume and profit per transaction.

formal policies of their organization. In such situations, the lead from top management is crucial. Without it, all down the line, managers will be faced with other priorities. These include short-term cost control or immediate sales achievement. There is then a need for strong, frequent reinforcement of the philosophy.

Strategic focus is therefore essential to the success of relationship marketing. However, strategic focus by itself is not enough. Top management must also be committed to the role of relationship marketing in achieving the desired focus and in contributing to competitive positioning. If relationship marketing is considered to make only a marginal contribution to return on assets, the message will be clearly transmitted down the line!

Too much has been written and spoken about 'top management commitment' for any line manager to suspend their disbelief when they hear the phrase. Commitment means walking the walk, being consistent with policy and providing adequate resources to do the job well. It is easy to subscribe to slogans but more difficult to implement policies that require fundamental changes of attitude. These take time as well as money. Thus top management must have a clear and full knowledge of the time and resources that will be absorbed and the problems that will be encountered along the way.

THE IMPORTANCE OF A CLEAR CORPORATE STRATEGY

It is easy for an organization to become confused about relationship marketing. Today, relationship marketing consultants are two a penny. Articles extolling the virtues of relationship marketing are part of managers' daily diets. There is tremendous pressure to rush into an ill-considered relationship marketing programme. This would be exactly the wrong thing to do. It often leads to ill-judged, hasty investments in technologies or systems that are inappropriate.

Relationship marketing is a total approach to looking at how your organization works. You can only determine whether you should be investing more time and money in relationship marketing through a proper analysis integrated into your normal planning process.

The key leadership role is to ensure that commitment is properly sustained. This requires developing a power coalition of high-level managers to provide support and producing evidence that relationship marketing pays. Essentially, the evidence of success must be in terms of the vision and the goals.

As the organization starts to respond, things can go badly wrong. Once an organization, however large or small, has accepted the need for improvements to relationship marketing, the next step is definitely *not* a relationship marketing programme. The next step is to take the idea and benefits of relationship marketing into the core policy-making process. Once the philosophy is absorbed into this process, then leadership is required to challenge the procedures and systems of every department.

GETTING COMMITMENT AND UNDERSTANDING

It is not sensible to ask top management to be committed to relationship marketing unless they understand your organization's current relationships with customers and how they can be improved. It therefore makes sense to involve senior management in some of the activities that usually form the 'front end' of a commitment to relationship marketing. It is not realistic to expect commitment other than on the basis of understanding. In addition to presenting results, ways to involve top management include:

- Attendance at internal discussions or customer focus groups.
- Listening to call centre conversations, live or taped.
- Visits to internal departments and discussions with customer-facing staff (along with visits to competitive sites).
- Exposure to the relationship provided by your company and by your competitors (get them to mystery shop their own company and your competitors).
- Involvement in the research design, which underpins strategic relationship planning.
- Exposure to examples of successful and unsuccessful relationship marketing programmes. The latter are important since they show that such programmes are not easy to develop successfully. It is also important that top management examine the numbers (the performance indicators and financial results) associated with these programmes.

Depth and continuity of commitment

Commitment must be sustained realistically and for obvious reasons. New ideas easily displace superficial concepts. Exposing senior managers to hard evidence and carefully piloted programmes is the only foundation for relationship marketing. Once such a foundation is built, it provides the basis for an enduring commitment.

The commitment must also be deep in the sense that it leads to the concept of relationship marketing permeating all plans and delivery of those plans. This may raise a few problems when the commitment results from a top manager's own conviction. A programme of communication and education is required. In particular, the 'seasoned operators' who form the core of the delivery apparatus may feel they have 'seen it all before', as indeed they usually have. Confidence is quickly lost if the new approach seems to deliver few benefits at the operator level or even if it increases the frequency of failures or half-implemented strategies. To avoid this, the relationship marketing programme must provide both immediate and longer-term benefits for all staff in the line of command. Steady, regular communication of the philosophy and practices of relationship marketing is a much better solution than quick blasts of publicity with no follow-through.

No strain, no gain

It is not realistic to expect senior managers to live, eat and breathe relationship marketing all the time. They have many other responsibilities and their role in developing and supporting relationship marketing is to:

- provide overall direction and guidance;
- set relationship marketing objectives and define quality standards;
- support these standards by meeting regularly with staff to discuss problems and opportunities in relation to the standards;
- create a style of teamwork that encourages staff to take responsibility for relationship marketing and work together to improve it;
- act as a role model (particularly through visiting company locations);
- accept responsibility for the quality of relationship marketing;
- help evaluate ideas on how to improve relationship marketing;
- help create a culture within which relationship marketing objectives can more easily be met;
- ensure that time is spent with new employees to introduce them to the culture and support them in their attempts to build and sustain customer relationships.

BOTTOM UP MANAGEMENT

Two obvious constraints often inhibit managerial support for the new vision by bottom up performance improvement.

The first is the assumption that once the top down directions have been given, all that is needed is a new training system and a related rewards matrix. So we imagine that all we have to do is show someone how to set up a loyalty grid or to send out a questionnaire and the rest will follow automatically. This is a reversal of what is actually needed. Attitudinal change must precede and pre-empt knowledge change which, in turn, precedes skills developments. In other words, skills come last!

The second is possible inertia from line functions. The first bottom up cycle will be lengthy and uncomfortable. Most people like to do their job as they are doing it now. Instilling a relationship marketing philosophy requires patience, determination and the resolve to recognize that this is a long haul, not a quick trip.

To remove these constraints, senior management must realize that orders and incentives are only effective if the desired results lie within the firm's existing capabilities. This includes what people are inclined to do as well as what they are able to do. When fundamental change is required, such as a move from product engineering to a customer value focus, then bottom up improvement has to be encouraged in a very explicit manner. Table 3.2 shows how this might develop.

Table 3.2 Encouraging a bottom up response

Management Function	Intention	Dangers
Performance Targets	Established based on customer relationship marketing metrics such as reduced churn.	Based on prescriptive marketing metrics such as market share, sales volume or number of contacts.
Goal Setting	Based on external customers, internal customers and suppliers.	Based on external customers only.
Benchmarking	Set against best in class regardless of area of activity, eg Disney for 'hearts and minds' campaigns.	Set against other similar, current organizations.
Problem-solving Methods	Chosen as appropriate and reviewed for success.	Based on approved, existing techniques.
Involvement	Every person in the enterprise.	Customer contact staff who are considered to be in a selling role.
Implementation Drivers	Resources allocated to support new initiatives and taken from initiatives that are less important.	New initiatives set up ('we will go for zero defects') but no new resources allocated.
Work Redesign	Driven by the operators of each process.	Imposed by management.

PERFORMANCE INDICATORS

If commitment to relationship marketing is not translated into the way staff are measured or managed then little will change. If managers and staff hear messages about commitment but see no change in the way that their performance is judged, they will be deeply suspicious of the message. Some early move to change performance indicators in the direction indicated by the relationship marketing concept is therefore recommended.

The acid test of these indicators is how top management reacts when relationship marketing performance indicators clash with others, such as financial indicators. This does not have to mean a sudden move into the red. Take a small example. It is easy to measure the performance of a call centre in a cost-oriented way with measures such as time taken to respond to calls, number of calls per agent, duration of calls and so on. It is much harder to measure it in terms of customer satisfaction levels, cross-selling or retention rates.

Integrating performance indicators with performance

Top management has a particularly important role when it comes to integrating financial, technical and relationship marketing indicators. One common problem is split responsibilities for achieving the following tasks:

- Delivering quality according to specifications, eg technical performance may be the responsibility of engineering but sales promised the performance.
- Delivering financial results such as a level of profits or meeting a budget constraint often falls across a number of functions.
- Achieving relationships which customers regard as satisfactory has several dimensions. For example, product quality and reliability or response to calls and use of information previously supplied by the customer.
- Pricing, credit terms and chasing debtors may fall to finance rather than to marketing.
- Engineers may be responsible for performance of installed equipment rather than sales.
- Marketing and sales staff may be responsible for finding new customers and getting more business out of existing customers but production and service are responsible for operations.

Each group has potentially a strong influence on relationship marketing but can end up pulling in opposite directions. Finance staff may alienate customers by chasing debtors. Service engineers may create dissatisfaction by questioning customers' choice of equipment ('Who sold you this, then?'). Sales staff may respond to inventory shortages by selling equipment that is not suitable for the customers' use, perhaps raising the customers' service costs through inappropriate usage.

The lines of control through which these different staff are managed may only merge near the top of the organization. Some thought must be given to creating an organizational form that allows the impact of each of these functional areas to be brought together, for example by the creation of customer management teams.

CORE PROCESS REDESIGN

Whilst both large and small organizations face the same problems in implementing the relationship marketing philosophy, a large organization, with many tiers of management or with many branches or subsidiaries, has to think more carefully about its processes in a formal sense. The planning framework in Figure 3.4 illustrates the scope of the core processes that may need to be reviewed.

LINKING STRATEGY WITH OPERATIONS

Linking strategy with operations, engaging individuals and focusing day-to-day activities on achieving objectives requires some discussion of relationship marketing planning and the hierarchy of key performance indicators.

The process flowchart in Figure 3.4 tries to illustrate the links between the objectives that emerge from strategic planning, the way that these are translated into measurable outcomes and the monitoring procedures needed to ensure that these are implemented as intended on a day-to-day basis.

The aim of this operational planning process is to enable the planners and executors of the actions to understand:

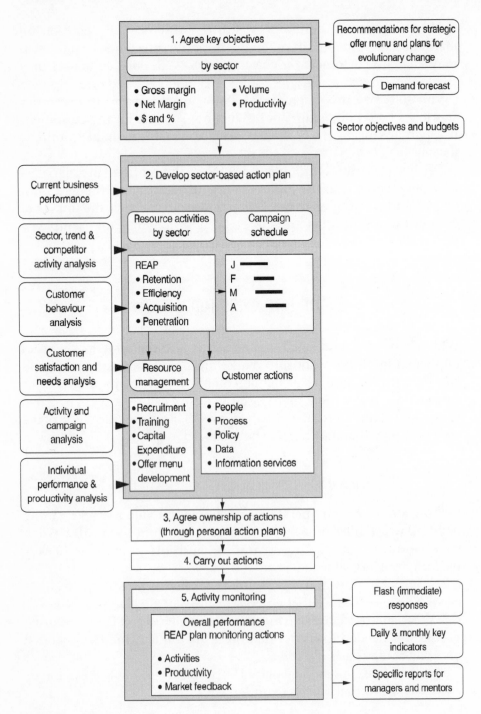

Figure 3.4 Planning framework for customer relationship marketing

- **What** needs to be done.
- The **purpose** of the action.
- The **benefit** that it is expected to achieve. Some of these benefits will be clearly quantifiable. Others will be less so, perhaps not at all, so that qualitative measures must be designed.

Most managers are familiar with the concept of responsibility accounting. The principle of responsibility accounting is that levels of management are associated with levels of profitability. For example, a departmental manager cannot be held responsible for capital over-heads as these decisions are made at a higher level in the company. A departmental profit and loss account must be constructed based on revenues and costs that fall within the control of the departmental manager. The same is true for relationship marketing. Each activity should have a clear key performance indicator (KPI), or set of KPIs, associated with them that can be monitored. Each of these must be allocated to individuals who will be accountable for achieving them.

Developing the analogy with accounting, it is also important to recognize the difference between auditing and control. Many of the procedures that businesses think of as controls are, in reality, audits. Control is only possible if performance indicators are available that can be understood, suggest a direction for action and allow future outcomes to be influenced. A daily profit and loss report, produced at the end of the day, no matter how quickly, is an audit tool. You cannot influence what has already happened. It is therefore essential that KPIs are reviewed regularly (how regularly depends on the type of action that might be required) through a dynamic monitoring process which allows them to be modified or cancelled if necessary.

PROCESS SUMMARY

Task 1 – agree objectives

Obviously the first step but, perhaps not quite so obviously a highly political activity. It is easy to overlook the fact that not all members of the enterprise will necessarily see it in the same way, no matter how hard senior management work on communicating shared values. At the same time, people usually have a personal agenda in terms of their needs and their jobs which affects their perspective. Agreeing a set of prioritized, shared objectives is therefore a question of negotiation and agreement.

For larger enterprises, pressures from other political (with a small *p*) groupings need to be taken into account. These might be geographic divisions (Europe, United States), functional (marketing, finance) or product (industrial, consumer). We will refer to these as sectors. Each of the objectives coming from another sector needs to be understood in terms of volume, margin or GOP (gross operating profit). These are negotiated and agreed through the top down, bottom up process that has been described. The whole planning process is clearly iterative because the implications of each objective become clearer as the level of detail increases. Each stage of the planning process increases the level of detail. Three outputs from this stage include: the strategic menu or offer (which configuration of products and services we will offer and how that will evolve in relation to the external environment); a volume or demand forecast for each; and agreed sector objectives along with their operating budgets.

Task 2 – develop the plan

This is where the planning process becomes more dynamic. The initial plan is developed well before the beginning of the year to which it relates in order to be able to influence outcomes. Thus, nine months to a year after it was written, when the enterprise might be only halfway through the current year, many things may have changed. It will therefore need to be adjusted during the year. The plan needs to consider:

- **Business performance** – an analysis of current business financial performance compared to the previous plan should indicate the performance of each sector. This leads to an identification of the gaps between likely, actual and the plan for the coming year. Note that the comparison is with previous plans, as well as previous actual outcomes. It is important to refine the quality of the planning process. It is also important to avoid crude comparisons of year on year performance that may not be meaningful. Market conditions this year can be quite different from last.
- **Sector trends** – this includes an external analysis on market, product and competitor trends, including a limited amount of SWOT (strengths, weaknesses, opportunities and threats) and PEST (political, environmental, social and technological) analyses, which are carried out in each sector market.

- **Customer behaviour** – ie customer behaviour in terms of retention rates, acquisition rates, cost to serve and other related performance indicators are analysed to determine areas for action.
- **Customer satisfaction and research** – external customer feedback, attitudes, complaints and requests are examined to understand the areas where our offer can be improved.
- **Activity analysis** – internal performance indicators are examined next, using customer databases or other sources of customer data to understand where improvements can be made internally. This includes activity analysis where retention, acquisition and penetration activities are examined for effectiveness and campaign successes or failures. In addition, the key offer performance (aspects such as delivery, invoicing accuracy, returns rates, statementing) is reviewed.
- **Individual performance efficiency** – the efficient use of field sales forces and telephony is analysed to see where time can best be spent. This process will include the consideration of formal (eg via workshops or questionnaires) and informal (eg via Intranet or conversation) employee feedback. The employees invited to these meetings should include key operational employees who have actually dealt with the customer groups being discussed. It is vital that they have actual experience of customer management activities and offer activity.
- **REAP** – a matrix of sector-specific actions can now be developed and categorized in terms of retention, efficiency, acquisition and penetration (REAP). A REAP checklist is provided at the end of this chapter. This is the first matrix that clearly identifies the actions required and must involve input from the market, service and sales people involved in the sector. Four sets of guidelines for improving the creative approach to each of these dimensions are included at the end of the chapter.

The REAP analysis, in turn, gives rise to two streams of operational development. These are in the areas of resource development (shown as resource management activities in Figure 3.4) and customer actions. Customer management resources include recruitment, training and capital expenditure. Customer actions cover sales, service and marketing campaigns and are enabled by policies, people, processes, data and IS (information services).

Task 3 – agree ownership of actions

If relationship marketing is to be pursued, each responsible manager must take ownership of the actions agreed. The team involved will already have developed the plan but a formal session is needed where action ownership is agreed.

Task 4 – carry out the actions

At this point, there is an interface with the human resource development system. This includes areas such as task allocation, commitment, monitoring and reward, which we shall not pursue here. Wherever possible, the action steps that result will be system driven. For example, contact management tactics or contacts for campaigns will be recorded via the same systems that generate the action and record the results. However, while systems might propose, it is still people that (usually) dispose, so actions should be reflected in personal objectives.

Task 5 – monitor

The plan is then monitored against the key performance indicators identified in task area two. As part of this monitoring, formal and informal feedback from customers, employees or from the market generally is used to ensure the activities are as effective as possible.

Performance, activity analysis, individual productivity and quality will also be monitored as part of the customer relationship marketing environment. As in any project work, the main danger at this point is that of ill-considered change. A change management process must be established so that any inclination to adopt a 'shoot from the hip' management style is suppressed as far as possible. A change management procedure ensures that any alterations in direction and responses to current market conditions are still consistent with the overall strategic direction. For instance, campaigns may be halted or expanded, processes may be changed or additional coaching may be necessary.

KEY FEATURES OF THE PLANNING PROCESS

- It seeks to use knowledge of actual customer behaviour and activity through customer databases, market intelligence and the corporate Intranet.
- It uses both formal and informal feedback from employees and customers.

- Plans developed by this method are quicker to produce and easier to change.
- It is developed by sector managers, with input from all operational personnel involved in the offer activity.
- In consequence, there is a higher level of buy-in from customer-facing personnel.
- Completely action oriented; it actually affects what people do on a day-to-day basis.
- Dynamic monitoring of actions makes the plan more tangible.
- Flexibility is maintained with little loss of internal coherence. Changes are based on monitoring current market responses, which are assessed in relation to long-term objectives.

In relation to the other two elements of the transformation triangle described earlier, the procedure implements the twin thrusts of top down, bottom up planning. The planning process then appears like Figure 3.5, with the operational side forecasting the customer inventory and number of sales per customer for the next few months while senior management review the effectiveness of relationship building within the context of the overall business.

The senior view may not always be reflected exactly by the operational view at first but through negotiation and interaction the two views will merge. Both 'parties' then agree on the objectives and actions for the year. A team approach is fundamental to eventual success and the notion of planning as a 'mirrored' activity emphasizes the fact that good planning, with maximum buy-in from the whole team, is best carried out through a process of discussion and negotiation.

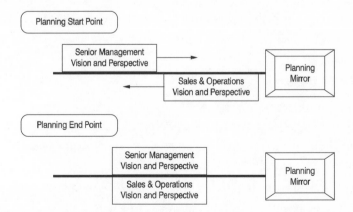

Figure 3.5 The move to shared values: a reflective/supportive planning approach

SUMMARY

Effective customer relationship marketing requires an enterprise in which decision making and resources are much closer to the customer than in most organizations today. Closeness does not necessarily imply geographical proximity but simply a point of contact, physical or virtual. Senior managers cannot hope to control all the interactions between customers and the enterprise directly. This means that they have to create an organization culture where the philosophy of the approach is widely accepted. Purpose, people and process must fit together.

The transformation of the enterprise in this direction proceeds by a combination of top down and bottom up approaches. The core processes needed to implement the directions agreed as a result of this integration ensure that systems, management procedures and control processes allow staff to meet customer needs.

Creating a structure to deliver relationship marketing means placing the authority to deal with individual customers as close to your customers as possible, empowering those with direct contact. At the same time, responsibility must be accepted by those with key roles to play. A planning process is needed to ensure that resources and information to support and monitor achievement are properly directed.

The key test of management commitment is whether intentions are translated into resource. In the short term, an investment may be required in the form of training, systems development or even new approaches to customers that do not produce an immediate return. The next step, therefore, is to produce evidence of benefits.

CHECKLIST FOR REAP PLANNING

Topic	Reap
Strategic Analysis	
• Are there market segments that appear to be more or less loyal than others (or more or less vulnerable)?	R
• What are the main reasons for customer loss? What can we do to put this right?	R
• Can we identify prospective lost customers sooner?	R
• Does the profile of our new customers fit the profile of our loyal customers?	A

- Based on the above, are we attracting the right customers? A
- What are the main reasons for customer gain? A
- What are the main reasons for near misses? Do we know when they take place? A
- How did we gain most of the good accounts this year? A
- What activities / media / contact strategies / lists / timing / segments really performed? A
- Which sectors were the best performers (individuals or teams) in acquisition last year? Use the best performers this year to coach marketing and other sales people. (In other words seek to share expertise and best practice.) A
- Have there been any events or trade shows in the last year where we could obtain the list of attendees/enquirers? A
- What are the lifestyle/business decision triggers that help us to acquire a customer? A
- Are there any market segments that appear to be more likely to buy other products or services? What are the characteristics that define these segments? P
- What impact is inbound cross-selling having? How can it be improved? P
- What impact are our cross-selling campaigns having? Who converts and why? P
- Are there any lead products that act as a precursor to a purchase of our products and services? P
- Are there any obvious (or not so obvious) product or service purchase combinations? P
- What are the trigger criteria for cross-selling? P
- Have all of our larger customers been qualified so that their potential for cross-selling is fully understood? P

Customer/Prospect Feedback

- What does our research show about the customers' perception of our service? Is there any feedback from customers that may be used to retain customers? R
- What complaints have we received about our service? R

79

- What do our mystery shopping experiences tell us?   R
- What do prospects say about their understanding of our
  offer when they research our products and services?   A
- What aspects of the offer have prospects requested that we
  cannot provide?   A
- What other products have customers in this market segment
  asked us for that we cannot provide?   P
- Should we provide them?   P
- Are there any customer-qualification, training or channel issues
  here?   P
- What are customers telling us about the frequency and type of
  contact?   RP
- What are customers telling us about the information we
  give them?   RP
- Is there any feedback from customers that may be used to
  help us be more efficient?   E
- What complaints have we received from prospects (volume,
  type and focus)?   R
- Is there any feedback from customers that may be used
  to help acquire new customers?   A
- What can we do to improve communications with customers
  who are thinking of leaving to encourage them to stay?   R
- Is there any feedback from customers that may be used
  to help penetrate market segments more effectively?   P

Competitive Situation

- To which competitors have we lost most customers?   R
- What do they offer that we do not?   R
- What are competitors doing that may influence the loyalty
  of our customers?   R
- How can we redevelop our offer to compete (if we want to)?   R
- From whom have we gained most accounts?   A
- Is there an opportunity to target this competitor's customers?   A

Co-ordination

- What is the rest of the company doing that may
  influence the loyalty of our customers?   R

- For example, can we link in with promotions or loyalty
  programmes from other sectors?   R

Employee Feedback

- Is there any feedback from employees that may be used
  to help retain customers?   R

- Is there any feedback from employees that may be used to
  help us be more efficient?   E

- Is there any feedback from employees that may be used
  to help acquire new customers?   A

- Is there any feedback from employees that may be used
  to help penetrate other market segments more effectively?   P

Financial Analysis

- Does the profitability of each product/customer combination
  look acceptable?   E

- Does the margin differ widely between types of customer?
  Can we obtain a greater price or reduced cost through
  our relationship marketing activities?   E

- Are there customer/product combinations on which we make
  losses?   E

- How can we manage to reduce service costs while
  maintaining core value added?   E

- Can we pre-qualify customers better?   E

- What is the forecast future margin of new customers gained
  this year over the next one, two or three years? Where does it
  put them in terms of high-, medium- and low-value customers?   E

- Does the apportionment of fixed cost (by invoices, activity
  analysis, cost allocation codes) to different sectors or
  products look reasonable?   E

Resource Focus

- How much time are we spending on each section of our
  customer base categorized by high-, medium- and low-value
  customers?   E

- How do we define customer value?   E
- How much time are sales people and other customer-facing staff spending on retention, acquisition or penetration activities and is this bearing fruit?   E
- Do we need to alter the allocation of effort and adjust pay, planning, appraisal systems and incentives?   E

Processes

- What seem to be our most complex processes?   E
- Can these be simplified without loss of value to any customer external, internal or supplier?   E
- Which activities take up most of the time in administration and support?   E
- Can we do anything about stopping the root cause (do we need to do it?) or can we improve or automate processes?   E
- Carry out some 'what if' analyses on the productivity, numbers of staff, sales conversion rates and activity mix. What does this tell you about resourcing and activities?   E
- How well are enquiries handled (speed of response, follow up, feedback, qualification, conversion rates)?   E
- What are the characteristics and costs of the sales cycle? Can it be shortened or improved?   E
- What is the proportion of wasted calls such as those to unqualified customers, eg those with no money available or those who generate little or no profit (worthless customers)?   E
- Are abandoned-customer rates and call centre service levels within targets?   E
- If not, what changes do we need to make to systems and resourcing?   E

4

Measuring the impact

TEN GUIDELINES FOR A RELATIONSHIP MARKETING STRATEGY

There are only three simple rules for ensuring the success of customer relationship marketing. Measure, measure and measure. Direct marketers are accustomed to these rules but traditional marketing planners have sometimes found this more difficult. Market feasibility studies that lead to a product or service specification, followed by an investment feasibility study, are used for large, complex problems especially where innovation or novelty is a big factor. There are many uncontrolled variables in such situations that make the task of precise measurement enormously complicated. The key to success for customer relationship marketing is data of as high a quality as can be obtained, constantly refined, associated with a series of marketing actions whose effect is constantly monitored.

Before developing a relationship marketing strategy it is useful to consider 10 guidelines to ensure that evaluation and measurement can be carried out effectively.

1. Is it the right thing to do?

The most important first question is, 'Should we do it?' Relationship marketing has become increasingly important as the benefits that it brings to both suppliers and customers are increasingly recognized. Advances in information technology have provided ever-improving tools. It is therefore easy to get caught up in a tide of populism. Nevertheless, relationship marketing is not necessarily the right approach for every product, service or brand. There are limits to the number of relationships that an individual or a business can sustain. Sometimes, the consumer just wants to pay $20 for a spade without entering into a relationship for lifelong horticultural management! We look at this again in Chapter 12.

Before you start, therefore, determine whether the product, service or brand meets the criteria for a relationship marketing approach. Is there sufficient scale, frequency, competitive pressure, positioning and differentiation to warrant the effort? Is it compatible with long-term strategy? If we are just planning to dump products or to blow a competitor away with an aggressive price war then relationship marketing will be over expensive. If we are positioning ourselves as an ultra low-cost, no-frills supplier, consumers will not expect it. Sometimes the nature of the product, or the market, can make relationship marketing seem over intrusive. For example, teenagers may not welcome direct mail from the company that supplied them with their first contraceptive products. Sometimes we may recognize that the resources required to sustain a relationship effectively, at parity with our competitors, are beyond the current scope of the enterprise. If relationships are not sustained with apparent equality, we run the risk that some customers will be made to feel second rate.

2. Start with the customer

Start with a customer perspective. The needs and attitudes of the key decision maker in the customer's buying process are going to be central to strategic communications planning. Take time to identify some crucial insights into where customer value lies, identify a point of difference between your product or service and competitive offers and seek to understand the differences that will exist between business to business and business to consumer.

The better that the key decision makers' needs are understood, the more likely that the features, benefits and advantages that will enrich the perceived value of the relationship can be properly developed and communicated.

3. Use research to give direction constantly

Use research and feedback to give direction continuously, not just when something goes wrong. Relationship marketing is based on a proactive marketing approach sustained by an open dialogue, a two-way communication.

At the inception of the strategy, it may be necessary to use research and sales forecasting companies, such as NOP in the UK or AC Nielsen Bases in the United States to provide pre-market assessment measures for planned programmes. These should then be supported by a combination of internally produced quantitative and qualitative measures. Be especially careful with the qualitative research. While focus groups are fast and inexpensive, they are not the ideal choice for this sort of problem. Qualitative research with greater predictive value, such as depth interviews or observational studies, might be better.

4. Don't get carried away

Do not get carried away by the tools of the trade. Technology is a fine servant but a poor master. The most frightening claim in relationship marketing is: 'Of course we believe in relationship marketing, just look at our new call centre' (mainframe computer, data warehouse, etc). In a large organization these tools are certainly essential but putting them to work effectively is a whole different ball game. Are the people, processes and procedures in place?

5. Do not lose sight of the basics

Do not throw out the baby with the bath water. The call to action for the customer is probably going to be face-to-face contact, mail or the Internet. When designing your strategy, keep the movement towards the act of purchase in the front of your mind. Use a cascade approach of integrated, overlapping marketing activities, in tune with the customer's preferred contact media, actions to ensure that a planned number of customer hits takes place in the right sequence. You do not have to look very far to find major corporations that launch expensive advertising campaigns, back them up with glossy brochures or expensive Web sites, and then have no procedure to allow them to follow up prospects by telephone.

6. Target and customize

This leads to the next guideline. Relationship marketing entails a targeted, customized dialogue between marketers and customers or potential customers. It enables the dissemination of appropriate messages for the initial conversion of suspects into prospects or sales and for compliance with the right audiences. This means that the dialogue may not be identical for each audience, even in promotional print like a newsletter. Relationship marketing can be the means for building a customer database not only for a single product but also for other corporate brands that benefit the target consumer. Marketers often employ mass media in the short term to trigger a sustained, direct, response-driven database marketing effort. The response is best channelled into dedicated teams with the right IT support and access to relevant data. Training for these teams, coupled with computer-generated scripts, ensures consistency of response. Make sure that everyone in the enterprise knows where these teams are and what they do.

7. Be consistent

Consistency is vital. Relationship marketing campaigns are often multifaceted. It is therefore important to ensure commonality of message and design across all contact vehicles, including people. The more consistent the customer interface, the greater the impact and the greater the opportunity to build a long-term competitive position. This implies continuous training and excellent internal communications. It also implies measurement across the whole range of these interfaces.

8. Stay legal

This is getting harder. Under European Union Directive 95/46, brought into effect in October 1998, companies are permitted to transfer personal information, including names, addresses and personal profiles, across borders. However, the country to which the data are being exported must have in place a national law on privacy and a regulatory agency monitoring the use of such information. Some countries, such as the United States, do not have such laws.

Customer relationship management depends on the collection and use of individual customer information. In addition, as companies become increasingly global, it is vital that this information is accessible to sales, marketing and customer care agents worldwide. Call centres or Web sites in Eire might serve consumers in the United States or Bahrain as well as other European Union countries. Legislation, such as the 1998 Data Protection Act in the UK, also applies to all types of personal records, not just those held in machine-readable form. A name and address book is as subject to the legislation as a computer database.

This may very well affect the marketing offer that it is possible to make. Sweden's privacy agency told American Airlines in 1997 that it could not transmit information about Swedish passengers to its US-based Sabre reservation system. This, in effect, prevented the airline from individualizing its service offering to Swedish passengers.

9. Keep it simple

On the other hand, most customers are more than willing to give you information, if you just give them the opportunity. These opportunities for data collection and measurement occur much more frequently than most companies allow. This does not necessarily mean that they wish to complete a long questionnaire at each point of contact. A few simple, clearly worded questions can yield a build up of data that provides the basis for monitoring important trends in customer needs.

10. Stay alert

Just because you own a hammer, don't imagine that everything is a nail. Not all marketing problems are relationship based. One UK charity decided that data protection laws were restricting its appeals for funds because it could not legally use the beneficiaries of its awards to target possible donors. In this case the beneficiaries were mentally ill and it was believed that their relatives and friends would make the best targets. The problem here is really one of positioning the product (charitable donations) rather than relationship building.

KEY PERFORMANCE INDICATOR (KPI) MEASURES

A key performance indicator (KPI) may be defined as a driver that is critical to the future financial success of the enterprise. Probably the most well-known set of KPIs are those proposed by Kaplan and Norton (1996) for their balanced scorecard. The balanced scorecard develops a series of measures based on four perspectives of a business:

- **customers** – how do they see the firm?
- **internal** – what does the firm excel at?
- **innovation and learning** – can the firm continue to improve and create value?
- **financial** – how does the firm look to shareholders?

The principles behind the balanced scorecard are worth reviewing. First, the approach seeks to avoid information overload by restricting the number of measures used, so as to focus only on those that are seen as essential. The idea is to bring a possibly disparate series of measures together on a single management report. Second, it aims to guard against sub-optimization by forcing management to examine operational measures comprehensively. Third, it requires management to translate general mission statements into a set of specific measures that reflect factors of strategic concern.

Our definition of a KPI is somewhat general and unspecific. This is deliberate. KPIs vary according to purpose and situation. The first five steps in implementing the balanced scorecard approach involve: definition of SBUs (strategic business units); interviews with senior SBU managers; an executive workshop; a second round of interviews; and then a second workshop. This process is designed to elicit the important drivers for each SBU and to ensure buy-in from each of several levels of management. Stage six is implementation and stage seven is the review process. KPIs will change as the business environment changes.

Dynamic monitoring of KPIs is the key to their successful implementation. Customer relationship marketing is essentially a responsive discipline. A rigid plan, which is unable to take customer feedback or changes in the external environment into account, will not be helpful. The planning framework described in the previous chapter suggests a systematic approach. The importance of developing specific and clearly understood performance outcomes is also important. However, the most decisive factor of all is that responsibility for each marketing action is assigned and accepted by the managers responsible for their success. These are the most important enablers of an effective monitoring process.

To be useful, KPIs must meet certain criteria. They should be:

- Clearly and unambiguously defined so that everyone understands them in the same way.
- Based on data that are easily obtainable. A great deal of vital customer data are captured at the point of contact by people who may not recognize its importance. For example, a slightly misspelled name may not seem terribly important to either the customer or the sales clerk in a retail environment. After all, the toaster or the TV is being sold. In a different situation, people react quite negatively to letters received at home that are wrongly addressed.
- Based on data that are captured easily. To encourage accurate data capture it is better to redesign the workflow if necessary. When the data are being captured by individuals, it is important to provide the time and the resources so that the procedure is part of normal working behaviour. Therefore, wherever possible, the KPI should be based on data that are captured as a normal part of the process of managing the relationship. Ideally, if the data are not transferred directly from an electronic system, it may be better to have the customer enter their own information to the data capture point.
- Of an acceptable level of accuracy with no chance of fraudulent capture, particularly if the KPI is to be used as a 'target' achievement or as part of the payment plan. The data must conform to the performance plan. In other words, they must be up to the job. During the Vietnam War, one US senator famously observed that by adding together all the reported casualty figures, the US military had killed the entire population of North Vietnam several times. Notice that we used the word accurate, not precise. Over attention to precision can produce a spurious sense of accuracy. Telephone numbers have to be exactly right but age can be captured as part of a range.
- Systems-validated immediately at the point of capture, to ensure that mandatory data used for KPI developments are recorded at the point of capture.
- Set up in such a way that we can 'drill down' into them to determine the underlying explanations for actual performance. Drilling down is a technique most easily recognized by accountants as a ratio pyramid. A high-level ratio is measured, such as return on investment, and then successively analysed by a series of supporting ratios to determine the cause of problems. The same

technique can be applied to large data sets in marketing. The technique is illustrated in Table 4.2.

THE KPI HIERARCHY

Monitoring the current plan is carried out at the same time as monitoring overall business indicators. Monitoring involves analysing three internal areas and one external area. To achieve the planned objectives in this new data-driven environment, we need to ensure that we have the right *resources* and that we are carrying out the right *marketing activities* in order to produce the required *sales performance*. Balancing these three areas, shown in Figure 4.1, is never easy.

A resource that is carrying out the wrong activities will be unproductive. For example, if the field sales team is meant to be order makers, they will be somewhat underused if they spend a lot of time as order takers. Sometimes, media such as mail or the Internet can handle order

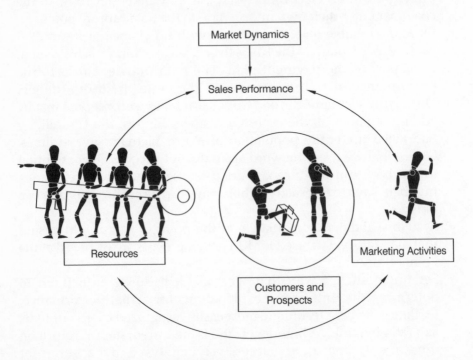

Figure 4.1 The balance of market dynamics

taking more effectively. An underskilled or unproductive resource carrying out the right activities will not perform as well as an appropriately skilled and productive resource.

MARKET FACTORS

Market factors may affect the plan through no fault of our own. Customers may close down, a new competitor may enter the market, production costs may become intolerably high due to an alteration in exchange rates or new forms of taxation. Again, we can borrow two useful ideas from the world of finance. The first is sensitivity analysis. When planning, some consideration must be given to critical success factors and their susceptibility to change. The second is to separate controllable from uncontrollable factors. It is perhaps forgivable to have made a careful but, as it turned out, incorrect analysis of likely tax changes. To have overlooked this aspect of government behaviour (or foreign government behaviour) is less understandable.

SALES PERFORMANCE

This is what the plan will be judged on. It represents the first two levels on the KPI hierarchy described below. It covers the gross and net dollar margin and probably looks at volume, margin percentages and market share by value and volume. An ability to drill down from the corporate to the individual customer level will enable the business to concentrate when necessary on those current or expected future high-value customers that we really want to look after. It will also save effort on those that we do not want to actively manage.

MARKETING ACTIVITY

Levels three to five of the hierarchy in Table 4.1 reveal the importance of developing detailed sector activities in an action plan. A temptation that everyone faces in their job is to devote too much time to those things that they most enjoy or that they find easy to do. Another problem is that of managing time. Too much unplanned activity, especially in the form of fire-fighting, can leave too little time for what is actually needed. At this point, therefore, the KPIs are acting like a road map to make sure the enterprise is headed where it planned to go.

For instance, too much emphasis on retention will not achieve high levels of new business. Too much emphasis on acquisition may leave existing customers vulnerable to competitive approaches. At a more detailed level, the plan may be to deliver a number of campaigns aimed at cross-selling to existing customers. The way this is done in terms of timing, offer and contact strategy will affect conversion rates. Testing different approaches and altering them to make them work better in real time, that is, instantaneously, will improve performance.

RESOURCES

There are two different elements to monitor here. Both examined at level six in the KPI hierarchy. These are productivity and quality.

Productivity measures are a double edged sword. They can easily be misused or can even be counter productive. For example, call centre environments may be very productive in terms of volume of calls or cost per call. However, if productivity targets are too high they can be very demotivating for call agents. Worse, performance and call quality may decrease as a result. Spending longer on calls, and in consequence handling fewer calls, can give agents more time to cross-sell or to deal effectively with customer feedback. As always, it is up to management to find the balance between productivity and performance.

Productivity is therefore only meaningful when considered with quality standards, such as call quality. A call centre may have extremely high productivity but if call quality is low, customers will be unimpressed and sales rates will suffer.

RELEVANCE AND DRILL DOWN

Many of the KPIs will be suggested by the REAP (retention, efficiency, acquisition and penetration) guidelines described at the end of the previous chapter. The ability to drill down into the data is important here. Different managers will use this in different ways. Senior management is usually interested primarily in the top two or three levels. Marketing managers would be interested primarily in levels two to five whereas sales managers might be interested in two to six.

Inbound and outbound call centre supervisors might be primarily interested in levels four to six.

Table 4.1 describes the hierarchy in more detail. Table 4.2 illustrates the progression from data to information to knowledge and then to action.

Table 4.1 KPI hierarchy levels

KPI Hierarchy Level	Description	Example KPIs
Business Performance	How is the enterprise performing against plan?	$ gross, volume, $ margin, $ cost.
Cost and Margin Performance	Where is the profit coming from, where are we making margin and where do costs lie?	Sector, region, product and marketing performance.
Customer Performance	How good are we at managing customers? What do they think of the way we manage them?	Retention %, acquisition %, penetration %. Reason for customer loss and gain summary. Attitude measures, satisfaction measures, complaints number and type.
Activity Summary	Which customer management activities are most effective?	Proportion of time spent on retention, acquisition, penetration and knowledge building compared to the revenue generated. Percentage of time spent on top five support activities.
Activity Detail	For each major relationship marketing activity, analyse detail.	Campaign identification, cost, response %, conversion %, sales revenue generated.
Individual Detail	Which individuals and teams are really performing from a productivity, performance and quality point of view?	Calls made, type of call, call preparation/talk/wrap time (time to close the deal), conversion %, employee satisfaction measures, morale measures.

Table 4.2 KPIs in action

Description	Illustrative Scenario
Business Performance Examine gross and net margins, volumes, market volume and value, plus costs in addition to overall market movement indicators, which show the status of the overall market.	Let us assume that gross and net margins are 5% down versus plan. The market is stable so we seem to be underperforming somewhere.
Cost and Margin Performance Enables a drill down into sectors or regions which are under- or over-performing against plan.	The drill down into SBUs shows that they are all performing well apart from one division – division X. A drill down into region shows that the southern regions are over-performing in division X by 3% but the northern regions are underperforming against target by 7%.
Customer Behaviour Looks at customer behaviour (retention, acquisition, penetration, volumes versus last year), attitude (satisfaction levels with our service and offer) and our cost to serve them.	Focusing on the northern region: Acquisition analysis shows that we have acquired many more new customers in the north than the south, although their actual volumes against projected 12 month sales revenue looks small. Penetration analysis shows that the penetration levels to division X customers are on target at 35%. Retention analysis shows that we have lost 10% more division X customers in the north, particularly in the middle segment. A drill down into customer loss reasons shows most of the losses are to competitors, mainly due to poor service.
Activity Summary Looks at the summary of activities undertaken with this customer group.	Field sales activity analysis shows that, although the percentage of visits spent on retention was targeted at 30%, only 18% of time was actually spent on this activity, the majority of time being spent on acquisition. Telemarketing activity shows the same bias. It appears that we have overdone the prospecting campaign focus and have not focused enough on retention activities.

Table 4.2 continued

Description	Illustrative Scenario
Activity Detail This shows activities in detail; looking at response, conversion rates and order values, for instance.	A drill down into detailed campaign results shows that our conversion rate in the north is similar to the south, but that the actual sales volume achieved from new customers is much smaller. The projected 12-month sales volume for these customers is similar between north and south. It appears that several actions need to be taken: Obtain a better balance between retention and acquisition (in line with targets). Look at the campaigns in the north. Why are we converting smaller customers? Is it a skills issue, a targeting issue (not calling the largest ones first), a prospect data issue (have not got the right prospects on the database) or a geo-demographic issue (there are bigger prospects in the south)? Investigation of this point may show that some northern sales people are sloppy when it comes to adding prospects onto the database or that they qualify them inaccurately. (Failing to qualify prospects leads to a waste of sales time.) We need to ensure that sales people are more realistic about the projected 12-month volumes that they estimate. This will affect the price we offer the customer as well as on demand forecasting. If sales people insist that the projected volumes are correct, we need to approach the customers to find out why we are only getting a proportion of the forecast volume.
Individual Performance Looks at the performance of individuals.	Analysis of individuals indicates that some sales people in the north do convert higher value prospects and are able to predict 12-month volumes more accurately. This knowledge enables us to identify which individuals we need to coach. Perhaps the best northern performers can describe what they do differently as part of this coaching (share expertise and best practice). However, something else emerges from this drill down that is interesting. The number of outbound telephone calls made by the northern team is generally much lower than for the southern team. The southern team can make 15% more calls with the same conversion rate. So another action emerges: The best southern telemarketers and sales people can help to coach the northern ones. If we can raise call productivity with the same conversion rate, we can spend more time on retention of middle volume customers, for example by telephone account management.

QUANTIFYING RELATIONSHIP MARKETING

In competitive strategy formulation, relationship marketing is most frequently used to achieve revenue defence and development or cost reduction. These are not mutually exclusive. Many of the opportunities opened up by relationship marketing affect both revenue and costs. Some lead to increased revenue while costs rise more slowly or remain static. Others lead to falling costs while holding revenue at the same level.

Many of the changes also have both a short- and a long-term dimension. For example, telemarketing may produce cost savings and revenue increases relatively quickly by reducing the cost of contacting and selling to customers and by increasing market coverage. These effects continue until competitive response matches your market performance. At this point higher levels of competence and expertise, gained though practice, may allow you to enter different markets. It may be possible to sell a wider product range to existing customers. It may also be possible to market in digital space since your databases may well be more refined than those of your catch-up competitors.

The revenue and cost changes that might result from different aspects of relationship marketing must therefore be identified and quantified by, for example:

- customer;
- product;
- type of relationship marketing tool (field sales force, inbound or outbound telemarketing, direct mail);
- direction of change (whether cost saving, revenue defence or market growth);
- time (short-, medium- or long-term);
- staff, function or marketing channel (for example, impact on field sales force, sales offices, retail outlets, physical distribution, marketing communications or market research).

The measurement process can be carried out in a number of stages.

STAGE 1: TARGET OPPORTUNITIES

The first step is to generate a shortlist of target opportunities for managing customers better. This is usually best achieved in a series of management workshops or focus groups. The workshops may be supplemented by a series of semi-structured management interviews. Sometimes a change agent such as an external consultant is used to facilitate this exercise but it is worth recognizing that in many cases the best ideas for new opportunities are already available to your company – you just need to learn what they are. An enterprise hierarchy can be regarded as a map illustrating the distribution of formal power. Quite often, the existing distribution of power, the current rules and the current procedures, discourage foot soldiers from offering good ideas. After all, someone who challenges the way we do things now may be branded as a troublemaker or a misfit. While everyone accepts that you can't make an omelette without breaking eggs, the destructive/creative cycle of organizational change is often frightening in practice.

New opportunities may threaten people's sense of position, their power base, their feelings of competence and their feelings of security. It is therefore very important to create an organization culture in which constant change and repositioning is seen as a normal condition of survival. A brief summary of the sort of opportunities that may be proposed may illustrate the scope and range of what is required. The list below progresses from high risk to low risk:

- changing organizational structure and reporting relationships;
- reorganizing workflows;
- policy development within existing functions, departments, or product groups;
- re-engineering processes;
- opening up internal communication channels by providing more access to information (it is surprising how many organizations expect an informed response to customer situations from a half informed work force);
- quality control measures.

The outcome of this stage should be a statement of target opportunities that provides the focus for the next stage.

STAGE 2: REVENUE DEVELOPMENT OPPORTUNITIES

Existing marketing plans should now be reviewed in the light of target opportunities to identify long-term revenue growth objectives and to clarify the basis for revenue growth plans. Revenue growth plans may be based on factors such as overall market growth, specific marketing strategies in relation to product range, pricing, distribution and marketing communications or anticipated competitive changes. Areas that might be selected for measurable changes include:

- **Improving retention rates** – even small percentage improvements may have a very large impact on the bottom line.
- **Cross-selling** – this refers to the proportion of customers who buy more than one product from you. If this percentage is increased, existing marketing and administrative costs are spread over larger revenues.
- **Upselling** – as the term implies, this refers to the sale of an enhanced version of the product or service or a longer term contract. This may be relatively easy to measure for an existing customer but is harder to capture for a new customer. After all, what evidence is there that the customer originally intended to buy a cheaper or smaller version of the product?
- **Lapsing prognosis** – the ideal time to retain a customer is before they lapse! By analysis of the customer database, it may be possible to identify triggers, profiles or patterns of purchase that act as predictors of likely lapsing behaviour. An obvious, easily recognized signal might be an increased rate of complaints but even this is rather late in the day.
- **Improved winback** – becoming better at reactivating lapsed customers.

Case example

Many retailers are now using databases to detect when a customer might be defecting. These are then used to build loyalty/frequency programmes to reduce the number of lapsed customers, especially among the precious 20 per cent who generate 80 per cent of the business. In the United States, Pier 1, with $1.5 billion in sales from some 1,200 stores, built a multi-store customer base. The database helped them jump off the discounting bandwagon by tracking recency, frequency and monetary statistics to identify their 'best' customers. The company issues Gold and Platinum cards to the 150 top valued customers of each store. These customers now receive personalized mail and special information about new products.

The database has enabled Pier 1 to lower marketing costs dramatically while holding on to their best customers. The database is used to identify who should become members of this exclusive club. See www.americasbest.com/weddings/pier1.htm for the Pier 1 Web site.

(1996) *Direct Marketing* **59** (2), pp 10–11

STAGE 3: REVENUE PROTECTION OPPORTUNITIES

Quantifying the cost savings from relationship marketing prior to implementation is not easy. It is even more difficult if your existing market information is not well organized since the information required may have to be estimated. This may involve not only the reconstruction of figures based on estimates but also the use of pilot studies when particular applications are implemented.

Typically, a comprehensive exercise to gather and analyse cost information is required. It will normally cover every channel of communicating concerned with distributing products and services to customers, such as the sales force, branches, sales offices operating by telephone and mail, retail outlets, media advertising and direct mail. The aim is to quantify costs that may be changed by relationship marketing approaches. The exercise is based on interviews, questionnaires and an analysis of financial and operating information relating to the channels of communication and distribution. This analysis may have to be carried out by market sector and product line as well as for the whole business since some of the opportunities may be confined to particular products or sectors.

For example, suppose that you need to estimate the cost-reduction effect on a field sales force. The data needed includes:

- Sales force activity analysis, to find out how your sales staff are spending their time, in particular time spent on low productivity activities, such as prospecting and converting low potential customers, compared with time spent on high-productivity activities (time spent converting high-potential customers or preventing their loss).
- Sales revenue productivity statistics, to measure the productivity of the time actually devoted to your customers.

- Data on market size (overall and by product, number of customers and revenue potential), to enable you to estimate the proportion of the market (overall or for given products) left uncovered by your sales force.
- Data on how the activity profile of your sales force changes when you implement relationship marketing and put relevant applications such as telemarketing or direct mail to work.
- Data on the current costs of managing your sales force.
- Information on how the activities that generate these costs affect the productivity of your sales staff.
- Information on how relationship marketing disciplines will lead to a change in the nature and scale of these activities. For example, the costs of support staff in providing data.

Table 4.3 provides some examples of revenue generation or protection areas.

Table 4.3 Revenue defence and revenue protection areas

Revenue Defence	Revenue Protection
Field Sales Force	
Sales staff to concentrate calling patterns on higher revenue prospects.	Reduction in the number of field sales people needed for given market coverage through more efficient calling patterns. Less time spent identifying prospects and obtaining prospect information.
Less lost business and fewer lost customers due to improved customer care, as relationship marketing provides improved channels for customers to signal their needs.	Reduced staff support required, due to higher quality information available to sales staff.
Enhanced new product revenues due to an improved ability to target customers for new products. Eventually, consequent greater ease in launching new products.	Reduced systems support, due to the standardization of support systems. One large British retail chain store (Debenhams) saved £600,000 each year simply by moving all its 1,200 office-support systems onto the same operating system with identical applications software (*Computer Weekly*, 19th November 1998 p 2).
Greater ability of the sales force to handle a broader offer range, by using automated response-handling systems and database targeting to inform relevant customers prior to the sales call.	Reduced sales force turnover due to improved quality of support and consequent higher motivation.

Table 4.3 continued

Revenue Defence	Revenue Protection
Greater empowerment of customer contact staff allows more rapid, flexible responses to changing customer needs, higher customer satisfaction levels with lower defection rates and increased repeat sales.	A reduced number of reporting levels becomes feasible. This is due to better standards of information on activities and increased effectiveness of field sales staff, leading to lower management costs.

Sales Office

Data mining techniques generate increasingly refined segmentation profiles that lead to automatically configured product and service offers.	The reduction in time spent obtaining and collating information along with more efficient prospecting systems reduces the number of staff required to service a given level of customer contacts.
A customer management centre with interactive voice response and automated scripting allows inbound calls to be routed more efficiently and handled more effectively. Service and feedback calls are turned into sales opportunities.	There are reduced costs of handling customer enquiries due to the improved structure of response handling mechanisms. Customer enquiries go to relevant destination more smoothly without passing through irrelevant hands.
Better informed staff are more confident and positive when dealing with customers. This communicates itself in terms of the image of the enterprise.	Lower staff turnover due to higher level of support and consequent improved morale.
The balance between branches, telemarketing, automated sales kiosks, PC services and Internet e-commerce improves the effectiveness of contact channel management while increasing perceived service levels.	There is a reduction in the number of branch offices due to an ability to cover the market better yet more remotely.

Marketing Communications

Flexible reconfiguration of the offer, in terms of smaller market segments, increase the inclination of the customer to regard the enterprise as the first port of call, or a one-stop shop when seeking new products and services.	There are lower costs for achieving any given task, due to greater accountability and due to an improved ability to make communications more relevant and therefore more effective.

Market Research

Greater ability to identify potential for increased revenue among existing customers through improved profiling.	Reduced expenditure on external research, due to higher quality and relevance of information available on customers and prospects.

Table 4.3 continued

Revenue Defence	Revenue Protection
Business and Marketing Planning More coherent plans to address new revenue opportunities due to higher quality and relevance of information. Higher success rates with the launch of new products or services through better matching of distribution channels to customer needs.	Reduced costs of information collection and management, due to higher quality, more relevant and updated information on customers and prospects. This offers possible reductions in the cost of piloting new products or services.
Retail The ability to market additional products to existing retail customers, whether in-store or through direct mail, due to the quality of customer information (such as the Tesco *Clubcard* described in Chapter 1).	Improved site planning, which matches customer profiles to area profiles more accurately. This leads to a reduction in the number of outlets required to attain given revenue targets but also helps to maximize the profit per unit of space provided.
Higher sales volumes of existing products due to ability to target promotions in terms of cross-selling opportunities.	More effective utilization of space due to the ability to market special in-store events more precisely through use of the customer database. For example, when Sears, the US retail chain, launched its 'Best Customer Programme' the intention was initially to increase retention rates. It was estimated that an improvement of only 1% would generate $6m of additional sales. In practice, better targeting improved retention rates by 11% – do the sums! (Johnson, 1994)
Marketing Communications Greater effectiveness in communicating with customers and prospects produces a higher revenue for given cost.	Reduced customer service costs allow for more complete coverage such as 24/24 and 7/7 (24 hours each day, seven days a week) without commensurate increases in operating overheads.
Product Marketing Reduced costs of selling, due to better alignment of channels to customer needs improves the chances of capturing higher market share.	Reduced selling, due to better alignment between existing (personal contact, face to face) and new channels (Internet telephony or digital interactive TV), some of which are only possible using relationship marketing techniques.

Table 4.3 continued

Revenue Defence	Revenue Protection
Inventory	
Lower levels of stock-outs and therefore quicker revenue due to improved sales forecasting. Higher service rates also reduce the possibility of sales loss to the competition.	Reduced write-offs, due to reduced frequency of new product or service launches and to earlier termination of unsuccessful offers.
A different view of the enterprise eliminates artificial boundaries such as those suggested by a building or by an organization chart. Close synchronization with other suppliers in the value chain can eliminate the need for inventories as products and services are created in response to individual customer needs.	General improved forecasting accuracy of marketing campaigns, leading to reduced demands for tidal inventory peaks.

STAGE 4: REVENUE AND COST REVIEW

A review of marketing activity over the period of the plan should then be prepared. This should compare the effect on revenues and costs of employing existing methods to achieve targets, with those implied by the use of relationship marketing.

If the analysis indicates the need for a distribution channel change underpinned by relationship marketing, the result might be a wholesale change in the revenue/cost profile. For example, whole categories of cost may disappear through, for instance, the abolition of branches while new ones will appear if a customer management centre replaces them. Distribution channel changes may create further strategic marketing opportunities, such as the ability to address whole new markets or to launch completely different types of product. There may also be some more tactical changes. Refocusing the field sales force on larger customers and supporting their efforts by a telemarketing operation would be an example.

Relationship marketing may afford many opportunities for increasing revenue and reducing costs but unless they are built into operating plans as measurable targets, they are unlikely to be achieved. Since there needs to be enterprise-wide agreement to support relationship marketing plans, it is important for all these functional areas to be involved in the strategic appraisal process.

Case example: revenue defence

Consider the effect of a marketing database used by a discount men and women's clothing chain in the United States, as part of a winback campaign (Johnson, 1994).

Different retail situations experience a different customer cycle and therefore have differing opportunities for repeat sales. Grocery customers shop about every seven to ten days whereas in the outer garment clothing business this is typically about every three to six months. Obviously seasonal buying patterns underlie this behaviour. In other industries, such as automotive or electronics, the cycle might be longer, perhaps three to five years.

Consequently, each retailer has a built-in 'reverse horizon,' beyond which a customer might become lost to the competition if not reactivated. For this particular retailer, the frequency of visits averaged about four to six months, so if a customer had not been to the store in at least seven months they could well be lost.

Using the database, the store selected customers who had not shopped in the last seven or more months. The targeting was then refined by selecting only those customers who had spent over $100 per lifetime, on the basis that these were likely to be more valuable.

- Approximately 48,000 customers met the criteria and were sent a personalized letter directly from the president of the company. The letter invited the customer to bring an enclosed gift certificate into the store to receive 20 per cent off any purchase.
- 48,000 inactive customers were mailed. Nearly 4,000 responded to the offer during the 20-day event. This equates to an 8.2 per cent response rate.
- Over $836,000 in sales was generated by customers receiving the reactivation letter.
- Since these customers were lost, nearly all of the $836,000 in sales was incremental. If they had not been contacted, probably none of these customers would have shopped at all. Note that the key here was getting the customers to present the gift certificate and the subsequent tracking of their purchase.
- The average transaction value increased from $114 to $214.

Furthermore, the retailer was able to reactivate nearly 200 customers who had not shopped in the store for more than two years. In fact, it was this segment of customers that had the highest average transaction level, about $300.

The result might surprise marketers who do not believe in the value of mailing lapsed customers. One of the most powerful advantages of database marketing is the unmatched ability to measure the results of each and every marketing or promotional event. With appropriate measurement the results are provable. You know whether it worked or not.

Case example: revenue protection

In the late 1990s, the financial services sector was undergoing major structural transformation due to the impact of new technologies. Despite this, many banks failed to follow best practice or to adopt new technologies effectively (McChesney, 1998).

The convergence of technologies such as telecommunications, computing and television posed a major threat to high street banks' traditional direct access to customers. Many banks were introducing technology reactively and with an inappropriate perspective. For example, call centres that were used to reduce the cost per call rather than increase revenue opportunities. Security First Technologies of the United States provides Internet based banking services for companies such as Citibank and the Royal Bank of Canada. They argue that it is necessary to re-engineer banking services entirely around these new technologies, rather than attempt to offer Internet services as an add-on to other types of contact. Such a strategy could lead to companies such as Microsoft or search engine providers such as Google or Yahoo becoming the first port of call for customers. If this happened, the relationship with the customer would move from the bank to the Internet operator. The point is illustrated by Table 4.4.

Contact Strategy

Table 4.4 illustrates the importance of reviewing customer contact strategies carefully. In the light of technology changes, future contact options needs to be assessed in relation to the capability of existing channels to support revenue growth and the cost of resourcing those channels, and the incremental cost of the relationship marketing strategy needed to support that revenue growth target.

Table 4.4 Customer service costs in the US banking sector (1998)

Costs per Transaction		Customer Service Costs	Contacts per Month	Cost per Problem
Bank Branch	$1.07	*Self help*		
Telephone Banking	$0.54	Internet	4.0	$0.10
Cash Machine	$0.27	Telephone	1.2	$0.25
PC Banking	$0.015	*Customer Service*		
Web Banking	$0.010	Telephone	0.8	$2.62
		e-mail	0.4	$7.50

Source: McChesney (1998)

FIXING THE BUDGET

At one level, fixing any marketing budget is a remarkably simple exercise. As we indicated in Chapter 1, as long as the expenditure is warranted in terms of profitability then it can be justified. Thus the budget, like any budget, should be related to the task. If insufficient resources are made available then not only are the chances of success reduced but also the whole of what is spent may be wasted.

There is only one difficulty with this simple rule, calculating how much extra profit you might make as a result of your marketing actions. Sometimes, the calculation is simplified because you may be forced to improve relationship marketing just to meet competitive standards and stay in business.

However, there are all sorts of definitional problems in setting the budget and many important policy decisions to be made about goals, objectives and time horizons. For example, if the sales team contact a customer in January, are they to be credited with the order that is received in August? The integration of short-term objectives with longer term goals is central to eventual success. At the heart of the decision must be recognition by management of the close connection between relationship marketing and profitability. Using a systematic approach, the strength of this connection can be quantified, which in turn leads to new approaches to customer management. At a basic level, this begins with the identification of groups of customers who wish or need to be managed differently and ends with a long-term commitment to achieving differentiated and higher levels of relationship marketing in order to maximize profit. The essence of the new approach is a much stronger market orientation.

Technical feasibility

Technical feasibility is defined in terms of the level, frequency, type and quality of customer contacts. This must be considered in terms of the activities that are planned as balanced by their resource requirements. Thus the technology required to sustain that level of contact, both in social and technological terms, must be assessed against the size and nature of the customer base. The start of the technical assessment must be to approach it in terms of a wish list. Invariably, the wish list will prove to be more than the organization can stand or cope with in the short term. Thus the next step is to work out what levels of relationship marketing will be provided, measured against the rewards in terms of changed customer behaviour. The important point to note here is that the final solution converges towards an appropriate level of performance that is always set in relation to overall goals. It should never be based on a bottom up approach of the sort, 'This is what we have, therefore this is what we can do'.

Financial feasibility

Relationship marketing is an investment decision like any other and should therefore be subject to the same financial disciplines. It is possible to over-invest in relationships, with no real possibility of return. Assessing financial feasibility requires quantifying the costs of relationship marketing policies and setting them against the benefits. For example, the reduced future costs of query handling are weighed against the increased profit through increased sales. This is not always a question of simple calculations. It is not usually obvious or straight-forward to answer questions such as how customer needs will evolve, what products customers are likely to buy or what the future costs of provision of relationship marketing are likely to be.

Like some other business activities, relationship marketing has the capacity to act like a bottomless pit for hard-earned money, hence the need to justify all relationship marketing expenditure in terms of your financial objectives. The easiest justifications are to be found in increased business from existing customers, a reduction in customer losses and more new customers. Unfortunately, since relationship marketing is very much a holistic technique, it is often difficult to identify neat, individual chunks that can be treated on their own. There is not much point in having a call centre without the right telecommunications infrastructure, IT bandwidth (so as to handle the communications traffic), sufficiently well trained agents and a willingness on everybody's part to make it work. Investment feasibility should therefore consider:

- systems (hardware, software development and/or licences, telecommunications);
- specific training for managers and other staff;
- culture shift education programmes for the organization;
- process re-engineering;
- policy development time;
- set up of new business units, for example telemarketing centres;
- the cost in terms of both money and morale of 'destruction', such as the closure of branches.

These must be set against the marketing benefits, which lie principally in the areas of customer development, acquisition and retention and, in particular, improving the revenue/cost relationship. Your ability to acquire and retain customers depends critically on how well you satisfy their needs, the subject of these activities.

SUMMARY

- Are you sure your marketing problem is amenable to a customer relationship marketing approach? Have you checked off the 10 key points at the beginning of this chapter?
- Does your market situation lend itself to constant measurement and monitoring?
- Have you defined the relevant SBUs within your business? Did you sit down with your fellow managers to identify and agree a series of KPIs in relation to market dynamics, sales performance and sales activities?
- Do you know what resources are needed to generate and monitor those KPIs?
- Are your KPIs based on a hierarchy of measures, each of which allows drill down to determine the specific cause and remedy for any variance against plan?
- Can you test your KPIs by writing down a straightforward example (on one piece of paper) of how your managers would track through a problem if targets were not being met?
- Have you identified revenue defence and revenue protection measures across each of your SBUs?

- What budget setting procedure is used? Is it related to the nature of the relationship marketing tasks to be achieved?
- What are the measurable benefits in terms of profit or surplus that are expected to accrue, in relation to the total cost of the resource base required to support them?
- What customer relationship marketing metrics are being used routinely to measure development, retention, acquisition and attrition?

5

Segmentation and the top vanilla offer

TRADITIONAL AND RELATIONSHIP MARKETING PLANNING

We have already pointed out that a relationship marketing approach is not necessarily ideal for every sales opportunity, nor is it always the preferred platform for every enterprise. It is always sensible to take the best elements of every marketing and management idea and use them where you can.

Relationship marketing will work well when a relationship between the customer and the supplier will improve marketing performance. To some extent, we would argue that relationship marketing reflects some of the transformations that are taking place in society as a whole, due to advances in information technology. Quite simply, the world is becoming more 'wired'. This affects four dimensions of enterprise behaviour (Sweeney, 1998):

- **Transformation** – the network revolution is transforming governments, global businesses and personal lifestyles. Europeans can now shop efficiently and economically from an e-commerce super-market for home or office delivery within two-hour time slots.

- **People** – as a result, power is shifting to the end-consumer and to buyers. Your competitor in China is only six-tenths of a second away. In some industries, the old intermediaries are losing power to direct purchasers. For example, in the travel and transport industry it is increasingly easy to purchase directly from Web agents. On the other hand, some aspects of what travel agents and tour operators provide (the personal touch) is still unique.
- **Process** – networked enterprises are therefore focusing on value net linkages, market-facing systems and intellectual capital. Organizations are increasingly conscious of the importance of their digital resources in terms of the extra services they can provide by using the data they hold about people. However, many of them have not yet really figured out how to do it. It is also difficult to identify how much value these digital resources add.
- **Technology** – at the heart of these changes but in many ways the least important part of it. Nevertheless, it is ubiquitous and increasingly interoperable. It is now possible to interface a mobile phone with e-mail and the Internet for a full range of customer services. Eventually, this interoperability will become 'invisible'. People do not think about the various technologies, systems and processes that provide entertainment when they switch on a TV. In the same way it will become second nature to pick up the phone and do some e-shopping through a keypad on the phone or through interactive voice response systems.

TRADITIONAL MARKETING PLANNING APPROACH

In order to understand how a relationship marketing approach might better serve an enterprise in some situations, it is useful to consider how it might differ from traditional marketing planning. Table 5.1 summarizes the logic of a classical marketing plan in a simplified way. Of course, in practice, the process is more iterative and less linear than that illustrated as assumptions are revised or as parallel processes develop interim solutions.

The case example on page 113 illustrates how the traditional approach works in practice.

Table 5.1 Traditional approach to the marketing planning process

Stage	Process	Output	Timing
Situation Analysis	Gather, collate and analyse data on markets and company performance.	Agreed corporate version of the business environment and forecasts of future position (momentum forecast).	Work begins before the planning year, drawing on existing information infrastructure.
	PEST analysis and assessment of influences on the market. Analysis of competitors' strategies and performance.	SWOT analysis.	Intensive period of work to prepare initial position analysis, may last between two and three months at the beginning of the planning period.
Objective Setting	Set marketing objectives by matching the company's overall business and financial objectives to the situation analysis.	Actual marketing objectives. Which markets to serve (target market segments), what revenues and profits are to be achieved in each market. Broad range of products and services to be offered.	Starts in parallel with the situation analysis, building in intensity. One further month is allocated to finalization once an agreed version of the situation analysis is finalized.
Marketing Strategy Development	Development of strategies for the marketing mix – product and service, price, distribution, marketing communications.	An agreed set of interlocking marketing strategies is produced – overall and for each target market. Resource allocation is developed against strategies.	Starts in parallel with final month of the objective setting process. Usually completed after the third planning month in a large enterprise.
Action Planning	Development of detailed action plans to ensure the achievement of strategies.	Allocation of accountabilities for the delivery of each strategy.	Starts at the beginning of the last month of marketing strategy development.
		Development of detailed descriptions of the tasks required. Detailed budget allocation.	Completed perhaps as long as two months later.
		Human resource planning and integration – recruitment, training, motivation, reward package, performance reviews.	

Table 5.1 continued

Stage	Process	Output	Timing
		Detailed timings and scheduling, possibly in the form of network analysis to identify critical paths and float.	
Implementation	Planned actions take place and are reviewed against plan. Variance analysis and corporate learning begins.	Business results – revenues and profits are generated.	Certainly some months and possibly as long as 18 months after the beginning of the planning process.

Case example: part of the marketing plan of a large telecommunications company

Process step: Developing the calling pattern of high usage residential customers.

Situation analysis: Although the company is facing competition in what was previously a monopoly market, it knows that even its most frequent users (defined as the top 20 per cent of customers) are using their telephones for less than an hour a day. Market research has identified that many of these users are aware of what they are paying for phone calls but would respond to promotional pricing programmes that gave them discounts, particularly for longer distance and international calls. This promotional pricing would also make these users less likely to consider switching to competitive suppliers.

Objective setting: Increase the volume of calling by high-usage customers by 20 per cent a year.

Marketing strategy development: Pricing will be changed to encourage additional use. Marketing communications will be redesigned to draw these changes to users' attention.

Action planning: Specification of the discount programme (size of discounts, times of day, week or year, start date) to be agreed between the marketing director and the pricing manager. Approval required by the finance director.

Following approval, a detailed advertising and direct marketing campaign will be designed. A public relations programme to be specified by the marketing communications manager will support this. It will be implemented by advertising and direct marketing

agencies, and will include a full briefing of field sales personnel, call centre staff, telesales staff, operators and customer service agents who will have to handle queries about the new pricing plans.
A set of clear performance parameters is specified.
A second-level campaign by way of contingency planning is designed to stimulate take-up of the offer if take-up levels fall outside performance targets.

RELATIONSHIP MARKETING PLANNING

The example of the telecommunications company describes a logical, systematic approach to identifying a marketing objective and putting into place a series of actions, properly supported, which would seek to achieve it. The main weakness of the traditional approach is quite simply that it does not take into account a consideration of where customer value might lie. Why does this happen?

Organizations function on two levels, the strategic and the operational. The strategic level is about growth and development. It is about imagining the future and creating new products and services to provide customer value. The goal at the operational level is to produce and market products or services at a reasonable profit. The operational level is all about organizational effectiveness at the present time.

Planning efforts that lose sight of the interface between the operational and strategic levels can lead to problems. A failure to understand that these two levels coexist in organizations can lead to suboptimization, maximizing present performance at the expense of the future. This is usually because of a failure to maintain a clear transition between the two levels. Consequently, this leads to a failure to balance properly each level with clear lines of responsibility and authority. Traditional marketing planning can lead to a focus on needs and satisfactions at the expense of value. Envisioning what can be done to increase customer value should drive all strategic planning for the organization, including marketing planning.

Everyone knows the joke about the time and motion study of a symphony orchestra. Instead of using 80 to 100 musicians, you can reduce the personnel costs by converting to a chamber orchestra of approximately 40 players. Better still, you can cut personnel overheads even more by reducing to an octet. Of course, a string quartet or a trio is even cheaper. Indeed, why not have the piece played by a one-man band? A one-man band provides for a very cost-effective competitive position. Obviously, an enterprise using this approach could deliver very cheap music. The question is, would it deliver the same customer value? A silly example? In late 1997, the Boeing Aircraft Corporation implemented a major 'downsizing programme'. Cost containment was dramatically improved but its distinctive competences were changed. The reduced corporation was no longer able to deliver customer value in the same way and, in 1998, it posted its first corporate loss for fifty years. Boeing is not the only major corporation to have downsized too far.

In that case, is it sufficient to ensure that customers are satisfied with our products or services? Many businesses already track customer satisfaction, often with some form of rating scale. Higher levels of customer satisfaction are assumed to lead to the increased probability of repeat purchases and thus increased profits. They might even be regarded as a surrogate measure of competitive advantage.

Unfortunately, this too is something of a misunderstanding. Customer satisfaction and customer value are distinct although related concepts (Goodstein and Butz, 1998). Customer satisfaction is about attitudes, while customer value is about behaviour. Satisfaction measures indicate how customers feel about products and services, while measures of customer value are indices of how customers will act.

When General Motors' Cadillac division discovered in 1997 that more than 90 per cent of its customers were either 'satisfied' or 'highly satisfied' with their recent purchase of a new Cadillac, they were very pleased. These figures were comparable with those reported by purchasers of Japanese cars. Subsequently, Cadillac was quite dismayed to learn that only 30 to 40 per cent of these new Cadillac owners would buy another Cadillac, compared with more than 80 per cent of Japanese car buyers. GM had simply been asking about customer satisfaction. It had measured attitudes, which are generally not good predictors of behaviour.

Providing and maintaining customer value needs to be the primary driver of most marketing decisions. Providing customer value requires changes in the way the company conceptualizes and implements its strategy, how it focuses information technology, how it undertakes its marketing planning and how it develops itself subsequently. Customer value determines customer behaviour and changing or cementing customer behaviour should be the basis of (relationship) marketing planning.

In the late 1980s, British Airways found that its traditional hierarchical structure was a major factor in limiting customer value. The traditional structure consisted of a group of functions: reservations, sales, airport services (check-in, baggage handling and boarding/ disembarking), in-flight services (cabin staff) and food services. Each of these had a director and each enjoyed the usual frictions and territorial disputes. Once these functions were integrated into a single, horizontal process-based organization, it became possible for BA to realize its mission of becoming 'The World's Favourite Airline'. By the late 1990's British Airways had outsourced many of its support functions such as catering, baggage handling and vehicle fleet operations to concentrate on its core, value-adding activities.

Table 5.2 describes how a customer value approach is built into relationship marketing planning.

Table 5.2 The relationship marketing planning process

Process Step	Process	Output	Timing
Customer Analysis (identification of the needs and behaviour of existing customers)	Buying and usage trends. Rate of recruitment and attrition of different types of customer. Extent to which existing customers take up additional or new products and services. Responsiveness of customers to sales and promotional initiatives.	Quantification of customer inventory. Identification of customer groups most requiring management.	Continuous measures derived from the customer database with major summaries produced monthly.
Customer Strategy Development	Identification of groups of customers to be managed in specific ways. Development of relationship management strategies – how each customer will be managed over time, using the whole range of marketing, sales and communication channels.	Clear relationship management strategies for each target customer group.	Permanent strategy determined once only, then modified responsively as customer needs evolve.
Customer Management Policies	Details of how different contact media such as face to face, telesales, customer after-sales service, advertising, direct marketing and so on will be used to achieve relationship marketing objectives.	Specification of targets and work processes for each channel of distribution and communication. Specification of campaigns.	Quarterly cycle of planning and review for campaigns. Channels subject to major review once every two years or when there is evidence of performance problems.
Implementation	Planned actions take place.	Business results – sales and profit.	Ongoing.

If we now consider how this would work for our telecommunications company the differences between the two approaches will become clear.

Case example: part of the relationship marketing plan of a large telecommunications company

Process Step: Developing the calling pattern of high usage residential customers.

Customer Analysis: Identification of needs and behaviour of existing customers. All high usage customers are identified by name. However, they are not simply grouped as one category of high volume users. The rise and fall in calling patterns is monitored and analysed according to the length of time the customer has used the service. People often become high volume telephone users for short periods, for example at times of family crises or, in organizational terms, during an intensive calling campaign. For about a quarter of high volume users, this usage pattern will then fall off. The campaign aims to identify persistent high volume users. Demographics such as family structure are examined, plus the rate at which customers are switching to rival services. Responsiveness to previous promotional efforts, particularly price offers, is assessed. Test campaigns for different types of customers within the frequent calling segment is mounted and results are analysed.

Customer Strategy Development: Confirmation that some high usage customers represent a good target is obtained. Use of previous response and test data is then checked to see which types of campaign are likely to be successful. A contact management plan is designed which establishes how the relationship for the target set of customers is to be developed using direct sales, mail, telephone, etc. The associated systems support to enable the price promotion campaigns to be delivered is put in place.

The main contact strategies are then developed in detail with timings and target outcomes. The overall budget is set to achieve the task.

Customer Management Policies: Detailed campaign planning decides which individual customers will be contacted with the price offers, by what medium, when and with what incentive. Detailed campaign objectives and performance measures are established. Roles for both internal and external processes are assigned including outsourcing agencies. Budgets are allocated to each campaign.

Implementation: The plan is put into effect on a continuous basis. Results are also measured continuously and tactics are modified according to customer responses.

DEVELOPING THE CAPABILITY FOR RELATIONSHIP MARKETING

There are six major techniques for developing a relationship marketing capability:

1. **Strategy development**: The general approach to managing customers is developed from overall corporate strategy and marketing strategy. The link to high level strategies is important as significant investments and changes in many areas of policy, processes and structures are required. These must be considered as part of corporate strategy so that senior managers can assess the investment needs and risks.
2. **Data management**: Procedures to identify, collect, clean (ensure accuracy, avoid duplication, cross reference to existing data), analyse and interpret data.
3. **Communications development**: Draws all the analyses together to produce a case for changing how you manage your customers in relation to the associated investment and profit implications. Develop a project plan to manage and monitor implementation. This includes achieving buy-in to the concept from all levels of the organization. The messages and the 'selling levers' to different groups in the enterprise will vary. For example, the field sales force will be looking for different things from the finance director.
4. **Capability development**: Develop the main processes and systems to support the customer relationship marketing strategy. Organization development in terms of culture (training and recruitment) infrastructure and skills, which will provide the resources to deliver relationship marketing. Changing culture may be a long-term process. However, culture underpins performance capability. It is not just a case of providing tools: people have to want to use them and then know how to use them.
5. **Tactical planning**: Plan and develop marketing programmes designed around the relationship marketing planning processes described earlier. These will use the customer data to target individual customers, communicated through various media and contact customers or invite customers to contact you through the resource capability.
6. **Implementation**: The essence of relationship marketing is measurement, which includes not only monitoring and control but also feedback to objectives and strategies.

CUSTOMER MANAGEMENT DIFFERENTIATION

Fournier, Dobscha and Mick (1998), writing in the *Harvard Business Review*, sounded a warning for would-be relationship marketers. They suggested that relationship marketing is powerful in theory but troubled in practice because many organizations do not fully understand what building a relationship really means. In their rush to cash in on the rewards offered by 'customer intimacy' and 'trust', they argue that many companies are simply overstepping the mark. Among others, they cite the example of a man who bought some presents for the medical team looking after his seriously ill mother. Subsequently, on the anniversary of that stressful and worrying situation, the supplier sends him a reminder to buy presents for the people on that list. Despite repeated attempts to have his name removed and explaining why he does not want to be reminded of that time, the customer seems unable to get a response from the company.

They suggest, too, that in their attempts to differentiate their products in an increasing variety of ways, companies are actually confusing the customer. In 1998 Coca-Cola was apparently available in 50 product and packaging variations and Crest toothpaste in 55. Based on this approach, they suggest that instead of bringing people closer to the companies with which they do business, relationship marketing has actually pushed them further away. By violating several basic rules of friendship, such as emotional support, respect, privacy, the preservation of confidences and tolerance for other friendships (relationships with other suppliers), they suggest that relationship marketers have forfeited the right to consumer trust.

To some extent, this argument betrays only a partial understanding of what relationship marketing is about. These examples are not representative of good relationship marketing but of hyperactive traditional marketing (Peppers and Rogers, 1998). Relationship marketing is not about buying customers with special offers, confusing them with product-line extensions or bombarding them with junk mail, junk 'phone calls or 'spam' (junk e-mail). Using computers to target either existing or new customers in some particular fashion is not an example of a relationship. In the same way that a person does not ask their spouse how they like their tea or coffee, a relationship marketer recognizes that not all relationships are the same, they change over time and that change is reflected in a dialogue between both parties. Once they have been told something important, a friend remembers. Relationships are individual and they are modified by both parties as

119

the relationship builds over time. Every relationship is different and contextual. As a result, the methods used by traditional marketers for mass marketing or target marketing are inappropriate.

Customers have some idea of the kind and level of relationship they want at any moment. Between neglect and over attention lies a wide range of possibilities. This poses some special considerations. How can the marketer possibly allow for the wide range of requirements that customers might have? The answer to this lies in the many different ways of differentiating the relationship.

TEN WAYS TO DIFFERENTIATE YOUR CUSTOMER RELATIONSHIPS

1. Consider whether there is a *personal* relationship between the customer and the account manager and decide what the character of that relationship should be.
2. Ensure courtesy and professionalism in all contacts with the customer.
3. Provide information, not just about products and services but about the current status of the relationship. Make the company accessible, by interactive fax, EDI, Internet, e-mail, DITV. Explain how customers can get more information about how to use the product and how to buy it; for example offer helplines. Provide for different ways of paying. Recognize that different kinds of relationships are possible and be open to customers who want to set them up, for example partnerships, alliances, multi-supplier deals, offsets, co-operatives and facilities management.
4. Obtain information about the customers' needs and problems and then use it. Make sure they know you are using it (responding). Improve key elements of the service such as delivery reliability and timescales on the basis of customer feedback. Make sure that complaints are channelled to someone who will respond rapidly and directly.
5. Be considerate in how you contact people; do not schedule outbound telemarketing so that you will call the UK at 6 o'clock in the morning or Saudi Arabia on Fridays. Ensure that the frequency of contacts is monitored so as not to be either too intermittent or too remote.
6. Give a commitment to supply. If it helps, offer to do this automatically, for instance.

7. At the same time, seek commitments to buy in the form of contracts or standing orders. Both of these actions (6 and 7) are facilitated by electronic interchange.
8. Provide reassurance about technical quality and service standards (and mean them).
9. Help the customer to try, buy or use the product so that they can obtain the maximum benefit. Do not seek to retain the supplier position at all costs. Encourage the customer to use your company as the first port of call on the basis that if you cannot supply, you will refer the customer to another company that can meet their needs more closely.
10. Reward or incentivize loyalty. This does not always mean giving money away. A premium call line to a call centre may actually cost the customer more but they are rewarded with privileged access. Incentives can take the form of less paperwork, easier purchase conditions or more value added in the form of different packaging, for example.

SEGMENTATION

THE IMPORTANCE OF SEGMENTATION

Segmentation is just another word for putting customers into groups that share similar characteristics. Segmentation is used because it can bring benefits of focus, concentration, specialization and differentiation. As a result, revenues are better protected, profits are increased and barriers to competition are raised. There may also be some cost savings. This is because a focused marketing policy allows a supplier to meet the needs of chosen market segment(s) very closely. If the relationship needs of each segment are analysed in depth then the relationship offering can be very finely tuned. The concept of 'mass customization' is based on this idea. In mass customization, the company seeks to both enjoy the cost economies of standard components and the marketing advantages of an individually customized product or service. The case example of Andersen Windows shows how mass customization works in practice.

Case example: Andersen Windows

Based in Bayport, Minnesota, Andersen is a $1 billion a year manufacturer of windows for the home building industry. Until the mid-1980s, Andersen was a mass producer of a variety of standard windows in large batches. In an effort to meet customer needs, Andersen kept adding to its product line, which led to fatter catalogues and a bewildering set of choices for both homeowners and contractors. Over a six-year period, the number of products almost tripled. Order systems became so complex that calculating a price quote for windows in a new house could take several hours and run over a dozen pages. Furthermore, this complexity almost doubled the error rate, which began to damage the company's reputation for superior quality.

In order to bring order out of chaos, Andersen developed an interactive computer version of the paper catalogues it sold to distributors and retailers. With this system, a sales person could help customers to choose precisely the windows that met their needs and generate a price. The system also allowed for some structural checks in the design. The time involved for creating a quotation was reduced by more than 75 per cent and the error rate was drastically reduced. In addition, customers got precisely what they wanted, promptly and easily. There was therefore a perceived increase in customer value.

However, developing the new system required a considerable investment of time and money. In each of the company's 650 showrooms, a computer running the system had to be connected to the factory. Customers were assigned individual reference numbers to allow their orders to be tracked through the production process and assure an error-free, on-time order. Furthermore, Andersen had to develop a manufacturing system that used some common finished parts (such as mullions, the vertical or horizontal strips separating window panes and sashes) but which also allowed considerable variability in the final products. This was a far cry from the old batch manufacturing process.

Andersen's next step was to develop a 'batch of one' manufacturing process in which everything was made to order. This reduced the inventory of completed products (windows) and therefore reduced holding costs. Making these changes was expensive and required profound readjustment throughout the organization but Andersen regarded the changes as necessary to retain its image and market share.

Source: Goodstein and Butz (1998)

The changes at Andersen Windows clearly depend heavily on substantial IT support. This involved not only developing the software to enable customers to design and price their choice of windows but a communication link with the main factory and an integrated approach to manufacture. The systems support requirements in themselves clearly present a considerable obstacle. However, they represent only the tip of the iceberg. The best IT system in the world will provide minimal customer benefits if the culture and processes of the enterprise are not inclined to use it properly. Thus some distinction has to be made between an ability to *identify* differences in relationship needs at the individual level and an ability to *deliver* those different relationships.

Customers may need a relationship that cuts across industry and sector boundaries. If this relationship is an important part of a complex product or service offering, then it is important to apply the principle of mass customization. Based on the same core offer, the relationship offering can be fine-tuned so as to meet the needs of increasingly refined chosen segments. Under some conditions, this refinement can give the appearance of marketing to each person individually, the so-called 'segment of one'. The notion of a market segment comprising one individual highlights very clearly the contrast with traditional marketing where the search is for segments comprising the highest total value based on volume.

Having followed the 10 steps to differentiation, it is now useful to look at the 10 steps to segmentation.

TEN KEY QUESTIONS THAT DETERMINE SEGMENTATION

1. With which customers do you want to create and manage a relationship?
2. What are their behaviours, needs and perceptions? Do we know where customers perceive value to lie? What may seem valuable to us may not be important to our customers, as illustrated by the Cadillac example.
3. Do we have a clear definition of a high value and a low value customer? What are the determinants of value and goodwill? Do we have a concept of 'good' and 'bad' customers? Do we know how to respond to various types of customers differently?
4. To what extent are the processes and procedures in place to execute effective relationship responses? For example, is there a standard procedure for dealing with customer complaints? Are we able to

distinguish regular complainers and low value complainers from reasonable complainers?

5. What are the relevant competitive offerings against which we should position ourselves?

6. Do we know how our customers experience our products and services? What do they think of the relationship as a whole? As the customer expects this relationship to change, are we able to respond?

7. What do our staff believe about their role in the relationship with customers? Do the staff believe that they can make a difference to the relationship?

8. What do our relationship metrics tell us about how well current policies are working? For example, what is the trend of retention, attrition and winback?

9. How can we best group the customer base so as to exploit the principles of mass customization most effectively?

10. What are the implications for information services strategy and IT needs?

MAKING SENSE OF CUSTOMER DATA

The easiest way to illustrate the importance of answering these questions thoughtfully is by examining a couple of applied examples.

Case example: value segmentation in a utility industry

The utility industry is often cited as an example of a product where customer loyalty is traditionally very low. After all, if you supply a product such as electricity, it is very hard to differentiate that from the electricity supplied by your competitor. As a result, competition is generally based on price.

Customer value segmentation provides a basis for improving competitive positioning but few utilities are actually equipped to take advantage of it. Typically, they segment their customers very broadly on the basis of usage rates. As a result, they end up with categories that describe the volume of electricity consumed such as domestic or commercial, without considering where value lies for the many different types of customers within those categories. Thus commercial customers might include such disparate organizations as hospitals, laundromats or restaurants.

Value-based customer segmentation would classify customer groups based on needs and values. In the energy market, customer service, price and reliability are three primary customer values (Lavinsky, 1997). Each of these has three levels of priority, key, not key and indifferent, which results in 27 potential energy customer types as shown in Figure 5.1. By researching customer needs and values, a utility can determine in which of these segments its current and potential customers lie. This enables them to position their marketing relationship with each segment to achieve three main objectives:

- **Attracting new customers**: Some commercial customers may seek a 'low-cost provider', others may prefer a 'quality customer service provider'.
- **Improve customer service, satisfaction and loyalty**: In general terms, each of these needs can be met with customized facilities. For example, customer service oriented consumers may be offered a telephone hotline. However, by discovering more about individual customers, loyalty, satisfaction, service and profitability can all be enhanced. Suppose our customer data shows that the owner of a local restaurant values reliability over customer service and price. This customer is then offered reliability guarantees, back up systems, a service for equipment monitoring and a special priority restoration service. The restaurant owner is pleased to pay a small premium for these value-added features because they meet his or her needs. Loyalty is enhanced. Moreover, this service creates a barrier to competitive entry. When competitors enter the market they will not know how to attract this customer. Should they use price, service or reliability? By building the relationship based on information about needs, the marketing position is greatly strengthened.
- **Introduce specialized products and services**: In the competitive, downstream energy market, gas, electricity and oil commodities will generate little, if any, profitability. Value-based segments present a unique opportunity to identify and introduce new offerings. Reliability conscious customers more generally can now be offered this unique service at its premium price. Note the reverse of this proposition. While quite profitable if offered to reliability conscious customers, the premium reliability service may fail if offered heterogeneously to all commercial customers.

It is quickly evident that, even with a relatively small number of dimensions, a segmentation pattern produces a large number of combinations very quickly. A utility product is relatively undifferentiated with a correspondingly low range of customer values. By contrast, as the next case example illustrates, the problem for financial services can be quite different.

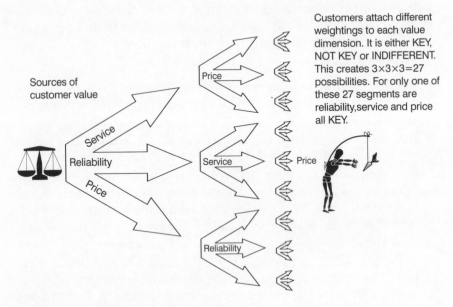

Figure 5.1 Value segmentation in a utility industry

Case example: value segmentation in financial services (banking)

The problem for banks in the financial services sector is that only a relatively tiny proportion of small and medium businesses or individual customers is actually profitable. Targeted customer development can help by focusing on building relationships, therefore increasing share of wallet (measured by their share of available financial services' revenue from any one customer). Targeting prospects that fit into a bank's predetermined profile for profitable relationships can do this. A sales and service delivery must then be devised to sustain that relationship supported by aggressive retention programmes that target profitable relationships.

The challenge is to know which current customers are profitable, to maintain and enhance those profitable relationships and to add customers with strong profit potential to the customer base. This task is formidable. It is necessary to develop a segmentation approach that targets high-value, small-business customers by estimating the lifetime value of each customer and to develop a customer relationship marketing approach accordingly.

Usually, 10 per cent to 20 per cent of a bank's small-business customers account for 80 per cent to 90 per cent of the bank's profits in this market. However, there are many effective ways to segment small businesses. They include current value to the bank in terms of relative profitability; projected value to the bank on a longer term, or lifetime, basis; channel preference; relationship stage with the bank (eg prospects, new customers, developing customers, mature); propensity to buy specific products and company characteristics.

Rather than assign a small business customer to one segment or another on a mutually exclusive basis, given customers can be described in terms of segmentation themes. In the bank sector, these themes might be in one of the following seven sectors (Berry and Britney, 1996). The list is illustrative and could be longer.

- **Recent value**: customers are in the high, medium, low or unprofitable segment based on their profitability to the bank over the past 12 months.
- **Future value**: the customer is projected to be in the high, medium or low segment based on their potential profit to the bank for the next five years.
- **Industry growth**: this reflects the business customer's absolute size and recent growth in terms of revenues, profits and number of employees by type of business. For example, large growth all industries, large no-growth all industries, small growth service industry, small growth non-service industry, small no-growth all industries.
- **Channel preference**: classifies customers into segments based on their relative use of the bank's services and sales channels such as telephone, personal services, night safe, direct connection, credit card, loans, etc.
- **Transaction frequency**: measures total transaction volume with the bank over the past six months in terms of high, medium or low.

- **Product propensity:** seeks to measure the propensity for product cross-selling and upselling based on three likelihood segments, high, medium and low.
- **Credit worthiness:** the relative credit risk of the customer.

Banks can apply these segmentation themes in many ways. For example, if a bank were to conduct a special marketing campaign to cross-sell, it might only target those prospects who are in the 'high likelihood to buy + high growth + high future value + high credit worthy' segment for that product. Within this group, it might develop two sales led acquisition programmes. The first might be a more expensive approach such as direct mail followed up with a phone call from a relationship manager for high potential value customers. The second might use direct mail only for lower potential value customers.

Deciding which segments to target and aligning the bank's resources optimally against these segments requires disciplined relationship marketing and performance measurement. Banks generally use database marketing tools to support the implementation of segmentation strategies such as this.

DETERMINING CONTACT STRATEGIES

As the bank example illustrates, a contact strategy needs to be devised for each customer group. Since each segment has different characteristics, the contact strategy needs to consider a number of elements. Channel strategy must take into account the sequencing of contacts and which combinations will achieve the best results. It therefore embraces issues such as the suggested outbound contact frequency by face to face, mail, telephone, e-mail, Internet or TV and the timings of those contacts. The strategy must provide for the need for irregular contacts, too, such as those that might be needed at the end of a contract or after a complaint.

Who should make the contact, whether it is a sales specialist or someone like the account manager, then affects the planning for the type of contact. These will vary according to the stage of the relationship with the customer, life stage of the customer and the value/loyalty situation, as indicated in Figure 5.2. If the customer's relationship to the

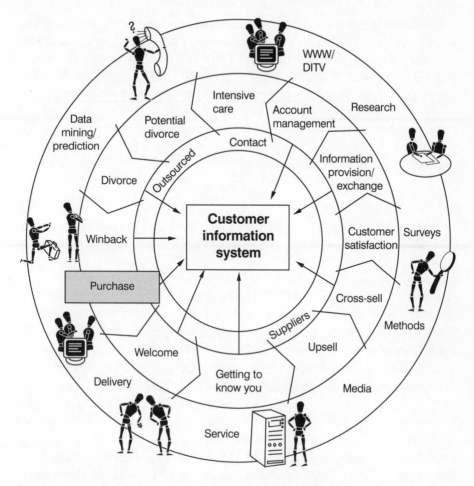

Figure 5.2 Supporting each stage of the customer relationship

offer is not well understood, determining value needs is of key importance. For established, loyal customers there is an opportunity for cross-selling and upselling.

It is apparent that the contact strategy will be determined by a combination of factors. It will flow from a good understanding of where customer value lies and a thoroughly indexed and cross referenced customer database, on paper or on a computer. The exercise will also have identified other elements of the offer that are considered important in your customers' minds. Some of the elements can be put together very quickly for little cost, others may require more research and investment.

Finally, it is necessary to agree the way forward with the front line teams whose job it will be to implement the policy. Feedback from them on whether something will work or not is useful, although they may not fully appreciate the strategic reasoning behind some of the decisions. However, they should help shape the approach and make some of the decisions themselves. They should also help identify what the critical success factors might be in managing customers in the ways described. They will feel more ownership for the process and can identify any training requirements.

A PRACTICAL APPROACH TO SEGMENTED RELATIONSHIPS

A number of writers, such as Jones (1997), have observed that the pressure on managers to create a clear and enduring segmentation of the customer base overlooks the fact that many managers can improve their customer relations even before beginning to do so. For example, Darby (1997) cites the case of Virgin Direct, a financial services company, which was attracting people who had 'a horror of dealing with sales people and jargon'. More worrying for these managers is the extent to which some of the new breed direct marketing companies have creamed off the better customers. They have done this by providing a service offer which concentrates closely on customer value (low cost, reliable service) and stripping out elements of the service offerings such as advice, which were not valued (Saunders, 1997). Indeed, these advisory services were very expensive to provide in financial services, since they were required to be regulatory compliant in terms of factual accuracy. Dropping this element was a key reason for the success of the direct marketers. The lesson in practical terms is very clear.

It is usually misleading to look at the current or past value of a customer without looking at expected retention rates and the cost of management. Lifetime value is an important discriminator between customers yet many companies only use as a segmentation criterion past or (at best) current value. Customers have different service needs but there is a core set of needs that almost all customers have that is often very well defined. For example, the following needs are common:

- A competitive approach but not necessarily the lowest price. Value for money is often more important.
- Speed and reliability of all interactions such as marketing communications, product or service delivery and complaint handling.
- Information availability and clarity at all stages of the relationship, over each transaction and however they may be interacting.
- Use of prior given information in all interactions, in others words listen to customers and be seen to be listening.
- Product quality or, to put it more simply, an expectation that the product or service is honestly represented in a way that is clearly understood by the customer.
- Most day-to-day customer contacts, in many businesses, are over the telephone. It is an accepted way of doing business. Retail is the exception, although this is increasingly supported by telephone and Internet. Field sales teams or face-to-face contact is only required for some customers and for some parts of the sales and service process.

BASIC RULES FOR SEGMENTATION

Segmentation is carried out for a number of different reasons. Primarily it is used to help target products, customer portfolios and promotional offers. It has a lesser value in determining service and communications strategy. This is because complex segmentation methodologies aim to find relatively coherent groups of customers whose needs are significantly different from those of other groups and for whom a complete proposition could be devised. This allows larger organizations to relate to these groups in a standard way, which makes life much simpler.

Segmentation is most useful where a company has to make any long-term commitment in order to provide different offers to customers; for example, in complex engineered products such as cars, where processes take a long time to set up and are difficult to manage. The benefits of a segmented approach enable a large company to align its products, processes, infrastructure and staff with each target segment cost-effectively and competitively.

This segmentation approach should not be confused with the customization and personalization of products frequently used in direct marketing. These techniques, which have been facilitated by the use of information technology, do not necessarily represent a segmented relationship approach. The basic rules to be followed can be set out as below:

- **Plan the customer portfolio** – understand which customers the company wants to serve or manage actively and which it does not.
- **Develop infrastructure (people, process, and systems) for core customer management** – define the support infrastructure and skill sets required to manage particular types of customer. It is likely to be too costly to set up completely separate infrastructures to manage many different sets of customers.
- **Vary pricing** – develop segmented pricing policies.
- **Develop customized products** – develop one or more products or product modules specifically for each segment.
- **Develop service** – meet customer needs better than the competition by developing specific service propositions for each segment. Establish a policy service level and make sure that both your staff and your customers know what it is.
- **Offer segmented communications or promotions** – develop communications and promotional offers that are relevant and attractive to specific segments.

THE TOP VANILLA APPROACH

The 'top vanilla' approach to products and services aims to incorporate the key elements of segmentation along with the rules just described. The term vanilla (as in plain vanilla ice cream) implies a broad appeal to as much of the desired market as possible. Top vanilla can best be explained if we examine how it works for two of the most important market segmentation criteria: value and service.

WHAT PRECISELY IS 'TOP VANILLA'?

Figure 5.3 illustrates the difference between the top vanilla approach and the old-style segmentation approach. Its central idea is that instead of a heavily segmented offer applying to each market segment, the top vanilla approach is offered for, say, 90 per cent (of the customers you

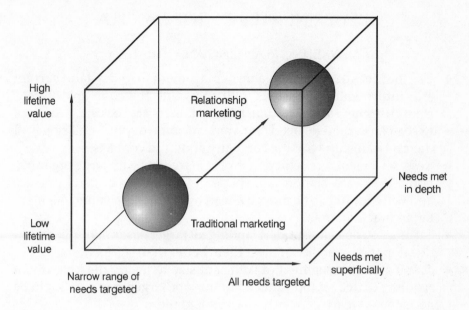

Figure 5.3 The top vanilla approach

want to deal with), with an additionally segmented approach for the other 10 per cent (Stone, Woodcock and Wilson, 1996).

The top vanilla approach is characterized by the following:

- It is vanilla because it is offered to all customers.
- It is top because it offers more than most customers require and is better than competitive offers for, say, 90 per cent of customers.
- Its well defined and clear processes help manage the costs of service delivery.
- For the other 10 per cent of customers, it is still top most of the time because for most of their dealings with the supplier the top vanilla approach is fine.
- It is flexible, allowing for personalized or segmented delivery of the message at the point of contact.

Essentially, all customers require the same set of core values. To become number one, the company needs to offer them brilliantly. The overall approach is top vanilla for everyone and, for selected customers, a service even more closely aligned to their needs.

KEY PRINCIPLES OF TOP VANILLA

MARKETING PLANNING AND STRATEGY

- Use the ideas of customer value management to understand current and future value. Consider both the value the company obtains from customers and the value that customers are seeking.
- Research customers' needs for value in some depth, at all stages of their relationship with the company and in all contacts.
- Research customers' experience of transactions with large organizations. Their expectations are shaped by examples of good practice and will continue to be moved ahead by leading top vanilla segmentation practitioners.
- Set as a key objective understanding all target customers' needs and develop the capability to meet them better than competitors.
- Target a market segment of sufficient size to justify the investment required to deliver top vanilla. This may be larger than you might be accustomed to for conventional segmentation.
- Measure only the most important performance indicators and develop systems to monitor movements and the underlying causes of movement.
- Move away from traditional marketing planning to customer relationship planning.
- Ensure that all the outcomes of relationship planning are tested for their deliverability using the top vanilla approach.
- Develop a core offer that is simple and modularized in large chunks.
- Brand the company and the offer and create a strong customer expectation about the quality of the offer. These may be the only factors that differentiate the company from its competitors. Remember that copying the offer is much harder than it seems, especially if the offer is rooted in corporate culture and effective knowledge management.
- Seek special insights into the customer base and its relationship with the company to develop parts of the offer that are hard to copy, for example, deep knowledge of customer needs or particular competences that are hard to match.
- If the company accesses customers through intermediaries, develop a top vanilla proposition for these channels. Encourage and support the intermediaries to do the same for their suppliers, agents and partners, too.

CUSTOMER MANAGEMENT

- Develop profiles of customers you want to recruit and develop data, systems and processes that allow customer facing staff to identify these customers quickly. Give these customers no reason to leave and deliver their core needs brilliantly.
- Develop profiles of customers you want to lose and develop data, systems and processes to allow the dismissal to occur with minimum risk.
- Develop targeted recruitment strategies and processes for those customers you want to acquire. Have robust and watertight enquiry management processes.
- Seek to really understand why customers are lost and act upon the information.
- Identify customers with potential for development and ensure that they are well informed about the whole range of products and services you can offer.
- Agree and share definitions of each type of customer such as 'new customer' or 'lost customer'. This is essential for measurement. Develop procedures for responding to each condition.

SYSTEMS AND DATA

- Operational systems must respond fast, be easy to navigate, provide the right information and allow for sharing of information quickly.
- Ensure data quality is maintained. Develop a clear data strategy and assign responsibilities for action.
- Make sure customer data is held where they can be accessed quickly by any customer facing personnel such as counter staff, call centre staff and field sales teams.
- Ensure data includes information on the state of the relationship between the company and the customer and the life stage of the customer.

MEASUREMENT AND COST CONTROL

- Challenge each function and activity in terms of the value it adds for customers, particularly for valuable customers.
- Focus on key indicators at each level of the business; use the concept of responsibility marketing. In finance, responsibility accounting

associates each level of profit within a business unit with a particular level of management. Indeed, delivering a figure can sometimes be associated with a particular person. Responsibility marketing adopts this idea by associating specific responsibility for tasks and outcomes with identified managers.

- Train and empower people to act on measures outside accepted norms. Establish acceptable parameters for action for each role and ensure that responses, limits and consequences are thoroughly communicated through training.

PROCESSES

- Develop a clear model of customer management through all stages of their relationship with the company. Use this to define customer management processes. Keep the model under review. Companies often get into difficulties either because their model becomes diffused, confused, neglected or undermined. A company's ability to develop, change and implement new models is a core part of its survival capability.
- Define cost-effective processes for managing customers that take the customer securely through all stages of the process. Beware of hand-over gaps between processes. Remember the process is what the customer sees and what effectively defines the strategy in everyone's mind. The processes must be checked against key criteria such as customer friendliness, cycle time and cost of operation.
- Keep customer management processes under review for their cost-effectiveness and quality.
- Where possible, develop processes to allow customers to manage their relationship with the company.
- Make sure that processes work well through all 'conventional' media and channels. Slow and/or inappropriate responses are dangerous wherever they occur. Like excellence, slowness is relative and contextual. The perceived need for speedy responses is increasing. For example, e-mail acknowledgements can be automated so that the initial response to a contact appears instantaneous. Beyond the automated level, the follow-up actions must be taken promptly.

ORGANIZATION

- Ensure the organization is lean and mean with small groups or hot teams driving policy forward. Keep in mind, though, that people are the main source of added customer value. Some redundancy in organization 'surplus staffing levels' provides for vital continuity in times of stress or difficulty.
- Determine a clear customer value-adding role for each level of the organization.

CULTURE AND PEOPLE

- Develop a culture that encourages appropriate treatment of all customers who have been accepted and all prospects who have been targeted and have responded.
- Encourage staff to respond to customers. As customers' needs evolve, the company must stay ahead of them. At the same time, make people understand what it means to lose a customer. Focus change on customer value and ensure energies are channelled outwards to continually improve the customer offer, not inwards to organizational politics.
- Develop the right blend of people, not all planners, not all doers, not all thinkers and not all 'feelers'. Create a team orientation, not individualism.

THE RISKS OF TOP VANILLA

The ideal is, as far as possible, to go for transparent marketing. Here the customer is able to decide whether to go for the segmented or the top vanilla offer according to their needs at the time of choice. The benefits of the approach are very simple. The main gain is in market share, whether this is achieved through using top vanilla to improve service levels or in terms of increased margin. The risks of the approach are summarized in Table 5.3.

Table 5.3 Possible risks in a top vanilla approach

Risk	How to Avoid the Risk
Relying on technology based solutions such as call centres to deliver top vanilla can lead to the customer relationship becoming too 'remote', impersonal and perhaps hard to access.	Recognize that people are the key to the delivery of the proposition and that excellent systems with reliable clean data are there to support them. Advanced self-service may be the key here.
Too many of the core competencies and capabilities necessary to achieve this model do not exist in the company.	Take time to phase in the approach, train staff, build capabilities.
Too long is spent on planning, causing uncertainty in staff and customers.	Begin with pilots as soon as possible but have a clear, visible roll-out plan.
Managers are too remote from what is happening at the sharp end and the company is too slow to react to market changes.	Develop and implement relationship marketing measures. Set up continual research of the customer experience and communicate results. Monitoring competitive and parallel industry leaders continuously. Set up a 'hot team' to engender and facilitate continuous change.
There is an assumption that adopting top vanilla necessarily implies a complete change in distribution channels. Disintermediation or change of this kind usually occurs when channels perform very badly in terms of meeting customer needs, not because in principle they cannot add value.	Focus first on how to turn existing channels into top vanilla, then on whether the company needs additional channels.
The introduction of the concept is mismanaged. Possibly there is an attempt to reduce the pain by cutting off the dog's tail a centimetre at a time. Thus the concept is prototyped in a 'direct-only' operation, with the aim of applying the principles in agent management later. The risk is that this partial approach does not permeate other parts of the company culture and never affects the overall operation.	Develop internal mechanisms for sharing best practice. Create a learning organization that values knowledge.

SUMMARY

- Have you sat down with your fellow managers and identified what changes will be needed in your organization as it becomes more 'wired'?
- Do you understand the basis of customer value in your products and services (see Chapter 8 for some more ideas on this)?
- Does top management have a clear vision of the way in which customers are to be managed? Can this vision be communicated in, say, less than five minutes? (If not, go back to the drawing board.)
- Does your top management devote time to buy-in? Top management only provides the strategy and context for the organization. It must engage all staff with a hearts and minds campaign if top vanilla is to have any chance of success.
- Do you have a clear idea as to how you will differentiate your relationships with customers from those of your competitors?
- Do your systems and processes allow you to segment customers into small groups (possibly as small as one customer in some cases)?
- Do you understand where you will provide elements of value that are difficult for competitors to identify and copy?
- Is your IT infrastructure up to the job? Relationship marketing planning is data intensive and depends on excellent systems support. This does not necessarily require the extensive deployment of IT but, in an organization of any size, an effective technology infrastructure is probably essential.
- Is a top vanilla approach most practically suitable for your enterprise, rather than segment of one? Top vanilla is based on meeting the identified value needs of the majority (say 90 per cent) of desired customers with segmentation variations for the remainder.
- Can you apply the principles of top vanilla in areas such as marketing planning, customer management, systems and data, measurement, processes, organization, culture and people?
- Once the top vanilla offer has been designed, do you have a clear and visible roll-out plan for deployment of the successful prototype?
- The essence of success then lies in learning. Corporate learning is needed to evolve a culture that will respond fluidly and responsively to change. Do you understand how your organization learns? (See Chapter 9 on knowledge management for more ideas on this.)

- Do your management reports give high importance to key relationship indicators?
- What measures have you established to assess the response of the organization to changing customer requirements in terms of relationships and values?

6

Getting the show on the road

INTRODUCTION

While relationship marketing focuses on producing added value for both external and internal customers, it also results in real financial benefits. We have referred earlier to the following benefits:

- *Revenue protection* against competitive approaches is strengthened through increased loyalty and therefore better retention of existing customers.
- *Revenue extension* in the form of higher sales volumes is achieved as the amount and frequency of purchases from existing customers increase.
- *Revenue development* is more effective as improved lead generation enables new customers to be acquired.
- *Revenue retention* is higher since the overall cost of sales is reduced as a percentage of the margin supported.

BARRIERS TO IMPLEMENTATION

Perhaps the best way to start thinking about implementing relationship marketing is to consider the opposite approach. What prevents an enterprise from marketing more effectively by using these ideas? For a large organization, the biggest barrier to implementation will probably be the past. A traditional marketer tends to be entrenched in its current position in the marketplace through existing products and services. It may not regard managing and developing broader relationships with the customer base as a primary task. A change in approach challenges every aspect of the current posture. On the human side of enterprise, the skills of those dealing with customers, the reward and recognition of people, operating policies and control procedures must be altered. On the systems side, information services strategy and data capture through to strategic plans and budget control will need to change. There will therefore be a number of potential barriers to overcome.

Clearly this may require a major organizational transformation. In any change exercise, it is always easier to start with external and to some extent superficial factors before tackling the human problems. This is a little bit like changing the uniform of a football team in order to improve morale. It may help in the short term but the effect will really be superficial. In relationship marketing, the temptation is to start by developing databases and its associated systems. However, these are just one building block. The team will not necessarily play better unless the attitude and training is changed. Table 6.1 sets out to describe the critical success factors for successful implementation.

Table 6.1 Critical success factors for implementation

Barrier	Issue	Keys to Success
Organizational buy-in, high levels of ownership.	The majority of employees do not feel responsible for the customer relationship, certainly not across the organization. Few people understand or see the real need for this change, particularly if business is going well at the moment.	If the introduction of a relationship marketing approach is not seen as a strategic issue for the organization it will be very difficult to convince people to become involved and own their part in the process. Senior management sponsorship is critical.
People skills and competences.	Skills and attitudes are key, particularly related to recognizing customer responsiveness, the importance of accurate data capture, relationship development and acquisition.	A 'hearts and minds' campaign is needed to influence and change attitudes though it is likely that some people will not be adaptable. These people should be removed from the enterprise in a way that is consistent with the new values. People should be monitored and appraised differently.

Table 6.1 continued

Barrier	Issue	Keys to Success
		Understand the impact of change on staff morale – don't expect too much too soon. Recognize that sales people can be resistant to the control that may be implied by the new systems. Provide continuous training as a resource and encourage the development of new skills.
Reward and recognition.	Reward and recognition programmes are often focused on rapid customer acquisition or fast reactions rather than retention or business development. Customers are rarely rewarded for being long-term loyal. Long-term suppliers should benefit from changes in contract and different sorts of measurement of performance. Sometimes even long established suppliers are pressed to compete with new companies using tactics designed to achieve a short-term expansion of their customer base, in the belief that this 'keeps them on their toes'.	Analysis and feedback from the key players in the relationship programme will be very important for the identification and development of rewards. At the very least, new procedures should be established to recognize long-term customers and long-term suppliers since to continue a reward system based on the old way of doing things could be very destructive.
Product design and development.	New product development is traditionally built on risk based approaches to the marketplace, with good ideas building on previous products. This is not wrong but clearly a more dynamic, interactive and responsive approach based on customer involvement is needed. In particular, real customer behaviour must be recognized and understood. It might be a mistake to assume that customers will be responsive to relationship marketing if all past contacts have been based solely on product and price.	Data must be brought together and analysed for behaviours. Additional research may be necessary to refine product and service ideas. The approach to product development will have to become much more flexible. Product cycle times (the time from conception to marketplace) need to be as short as possible. Products and services must be integrated with customer relations.

Table 6.1 continued

Barrier	Issue	Keys to Success
Business policies.	The core issue here is customer ownership or rather customer stewardship. Business policies and processes may require changes in how customers are viewed, the segmentation process, marketing planning, marketing budget allocations, communication activities, data capture policies and customer profitability cut-offs.	Managers must understand why policies and processes need to be changed. They must commit to working with functional managers to change current processes. They must be willing to change work practices and ensure supervision of that change. Again, it is important not to under-estimate that rate at which the organization can absorb change. New policies take time to be accepted and need constant reinforcement. Buy-in is vital.
Business processes and programmes.	Business processes have a tendency to evolve in a way that makes life easy for managers and staff, not customers. This establishes a potential conflict with the customer relationship management approach. It can be extremely difficult to integrate existing processes into a cohesive programme, even more so if those involved are in isolated departments.	The relationship cycle with the customer groups targeted in the strategy must be analysed and processes aligned accordingly. This will require cross-functional team involvement and management. Core information and knowledge management around the cycle must be identified and a new approach to managing knowledge agreed.
Measurement.	Measurement can be an enabler or blocker for implementation. Many process measures in current use are focused on speed and efficiency such as response rates in a call centre. Few measures extend across functions to the customer base. In some instances where organizations begin to implement customer business measures they can impede development by being too ambitious. For example, seeking to improve customer retention for the entire customer base can be expensive and may even result in retaining unwanted customers.	Measures from processes through to business controls should be reviewed with the customer relationship management programme in mind. The main areas to look for are: • retention of wanted customers; • customer development; • customer value; • acquisition of wanted customers.

Table 6.1 continued

Barrier	Issue	Keys to Success
Data and databases.	The quality of current data is often variable. Databases are sometimes not customer focused and much relevant customer data is paper based. System functionality and surrounding processes such as data input and data quality will be a major factor in a successful outcome.	Managers must be willing to invest time and resources in database development. Everyone must understand the importance of the database and their contribution to it. Good quality customer data must be established, based on clear data definitions or at least clear plans to improve customer data quality must be put in place.
Information systems.	Information systems are often diverse and disparate. They do not lend themselves to integration and they do not support fast responses to the market. For example, sales data and accounting data are not matched, so sales calls are made to a debtor.	The system and interfaces must be proven and reliable. Systems must be easy to use and simple. Intranets or extranets can often provide a useful tool for bringing relevant customer information to contact personnel.

THE IMPLEMENTATION PROGRAMME

Relationship marketing is more of a journey than a destination. Personal and corporate learning are the vehicles that will ensure progress. The journey may take many years and may never be complete. Implementation will involve several interdependent projects, often carried out in parallel. Some of these projects will be substantial, enterprise-wide exercises that involve business processes, information services strategies and competitive positioning. Others will take the form of a series of pilot projects, selected to demonstrate or test certain capabilities; for example, full relationship marketing cycle management for a selected customer group or a large scale implementation in one dimension such as an enterprise wide welcoming programme.

For each of these pilots, the usual project management structure, tools and controls should be used (Lock, 1996). Programme management is the co-ordinated management of a portfolio of projects to achieve a set of business objectives. It provides the framework for implementing the whole range of business strategies and initiatives and for managing multiple projects. The starting point is a board level, strategic plan. Major business change of this sort is all-embracing, covering a wide range of internal and external factors. The plan must encompass changes to business culture, organization, skills, processes, systems, technology and infrastructures. Programmes such as this are characterized by long implementation periods, usually in excess of five years. They therefore need to be implemented in stages. Two levels of evaluation are required as the programme progresses. Each stage must produce measurable deliverables and each stage must produce outcomes, which contribute to the overall goal. The key issues that need to be addressed in managing a programme consisting of multiple projects are:

- A consistent business blueprint that recognizes business process requirements and provides the framework for co-ordination between projects.
- A basis for prioritization and adjudication between competing projects, particularly for shared or scarce resources.
- A high-level or meta project framework that controls sequencing to achieve optimum business benefit and provides for interdependency and co-ordination across projects.
- A defined common architecture for applications, data, technology and information services infrastructure across projects to allow for interoperability of platforms.
- Excellent communications and a commitment to the long-term goal. Sub-optimization or a reluctance to participate in and share risks will inhibit the enterprise wide transformation that is needed. However, everyone must understand the purpose and contribution of each sub-project.

A programme management approach yields a number of advantages. It produces better support for executive management and should improve both communication and the consistency of decision making. The latter is very important throughout the long life cycle of strategic programmes as the changing business environment or even intermediate project initiatives can distract from the long-term goal. It provides for improved resource management and better management of risk across the whole range of activities. It maintains focus on delivering business benefits through a formal programme of management and measurement and provides for overall control through a framework within which costs, standards and quality can be justified, measured and assessed.

Although the initiator may be an IT manager or a middle level marketing manager, the key internal client for relationship marketing projects must be the marketing director or even the managing director. However, the project manager is likely to be a marketing or a business development manager.

EVALUATING CURRENT PRACTICE

The second major task in implementation, after the establishment of the vision and the long-term goal, is to undertake an audit of current practice. Only once the present situation is well understood is it possible to grasp the size of the gap between the actual and the desired position. This analysis also acts as the basis for establishing early priorities. It determines the scale and scope of the resources that will be needed to achieve effective competitive positioning. Table 6.2 provides a framework for a structured evaluation of current practice.

Table 6.2 Structured evaluation of current practice

Business Definition

- Describe your main business. How do you define what you sell?
- If we take the four dimensions of the product as creation, delivery, information and operations, where do your main strengths lie in each area?
- Do you know who your main customers are? Do you have reliable, accurate profiling and identification data? How often is this updated?
- Who are your main customers? User/choosers, business-to-business, intermediaries, individuals?
- Who do you see as primarily responsible for building the initial relationship with the customer?
- In terms of brand strength or customer ownership, if the top consumer brand in your market were scored as 10, what would you score yourself?
- In terms of electronic delivery platforms and technology assets, if the top e-business supplier were scored as 10, what would you score yourself?

Customer Management Strategies

- What is your overall customer management strategy?
- How does this vary according to customer segments or profiles? What is the customer value proposition in each case?

- How does it vary according to product type? What is the customer value proposition in each case?
- How would you define an important customer? Does the customer management strategy vary according to the importance of the customer?
- How close do you think your company is to establishing a top vanilla offering? In other words, can you vary your generic offering on a personalized basis either to end-users or business-to-business?
- How high is the profile of customer relationship marketing at the top level in the organization?
- How do you assess or judge whether the relationship with customers (or groups) is being managed according to policy?
- Have you an agreed set of 'rules and rights' for access to your customer database by your own staff for customer management purposes? For example, can customer contact staff pull up a customer record?
- Can any of your suppliers access your customer database? How would you describe the main emphasis of the rules and rights for accessing customer information?
- Can you integrate your main customer database with other databases such as your complaints database in order to facilitate the implementation of policies?
- How do you manage customer retention and loyalty?
- How would you describe the position in respect of customer attrition and how do you manage this issue? Do any of your intermediaries inform you about attrition or help you recover lost customers?
- What strategies are adopted for recovering lost customers? What are the relative roles of the company or the intermediaries?
- In your business, which company would you say had the most effective strategies for managing customers? Why?
- If this company were given a score of 10, how would you score your own company?
- Have any of these strategies been modified substantially in the last few years? How?
- Would you judge these strategies effective? What would you change?

Customers: Knowledge, Value and Perceptions

- Where is most of the formal knowledge about your customers held? How is it collected? What process is used? Who owns it?
- How would you rate the quality of this knowledge in terms of accuracy, relevance, recency and timeliness?
- How is formal knowledge about customers inventoried? How is it shared, made accessible to other members of your organization?
- What methods are used to identify and share best practice in dealing with customers on a face-to-face basis?
- Do internal organization issues ('turf wars') affect the use and value of your customer knowledge?

- To what extent do you share knowledge about your customers with your customers? Can they access their own records?
- What rewards are available to members of your company for developing and sharing new knowledge about your customers? How do you assess the quality of this new knowledge?
- If you had to put a value on your customer knowledge assets, what would it be? Do you have procedures to revalue and protect this valuable asset?
- How do you analyse your customer knowledge?
- Do you think your customers are aware of the different contributors to the value chain in providing your service? What part of this chain do you think is part of your core business?
- What value do you think your customers attach to different providers? Do you think this is important?
- Do you think that you listen to your customers? To what extent do you think you vary the total product package in response to what your customers tell you? How quickly can you do that? How much of a variation do you make?
- Do your customers like the total value package that you provide? Do you think that it is possible for them to like it more? What needs to be done to increase their liking?

Channels and Intermediaries

- In terms of disintermediation effects, where do you think the greatest opportunities lie for your company in the future?
- In terms of disintermediation effects, where do you think the greatest threats lie for your company in the future?
- What would you say is the most important marketing channel for your company? Why is it the most important? What are the next two? Why are they important?
- If we score the most important channel as 10, how would you score channel 2 and channel 3?
- How does each of the channels deliver different value to the customer?
- How is the balance between different channels maintained?
- Are there any conflicts between channels?

Value Chain, Systems and Data

- In terms of its customer relationship marketing activities, what are the main processes that your company outsources? On what basis does it choose to outsource these processes?
- What changes do you think you would make to this policy? Would you outsource other processes or bring some of these back in-house?
- What are the key internal systems for managing customers at the moment? How will these change in the future?

- What are the main resources that you will need to develop in order to implement these new systems? (Possible suggestions: technology, management skills, knowledge, market development, supplier relationships.)
- What are the key customer-facing systems for managing customers? How will these change in the future?
- What are the main resources that you will need to develop in order to implement these new systems? (Possible suggestions: technology, management skills, knowledge, market development, supplier relationships.)
- If you consider your operational support systems, where do you see the greatest opportunities and threats in the next five years?
- How important do you think these issues are?
- Thinking of integration between systems, do you believe that technology decisions, marketing needs and sales are working well together?
- To what extent do you set out to integrate marketing and sales systems with your major suppliers and partners?
- What are the major barriers to increasing your control over the value chain in the next five years?

Technology Management

- Who takes the lead in the specification of systems for managing customers, eg database, Internet, call centres, digital interactive TV? How far do systems people and marketing management agree about priorities?
- To what extent are you able to deploy the technology to enable customer-assisted purchasing? (For example, a kiosk or Web site that enables customers to assemble the service and product package that they need at any time.)
- To what extent does your company employ intelligent algorithms (rule-based software procedures) for responding to customer needs? How adequate is the current technology for supporting your customer management plans?
- Do you have a process for developing and aligning visions for the use of technology in managing customer relationships? If so, what is this process?
- What technology or medium offers the most potential for improving your competitive position in the next three years?
- What barriers do you think you would have to overcome to exploit this technology most effectively?
- In what way could the current systems be improved?

Response Management

- What reports does your company produce on how it manages its customers?
- Does the proportion of 'problem' customers vary according to segment, product or region?
- What is the best medium for encouraging customers to consider additional services? Why? How?
- What steps are being taken to respond to new technologies in developing future customer relationship techniques?

Evaluation

- If you had to name a company that had integrated its policies, procedures and systems for customer relationship marketing at the leading edge, who would you name?
- In what way would you say they were ahead of the field? How far are they ahead? Is there a competitor that you consider to be especially vulnerable in this area?
- What is the overall procedure for reviewing customer relationship marketing strategies? How is the review process triggered, for example by the planning process?
- What would you regard as the most important critical success factor in defusing problems in customer relationship marketing?
- What has been the most significant influence on customer relationship issues in the industry in the last three years? In your company?

DEVELOPING THE BUSINESS CASE

Once the data has been collected, the next stage is to develop the business case for a possible customer relationship marketing programme. The first step here is to analyse the data so as to understand the customer base.

UNDERSTANDING THE CUSTOMER BASE

Clearly, to determine your strategy you need to understand who your customers are, how many and what kinds of customer you are recruiting, developing and losing, what your sector and geographical strengths are and where possible problems such as high attrition rates might lie. In addition to these descriptive analyses, customer attitudes to your management approach, compared to that of your competitors, is needed. The sensitivity or responsiveness of your customer base to competitor actions must also be assessed. Finally, it is useful to seek some understanding of how your customers would like to be managed, both now and in the future.

At the heart of all this is the need to understand the real value of different customers and to determine which ones you want to manage better. The analysis will reveal many things you thought you knew already but it is important to recognize that much of this knowledge will not have been quantified and used to determine a customer relationship strategy previously and some may have been known 'anecdotally'. The analysis will also show where the quality of some historical data is poor (unfit for the purpose). The main analysis should focus on ranking of customers by some criterion of importance. For example, retention rates, acquisition rates, lifetime value, customer satisfaction and customer perceptions of value. This will aim to produce a categorization overall, by channel, by staff group within channel, by segment, by value and by profit in deciles. In many cases, data mining techniques will be the key to competitive advantage as these may reveal segments that have not so far been recognized.

The findings of the analysis should be discussed in a working session with the people who work with each customer group. This confirmation step is important for two reasons. There may be a defensive reaction from some employees who may see themselves being blamed for not knowing their customers well enough. Secondly, underlying assumptions about customer behaviour, 'conventional wisdom', may simply be untrue. It is important to emphasize that the messages come from the data and that they represent opportunities for better marketing.

The next step is probably to hold a workshop or a series of workshops to agree relationship priorities. Open discussion facilitates buy-in and may encourage more creative thinking if it is conducted in a supportive style. Thus, for example, the group may identify where additional research or better procedures are needed to provide missing information. In the interim, action steps will be associated with a critical review of processes and procedures. These will range from the development of marketing programmes aimed at recruitment, retention or cross-selling to a complete review of contact channel strategies to refocus or improve the style and level of two-way communications. It may also lead to greater support for enhancing the organization's database capability as the engine for improved future strategy.

BENEFIT DEVELOPMENT

Hard business cases are difficult to produce initially as they depend upon predicting how customers will react to different ways of being managed. At the beginning of the programme, the case will be somewhat tentative but it should become firmer as the quality of data improves and as results are measured. We look at this more closely in the final chapter. The business case plays a key role in achieving buy-in from senior management. The key justifications in marketing terms are revenue based, as described in the first section of this chapter.

Revenue protection

If customers are better managed and their needs better met it seems reasonable to assume that they will stay with you longer and buy more. The enterprise is thus less vulnerable to competitive attack. This is a strategic benefit that results in an increased customer lifetime value but unfortunately its effect on the bottom line cannot always be calculated reliably. Three key measures might be used to demonstrate improvements:

- **Attrition rate** – the rate of customer loss. This is a key measure of *behavioural* loyalty. Behavioural loyalty is concerned with what customers do in their relationship with you: stay, go, buy more or buy less.
- **Satisfaction levels** – measure the *attitudinal* loyalty but this is only partly linked to purchase behaviour. Attitudinal loyalty is what customers say about their relationship with you.
- **Lifetime value (LTV)** – is a function of how long customers are retained and their purchase rate. This does not refer to customers' real lifetimes but their likely value as long as they stay with you!

Perhaps the most important of these three is attrition rate and its impact on margins. Attrition can be measured fairly easily. The effect of reducing attrition can therefore be calculated simply by estimating the profit from customers that would have been lost if attrition had remained at higher levels. The extent to which attrition is reduced and the degree to which this is attributable to better customer relationship marketing can usually be established through comparative tests of different contact strategies.

Revenue extension

A regular contact strategy with the right backup should produce a bigger share of customers' spend and a higher LTV. The right backup in this case refers to logistics and operations. The sales assistant who explains that something is out of stock 'because it's Christmas, what do you expect?', is illustrating most acutely what happens when the backup is deficient. The four activities most commonly used to extend revenue are:

- **Cross-selling** – selling other products to existing customers.
- **Upselling** – an enhanced version of the product or service, often with a higher margin.
- **Increased share of wallet** – for products or services where buying is continuous, this refers to building the proportion of purchases made by existing customers.
- **Reactivating customers** – if they were lost to a competitor.

The benefits are best calculated for customers whose purchase history extends perhaps 12 months or more (the actual period depends on the length of typical buying cycles). Those under this period are still considered as new customers. If all customers were used in the analysis, gains and losses in the current year might hide the underlying figures.

Revenue development

Even if retention rates have been improved, a steady flow of new customers will be required to replace those lost. Profitability can be improved by recruiting new customers of the right quality and potential. This is an important part of the business case. There are two sets of measures here, final outcomes and improved processes. Processes are dealt with in the next section. The final outcome measures are calculated by comparing a momentum forecast (what would have happened anyway) to actual results. This will produce a short-term measure based on first year volume and margins generated by new customers. More speculatively, based on profiling data and matches with existing (known) customer groups, it is also possible to compute new customers' potential. This is a longer-term measure that takes the quality of new customers into account. From these measures, it becomes clear that the revenue development is assessed at two levels.

Level One, where revenue development is quantified financially. It can be reliably measured against a 'stake in the ground' benchmark, such as reduced attrition rates. Measures such as these are attached to high levels of confidence and will probably be achieved in the short to medium term.

Level Two gives a strategic assessment of revenue development and is more difficult to measure with certainty. It assesses development against, for example, increased sales through more loyal customers or new customer potential spend. However, the benefits are certainly quantifiable and are amenable to retrospective verification.

Revenue retention

Essentially, as the targeting and return on marketing activities is improved, there should be a better return overall due to improved effectiveness and fewer misdirected actions. Two measures may be used on either a current or a lifetime basis. The first is the absolute cost of sales, marketing and service. The second is the cost of sales as a percentage of profit.

The overall cost of sales may increase in absolute terms but, of course, if the overall sales volume has also increased, this may be welcome. A relative measure helps create the right perspective. The cost of the direct sales effort depends critically on customer contact strategies. As an example, the costs for a field sales team could include a wide range of factors such as:

- **direct costs** – salaries, bonuses, expenses, benefits (cars, health insurance, vacations) and equipment (laptop PCs);
- **management overheads** – to support direct sales;
- **office support costs** – administrative staff support for the sales process;
- **marketing costs** – for customer acquisition and retention such as promotional media, database operations and analyst costs;

- **office overhead allocation** – rent, insurance, city taxes, inventory, cleaning services.

To maximize revenue retention these figures must be calculated for each contact strategy. The efficiency of each channel should then be monitored continuously. As in any operational area, the intention is to push the contact strategy down to the lowest (and preferably the cheapest) level. If costs were measured on a scale of 0 to 100, face-to-face sales would assume pole position at 100, telephone sales might weigh in at 7, direct mail at 1 and electronic media at 0.1. A direct sales call is therefore about 1,000 times more expensive than, say an e-mail and needs to produce a high return to be justifiable. Indiscriminate or unmeasured face-to-face selling can be very wasteful of resources.

Contact strategy costs can be greatly reduced by careful allocation of customers to sales channels. If least cost substitution is applied to all customers and prospects then the total impact can be very significant.

CUSTOMER CONTACT STRATEGY

A moment's thought reveals that high value customers normally warrant a different contact strategy from low value customers, yet many organizations fail here. It may be that they have little or no idea about the value of their different customers or it may be that they have not thought about the nature and cost of their contact strategies. They therefore use the same rather spendthrift approach for all customers.

The main tool here is once again the database. The database helps you plan, implement and monitor contact strategies. The strategy should be based on customer programmes designed to maximize each individual customer's profitable lifetime value and so maximize the value you get from the customer base. The complexity and cost of the strategy will vary for different channels in order to meet this goal. Thus, for example, in a business-to-business marketing operation there might be:

- a key-account management programme to support the needs of the largest customers;
- basic field or branch sales with personal account management for substantial medium-sized customers;

- a two-pronged approach coupling personal sales with telephone account management for new customers;
- a telephone account management programme for small- and medium-sized customers;
- a direct mail approach with inbound telemarketing for very low-value customers.

The contact management strategy should work in two dimensions: 'what' and 'how'. The first concerns the customer relationship cycle that we introduced as Figure 1.3. The relationship begins with targeting customers for one or more recruitment contacts, followed by a welcome to the company. The relationship builds, like any relationship, by getting to know each other. This is when further customer needs are identified and when the customer is learning to get more from the relationship. After qualification, formal and continuing account management programmes are set up to watch over the relationship. Any contact that is not well managed may threaten the relationship instead of enhance it. At the other end of the relationship come problem management and winback. The second dimension, 'how', concerns the social and material technology (people and processes) used to build and sustain the relationship.

ACCOUNT MANAGEMENT – WORKING THROUGH THE RELATIONSHIP CYCLE

Welcome or qualification programme

Shortly after recruitment, there is an opportunity to welcome and reassure new customers. Not only does this begin the relationship-building process but it also gains additional customer information, which helps to qualify them and perhaps define how they want to be managed. The word 'qualify' in this sense means to understand what the customer might be inclined to buy as well as what they can afford. It is an opportunity to provide the customer with initial benefits. A standard programme which identifies first orders and triggers a contact, normally through the telephone, followed by a mail pack giving key contact numbers and information, may pay enormous dividends in terms of the professional image it creates in the customer's mind. The welcome stage is important but is sometimes overlooked. When this happens, it is more difficult to decide on the account management process for each customer. Learning about the customer and developing the relationship is more difficult and the chances of skipping rapidly to the problem management and divorce stage are increased.

Getting to know (learning)

Given a positive reaction, the natural next step would be to promote higher-value products or services for the same category of purchase or to try to increase the frequency or volume of purchases. In other words, to upsell. There are two distinct approaches here: gradual customer education on the benefits of your products or services, for example to attempt to convert them to higher-margin products; and incentivizing them to buy more.

Incentives are usually applicable in three situations: where you only have a small share of spend, when a customer is trading suppliers off against each other and with intermediaries in the sales channel.

Customer development (account management)

Most organizations assume this to be the most important and longest phase of the relationship. In many cases this is true but there are also many products where short duration, intermittent or infrequent purchase patterns are inherent in the product or service. Examples such as baby products, furniture or tractors spring to mind. Loyalty programmes and cross-selling are more difficult in these circumstances.

Rewarding loyal customers for their continued custom is both cost effective and appreciated, and it is expected in some markets. Customer loyalty programmes are the most complex programmes of all to develop and need to be carefully targeted with clearly stated, realistic objectives. The behaviour of key groups of customers whose loyalty is particularly important must be researched and a long-term series of campaigns designed to achieve the objectives.

Cross-selling is a conscious, formalized, planned strategy to encourage customers to buy additional product categories. It can take place within a business and across businesses.

Customer development will also be characterized by data driven contact activities. Database analysis aims to identify potential problems or opportunities and route information to the right contact channel for action. For example, the sales history on the marketing database will identify **FRAC** data:

- Frequency of purchase;
- Recency of last purchase;
- Amount of purchase, both as volume and margin;
- Category of product.

These data are used to monitor any significant volume changes both in the short term (sudden changes in order frequency) and the long term (year-on-year changes in trend).

For higher value customers, it is useful for the database to record key relationship sales and service objectives so that actual results can be compared to planned figures. Variations from the plan may then trigger an account management action.

In addition to internally generated triggers, two important external triggers may also require a response. The first of these is a change in tactics by a competitor. If competitive activity is targeted at current customers, a defence contact is needed. It is worth bearing in mind that competitors will be most successful where the product or service offering is poor. So this may be a symptom of some decline in the quality of the company's offer that needs attention. The database should record the competitive approach. Identified trends can then be used in turn to trigger contacts designed to weaken a prospective competitor's future offer. An easy example might be a specification upgrade prior to a new model release by a competitor.

The second external trigger is activities stimulated by the customer. Here the database must record, analyse and route customer feedback for speedy review and possible action. Take, for example, a sales enquiry. Each sales enquiry must be handled well, qualified and passed to the relevant sales staff. At this point, qualification may involve a standard set of questions to improve understanding of needs and potential. After qualification, where responses are recorded on the database, the follow through should be smooth and efficient. In this context, speed is relative. An electronic enquiry must be processed more or less instantaneously by an electronic response. Written quotations, brochures and direct sales calls may then follow this.

If the enquiry is accompanied by an order, access to sales history and data on needs may allow a qualified order-taker to check the order against past purchase patterns ('Do you want the red cover with that, as usual?') and to cross-sell other products. Cross-selling during inbound order or enquiry taking can be very beneficial.

Problem management

If the database is doing its job, supported by an effective contact strategy, the need for problem management is minimized. In some ways, if the customer actually raises a reasonable complaint it is like being hit on the head with a hammer. The time to take action is before the hammer makes contact, not after it has landed. Good customers will not complain without cause. At the same time, individual complaints vary in severity. The severity of a complaint therefore depends on whether it is justifiable, whether it is the result of a previously unresolved complaint, who actually makes it and the frequency with which it is made. Obviously, even a series of minor complaints within a short period is a bad sign. This is why all complaints should be recorded on the database and possibly actioned either directly or during the next account contact.

It is very important to record the date of present and planned contacts, trace dates (when follow-up action is needed) and a feedback code that identifies future required actions. For example, not all sales enquiries are serious and valuable. The feedback code records whether the enquiry resulted in a sale, may result in a sale or was merely an enquiry with no intent to purchase. For complaints, the code will show whether the matter was handled to the customer's satisfaction or whether an escalated response is needed. Problem management is designed to ensure that all activities or contacts remain on an action list until they have been resolved.

Winback

Reactivating inactive customers is usually more cost-effective than recruiting totally new customers, depending on the reason for the 'divorce'. If the relationship lapsed because of a fundamental problem, such as bad product or service quality or because customers have passed out of the target market, then winback may not be possible. However, much more is known about lapsed customers than prospective or even new customers, so winback actions can be very profitable.

There are two elements to this programme. First, identifying customers who are becoming inactive, before they lapse. Second, reactivating customers who lapsed some time ago. Data on inactive customers can be tested or revalidated through telemarketing. This helps to target re-activation promotions more profitably.

Contract renewal or finance completion (such as the final payment on a car purchase loan) represents a special case for winback. There are many sales and service opportunities at this point but several timed, relevant and personal communications may be needed before and after renewal.

CONTACT TOOLS AND TECHNIQUES

It is essential to evaluate the importance of different relationship components. Managing these components involves determining:

- **Customers' requirements** – the determinants of buying decisions.

- **Customers' perceptions** – of each offer, as promised and delivered.

- **Customer levers** – which components of the relationship can be acted upon cost effectively to improve the position?

Sales team and face-to-face

The methods of communication available to a field or branch sales force for communicating with customers include: face-to-face, telephone, fax, letter, e-mail and, increasingly, portal home page. This activity must be linked to the customer database. Face-to-face customer management is normally employed for the most valuable accounts, though even here increases in efficiency and effectiveness are usually achieved by substituting other media for some face-to-face time. Field or branch sales staff often carry out both planned and unplanned activities. The database helps schedule, trigger, prioritize, log, communicate and follow them up.

Mail

In an electronic age, surface mail is still an important contact tool and surface mail volumes continue to grow. In many sectors, this is still the lowest cost method of managing customer communication and sometimes achieves very high impact. For example, financial services companies often find it the best possible medium for cross-selling. American Express's customized statementing programme is probably rivalled only by British Telecom's in terms of the delivery of a totally personalized relationship that results in good cross-selling performance. The latest developments in fully customizable, high volume laser printing are giving additional impetus to the use of mail.

Telephony

Telemarketing, telesales (telephone selling) and telephone account management are probably the most commonly used methods of communication with prospects and customers. Used correctly, the telephone is a powerful tool, fast, immediate and cost effective especially compared to face-to-face contact. It is also more interactive, personal and flexible than direct mail, though the two working together can be very powerful. As field or branch sales forces shrink under growing cost pressure, the telephone is becoming increasingly important in customer acquisition and retention. Telesales and Telephone Account Management (TAM), though not necessarily appropriate for all customer segments, have a clear cost advantage over field or branch sales. They allow you to manage actively those customers who prefer telephone calls to visits and also to manage those whom it may not be economical to visit. Telesales may increase sales force efficiency when the telephone is used for both outbound work, such as customer qualification and service calls, and for inbound work, such as technical queries, service calls and complaints handling.

Online activity

Online activity has moved from 'nerd' to 'herd' very rapidly since 1995. This is a huge area and warrants a contact strategy of its own. Virtual markets and extended enterprises have five important characteristics (Hagel and Armstrong, 1997):

- *A distinctive focus on membership.* Internet service providers tend to target specific types of member, so users of Compuserve and America Online have different characteristics. Within each community special interest groups (SIGs) often develop with a particular type of transaction interest (personal finance, forensic medicine, travel and so on). These virtual communities are not only gathered together electronically but have access to much more information than in the past and a much greater ability to purchase literally from anywhere around the globe. There is, therefore, a significant shift of power to the consumer.

- *Integration of content and communication.* Many media are one way, delivering content to an audience. Those that are two way (like a field sales team or telephone), tend to be expensive, slower (such as mail) or uncertain (eg fax). Online activities are more like the telephone but with an enhanced capability to capture, store and compare data. This means that the consumer has a greater ability to shape their communication environment. A person interested in travel can draw in brochures from hotels, airline schedules and even resort information. Of course, this also means that online users can quickly suffer from information overload, which provides an important value-added opportunity to some vendors.
- *Emphasis on member-generated content.* This is a double-edged sword. Customers can more easily share information about products or services with each other online, a feature that has been dismissed by some vendors as trivial. They suggest that people in a restaurant would rather have their meal prepared by an expert chef than by the person who happens to sit at the next table. However, this tends to ignore the success of member-generated content, which increasingly shapes choices. Book sellers such as Amazon.com and BarnesandNoble.com encourage readers to contribute book reviews for their Web site, with offers of prizes for the best submission.
- *Choice of competing supplier offers.* Also a difficult area. While a supplier may encourage electronic links into their site, customers are soon likely to tire of a narrow provision of information and services. Since a new supplier is only one or two clicks of the mouse away, a badly constructed site will actually drive customers to other suppliers. This turns the traditional market on its head. Suppliers do not seek customers so much as the other way around. Thus, in order to maintain the relationship, it may actually be necessary to form strategic links to other suppliers. Amazon.com provide a search engine called Eyes that automatically sends an e-mail when a book comes out in paperback or when a favourite author publishes a new work. In a variation of the online greetings card, when someone buys a book as a gift, they can specify a message to be sent by e-mail from Amazon, notifying the recipient that a gift has been picked out. If the recipient accepts, they are asked to respond to the e-mail with

a postal address. This little bit of value added also allows Amazon to obtain information on a prospective new customer.

- *Motivated intermediaries.* These are commercially motivated, elec-tronic community organizers. A motivated intermediary may affect the relationship between a supplier and a customer. For example, a personal finance service may collect together information on interest rates and provide an interactive tool to advise customers about investment decisions. A financial services provider would need to find ways of disintermediating or working with this activity. Clearly, the intermediary also has the option of aggregating consumer power so as to achieve a position of power. Notice that vendors of books, CDs, travel services, wine and all the other Web-based products and services are intermediaries. Their entire business depends on people visiting their (virtual) store just like a classic retailer. In the same way, the basic attraction is that they provide variety of supply in one convenient location. It just happens to be on the Internet, not in the shopping mall. However, unlike a classic retailer they work in a richer (more complete) information environment, which puts the customer in a more powerful position.

CUSTOMER EXPECTATIONS AND RESPONSES TO RELATIONSHIP BUILDING

Customers increasingly expect companies to use the information they have provided at various stages in their relationship to be used positively in managing their account. For instance:

- When customers require service, they expect details of their rela-tionship to be available to whoever is delivering the service and to be used if relevant.
- If they are ordering a product or requesting technical service, they expect information they have given about their needs, not just recently but over the years, to be used to identify which product or service is best for them.
- If they are in contact with several different members of an enter-prise, they expect the actions of these staff to be co-ordinated.
- They expect the enterprise to consider their needs for a long-term relationship, not just for individual transactions within the rela-tionship. They want an appearance of care.
- If there are problems on the customer's side, such as meeting payments or service problems that are the customer's fault, they

expect their past relationships to be taken into consideration in resolving them.

- Loyal customers expect to have better relationships than if they were not loyal.

CUSTOMER MANAGEMENT KEY PERFORMANCE INDICATORS

Effective implementation can only be judged against the right measures.

Table 6.3 identifies some key performance indicators that should be compared against the predictions made in the business case. These indicators should be measured routinely against business objectives, trends from previous years, market performance and business case predictions. As with all KPIs, they should be designed to allow drill down so that a causal explanation for variances can be developed.

Table 6.3 Example key performance indicators for customer management

High-Level Key Performance Indicator (KPI)	Notes	Suggested Frequency
Volumes and margin overall	Ensures that overall business objectives are being met. Drilling down into the data reveals variations in performance by segment. By examining deciles, top end or bottom end shifts in customer groups can be identified. Decile analysis helps to identify the resource required to support the customer base. This should be compared with market share or growth figures.	Monthly
Cost of sales overall	Cost of sales monitors the effectiveness of the contact strategy, to determine whether different segments are being managed through channels with the most appropriate cost structures. Drilling down to examine channels against margin, cost per segment and cost per decile may indicate where to modify channel strategy.	Annually

continued overleaf

Table 6.3 continued

High-Level Key Performance Indicator (KPI)	Notes	Suggested Frequency
Number and value of new customers gained	Numbers of new customers, likely annual volumes and their potential lifetime value are also key measures. Drilling down by segment provides an indication of where the new business is coming from. Initial estimates of potential should be compared with actual performance after 12 months. Variances should be explained so as to improve forecasting.	Monthly
Existing customers – changes in volume from last year	Share of wallet (spend) measures behavioural loyalty. People who have been customers for more than 12 months should be identified and monitored. Decile analysis will indicate, for example, whether larger accounts are buying less but smaller accounts are buying more.	Quarterly
Retention rate percentage	The retention percentage over the whole customer base can be a misleading figure. It is important to examine trends by sector and size. Decile and segment analysis can show where relationship management needs more attention.	Quarterly
Attitudinal loyalty	Customer loyalty, the key to future business, is reflected by two measures. First by attitudinal loyalty (satisfaction and customer value). Second by behavioural loyalty, which is assessed by retention rates and variations in buying volumes. The one follows the other. Understanding customer satisfaction and the view of your offer is an important measure of future success. Drilling down by segment is vital here, as is comparing this measure with attrition rates.	Rolling quarterly or annually
Complaint numbers, percentage resolved and timescales	Monitoring the level of complaints and compliments is done to identify trends. Drilling down to segment, type of complaint and eventually to individual customers will pinpoint areas for action.	Monthly
Marketing cost	The marketing spend must be justified against objectives and achievements. Analysing by generic campaign type and by individual campaign will improve future allocation of marketing resources.	Monthly

SUMMARY

- What are the potential barriers to implementing relationship marketing in your organization? What do you need to do to address those barriers?
- Your implementation programme might be envisaged as a series of projects. Have you made a project plan for each phase?
- Run through the *evaluation of current practice* checklist for your company. What conclusions did you draw? Can you see structure, integration and consistency in your relationship management practices?
- Now that you have the data, what is the basis of your business case for relationship marketing: revenue protection, revenue extension, revenue development, revenue retention or a mixture of these?
- Different emphases are appropriate as the relationship with customers develops. Taking FRAC data for each segment, can you identify clearly what your contact strategies are? Which tools and techniques are most useful to you at each stage of the relationship? Thinking particularly about your e-business, how will your contact strategy change?
- What alterations are needed to your products and services to market them successfully online?
- Do your staff clearly understand how customer expectations might change as your relationship strategy rolls out?
- Have you made a list of KPIs to monitor the performance of your implementation programme? Are these built into your regular business reports?

7

Customer loyalty and continuity

WHAT IS CUSTOMER LOYALTY?

The word loyalty conjures up the image of unquestioning commitment. It is, in that sense, a thoughtless condition. However, loyalty is not mindless. The dog is loyal to its owner, the patriots to their cause, the customers to their supplier. Does the last phrase go one step too far? The feelings that engender loyalty in other situations are hard to reproduce in marketing. For our purposes, loyalty can be defined in two ways:

A state of mind, a set of attitudes, beliefs and desires. We could call this 'emotional' loyalty. Companies benefit from customers' loyal behaviour consequent upon these attitudes and beliefs. The focus of the resulting loyalty approach will be on maintaining a special place in the mind of the customer. It will try to make the customer feel that their loyalty is being rewarded by a stronger or better relationship, visible perhaps in a higher level of recognition or service. An emotional loyal may buy from a supplier because of the relationship, even when the purchase does not meet all objective criteria.

Loyalty is also a behavioural inclination. It precludes loyalty to some other suppliers but not to all of them. A customer can be loyal to more than one competing supplier. We could call this 'rational' loyalty since it makes sense for some types of situations. Here, the focus of the loyalty approach will be on incentives that reinforce behaviour patterns.

The consequences in marketing terms of accepting each definition are shown in Table 7.1 but, as in all good marketing, it is probably better to use both approaches in combination, as they suit different customer situations.

Table 7.1 Basis of customer loyalty

Basis of Loyalty	Basis of Relationship Marketing Approach
Emotional	Managing loyalty is a constant *theme* of the company's approach to managing customers.
Rational	Loyalty management takes place through *schemes* to reinforce 'loyal' behaviour.

CUSTOMER SITUATIONS AND LOYALTY

There are no necessary conditions for loyalty

Loyalty is a composite, as is loyal behaviour. It fits with other attitudes and beliefs that a person may hold and other cognitions. Loyalty may not always be the primary driver of behaviour. Loyal customers can sometimes appear disloyal. For example, a loyal customer, when coming up to a major purchasing decision, may solicit information from competitive suppliers. They may do this in order to justify the decision, to benchmark, to conform to standard company purchasing procedures, or to develop a stronger negotiating position. Loyal customers may also buy from competitors if their preferred supplier does not have the right product or service to avoid over-dependence or if a fundamental basis of customer satisfaction is temporarily absent. For example, connecting trains or buses that do not connect remove a key-product attribute.

Degrees of loyalty

Not all customers are equally loyal, nor will any one customer always demonstrate the same degree of loyalty all the time. Loyalty is developed by approaches that reinforce and develop a positive state of mind. The aim is not to make all customers loyal but to improve the loyalty of those customers most likely to respond. Different people respond to different things. Some respond to incentives, some to differentiated marketing, some to high general standards of service, some to product excellence and some to strong branding. In addition, some customers will accept switching barriers more easily than others. The relationship between loyalty and purchase behaviour is not linear, as Figure 7.1 illustrates.

In product areas such as banking or utilities, many customers go through their whole lives without experiencing supplier variety, so their loyalty is never really tested. Under conditions of deregulation and new competition, it may take some time before any real emotional loyalty builds up. It may therefore be important to build behavioural or promotional loyalty schemes quickly if competition is about to be introduced, simply because the customer loss rate while competitors are sampled could not be afforded. Such loyalty is best sustained by providing excellent customer value so that any comparisons that switchers may make show the original company in the best light.

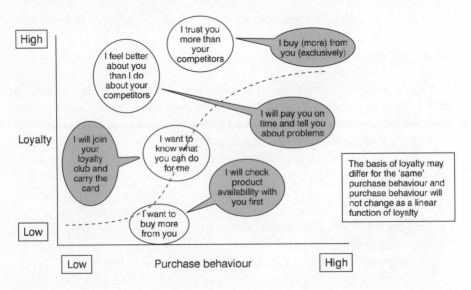

Figure 7.1 Loyalty, beliefs and customer behaviours

The exchange of information is the key

The exchange of information provides a critical bridge between emotional and rational loyalty. Loyal customers are more likely to provide data because they trust the supplier, expect it to be used with discretion and to their benefit. They also expect the supplier to be able to access that information during transactions. The importance of information technology as the corporate memory of customer information cannot be overstated. Loyal customers also expect to receive more information. Privileged communication is an essential element of loyalty programmes.

Loyal customers are not always the best customers

Net customer value and loyalty are correlated but not always closely. Some retailers, for example, have customers who buy very little but complain easily. These customers complain at the slightest excuse and expect to be rewarded for their loyalty by over compensation. Conversely, some high value customers are completely disloyal. They buy so much of a product or service that it is very important for them to get the best value for money or most appropriate version each time they buy. Since many companies have not defined what they mean by a 'good' customer, this makes it hard to design loyalty schemes to attract them. Often, good is equated to high volume, though such customers may be inherently fickle and might not even be profitable. For example, large consumers of energy frequently switch sources to gain lowest cost supply.

It is only worth adding a loyalty dimension to your marketing platform if there are enough high value customers (individually or as a group) who will respond to being managed in a loyalty relationship. Their response may be just to purchase regularly rather than to buy more but retention can be a productive marketing investment.

Loyalty must be understood in context

It's very rare for a customer to inherit loyalty, although bankers used to believe that they did! Loyalty develops along with positive experience of the product, service or company. So a critical time for loyalty management, in terms of influencing both emotions and rationality, is at the beginning of the relationship. This is most likely to be when customers first start buying the product or indeed the product category. At this time, the customer has the highest lifetime value but often the lowest current value. This is why airlines are increasing focusing on the newly 'graduated' frequent flyer. Banks, on the other hand, are still trying to identify the ideal time to start attracting and managing the customer. The problem is that when young people get their first job they often switch banks, which makes all the investment made in them as students (when they were loss making) a waste of money.

Case example: the British retail clothing market and the generation transition

In the late 1990s, the battle for 'share of wardrobe' was intense. Marks & Spencer held the middle ground. It pursued a product led approach based on an undifferentiated relationship open to any customer who wanted to join via its storecard. Although the relationship was enhanced by financial services and mail order offerings, these were also undifferentiated. The main variations were based on traditional direct marketing according to the products taken and promotional responses. At the beginning of this period, Marks & Spencer held a dominant share of the women's clothing market.

Upmarket from Marks & Spencer were to be found companies such as Jaeger. Jaeger positioned itself above Marks & Spencer, although they shared many customers. Jaeger customers tended to turn to Jaeger for high quality, durable outerwear and leisure wear. They regarded Jaeger clothing as an investment. Many customers held the Jaeger storecard, which rewarded them according to their spend. A loyalty card was also added. However, Jaeger became conscious of the fact that one of the key sustainers of their market was weakening, namely the transfer between mother and daughter generations of the 'Jaeger habit'. In certain families and social circles, there would be a time when the mother would say to the daughter, 'It's time for your first Jaeger outfit'. The mother would then escort the daughter to 'her' Jaeger store, where she would be known personally by the assistant. However, with the breakdown in cross generation influence, many daughters would not, as a matter of principle, be seen wearing the same type of clothing as their mothers. This created a product problem for Jaeger, which was resolved by the introduction of the Jaeger London Collection, targeted at younger women. In order to ensure that the buying habit was transferred, Jaeger had to use its customer information systems to support promotions aimed at encouraging daughters of 'Jaeger women' to take up the habit.

At the other end of the scale, Next attacked Marks & Spencer through a variety of more specialist product and store concepts targeted at the younger buyer. However, its buyers were ageing, becoming more similar in profile to the classic Marks & Spencer buyer. This presented both an opportunity and a threat to Next. The opportunity lay in continuing to recruit new, younger customers while holding on to its older, higher value customers. The threat lay in the difficulty of compromising its product offering, so in trying to serve both markets it might fail to meet the needs of either. The alternative strategy was to stay closely in touch with its older customers, using relationship marketing techniques, and modify the core Next proposition to meet their needs. It could then introduce other product and store variants for new, younger customers avoiding where possible the alienation of the older customer. Next placed great emphasis, relative to Marks & Spencer, on the use of its marketing database.

Finally, BHS (British Home Stores), positioned itself slightly downmarket from Marks & Spencer. They decided that their only chance of long-term survival against Marks & Spencer was to fine-tune their offer to mothers with children at home. Product ranges were redesigned with this in mind and the Choice loyalty card targeted these customers very strongly. Store staff were instructed to encourage mothers accompanied by children to take the card if they did not already have one. The effort resulted in a consolidation of BHS's market share in this segment.

Marks & Spencer famously refused to engage in 'sales'. Indeed, one of their directors was quoted as saying, 'Every red sticker represents one of our mistakes'. In 1998, the company reported its first downturn in profits. By mid-1999 profit levels were half those of the previous year, an unprecedented event. A new CEO, strategic repositioning, new lines and store layouts led to a remarkable rebound by mid-2002.

LOYALTY AND PRODUCT TYPE

Customer loyalty is, at its best, a consequence of how the entire business is conceived and managed. The key to differentiating an offer from that of competitors is to focus on customer value management. This will ensure that customer facing processes deliver customer-defined value during normal interactions, which will both attract and retain customers. The basis of customer value, and thus of loyalty, will vary with the product or service.

RENEWABLE CONTRACTS WITH FIXED TERMS

Examples – insurance, subscriptions, clubs and maintenance contracts.

Risk – the customer may go to the market when the contract expires.

If the need for the service ends at the term of the contract, such as a life insurance policy, then the retention risk is associated with contract cancellation. The customer may suffer from a penalty but loyalty incentives could still be profitable if customers have a known tendency to cancel. Offering the incentive may reduce cancellation rates and thus reduce the costs associated with replacing lost customers. If the need for the service continues – an outsourced IT contract, for instance – then some loyalty incentive to renew is appropriate. Best practice suggests that this incentive should be in the form of increased value rather than a discount.

CONTRACTUAL WITH ROLLING NOTICE

Examples – utilities, term deposits.

Risk – cancellation may occur at any time.

Similar considerations apply as with fixed-term contracts, except that the customer needs to be kept aware of the costs of cancellation. This is harder than with renewable contracts, when the customer's thought process is concentrated by the renewal date. One method that seems to work in financial services is the idea of a loyalty bonus given for each year that the customer maintains the contract.

ONE SUPPLIER AT A TIME

Examples – insurance, personal services (hairdressing, healthcare, vets).

Risk – customers may switch.

If the customer switches, the commercial relationship with the customer is lost, although a promotional relationship can be maintained. Where a renewable contract is concerned, at least the supplier can target the customer again for winback at renewal time. However, in transaction-intensive relationships, the loss of knowledge of the customer's transaction pattern reduces understanding of current behaviour. There is therefore a particular need for suppliers to offer loyalty incentives to good customers. Also, for this kind of service, winning increased business means getting competitors' customers to switch. Avoiding the need to replace good customers should be taken into account when fixing the budget for retaining customers.

SCOPE FOR A MULTI-PRODUCT RELATIONSHIP

Examples – financial services, travel, consumer electronics.

Risk – buyer fatigue, one out, all out.

While cross-selling incentives can be used to offer the customer discounts for additional products bought, there is a danger here that if you lose one product sale you may lose them all. An example of the method might be to offer discounted hotel space when flights are bought. Note that targeting all customers for cross-selling in this situation can be very wasteful as they may not be good prospects for each product in the range. In most fields, cross-buying is associated with reduced attrition but this does not mean that cross-buying actually reduces attrition. Retention and cross-buying might both be outcomes of good branding and service. However, it is also clear that an extensively cross-bought customer effectively provides the margin to allow the supplier to focus its marketing efforts more intensively on each customer. This might include some loyalty bonus.

A SINGLE INTERMITTENT TRANSACTION

Examples – cars, holidays, furnishings, white goods.

Risk – suppliers lose touch due to long purchase intervals.

Widely spaced transactions pose greater problems in loyalty management because of the greater chances of losing touch. Suppliers in this group need to create additional relationships based on more frequent contacts. These may be self-funding because they are based on other products or services or because of the reduced cost of replacing lost customers. Offering financial services is a typical technique. Customers buying a car are offered special financial terms that encourage replacement trade-in for a new model from the same manufacturer.

A STREAM OF TRANSACTIONS WITH CHOICE AT EACH PURCHASE

Examples – groceries, stationery, computer consumables.

Risk – many opportunities to distract with point-of-sale promotions.

Many customers will maintain relationships with a number of suppliers and order from the one offering the best value for money at the time of purchase. In such cases, overriding volume incentives are often used, either in the form of discounts or improved service levels.

COMBINATION OF FACILITIES AND USAGE

Examples – telecommunications, security systems.

Risk – many opportunities to distract with point-of-sale promotions.

Similar to the above, except that the customer obviously has an incentive to concentrate business with a limited number of suppliers. A similar solution is possible with the additional incentive of a reduction or waiver of the cost of the facilities component.

WHICH CUSTOMERS DO YOU WANT TO BE LOYAL?

In Chapter 5, we discussed the importance of segmentation and the nature of the top vanilla offer. Since managing a 'market segment of one' is often practically impossible, companies need to group customers according to their likely value. Customers are not equally valuable, nor are they equally attractive. It is therefore important to consider which customers you want to attract and how you want them to behave. Unless a loyalty scheme designed to change behaviour reinforces and adds value to the brand, the changed behaviour will last only a little longer than the scheme. Customer loyalty schemes, by definition, are not of this kind. Many schemes are effectively data based promotional continuity programmes.

Case example: Tesco Clubcard

In 1995, Tesco introduced its Clubcard loyalty scheme. Shop visits increased by 16 per cent and share of total grocery spend went from 43 per cent to 46 per cent. By May 1996, Tesco had displaced its main rival Sainsbury's in the top spot, partly due to its loyalty scheme. However, it had issued £202 million in vouchers and a further £100 million plus was spent on the Clubcard infrastructure. Tesco claims a justified return on its investment but some analysts wondered whether the company had in effect simply computerized a long-term promotional scheme. Huge amounts of data were generated and the task of analysing it was likened to trying to drink from a fire hydrant. Nevertheless Tesco continued to develop the scheme and by 2002 was not only dominant in the UK grocery market but had made significant progress in several other countries..

Loyalty schemes have the benefit of yielding customer data that can be used for targeting and may therefore save other forms of marketing communication spend. The Tesco scheme was regarded as successful by marketers because, for the first time, certain groups of women received personalized promotions targeted specifically at them and they responded by increased purchasing.

It is usually helpful to distinguish categories of customer, so as to influence emotional or rational loyalty more precisely:

- **True frequent users** – of the product, service or company.
- **Affinity customers** – are not such frequent users but like to identify with the company. Active affinity customers are responsive to offers from the company and may focus on collecting the scheme's currency. They have a high propensity to recommend other customers or involve a reference group such as family or business colleagues in using the same products or services.
- **Intermittent customers** – buy very infrequently and base their decision on the offer at the time of purchase.

Case example: frequent flyers

Among frequent flyers, hyperusers usually stand out and must be managed differently because they tend to have very different service needs. For example, the frequent flyer typically requires basic personal recognition and to get 'to and through' as quickly as possible. Hyperusers typically qualify for the top tier loyalty scheme of more than one airline, hotel or car rental company. Marketing to them needs to be more competitive. They provide very high net present value. Intermittent customers may have what might be called 'burst travel characteristics'. That is, for a short period, they are travelling very intensively. They only just make the higher tiers of frequent flyer ranks and are therefore almost captive.

This demonstrates the importance of understanding the fundamental usage pattern of customers before deploying a loyalty scheme. If most of the business is channelled through the company, then the main value of a loyalty scheme is defence of share. The loyalty scheme must compete for resources against other ways of achieving the same objective, such as branding and customer service. However, if average life as a customer is short, the service component of a loyalty scheme can be key in attracting new users and encouraging them to give most of their business to one airline as quickly as possible.

Most individual flyers fall into the active affinity group. This figure can be as high as 50 per cent for some airlines with passive affinity being another 20 per cent. Here, a loyalty scheme with a small amount of service differentiation ('stroking') can be a good way of getting these customers to identify themselves. It will also help the company identify future frequent flyers. The scheme can be funded by targeted promotional offers.

Data mining makes it possible to identify the characteristics of different kinds of 'good' customer. These might be emotionally loyal, high value, cross-buyers or brand respecters. The aim is to predict customers of higher future value, who can then be targeted by loyalty scheme offers. The customer database should therefore be widely accessible to other areas of the company to support this role, a requirement that tends to be grossly underestimated! The power of this approach is particularly great when customers elect into such relationships and (ideally) pay for membership because of the benefits they receive (Butscher, 1998). People who join these sorts of affinity clubs tend to be emotionally loyal and share information about themselves openly.

THE LOYALTY GRID

Understanding the loyalty position is the key to developing a more tightly targeted communications plan. Table 7.2 illustrates how data mining can be used to draw up a loyalty grid. In this example, three types of data might have been used:

- actual sales history based on FRAC;
- share of wallet calculations;
- measures of emotional loyalty based on simple attitudinal research.

The exact form of the grid depends on the nature of the business and the competitive position within it. If customers can be mapped on to a loyalty grid, a basic orientation for the loyalty scheme can be determined along with an indication of where to spend the marketing communications budget.

The intended effect of these actions is illustrated in Figure 7.2. This relates spend based on rational loyalty, which the scheme is designed

Table 7.2 The use of data mining to build a loyalty grid

Actual or Potential Profit	Loyal	Switchers, Multi-sourcers	Competitor Loyal
Large	Retain via account management, maybe cut management costs	Spend most to make loyal	Manage cost-effectively but look for moments of truth (such as contract renewals)
Medium	Capitalize on loyalty by incentives and product bundling	Spend to make loyal	Manage them but very cost-effectively
Small	Consider other channels or minimal management	Consider passing to other channels	Pass to other channels

to encourage, promotional responsiveness (measured in terms of the additional profit yielded by the customer's response to promotions) and emotional or attitudinal loyalty. The general thrust of the marketing effort is to push customers from bottom to top (increase behavioural loyalty) and from left to right (increase emotional loyalty).

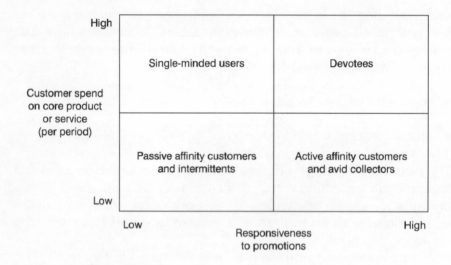

Figure 7.2 Effect of a loyalty scheme on users and responders

CUSTOMER ACQUISITION – SIX STEPS TO SUCCESS

Most strategies in customer relationship marketing are based on the ideas of customer acquisition and retention. Almost all companies suffer some customer attrition. To stand still, they need to acquire more customers, which is the purpose of acquisition programmes. Acquisition is therefore used to offset attrition. The attrition rate is measured as the number of customers at the beginning of a period who take their trade elsewhere, expressed as a percentage of the total number of customers. The significance of the figure depends upon factors such as the average length of the buying cycle, frequency of purchase and the range and value of products bought. For example, a customer might be regarded as lost (from a segment) if they switch from buying high value products to infrequent purchases of low value products. Customer acquisition is the process of gaining new customers and it proceeds usually in six stages.

1. SET OBJECTIVES

The starting point for any acquisition programme is a simple financial calculation to determine the allowable marketing cost per acquisition. In other words, how much you can afford to spend to acquire a customer. It should be determined by the expected lifetime value of a customer, as opposed to short-term profit. Lifetime value is the profit expected from a customer over their expected life with you. Emotional loyalty (which produces recommendations), upselling and cross-selling all increase lifetime value. Strictly speaking, it should be calculated using discounted cash flow techniques but most marketers use a figure based on spend over a fixed number of years. The duration of this term is related to the duration of the 'lifetime' and the length of the buying cycle.

For example, a parent is likely to be in the market for high volumes of detergent while there are children at home, perhaps 20 to 25 years. Acquiring a customer at the beginning of this period can yield a very high lifetime value if loyalty is managed successfully. However, keeping the customer loyal in such a highly competitive market is expensive. Many quite loyal customers will switch to try out competitive offers since detergent falls into the 'stream of transactions' category and may switch back later. This reduces the lifetime value even of loyal customers.

If lifetime value cannot be calculated, it may be possible to use short-term approximations. For example, the cost of achieving the initial sale(s) or return on investment from the initial sale(s). However, lifetime value is a better criterion for targeting customers to be acquired. One reason why a good customer database is so valuable is that it allows you to track long-term buying patterns as a basis for lifetime value calculations.

2. PROFILING

If the customer database contains information about individuals, response rates and purchase histories, it can be used as the starting point to examine which media sources and communication strategies work best. Where little or no history exists, developing a profile of existing customers will help to target new customers. Many companies use customer satisfaction questionnaires for this purpose.

Market segmentation is essential in understanding and differentiating the market. Broad based research may not target the right customers. Pareto's 80/20 rule may well apply; indeed, in some cases research has shown this to be more like 90/10. The reason for the smaller proportion is that these are the high value or 'good' customers. It is usually more productive to pay more attention to your most profitable customers by focusing your market research and customer satisfaction research on them. At the same time, it is important to be alert to the meaning of consumers' precise stated requirements. Answers to questionnaires should be compared carefully. Normalize results, which allows the miserly scorer to be compared with the generous scorer, so that exceptions do not skew results.

3. TARGETING FOR NEW CUSTOMERS

Targeting should be based on profiling the customer base. The aim is to look for suspects with similar characteristics to your best customers.

A special case of targeting is 'member get member' schemes (known as MGM). This is often used by membership and credit card organizations. Members tend to recruit people similar to themselves. MGM is a good option if the quality of the database is poor or if mailing lists are hard to acquire. MGM is targeted word-of-mouth advocacy with a bonus built in for existing customers. For example, Preferred Direct is a direct selling motor insurer. For a two-year period it relied exclusively on MGM campaigns, using Marks & Spencer vouchers as an incentive.

4. MEDIA

The allowable media cost per sale is a component of the allowable cost per acquisition and, obviously enough, is a function of the lifetime value of customers. Other variables to consider in the media plan include:

- **Reach** – the larger the audience, the more viable mass media will be.
- **Media cost** – weighed against the likelihood of response.
- **Media availability** – you may have to work hard to find the right combination of media to suit a particular campaign.

- **Media accessibility** – do your prospects for recruitment pay enough attention to the medium for it to be a successful recruitment device?
- **Media weight** – this is a measure of the 'quality' of each medium. A component of most media models, it is a figure ascribed to the value of different market segments. In a sense it is a measure of effectiveness and response rates. For example, if the target is males aged 41 to 50 in the $101,000 to $110,000 income bracket, each hit on a target might be given a value of 1. A hit on a male in the $91,000 to $100,000 income bracket might be given a weighting of 0.95.
- **The number of stages** – required to achieve the right response. The more complex the product or service, the more complex the recruitment process is likely to be. For example, some industrial equipment products may require two or three letters, a catalogue, two or three phone calls and several direct sales visits.

Good media models take all of these factors into account as well as additional factors such as buyer fatigue and attention loss over a long campaign. Responsiveness to a particular medium diminishes as exposure increases. Generally, the more an advertisement is used, the lower the response. Doubling the size of advertisements, the weight of mailing packages or doubling their frequency, will less than double response rates. Multiple media campaigns are usually more cost-effective as they are less susceptible to the law of diminishing returns. However, they are more difficult to co-ordinate. For example, if the timing of a promotion through one medium slips, such as a letter referring to a TV campaign, then the effect may be counter productive.

In the past, many direct marketers focused on immediate impact as opposed to the cumulative impact of several communications. As far as instant results are concerned, selective market coverage where the same prospect is not hit twice will normally outpull high frequency. This contrasts to the philosophy of general advertisers, who prepare media plans based on reach (the total number of prospects covered) *and* frequency (how often the advertisement appears). The general approach is illustrated in Figure 7.3.

5. COMMUNICATION

The offer made to potential new customers is a function of buyer behaviour. Depending on the product or service, the campaign may target immediate buyers, trial buyers, highly qualified enquirers or

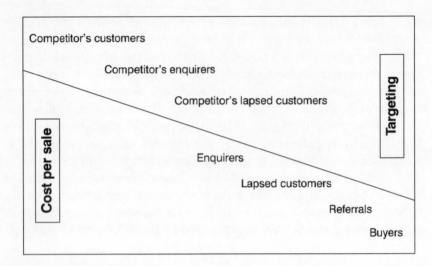

Figure 7.3 Balancing media costs per sale with targeting effort

loosely qualified enquirers. These decisions will affect the creative treatment, the offer and the number of stages needed to complete the buying cycle. The creative treatment also depends on the brand personality which determines, for example, whether a communication is product- or offer-led.

6. SALES

Once the sale is made, the process of developing the relationship and retaining the customer begins. A good first step, often overlooked by large companies, is to thank the customer for their order. On the other hand, this is not a good time to investigate whether the customer service and retention procedures are solid enough to cope with a large influx of customers!

CUSTOMER RETENTION – SIX STEPS TO SUCCESS

The customer retention rate is the obverse of the attrition rate. It is the percentage of your customers at the beginning of a period who are still doing business with you at the end. Once again, a single measure gives only a rough guide to the situation. Customer retention is the process of keeping customers.

The purpose of retention strategy is to maximize an individual's profitable lifetime value as a customer. Active customers can usually be identified from records of current transactions. The definition of lapsed and inactive customers varies according to transaction frequency for the product or service. To be cost effective, retention strategies have to be planned in some detail and can result in quite complex programmes. Thus someone who has not bought a bed for several years is not necessarily lapsed. If the product is durable and replacement takes place every ten years or so, then customers might consider themselves as loyal to a company even if they have not bought for five years. For this reason, companies with long replacement cycle products try to sell lower value items such as service, support or parts on a more regular basis. This not only generates revenue but also provides a basis for keeping in touch with customers. The longer the known lifetime or *potential* lifetime of your customer, the more promotional activities can be undertaken during the customer's life with your company. Retention activities will vary through the relationship cycle described in Chapter 6.

Welcome

Welcome and reassure customers, overcome any cognitive dissonance, build loyalty and gain additional customer information. It also opens up the opportunity of giving your customer initial benefits. Whether a welcome process is appropriate will be related to the length of the customer life cycle.

Getting to know (learning)

A natural next step is to upsell. In the case of a credit card, a gold card might be offered; for cars, an upmarket model; the CD buyer might be offered a boxed set. The timing of the offer can be determined by previous customer histories. Often this can be achieved by testing. A statistical analysis of test results can produce a score applied to the customer database that attaches a likelihood factor to each record, measuring their propensity to respond to offers.

Customer development (account management)

This is a conscious strategy to switch customers across product categories or cross-sell. A credit card company could promote a home shopping service or wine club. A car company could promote the second car for the family. A book club could promote a music collection. In both up- and cross-selling, loyal customers should be given some incentive to remain loyal.

Problem management

Cost-effective inducements are needed to reward loyal customers for continued patronage. Often a renewal cycle involves several timed, relevant and personal communications before, on and after the date of renewal. Customers who pass the final renewal cycle date become 'lapsed'.

Winback

Reawakening lapsed customers where feasible is usually more cost effective than recruiting totally new customers. The data on lapsed customers available to you from your database may be unreliable. Reactivation campaigns can be targeted better if lapsed customer data is verified (usually by telephone) so that the profitability of promotions to lapsed customers does not have to be guessed.

Cost effectiveness is a more critical issue for inactive customers. They have not bought or responded to a promotion for longer than lapsed customers. However, the answer is to test and compare the results to the acquisition programme in terms of cost justification.

There are six steps in retention strategy.

1. IDENTIFICATION

The first step is simply to identify and value the best customers against an agreed criterion of profitability. It may be that smaller but regular buyers contribute a greater profit margin and lifetime value than one time large purchasers.

2. ANALYSIS

Thorough profiling and tracking of customer purchase histories based on FRAC (**F**requency, **R**ecency, **A**mount and **C**ategory), promotional responses and sources of business are vital here. These analyses also help identify the potential market of similar customers for the acquisition programme. This is sometimes referred to as a marketing audit. Many financial institutions have been surprised to learn how many customers and families are multiple purchasers of their products when they have undertaken this kind of analysis.

3. STREAMING FOR TARGETING

Once each customer record has been analysed and scored for potential value, it is accessible for selection. The criteria for selection include not only potential profitability but also customer accessibility, by direct marketing or by other techniques. In addition to the usual range of marketing communications, most companies have access to a series of customer contact points at nominal cost. These are known as 'free rides' and are ignored surprisingly often. They include statement stuffers, product dispatch stuffers, invoices and account letters, opening and closing letters, catalogues, calls from customers and point-of-sale or service contacts. While some industry sectors take significant advantage of free rides (financial services is a good example) others do so only partially or not at all. Even a delivery note can be accompanied by a simple feedback form with three or four questions.

4. CONTACT STRATEGIES

Contact strategies were discussed in the previous chapter. The aim is to reward customer decisions to stay loyal and to increase purchasing. Different media are 'bundled' according to their relative strengths in order to achieve the greatest effect. For example, customers who are a long way from buying (they may have just bought) may need a gentle mail prompt. The task is to assess the most appropriate and cost effective contact strategy for each segment. The idea of putting the customer in a privileged position is common here. Many companies, such as British Airways and Capital One, the financial services group, now use this approach to determine the contact strategies for many different customer groups, particularly their best customers.

5. TESTING

It is always worth having a continuous series of tests to establish optimum timing, frequency, offer and creative treatments. Without these, the profitability of loyalty programmes can be difficult to establish.

6. EVALUATION (MODEL BUILDING)

The objective of a retention programme must be to make it worthwhile for customers to be loyal, which is why a thorough understanding of customers' behaviour is vital. It is sometimes necessary to achieve a delicate balance between marginal income and customer irritation. In any retention programme, all possible contact points with customers must be reviewed, competitive messages must be taken into account and optimal frequency must be tested. Evaluation is therefore based on a careful modelling exercise. The model should be refined continuously through links to the customer database backed by periodic but regular research.

LOYALTY MANAGEMENT – SIX STEPS TO SUCCESS

1. DEFINE OBJECTIVES

The need to develop a loyalty approach over and above existing marketing, sales and service approaches should be identified as part of an overall customer relationship marketing audit. This might reveal, for example:

- competitive attempts to target precisely your best customers;
- falling repurchase rates among your best customers;
- falling levels of emotional loyalty;
- increasing switching rates away from your products or services.

Research by the Future Foundation shows that customers are happy to provide information if it helps to manage the relationship. This is especially true if they then see that the information has been used in a relevant way, for example, by selectively targeting the promotion of products and services or by contacting the customer at intervals and at times that the customer has said are appropriate. Table 7.3 shows the factors where UK retail customers say they are most likely to respond.

Objectives for the loyalty approach should be quantified or the approach cannot be evaluated, whether by research or through business performance. Objectives should always contain a financial component or the scheme may be vulnerable to the criticism that it makes customers feel good but has no effect on profits.

Table 7.3 Factors affecting propensity to respond to promotional contacts

Sector	%
Home shopping	43
Air miles or points	43
Regular letters or magazines	50
Better credit terms	57
Thanks for being a customer	74
Free telephone service	75
Tailored products	76
Advance warning	77
Discounts	80
Recognition	82
Free delivery	87
Treated as an individual	90

Source: The New Information Trade, The Future Foundation (1996)

2. ADOPT A DEFINITION OF LOYALTY THAT MAKES STRATEGIC SENSE

There are circumstances in which emotional loyalty is not feasible. In some markets, such as personal computers, commodification has taken place. Companies and their products have become undifferentiated, although often this is due to the suppliers' own marketing and service failures. In such cases, devising incentives to reward specific loyal behaviours may be the only approach. However, it is usually best to start with the aim of building emotional loyalty, perhaps best paraphrased as the *desire* to do business with the company and not with its competitors.

3. UNDERSTAND CUSTOMERS AND THEIR PROPENSITY TO BE LOYAL

Whether using the loyalty approach pays, depends on customers, their needs, their basic attitudes to buying in general and to each particular supplier of a product or service. It is therefore critical for a company introducing a loyalty scheme to establish, usually through research and testing, an understanding of which groups of customers are strategically important. The propensity of each of these groups to respond to different marketing, sales and service approaches must be determined. FRAC analysis is needed and the customer database must be used to monitor responses. Based on the definition of loyalty adopted, measures must be obtained to show changes in purchase behaviour and changes in loyalty.

4. DEVELOP AND QUANTIFY THE LOYALTY APPROACH

4.1 Which aspects of the marketing and service mix can be deployed most effectively?

There is a tendency to concentrate first on promotional incentives such as discounts but these have the disadvantage of focusing on specific behaviours. Qualification to receive incentives is often fixed in terms of those behaviours. A key area of attention should be the service interface with the customer. Murphy and Suntook (1998) have pointed out, as have others, that satisfaction and loyalty are associated with different trigger points. A supplier who concentrates on high quality may reduce satisfaction levels if, say, delivery times suffer as a result. On the other hand, to increase product or service attributes beyond a certain standard may be wasteful. A computer keyboard has to meet certain minimum standards of performance but creating a truly excellent keyboard may not influence the majority of buyers, although it may well influence journalists or professional buyers. A low-cost Internet service that is always engaged will upset everybody. The most important thing to recognize is where customer value lies and to understand that the range of performance that influences satisfaction levels is not so much 0 to 10 but, say, 7 to 9.

Put simply, how you deal with the customer, in terms of managing their requirements and exchanging information, should hold the key to sustaining and building loyalty. It is important to measure the perceived value of potential benefits and then later look at cost. If a benefit has a very high value, cost should not be a knock-out criterion.

4.2 Financial evaluation

Develop a sound financial concept, taking into consideration all cost and revenue factors. Additional revenues might include membership fees, sales of advertising space in the membership magazine or on the Web page, sales of merchandise and new fee based services. Financial problems are a significant issue for loyalty programmes of any scale. The £100 million spent by Tesco quoted earlier is not unusual. This is not to suggest that schemes cannot be scaled to size and type of business but whatever approach is chosen, costs will be incurred that have to be justified. A sensitivity analysis based on different membership levels, or different benefit levels, is needed. One or two of the early loyalty schemes introduced by US airlines produced scenarios in which the airline would be flying the majority of their passengers free after a few years since no one thought to include expiry dates on benefits for frequent flyer miles.

4.3 Relate high perceived value to low cost of provision

This is the key to most successful schemes. Finance directors are not keen to give away profits. The justification of loyalty schemes is that they reduce marketing costs but these financial benefits may take time to emerge. Meanwhile, the costs of the loyalty scheme are all too apparent. Some good examples of loyalty scheme benefits might be:

- **Utilize spare network capacity** – under booked flights, weekend and evening phone calls, off-season holidays, night-time electricity.
- **Reward well behaved customers** – a car rescue scheme for customers who have their cars serviced according to the manufacturer's schedule costs less than when provided on the open market to non-loyal customers.
- **High marketing cost items** – where the marketing cost for the product or service disappears when provided as part of a loyalty scheme. For example, an invitation to a special pre-Christmas Sunday or late-night opening for a department store.
- **Part payment** – loyalty points plus cash.
- **Service touches** – cost very little to provide but differentiate you from competitors. These often have high perceived value, for example privileged information about new products or services.

4.4 Define qualification levels

This is where the loyalty grid is used to determine the qualification levels for different groups and types of customer. Conventionally, qualification levels are fixed in terms of how much customers buy overall but there are many other approaches. For example, how much customers buy of a key product or service, whether they buy at full or discounted prices, purchase frequency, future potential purchases, actual or potential importance as a decision influencer and whether there is any reciprocal buying.

It is common to set 'tiered' qualification levels, with increasing loyalty commitment matched by increasing service levels and bonuses. This makes sense when the customer's movement between tiers is upward. Being downgraded is not pleasant in any context but very disappointing for customers who have been nurtured upward for a long period. For this reason, a slow let down is recommended with early warning and proper explanations. It is important not to let temporary reductions in purchasing, which may be totally uncorrelated with loyalty, lead to downgrading. Demotivating customers by downgrading them immediately makes little sense.

5. DELIVER THE LOYALTY PROGRAMME

This is usually fairly straightforward because individual components of the approach are often a remix or enhancement of existing approaches. What distinguishes the loyalty scheme is consistency. This should come through in all the key areas, such as:

- briefings for marketing service suppliers such as advertising and direct marketing agencies or in-house magazine publishers;
- customer service definitions;
- staff training and motivation;
- acquisition or adaptation of customer facing information systems;
- setting pricing and terms of payments.

Delivering the approach internally is just as important as delivering it externally. Top management and all other employees have to support, understand and buy into it. The workload involved is, of course, significant but should be straightforward if there are clear objectives and well developed processes. Loyalty schemes can backfire badly if they are developed in a hurry to fix a short-term marketing problem, without regard for a carefully designed approach.

6. MEASURE AND EVALUATE

Loyalty approaches must in the end pay off by producing better sales and profits than would have been yielded without the approach. The term increase is avoided here because sometimes loyalty schemes are used to stem declining sales and profitability.

One measurement problem is opportunity loss. Since the scheme is aimed at the best customers, it is not possible to answer the question, 'What would have happened to these customers without the loyalty approach?' For this reason, the opportunity to test effectiveness should be taken wherever possible. The best time for this is at the launch. Customer groups should be divided into relatively watertight compartments so that results can be cross referenced with control groups. The scheme should, if possible, be rolled out slowly, being evaluated, modified and improved as it unfolds.

ARE LOYALTY SCHEMES WIN-WIN?

We have emphasized on several occasions the need for customer databases and the importance of analysing and sharing information. Customers realize, of course, that 'better' relationships are increasingly sustained by information systems. Indeed, in some cases, customers themselves are keying data directly into their suppliers' systems from the office or from home. However, there is evidence that customers have mixed feelings about being managed in a loyalty scheme, with a marked lack of enthusiasm in certain retail sectors (Evans *et al*, 1998). There is an awareness by some consumers that intrusions upon privacy incur personal costs that might outweigh the benefits of being a member. This is also associated with an erosion in trust that needs to be taken into account when the scheme is designed.

DO CUSTOMERS WANT LOYALTY SCHEMES?

Not every customer wants to be included in a loyalty programme. Some will respond well, in terms of maintained or increased loyalty, to individual elements of the programme. Others will want to keep the relationship at an administrative level. That is to say, they want the product or service at a good price with a relationship sufficient merely to ensure that contracts are fulfilled.

From an information systems point of view, it is an essential design requirement to be able to discriminate between these different types of customer. In many countries it is illegal to hold data on either a paper- or a computer-based information system without the knowledge and consent of the data subject.

CUSTOMER BENEFITS

For customers that choose to participate fully or partially with a loyalty scheme there are a number of benefits. Customers maintain their knowledge investment so that, irrespective of the amount they are purchasing, they always know how to get the best out of the supplier. They may be offered a wider range of relevant products and services, often on attractive terms (funded by the loyalty scheme). They may also feel more secure in the relationship. For example, credit card companies now use their customer databases to try to detect whether a card has been used illegally. This offers an extra level of protection for valued, 'good' customers.

SUPPLIER BENEFITS

The supplier benefits because the customer is more receptive to messages and offers. Even if an individual purchasing decision goes against the supplier, the customer retains this receptiveness. The opportunities for cross-selling are increased, even from third parties and this can help defray the costs of maintaining the scheme. Customers also have additional opportunities to express needs, improving the quality of the customer database. All promotional programmes can be integrated through the loyalty scheme to make more effective use overall of the information available for marketing.

SUMMARY – TEN STEPS TO SUCCESSFUL LOYALTY SCHEMES

1. Recognize that loyalty is a relative concept and the form it takes varies greatly according to the type of product or service involved. We have introduced the notion of emotional loyalty and rational loyalty. The approach to managing loyalty depends critically on the definition adopted. There are many different ways of managing loyalty, ranging from promotional schemes to much longer themes that run through a company's entire approach to customers. A straightforward and rational approach to determine which way of managing loyalty is right for the company is recommended. Loyalty management is not a panacea for all marketing ills. Nor does it necessarily imply radical change. Many companies are today

discovering that they are managing customer loyalty very well. However, there are also many companies that are not.

2. Analyse the market to determine whether it can be segmented using a few simple criteria that enable prediction of likely loyalty. Identify which kinds of customer are most likely to be loyal, given the right product and service. Determine how they can be managed within a loyalty scheme.

3. Research customer needs and attitudes in particular: what makes them satisfied or improves their image of the supplier? What makes them feel they are optimizing their use of the product or service in question? For small businesses, this might require briefing a professional researcher to run one or two focus groups or to design an attitude questionnaire. Remember to concentrate on the most important customers. At the same time, find out what is keeping customers loyal at the moment: why do they re-buy?

4. Translate business objectives and strategies into market targeting. Small businesses, being generally closer to customers, should have less difficulty in working out which customers they need most to succeed. Consider target volumes and target prices.

5. Install a measurement mechanism, whether it is research based (such as a questionnaire) or customer database oriented (such as an identification of repurchasing rates). Ensure that performance can be tracked both quantitatively and qualitatively.

6. Design a customer management business process involving people, processes and procedures in line with customer requirements. This may sound complicated but it is simply a question of understanding what customers need, how they buy and how the company is going to structure its relationships so as to help them buy. Too often companies that begin to invest in marketing and customer service see this as a functional process such as telemarketing, advertising or field service. It is more a question of redefining the structure and management of the customer interface into areas such as customer acquisition and retention.

7. Evaluate the performance of current IT systems in supporting these processes. Many businesses have no systems for customer management. Their systems are focused entirely on transactions and logistics. Today, good customer management systems, built on a marketing and customer service database that can help with acquisition and retention, can be built on a PC affordable by even a small business. If your customers number in the hundreds of thousands then be prepared to spend big bucks.

8. Develop customer management action plans for information management, systems support, marketing and service that have the clear objective of improving loyalty. Ensure that the success of these plans is trackable using the measurement mechanism. Thus individual sales levels, requests for information, proactive efforts to identify what customers are thinking and feeling about the company and the effect of incentives and rewards for remaining loyal should be monitored. In practice, most customers are so pleased to receive special service or a little incentive that they reward the provider with very high loyalty.

9. Pilot the systems, marketing and service with the key objective of identifying the customers' responses to the scheme. Unless it is essential, try to avoid 'big bang' launches. Try the scheme on some customers; if it works, repeat it with a larger group. The philosophy of testing and piloting is strongly established because of the risks of not doing it. Badly designed schemes that escape all internal checks are not unknown. One manufacturer of domestic appliances introduced a purchasing incentive that made it cheaper to buy an appliance and throw it away, than buy a London to New York airline ticket directly. The demand for the appliance could not be met and the company had enormous difficulties chartering whole aircraft!

10. Roll out, monitoring performance carefully, using internal quality and cost effectiveness measures to ensure that costs are matched by benefits. When developing loyalty relationships, the consequences of not knowing what works can mean reduced customer loyalty.

8

Transparent marketing, customer value and process management

TRANSPARENT MARKETING

In transparent marketing, suppliers try to make themselves more openly available to customers. Using technology, the customer can look inside the company and change how the company relates to them. The ability to make an actual change is important to the concept. Many companies allow customers to view passively, carefully controlled images. The supplier's role is therefore to:

- create a strong brand that invites confidence;
- provide various modes of access for obtaining products and services;
- influence customers to consider the benefits of different types of relationship;
- ensure that customers can get information easily.

Technology is beginning to allow suppliers and customers to achieve this kind of flexible relationship. Certainly on the enterprise side, where resources are properly deployed, a range of technologies and services are beginning to achieve synergy. This is especially true in business-to-business marketing. At the consumer level, progress has been slower but the pace is beginning to hot up rapidly. There is growing evidence of sophisticated groups of consumers in many countries who steer their way around these systems. These people are important opinion leaders. They tend to be frequent, possibly even loyal customers, so they quickly learn how to use the new approach. When they have learnt the access routes they use them often to get information and to buy. They are adaptive, being happy to discover new ways of extracting results from large companies. They are technologically aware and capable, not frightened of trying and failing. They are also persistent up to a point, because if they find other methods that work quicker or better, they will use them. These may include a well arranged old-style store. Finally, they tend to be wealthier and better educated since they have the required technology in the home as well as the workplace. Put simply, they are ideal customers for many marketers. On the other hand, being sophisticated and electronically enabled, they can switch quickly between suppliers.

Of course, this approach does not suit all customers or even all products and services. There are those who do not understand or like technology, have a strong preference for personal contact and who like to see, touch and feel the products or experience the service on a trial basis. High involvement products such as expensive jewellery or personal services such as counselling probably do not suit the new media so well. We might therefore conceive of market segments that reside within a sort of electronic fortress where they can use the new access media. The challenge for suppliers is to destroy their own fortress wall and increase accessibility. This will require a big drop in the cost to set up and use the new approach, possibly by transferring the costs to suppliers. It will also need some improvements to the speed of interaction and the simplicity of the user interfaces. Six technologies are probably the key to the future.

AUTOMATED CALL DISTRIBUTION CENTRES (ACD)

ACD actually refers to a set of related technologies such as computers, software, switches and network services. They are supported by new processes and techniques that allow companies to handle very large numbers of calls from (inbound calls to a *call* centre) and to (inbound and outbound calls through a *contact* centre) customers. While handling such call volumes is not easy, the most crucial element is to integrate internal data management systems so that they are available to the call agent, and possibly to the customer, during the call. This requires rapid, intelligent data access along with a sophisticated data capture facility for new information. Telemarketing capabilities based on call centres have already transformed distribution efficiency in industries such as financial services, insurance, utilities and travel. They have also allowed new intermediaries to emerge. In some cases, intermediaries have been displaced, especially where relatively frequent contact between customer and supplier is combined with large numbers of small transactions such as in banking. In terms of cost management, the option of outsourcing or of using automated response systems offers the option of transferring capital costs to revenue and of ensuring that costs are proportionate to the success of campaigns.

SMART CARDS AND E-CASH

In the same way that call centres owe their success to data handling, not telephone calls, the contribution of plastic cards was not just in easing the credit market but the fact that customers qualified themselves for a purchase. Armed with a card, customers could present themselves in a variety of different environments as a 'pre-validated' customer. The benefits of being a customer, completing a transaction, obtaining credit, getting discounts and earning loyalty points were immediately available. The card allowed companies to establish more secure relationships with much larger numbers of customers. Direct marketing in particular became easier through methods like mail order. While credit, debit and switch cards are now enabling Internet-based transactions, it is the smart card that is the key to true electronic commerce. The semiconductor in the card will hold a secure electronic signature, probably linked to retinal or fingerprint recognition. Such a card will then transform every aspect of life. Extremely low value transactions will be possible, which will encourage people to use networks more fully because the cost of use will be a fraction of a cent per page. All financial transactions will be electronic. (Bye-bye banks?) Invoices and statements will arrive in the form of spreadsheets for personal analysis. It will be much more difficult to lose your money as not only will the biological security be harder to defraud but a log of every transaction made by any person can be produced at any time.

These smart cards will also open up new possibilities for consumers. Intelligent agents, computer programs known as robots or WeBots, will search supplier databases electronically to provide new services based on each individual consumer's pattern of transactions.

CUSTOMER DATABASES

Improved database technology has allowed companies to appear to recognize and possibly to understand their customers better. The customer database enables companies to trade in digital space by establishing new businesses based entirely upon data. They have also helped to improve the efficiency of the contact media resources of direct marketing such as mail, telephone and face-to-face. The customer database is a good example of what happens when you grab a tiger by the tail. If you let go, there is real trouble. Unless the data are carefully and accurately captured and maintained, and unless the information service systems are supported by efficient logistics, the potential for disaster is high. Management attention is diverted to fire-fighting and very high marketing costs are incurred for little real return. The difficulties lie in the area of integrating all points of customer contact within the customer database along with external data suppliers. For example, a customer who walks into a branch office to complain about an aspect of service may be unimpressed to be the recipient of a mailshot subsequently encouraging another purchase from the same company. This sort of incident happens if the branch face-to-face contact is not captured on the database or if the complaints database for service A does not link to the prospect database for service B.

NETWORKS

It will be noticed that the common element for each of these three technologies is computer networking. This provides the ability to access and move large amounts of data products, services, transactions and customer information rapidly around the world. Particularly impressive are online transaction and processing (OLAP) systems. These systems validate and complete the transaction from both sides by, for example, checking the customer (for identification and credit purposes) and checking inventory databases (for availability) within a few seconds.

THE INTERNET

Expectations about the use of the Internet have run ahead of usage but there is no doubt that the e-business opportunity is starting to permeate management thinking. Those experimenting with the Internet as an addition to current practice are often treating it as a channel rather than integrating it into current business practice. Failure to exploit Web-based marketing fully can cause some customers to be less satisfied. A difference is emerging between companies taking a truly virtual approach and those using the Internet merely as an adjunct to conventional channels. Truly virtual companies tend to focus on issues such as identifying suppliers that can deliver virtually, establishing processes that produce a very rapid response and making customizable products. All this on a global scale.

Case example: buying clothes on the Internet

There are two problems with ordering clothes remotely, such as by mail order or over the Internet. The first is how will they look on you, as opposed to the model in the picture. The second is making sure they will fit. The problem with the Internet is that you cannot touch the merchandise until it arrives at your door. In 1998, a company called Lands' End (www.landsend.com click my model) introduced a service that allowed women shoppers to key in their personal dimensions. The system then generates an image of a model just their size. The software was developed by Public Technologies Multimedia (PTM), a company based in Montreal, to give Internet shoppers a three-dimensional look at several style collections, all on the shopper's own body type. Of course, the system also offers the possibility of customizing an item individually in terms of style and finish. Major retailer J.C. Penney developed a similar site in January 1999, also using PTM 3-D modelling software.

Call and contact centre technology should now be closely integrated with the Internet. While online, a net surfer can then click on the 'call me' button to be connected with a call centre agent. Using either a land phone or IP (Internet Protocol) telephony, the call centre agent can return the call and emulate, at the call centre, the image on the customer's screen. Information from the Internet session is then used to inform the agent about the customer's interests and needs.

Although the Internet is a different way of doing business, it has to observe some conventional marketing rules about brand image, look and feel, ease of navigation around the Web site and trust. Customers expect sites to be more welcoming and easier to interact with than other modes of contact, often hard to achieve in practice. The other problem is that the Internet has a culture of information for free. Payment based subscriber services are harder to establish and often do not do well. Giving information away in the form of, say, stock advice or used car prices is more in line with what customers want. Money can then be made on the product sale wherever it takes place, which does not have to be on the Web. Suppliers can make lots of small profits on a high volume of transactions, which is where e-cash comes in. Customers like to make their way to strong brand names in any medium so the competitive argument for letting customers find you on the Web is strong. The Internet illustrates transparent marketing at its strongest. Customers not only classify themselves but also arrange to get what they want from you, how and when they want it.

From a supplier's viewpoint, one of the key enablers is the 'cookies'. Cookies are small data files that contain a record of Web sites that a computer has contacted. They are a sort of electronic business card. Cookies allow suppliers to know more about their customers, perhaps more than they should. This raises issues of customer privacy and some of the ethical aspects of transparent marketing.

DIGITAL INTERACTIVE TV (DITV)

DITV is an emerging technology of the late 1990s and is still taking shape. From a transparent marketing perspective, the opportunities are similar to those presented by the Internet but more radical in terms of speed and reach. The very success of the Internet is partly its own undoing. The overloaded superhighway can be very slow indeed at times. DITV is fast. It is also associated with a source of strongly branded, trusted and successful services, television companies. For example, in 1998 CNN was getting 8 million hits a day on its site, even without interactive TV. Both Sky TV and the BBC reported similar volumes.

DITV allows the consumer to interact digitally with the broadcast information. In addition to using this source of feedback for entertainment programming, companies can allow viewers to download product information and to provide interactive responses about those products. This data can be digitally crossmatched with profile information about the viewer held on subscriber records. The greater power and larger potential audience of DITV allows us to conceive of more radical applications as a result of these interactions. In some countries, virtually every household possesses one or more televisions, a penetration rate that will be unmatched by the Internet for years. This will compete head on with existing mass media, especially conventional TV and press, since interactive, personally customized advertising will bring a new dimension to the marketing process.

DO CUSTOMERS WANT TRANSPARENT RELATIONSHIPS?

While companies often talk about their need to manage relationships with customers, few customers seem to use the same language. Even when they bought a brand repeatedly, few people seem willing to describe their feelings in terms of having a 'relationship' with it (Henley Centre, 1994). The only product types for which the proportion of customers agreeing with this statement was above 10 per cent are shown in Table 8.1. Even though new cars and holidays are classic high-involvement products, the figures are surprisingly low. Three of the top five are financial services, curiously enough one of the service industries that has received most public criticism for how it has managed its customers.

Table 8.1 Products or brands with which more than 10% of customers acknowledge having a 'relationship'

Product / brand	Per cent
Personal loans	44
Investments	28
New car	15
Car insurance	14
Travel agent	11

Source: Henley Centre (1994)

What is clear from the report is that the term 'relationship' has meanings at several levels. Although a marketing relationship is not the same as a personal relationship it has an importance and an effect on behaviour of its own. Some of these are demonstrated by overt behaviour (repeat purchases), others constitute states of mind, thoughts, perceptions and beliefs. This is a transactional, rather than a personal link. For the supplier, the key issue is not whether the customer considers that a relationship exists. Whether the relationship marketing approach is helpful depends on three things: the quality of the interaction between supplier and customer, the importance of these interactions in affecting the customer's purchasing pattern and the extent to which the supplier can affect the main elements of that interaction, compared to competitors.

A marketing relationship is therefore better regarded as a management concept used to analyse a marketing situation. Table 8.2 provides examples of elements of the customer interaction that affect the quality of the relationship.

Table 8.2 Elements affecting the quality of a customer relationship

Relationship Component	Factors Affecting the Quality of Marketing Relationships as Seen by Customers
Contacts with Company Staff	Easy contact accessibility with the right person, preferably the same person each time.
	Good physical accessibility by way of parking, opening times, limited queuing, etc.
	Using information previously provided by the customer.
	Personal recognition of the customer or prospect.
	The right level of friendliness, helpfulness, courtesy, sensitivity and empathy.
	Complete product or service information, eg price, location and delivery times that are clearly communicated.
	Control in the right place, with the customer or with the supplier, as required, ie recognizing where the customer wants to lead or to follow.
	Speed of service.
	Responsiveness and empowerment (to handle enquiries or complaints).
	Diagnostic skills (what is the real need) backed by flexible scripts in dialogue.
	Follow through, keeping the customer informed of status.
	Trust and confidentiality.

Table 8.2 continued

Relationship Component	Factors Affecting the Quality of Marketing Relationships as Seen by Customers
Outbound Contact Management (mail, telephone, sales, visits, deliveries)	Relevance and personalization. Intelligibility, communications must be easy to understand. Accuracy in the provision of services or products. Speed – time-based competition is a key factor. Frequency of contact (not too much or too little). Interest, keeping in touch with what the customer is doing. Timing in relation to the customer's inclination to pay attention or in relation to the timing of the buying cycle. Link with inbound contacts, in other words, taking account of customer feedback.
Physical Service Environment	Clean, ie an attractive local environment. Context, eg at a location where others are receiving service at same time. Easy to navigate to and within the supplier location. Comfortable, low stress.
Brand Image	An acceptable image in terms of security, value, empathy. Projected image matches perceived image, which matches delivered image. In other words, the supplier does what they promise to do, directly or by implication.
Transaction Value	Consistency across transactions. Quality and value for money of the product or service. Speed of delivery. Whether loyalty is rewarded and the incentives or terms of the reward. Safety – perceived to be risk free or low risk. Whether user costs are recognized. For example, if the supplier recognizes where effort or input is being passed to the customer by rewarding the activity. For example, if a customer sets up their own order by entering data, they get a faster service. Guarantee or warranty supported as promised without quibbles.

CONTROLLING THE RELATIONSHIP: TRANSPARENT VERSUS PRESCRIPTIVE MARKETING

Table 8.3 illustrates how the transparent marketing relationship might take effect at different stages of the relationship cycle, in comparison to the traditional, prescriptive approach. The table illustrates the extreme end of each point of comparison although, of course, in practice, companies rarely lie consistently at one end or the other. More seriously, many companies have no formal methodologies for managing the customer relationships at different stages. Looking at corporate information services to see whether the company actually has any data flows to measure which customers lie at each stage easily tests this proposition. By contrast, high levels of customer churn or loss are suggestive in themselves of the need for better data.

Table 8.3 Comparison of prescriptive and transparent marketing activities at each stage of the customer relationship cycle

Relationship Cycle Stage	Prescriptive Marketing Approach	Transparent Marketing Approach
Targeting	The supplier approaches customers as members of a target market segment, usually by using broad-band advertising media such as TV, print or mailing lists.	The customer decides which suppliers to consider, at a time of their choosing. The approach medium is also chosen by the customer according to the products and services required.
Recruitment	The supplier manages the customer through the recruitment process, following a schedule that suits the supplier. If the customer causes errors or delays (as defined by supplier) they are prompted by the supplier to correct them.	Having selected the supplier, following their own timings and using their preferred medium or channel, the customer provides the information they consider relevant. This may be more or less than the supplier actually wants.
Welcome	The supplier tells the customer how to manage the relationship and what to do if things go wrong, based on the supplier's previous research into what worked and what did not work with previous welcoming policies.	The customer makes clear to the supplier what information is needed to ensure that the relationship is conducted according to the customer's needs and provides this information. The customer also tells the supplier where there are initial problems in the relationship and how these can be resolved.
Getting to Know (Learning)	The supplier determines what information is required to manage the relationship and asks the customer for this information, at times and in a form that is determined by the supplier.	The customer gives further information about their needs and asks for more information about the supplier, according to customers' individual needs.

Table 8.3 continued

Relationship Cycle Stage	Prescriptive Marketing Approach	Transparent Marketing Approach
Account Management	The supplier develops a model of a 'well managed customer' for the segment to which the customer belongs. This is implemented without regard for individual variations. The timing and nature of contacts is determined mainly by the supplier's prediction of when it is appropriate to contact the customer and their estimate of the cost effectiveness of contact.	The customer, either directly or by inference, makes the supplier aware of their preferences for the basis of a 'steady state' relationship between them. There is a continuous exchange of information to which the supplier responds.
Account Development	The supplier targets customers for development, based on analysis of customer characteristics in terms of their propensity to buy more of same or additional products. The timing and nature of the contact is determined by the supplier's need to sell, the supplier's prediction of when it is appropriate to contact the customer and the estimated cost effectiveness of contact.	The customer retargets the supplier using their preferred media but takes into account the supplier's conduct of the relationship so far.
Problem Management	**Problem identification** The supplier tries to identify what service failures have occurred and implements a service-recovery programme based on a predetermined model, relating service recovery actions to improved chances of retention. **Intensive care** The supplier attempts to identify whether and in what respect customers have changed, based on predictive, segment level analysis.	The customer notifies the supplier of problems in the relationship through whatever medium the customer finds convenient. The customer also notifies the supplier of their expectations as to how the service recovery process should be managed. The customer notifies the supplier of changes they perceive as relevant whenever they begin to take effect.

Table 8.3 continued

Relationship Cycle Stage	Prescriptive Marketing Approach	Transparent Marketing Approach
Pre-divorce	The supplier has identified typical pre-divorce signals and when these are received swings into action with a standard retention programme. Usually the benefits and timings are standard for the segment to which customer belongs.	The customer signals to the supplier that poor performance in service recovery or in managing new information is causing problems. The customer expects an individualized response that recognizes this.
Divorce	The supplier identifies from its database that the customer is lost and reassigns the record to the non-customer segment for reprofiling.	The customer notifies the supplier that they are breaking the relationship. Based on the reason for the divorce, the supplier is able to assess whether the customer is likely to be in contact again and, if so, when and how.
Winback	The supplier sets in motion a standard winback programme, usually with benefits and timings that are standard for segment to which customer belongs.	The customer reapproaches the supplier.

CUSTOMER-CONTROLLED CONTACT

Although Table 8.3 seeks to exaggerate the extremes of each pole by way of illustration, it is apparent that in transparent marketing the initiative for making contact with the supplier lies predominantly with the customer. This feedback, channelled when and how the customer prefers, contains a stream of messages that actively tell the supplier where further sales or service opportunities might exist. If complaints or requests for help are interpreted in this light, a much more positive spin is placed on the relationship. The difference lies in who is perceived to control the contact.

Company-controlled contact

- **Definition** – contact takes place on the initiative of the company and may follow a set of defined steps, perhaps moderated according to customer feedback at each step.
- **Examples** – direct marketing campaign, advertising campaign, sales calls.

- **Typical media** – market research questionnaire, outbound telemarketing or inbound telemarketing following an outbound contact such as a coupon response to advertising, a response to a sales call or to TV advertising.

Customer-controlled contact

- **Definition** – contact takes place on the initiative of the customer. At each step, the customer seeks to identify or even specify the nature and timing of the next step and their preferred way of linking to it.
- **Examples** – complaints, comments, compliments, unsolicited sales contacts.
- **Media** – surface mail, often to senior management or to head office, helplines, customer service counters in-store, Internet, sales person, technician.

The distinction between the two types of contact is sometimes one of degree, not one of kind. The company may have triggered the customer-controlled contact in some way, for example by distributing comment forms. However, it is evident that customers increasingly expect to contact companies when they want, where they want, how they want. Sometimes they expect to be able to contact specific departments or individuals. This is forcing companies to be much more accessible and prepared for the contact, in short, to be more customer focused. It is also evident that these contacts are not going to be channelled in some neat, easily controllable manner. In addition, with flexible work practices, many customer contacts are dealt with by a variety of staff. It is not always going to be the customer services department that will receive the feedback. Many companies will need to re-examine the processes by which customers contact them and the nature of their customers' expectation about this contact process. Not only will contact patterns be irregular but volumes will also be higher. It also seems likely that customers will expect companies to be able to channel feedback to the functional area that can respond quickly and efficiently. These expectations have considerable implications for the design of processes and procedures.

EXAMPLES OF EMERGENT TRANSPARENT MARKETING

Improved customer/supplier interaction through the Internet does not necessarily imply a need for disintermediation on the basis that the customer no longer needs an intermediary such as an agent or broker to help them buy. In fact, transparent marketing works especially well when the relationship between the original supplier and the final customer is intermediated, even if the intermediary is in competition with a direct channel.

Case example: gas company

In this (anonymous) example, shaping the offer (proposition targeting) helps to plan communication messages and allows customers to choose a service level that best suits them. When Gas Co was developing a formal proposition framework for all its European businesses it faced two challenges. First, the proposition needed to be varied for different markets in different countries. Second, the message needed to be communicated simply but effectively to the staff who would deliver it. The approach adopted developed a central set of elements to the proposition by defining the basic European offer and quality standards for core elements. These included pricing, ordering, delivery, product quality and invoicing.

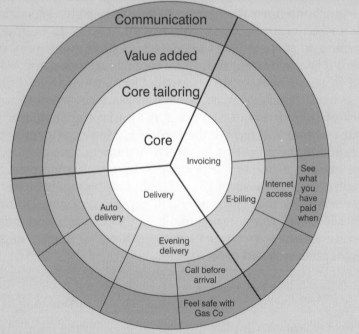

Figure 8.1 Gas Co's target device

Each separate European business could then tailor the core elements based on a 'shopping list' of features that could be altered for different customer segments but within Europe-wide quality standards. Thus customers enjoyed a highly personal product and service. Each gas business was then encouraged to develop market-specific, value-added additions to the centrally defined proposition elements. They then built communication messages around these value-added elements to form the basis of communication plans. The device used in each country to communicate all the elements of the proposition was a target (see Figure 8.1). This fitted well with the highly targeted nature of their business culture and with a very successful safety campaign called 'target zero accidents'.

Case example: real estate

A similar intermediary-focused initiative exists in Switzerland, where 17 of the country's largest real estate agencies, including divisions of major banks and insurance companies, joined forces in a co-operative group. They pooled details of empty residential and professional property and opened it up to the public. The site is available in English plus the three main languages of Switzerland and is therefore accessed internationally. Subsequent correspondence takes place via e-mail. This approach has increased the speed at which property is rented or sold and has reduced substantially members' expenditure on newspaper advertising, although one new role of this advertising is to promote the Web site (www.immopool.ch).

Case example: motor scooters

Piaggio, Italian manufacturers of the world famous Vespa motor scooter, uses its Web site not only as an electronic showroom for consumers but also allows them to order and pay using a secure payments system. Business partners can use the site to order documentation, file sales reports or gain access to selected applications on Piaggio's business systems. The IBM-designed site has 160 pages of text and fast graphics, as well as a virtual showroom with constantly updated details of Piaggio's product range (www.piaggio.com, www.vespa.com or www.gilera.com).

Each of these examples accentuates the need for an integration of strategy with implementation. A study by IBM (1998) has shown that creating a Web presence matching that created by other media, while adding interactive value, is not easy. In some cases, suppliers with powerful brands regard their Web sites largely as a vehicle for information giving. Others have recognized that the Internet is key to obtaining much higher-quality feedback from customers.

CUSTOMER VALUE MANAGEMENT AND PROCESS CONTRIBUTION ASSESSMENT

Transparent marketing works on the basis that products, services and information are accessible to prospective customers through various media. The supplier's role is to create a strong brand to invite customer confidence, to influence customers to consider the advantages and disadvantages of different types of relationship and to provide a range of access channels that suit customer preferences. Thus customers can get information about products, relationships and benefits easily without company intervention. This marketing model will only work if two conditions are met:

- The enterprise must be thoroughly attentive to customers' wants and needs or lose business to superior competitors.
- The enterprise must judge accurately which 'visiting' customers have a clear propensity to enter into a profitable relationship. Effort must then be concentrated on those visitors or the infrastructure costs of the approach will be uncompetitive.

Customer value management (CVM) and process contribution assessment (PCA), used by IBM, provide an analytical framework for aligning customer needs, customer value and enterprise processes.

CUSTOMER VALUE MANAGEMENT

CVM may be defined as:

A methodical approach for achieving the strategic, profitable and competitive positioning of a company's essential capabilities. It aims to align enterprise processes and infrastructure with the highest priority needs of current and future target customers, so as to deliver the company's products and services effectively. In order to do so, all those parts of the value chain that sustain the relationship with the customer will be managed to achieve this end.

This definition, after Thompson and Stone (1997), involves:

- Identifying the key moments of truth at every stage of the relationship between the supplier and the customer.
- Identifying the ideal value that target customers would like to obtain during, and as a result of, this contact.
- Identifying the gap between what the company currently offers and what the customer values most.
- Specifying the capabilities required to close the gap, then developing and identifying the enablers required to deliver them.
- Evaluating the costs of providing these capabilities and enablers against the additional value that would be created for customers. This is then evaluated against the profit that can be obtained from customers for providing them.

The three basic measurements for CVM are time, cost and quality. It is important to understand the relationship between cost and time, and how this affects quality. The balance between the three needs to be tested against different interaction characteristics to see how quality or delivered customer value moves against changes in time or cost. The ideal solution is not always obvious. A reduction in the time taken to complete a process does not always improve its customer value. For example, an electronics retailer discovered through having an immediate response (zero ring time on its order line) that customers were using this contact channel for product support and other issues. In the majority of situations the answers being sought were to be found in the manuals and catalogues already held by the customer. This therefore increased the costs of order line call handling. By breaking the process down, a target time and cost were determined, to maximize the value received. Determining a maximal position in this way is somewhat similar to an economist's idealized notions of pricing curves. Theoretically, higher supply leads to lower prices, higher demand leads to higher prices. If supply and demand can be plotted on a graph, an optimal price can be fixed which balances supply and demand. Maximal customer value is an equally idealized notion. However, the description serves to illustrate how it is intended to trade process time and cost against each other so as to maximize customer value. In the example given, the company identified the need to add a variable delay to calls on the order line (increased time). This discouraged customers from phoning the order line for product support. It was quicker to pick up the catalogue, research the products required and use the order line as intended.

The gap between the ideal and the current value represents the organization's needs for change. CVM is therefore closely linked to the second idea of process contribution assessment, which is used to determine the gap between the current and ideal process contribution.

PROCESS CONTRIBUTION ASSESSMENT

PCA may be defined as:

> An analytical approach to determine the maximum value that can be derived from each customer contact process. It focuses on the real opportunities for taking time or spending money at the point of contact, which will result in significant improvements in the customer's value to the enterprise.

In classic re-engineering terms, a process starts and ends with a customer (Hammer and Champy, 1993). Thus, by contrast to a function, such as finance or purchasing, the customer servicing process starts with an order and ends with a delivery. A process is therefore cross-functional. Conceiving an enterprise in terms of processes rather than functions often presents a number of dilemmas for enterprise members (Braganza and Myers, 1996) since formal boundaries and lines of authority have often to be set aside. The sales team may be unhappy with the idea that logistics cannot only make deliveries but also collect new orders from customers. PCA assumes that a clear understanding of the need for a process orientation has been achieved and then seeks to examine specific ways of improving processes so as to increase the value of the customer to the organization.

Taken together, therefore, the two approaches combine the ability to look into the organization from the customer's perspective (CVM) and to look outward to the customer from the organization's perspective (PCA). These two strands lead to a customer relationship marketing strategy that aligns customers' needs and wants with the desire to maximize potential customer value. The test of whether these objectives are realized is whether the processes actually deliver. Processes are the catalysts for all customer interactions with the enterprise. The speed, control and repeatability of the process are crucial. PCA aims to provide a structured approach to understand the components, nature and quality of each stage in a process.

Using CVM and PCA

Developing the two approaches into a methodology, we might therefore proceed as follows:

- Identify the key moments of truth. For example, the customer looks in the telephone directory to find a supplier, contacts a call centre to enquire about a product or has a difficulty with a service.
- Map the end-to-end process for each moment of truth, identifying where different layers of the organization in terms of people, procedures and systems are affected. It is important to understand this ripple effect as this is where the cost, time and value equation for the process lies. The key here is to map systems and data flows against the process. This identifies how well they support the process flow or whether they break it. For example, for a call centre or the Internet, the first electronic contact gathers customer information before the first hand off. The first hand off, the main one for the majority of contacts as far as the customer is concerned, might be to knowledgeable or experienced people for advice or authority to resolve the problem.
- A detailed examination of the scope of each process step is therefore needed, looking at the type of action related to the skill levels of the people involved. The information used to lead the customer through to the next step of the process is identified. The basis of the decision as to whether this is cost effective is traced. The information recorded and used for the next point of contact is identified.
- This analysis then provides an input to determine the current process contribution. It also provides a detailed framework for analysing the duration of each step, elapsed time and cost breakdown. The scope in terms of the ripple effect can be assessed and, therefore, so can its potential impact on perceived value. Finally, an indication of the revenue-generating points in the process can be determined.

This analysis provides a sound and clear basis for identifying the current capabilities and enablers that form the terms of reference for subsequent decisions. For example, to identify the cost of each step within the process we need to understand:

1. where significant costs are incurred;
2. the decision criteria for incurring the cost;
3. how customers are qualified;
4. whether we want to incur the cost with this customer at this point;
5. what the chances are of increasing customers' propensity to buy.

The measure of customer value, shown in Figure 8.2, is based on the worth, in monetary terms, of the technical, economic, service and social benefits of the market offering which is received in exchange for a price paid (Anderson and Narus, 1998). The first element in customer value is the monetary aspect (pounds per hour or dollars per unit). Second, there are the additional costs the customer incurs, excluding price, to obtain the benefits. Third, there is the value that the customer obtains in exchange for the price. An offer comprises two elements, value and price. Changing the price does not change the value, only the incentive to buy. Finally, there is the context, the extent to which alternative offers exist, such as purchasing from a competitor, providing the product or service in-house or not buying at all. Simply trying to compete on price has only one logical outcome, mutually assured destruction (MAD). In order to develop the ideal process contribution to maximize customer value, each of these aspects needs to be weighed in relation to the offer. Processes that support value can be categorized at three levels: basic, attractor or satisfier.

Process steps that are likely to cause the organization to lose control of the business or to generate bottlenecks if they do not work are *basic*. These are the organization's 'must-haves', the business equivalents of food and shelter. They are associated with a minimum acceptable level of performance. Over performance of basic processes, such as answering the phone in fewer rings than a competitor, will not usually enhance customer value. Typically, basic process steps offer considerable opportunity for cost reduction.

At the other extreme are *attractors* or differentiators. These process steps must be well defined and performed. They are central to customer decisions to remain and conduct more business with the company. Performed well, they will have a significant effect on customer value. Attractors are the processes that the company should target and where the leverage effect on customer value is greatest. An attractor might be based on recognition of the customer and their order pattern triggered from knowing the incoming phone number.

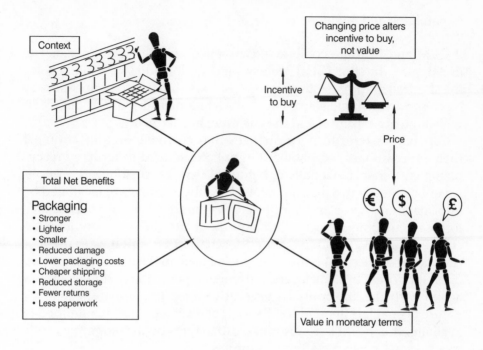

Figure 8.2 Customer value measurement

In between are the *satisfiers*. These are processes that can improve customer value but which generally do not cause any significant difference. They are traditional process steps that have evolved over many years and have been associated with the service. To change these might incur significant cost, with little or no effect on customer value.

Note that these categories are fluid; processes may change categories over time. An attractor may move to a basic process if everyone gears up to offer incoming caller identification. This might happen even if the change takes place in another industry since customers may carry expectations from one experience to another.

Thus the aim of the process contribution assessment is to identify which combination of processes – basic, attractors or satisfiers – provides the enterprise with the greatest value from customers. This is achieved by homing in on the critical moments during a relationship, where the company can obtain maximum value. The recommendations from this analysis can then be used to develop a competitive set of processes for maximizing the performance of the company.

Capabilities and enablers

If CVM and PCA are combined, two sets of gaps are recognized. The first depicts the shortfall in process contribution and the second shows the shortfall in the customer needs. The extent to which both gaps may be closed by a single set of capabilities is a measure of the degree to which the organization and the customer are aligned.

Capabilities refer to performances that customers require to meet their expectations. A capability might be described in terms of recognizing customers personally or being able to offer customized services. An enabler facilitates that capability. Usually, enablers are facilitated by information services and supported by training. Thus a database able to recall customer information rapidly at the point of contact is an enabler, linked to a training procedure that shows staff how to use it. A product or service that is individually tailored on the basis of a standard offer, supported by a sales person trained to guide the customer's interaction with the enterprise, is also an enabler. It is apparent that the nature of enablers depends on the capabilities that they are intended to facilitate. It is possible to prioritize capabilities by developing a crude scoring system. Here are some examples:

- The extent to which current enterprise capabilities are fully enabled on the basis of: not at all, low, medium or high. Example: we can recognize user/choosers but we cannot recognize family or group members.
- The relationship of current capabilities to needs – close, approximate or distant. Example: we can track complaints on our customer database but we cannot link future contact plans to complaints recording, so when an agent is talking to a customer the agent does not know if another part of the company is planning to write to them tomorrow or next week.
- The correlation between capabilities – if A is present, B is required. Example: if we have individually customized products, we need a method of varying the offer shortly before delivery if the customer has forgotten to ask for an important feature.

This approach helps to apportion improvement factors appropriately across capabilities. The capability gaps thereby created help to assign priorities when developing enablers. The linkage of enablers to capabilities is done in the same way, by apportioning the derived capability gaps that will make the biggest difference.

Implementation of capabilities and enablers

Moments of truth turn into moments of value depending on how the company's deliverables support the offer in relation to customer needs. The final stage is largely based on three elements – risk, cost and change:

- Some things are just too tough or too risky. Staged capability development in the form of a route map or journey towards the ideal might be a more practical method of closing the gap. Thus we might aim to recognize customers who make electronic contact but only recognize repeat customers in face-to-face situations.
- The cost of providing the capabilities and enablers must be measured against the additional value created (for customers) and derived (from customers) in the form of profit.
- A change programme must be designed to ensure that social technology keeps up with material technology. Generally, information services can be deployed more rapidly than a social system can be adjusted to absorb change through training or, even more difficult, through a culture shift. For example, GroupWare as a technology allows for the easy interchange of ideas and information. However, the availability of the tool, does not in itself alter the propensity of individuals in a company to share information with each other. People inclined to be secretive will still keep things hidden. A culture shift to reassure them about their own position and to encourage them to understand the overall benefits of sharing knowledge would be needed.

Case example: mail order

XYZ Corp was the market leader for high technology components. It had an enviable reputation for its order entry, warehouse and despatch functions. Customers were answered instantly and a highly disciplined order entry process captured customer requirements very quickly. Picking lists were then transmitted electronically to a sophisticated, automated warehouse. Goods were dispatched within one to two hours, typically for next day delivery. Stock control systems ensured high levels of order fill and line fill.

The customer help desk was designed to answer a range of queries ranging from simple product and stock enquiries, through technical specification questions, to advice on component usage. By contrast with the order systems, it suffered long answer hold times, even longer call transfer times and unacceptably high call abandon rates. Call agents worked with a relatively simple call centre system. This enabled them to query a very simple database of product data and allowed 'interesting' calls to be logged so that repeat queries about the same issue did not have to be researched again. All other documentation such as catalogues, technical manuals and data sheets were held in paper form. Agents had no access to the main business systems and data. There was no access to customer data.

The business issues

- The order line created expectations of a service level that the help desk then defeated.
- Potential customers were using the help desk to get product advice and then, forced to place another call to the order line, in many cases placed the call to an alternative, possibly cheaper supplier.
- Copies of technical documentation were dispatched manually by photocopying or reprint service from the central library.
- If call queues were long, agents would feel pressured into 'don't know', regret or even refusal types of response because the search through available material was too time consuming.
- Details of customer requests were not logged so that regrets or refusals, which actually might relate to a genuine need for a new product, could not be tracked.
- Front desk (first-layer contacts) might often, through lack of support systems and processes, spend too much time answering a question without realizing that they were getting out of their depth.
- However, call transfers to specialists would be avoided because the agent was afraid that the transfer time would be unacceptably long.
- If calls were transferred to another agent, the query would have to be repeated.

Customer value analysis

- Customer expectations of service levels were frequently not met, causing customer loss.
- Telephone response times and wait times during calls were long.
- The accuracy of information provided by the help desk was suspect.
- Literature fulfilment did not meet the high standards set by the order line.
- Customer needs and wants (in terms of product specification, availability and demand) could not be tracked, addressed or analysed.
- The customer was not identified and repeat issues were only partially tracked, depending on what agents considered to be interesting.
- Return calls to customers for responses to detailed research could not be managed centrally.
- Competitors were offering the same product at a cheaper price, again encouraging defection.

Basic needs

- Achieve decent standards of telephone response on the help desk.
- Give complete, accurate answers to straightforward product queries quickly and easily.
- Prompt and complete dispatch of literature.
- Take the order smoothly and accurately.

Satisfiers

- Confirm order, price, availability and take the order.
- Check on upselling or cross-selling possibilities.

Attractors

- Capture customer requirements quickly and make it obvious that they are being dealt with.
- If the exact product required is not accurately described by the customer, or if it is not available, map to the closest item available.

- If the call is transferred between layers, transfer all data captured so far and the substance of any feedback.
- Build up a pattern of questions and contact patterns so as to give the customer the impression that the company is on top of any potential problems and have worked out a fix.

Capabilities that *must* be provided

- Better and more comprehensive availability of information to agents.
- Improved search techniques.
- Automated literature dispatch.
- Order taking linked to customer, inventory and accounts-receivable databases.

Capabilities that *could* be provided

- A work control system to ensure fast and accurate follow up to unresolved issues.
- Automated capture of customer identity.
- Customer-call history.
- Fuzzy search, 'sounds like' capability.
- Calling system with data transfer.
- Feedback of customer requirements into business and product planning.

Enablers

These capabilities were prioritized according to an analysis of customer comments and feedback, which led to the development of the following:

- A new call-handling system based on different software that allowed linkages into a more detailed product database, directly integrated with the main business systems. This was to be achieved by extracting relevant product and customer data for display to agents.
- Conversion of paper documentation into a document management system using scanned images for concurrent display of document images on multiple-agent screens.
- Extension of the databases to enable automated cross-referencing of product descriptions to technical data.

- A continuous data capture procedure so that products, customer requirements and technical data were passed seamlessly between agents during calls.
- Greater integration of databases so that product data, order entry systems and stock availability could be linked without re-keying.
- Creation of customer and contact history databases to record call outcomes, notes and follow-up actions.
- A new structure for product naming and categorization together with advanced searching algorithms.
- Computer/telephone interaction for capture of calling-line identity.
- Automatic post, fax or electronic despatch of technical data.

Process change needs

- Product searching speed needs to be improved.
- Agent skill levels need to be more precisely matched to the complexity of the call, optimizing staff utilization so that skill levels are matched to the agents' ability and authority to give complex technical advice. The aim is to optimize the quality and accuracy of advice.
- Call wrap-up times need to be improved through automatic literature fulfilment and capture of call details during a conversation with a customer.
- Linked, direct order taking needs to more efficient than simple call transfer to the specialist order line.
- The time on a call could usefully be extended in order to capture customer feedback and other specific information for reuse in downstream processes. For example, product development, product quality issues for supplier management and safety issues.

This summarizes the findings of the first stage. Subsequently, new capabilities were added that needed higher priority on the implementation plan. These included a reorganization of work processes to channel the flow of calls and documentation to the appropriate agent. As a result, agent skills, experience and authority needed to be defined more accurately to match these criteria. Call scripting guidance was introduced to ensure extended capture of customer feedback and automatic capture of basic call details. This was associated with better control of call-backs and scheduling of research work by senior staff. The enablers required to support these capabilities included a departmental reorganization and reprofiling of skills. Extensions would be needed to the document management database to define document classification so as to match agent skills, along with software to control this. Screen scraping of host computer sessions, which provide for automatic menu navigation along with application to application data transfer through DDE (Dynamic Data Exchange), would also be needed.

SUMMARY

- Six technologies probably hold the key to the electronic future: ACDs, e-cash, customer databases, networks, the Internet and DITV. In respect of each of these technologies, what are your strategies for creating a strong brand, providing access to the enterprise and ensuring that customers can get information easily?
- How will each of these technologies help your company to manage customers at each stage of the relationship cycle?
- Which of your market segments are currently inside the electronic fortress? Which ones would you like to bring in?
- Which factors affect the quality of your organization's relationships with customers? Do you monitor and measure each of these elements regularly?
- Who controls the relationship at each stage of the cycle? To what extent is this in the hands of your customers? Can your processes and procedures recognize and respond to messages and feedback from customers that signal relationship changes?
- The nature of the contact, the timing and even the means of contact are less predictable when under customer control. Quite simply, are your systems flexible enough and fast enough?
- What are the main elements of customer value for your products and services based on time, cost and quality?
- What is the contribution to value provided by each process? Can you categorize which processes are basic, which are satisfiers and which are attractors?
- Are you providing basic processes as cost effectively as possible?

- What points of differentiation are there in your attractors?
- Have you operationalized each process in terms of capabilities (what the enterprise must be able to do) and enablers (how it can be done)?
- What technology is needed in order to support these capabilities? What are the implications for organization culture change (attitudes) and for training (skills)? What kind of information services must be in place to allow customers more open access to the enterprise?
- Do you need to re-engineer internal processes to allow customers to control the offer? This may require total company redesign to achieve a top vanilla, direct service.
- Is there any information loss due to the hand off between organizational layers? How do you know? How good are the internal transfers of information? Try tracing through the organizational response to different types of customer feedback.
- Are internal customers and suppliers also in transparent relationships? For example, do product planners receive messages directly from customers rather than from market researchers or database managers?
- What is the role of Intranets and GroupWare in supporting value chain transparency for your company?

9

Customer knowledge management

WHY MANAGE KNOWLEDGE?

'What you don't know won't hurt you.' Quite why this old proverb became popular is not very clear. Not knowing which foods to eat or which animals are dangerous has never been a particularly good recipe for survival. Even in political terms, it is usually useful to be able to distinguish friends and foes on the basis of what they might say. In today's world, where technology drives many products and services, very little commercially available technology confers a competitive advantage for very long by itself. Eventually, an enthusiastic competitor can use the same technology to match the price and maybe even the quality of the market leader. So, how do you stay ahead? The answer lies in what you know, that is, in the more effective utilization of knowledge. Effective relationship marketing depends on 'knowing' a great deal about your customers. As competitors catch up with their technology, knowledge rich, knowledge-managing companies can move to new levels of quality, creativity or efficiency.

Knowledge management seeks to develop the techniques and technologies for identifying, cataloguing and sharing existing enterprise know-how. The customer database is one such repository of possible knowledge. The central idea is that companies have a huge potential for new ideas and increased creativity but may not be able to access the knowledge that they already possess. A former CEO of Hewlett Packard once said, 'If Hewlett Packard knew what Hewlett Packard knows, we would be three times as profitable.' Quantifying or even cataloguing existing knowledge can be a daunting task but the results can be startling. Davenport and Prusak (1998) cite an example from a consortium of hospitals in New England that undertook a knowledge-sharing programme between heart surgeons. The result was a 24 per cent reduction in mortality rates for coronary by-pass operations. Indeed, they claim that even a simple company 'yellow pages' exercise can yield dramatic results. In one study they undertook, managers spent up to 30 per cent of their time just directing people to the right sources of knowledge. Once people with the same interests and problems are connected, this opens up a great potential for creativity and innovation. Even small companies have the tools to do this technologically. Most people are equipped with a PC linked to a network and to the Internet, they have personal productivity tools such as word processors and spreadsheets. They could therefore share information over an Intranet, a shared database or through the use of GroupWare. Yet very often, in companies both large and small, vital customer knowledge is inside someone's head. How can this be shared?

Conversations around the coffee machine by knowledge workers sharing what they know may well become the most important form of work. One of the greatest opportunities for the future lies in a company's ability to identify, capture, create and use the knowledge that they have of their customers, their needs and the relationship they share. By the same token, one of the greatest challenges facing companies is the management of customer knowledge. It is not easy, even in small organizations, to capture the knowledge passed on by customers. Data from perhaps dozens of points of contact with a single customer has to be codified in databases, managed properly and then recalled at the right time to benefit both the company and the customer. Nor is it easy to identify those people or teams in the organization who have very positive relationships with customers, understand the real elements of this relationship and then replicate them.

The core proposition in knowledge management is that competitive advantage is to be found in being able to marshal and exploit what is known not just by individuals but also by teams. Customer relationship marketing adds an additional dimension. It focuses not only on what managers know about their own customers and prospects and those of the competition but also on what customers know about their own needs. At the same time, customers may have varying states of knowledge about suppliers' characteristics and abilities to meet their needs. This means that they may have a different view of the current state of the relationship between themselves and their suppliers. For example, a mistaken belief about the level of a supplier's knowledge may lead to a worse relationship. The customer may expect the supplier to have knowledge of transaction patterns and of their requirements based on the customer's past behaviour, which the supplier is unable to action. Some pizza companies can 'recall' the preferred toppings of their regular customers. If the pizza company can do this, the customer may expect the utility company, the travel company and the financial services company to match that level of knowledge-based service.

Where intermediaries are present, relationship marketing also focuses on the transfer of customer knowledge through distribution channels. Put simply, the transparent marketing approach demands that the focus of knowledge management be broadened to encompass the knowledge of all the participants in the value chain, including the final customer.

It is apparent that this will generate a great deal of data. In some cases the data can be pulled together relatively sensibly, to produce information about the customer. However, the data does not, in itself, enable the organization to act knowledgeably in its relationships with the customer. The critical success factor is to develop a learning process that enables the organization to identify key customer relationship information, thus allowing it to act knowledgeably. Additionally, and very importantly, the company must identify the types of knowledge that impact positively on the relationship with the customer and nurture them.

As organizations have developed more cross functional integration around the customer, explicit knowledge is being accumulated more extensively. There is intuitively more reason to share and use it. In addition to this, interactions between different layers of the enterprise, such as marketing, sales and customer services has seen the barriers of departmental language break down somewhat. This has enabled the transfer of more tacit knowledge and therefore knowledge creation. The focus is no longer on delivering the offer but learning from the customer, using knowledge flowing in, through and out of the organization.

KNOWLEDGE MANAGEMENT IN TRANSPARENT MARKETING

What happens when we introduce truly interactive, transparent marketing? In one sense, it provides a spotlight for the customer. Customers can now call up the explicit knowledge, about them, which is held by a supplier. Customers can examine the relationship they have with the supplier. They can even assess how well that knowledge is being used, by making judgements about the suitability of offers that they have received, based on the knowledge held. The customer can provide more information and observe the effect of incorporating it into the supplier's database, not just by observation but by seeing the conclusions drawn from it. Interestingly, many customers indicate that this is precisely what they would like to be able to do. Indeed, it is what they used to do when their primary contacts with the enterprise were face to face. The customer would go into the local store and watch the clerk make a note that next time they ordered a slice, they want it from the centre of the cheese, not from the crust. More sophisticated business-to-business customers will certainly want to see the immediate application of shared knowledge, in new product and service offerings.

Of course, not all customer knowledge can be shared in this way. Like most relationships, some are good and some are not so good. If the relationship with the customer is considered to fall into the latter category, for whatever reason, it may not be sensible to share that assessment. The benefits of increased sales and improved customer loyalty must be set against the costs. This can be achieved through combining knowledge management with the CVM and PCA analyses described in the last chapter.

INNOVATION, KNOWLEDGE AND COMPETITIVE ADVANTAGE

Transparent marketing is an information-intensive way of doing business that recognizes not only responsiveness but also time-based competition. In some ways, this means that the enterprise is constantly reinventing itself, or being reinvented by the customer. With fast changing markets and technologies, this kind of competition is also innovation intensive. The problem is, how do you institutionalize (in an organization) something like innovation? Like any other endeavour, innovation takes talent, ingenuity and, above all, knowledge. It is, of course, exciting to think of innovators like entrepreneurs being struck by a flash of inspiration from which tremendously successful new ideas for new products and services emerge. Indeed, some corporations, realizing that the rate of product and service change is increasing, set performance targets in terms of the future revenues that are expected from PANS. PANS stands for **P**retty **A**mazing **N**ew **S**tuff. Unfortunately, like so many things in life, innovation also depends on diligence, persistence and commitment. If these are absent then most companies are unlikely to succeed at innovation. The history of invention is littered with good ideas and products that were brought to the market by one company but successfully exploited by others. Drucker (1998) cites the example of the passenger jet aircraft, brought first to the market by the British company de Havilland but exploited more successfully as a commercial product by Boeing and Douglas. De Havilland forgot to take account of where customer value might lie (payload and size for routes on which jet engines would give an airline competitive advantage). They also had no idea of customer value measurement in terms of pricing and financing. Curiously enough, these mistakes were repeated by the Anglo-French Concorde manufacturers a generation later.

It is certainly true that some innovative products and services are attributable to the sort of creative flair that we describe as genius or entrepreneurship. James Watt's steam engine might be a case in point but Drucker identifies seven areas where organizations might systematically discover innovative ideas:

- Unexpected occurrences arise when an invention for one purpose turns out to be useful for another. IBM outflanked Univac by redesigning a machine, which Univac saw as an advanced scientific device, for routine applications like payroll calculations.
- Incongruities depend on new insights. Making ships faster and more fuel-efficient did not produce enough benefits to turn around the ferry business. Redesigning them for faster turnarounds, using roll-on roll-off techniques, so that they spent less time in port, addressed the real cost burden.
- Process needs are a long standing application of PCA. Thus newspapers as a mass communications medium can provide cheap, almost free information because of the invention of the lithographic printing process and the social innovation of advertising. The advertising pays for the paper.
- Industry and market changes, which result from the following three factors:

- changing demographics;
- changes in perception;
- new knowledge.

Very often, these last three changes come together. IBM's entry into the PC market is almost apocryphal in this respect. Having attained dominance as the world leader in large computing, it failed to recognize the importance of the PC. In 1980, when it entered the PC market, it assembled a machine that used standard components and a bought-in operating system. The standard components allowed competitors like Compaq to reverse engineer the device and provide more cheaply a machine that now had respectability conferred upon it by IBM's presence in the market. The bought-in operating system gave birth to Microsoft. Within little over a decade, IBM had to reinvent itself twice to survive these changes, first as a manufacturer of small computers and second as a software and services company.

The PC is a good example of how innovations often depend on strands of knowledge from a variety of sources. All sorts of inventions contributed to the eventual development of the PC. These included new ways of thinking, such as the invention of symbolic logic by Bertrand Russell and Alfred North Whitehead at the beginning of the twentieth century or the work of the mathematician Alan Turing on the Enigma code breaking machine used in World War II. They included ideas that never worked, such as Charles Babbage's difference engine, and some that did, like the audion tube, an early form of electronic switch. They also depended on a host of other ideas and inventions that eventually allowed Ted Hoff of Intel to produce a microprocessor for an electronic calculator in 1971. At around the same time, in 1970, E F Codd, who was working for IBM at the time, published a seminal paper that is now credited as the origin of the entire relational database technology. While word processors are probably the most commonly used pieces of computer software and spreadsheets are the most transformational pieces of software associated with the PC, in marketing terms the invention of the relational database was the most significant. Customer relationship marketing in its present form would not be possible on any scale without all of these inventions.

What has all this got to do with marketing? Tracing the development of a technology so central to the modern world shows how streams of ideas, philosophies and concepts are interwoven with engineering and scientific advance. For the computer, these ideas and inventions spread from 1906 to the present day and derived from many sources. On a smaller scope and scale, they are a good example of the problems facing the innovative enterprise. There is a flow of ideas and expertise. People bring these to work. At work they think of new ways of doing things and they become aware of what other organizations are doing. Together, this abundance of ideas represents a huge, potential source of competitive advantage. The question is, how do you capture all of these ideas and use them for marketing purposes?

Relationship marketing, in organizations of any size, depends on the storage of enormous amounts of data. As a result, it is sometimes referred to as database marketing. The essential logic of what is meant by capturing these large amounts of data is well described by the term 'data warehouse'. A data warehouse aims to gather data from all over the organization and make it available for a wide variety of uses by groups and individuals. In computing terms this presents complex problems although these are not as acute as the cultural and social issues that we referred to when discussing PCA earlier. Querying these large databases from across distributed corporate networks can be very slow unless a careful choice of storage paradigm is used. The method used for data warehouses is typically based on online analytical processing (OLAP). In OLAP, the data storage principles of multi-dimensional analysis of data, from disparate sources, are employed to permit free-form user analysis without professional information services staff intervention.

To give a measure of the speed of this advance: in 1996, 98 per cent of finance directors in the UK had never heard of OLAP (*Computer Weekly*, 1996). By 1999, Microsoft were making a big play for the OLAP market with a product called Plato but already the technology was moving on. OLAP was being subsumed into knowledge management, which tries to merge technology and management theory. The idea here is to try to improve the corporate memory of the enterprise by bringing together that complex web of knowledge that includes the skills and experience of the staff, intellectual capital assets, such as research and development, and corporate information systems. Knowledge management on the whole is focused on unstructured information although there is an overlap with structured information systems such as decision support, data warehousing and data mining. If this flow of formal and informal information can be brought together coherently, the enterprise will be able to innovate and obtain a real competitive advantage. Knowledge management ultimately offers a perspective on the overall use of information in an organization. Tools are now being developed for the analysis of large amounts of unstructured information known as document mining. New versions of GroupWare such as Lotus Notes Sharepoint Server are particularly targeting knowledge management as a key concern and this technology area is a new battleground between IBM and Microsoft in the early part of the new millennium. The issues associated with innovation and knowledge management are summarized in Table 9.1.

Table 9.1 Issues in knowledge management

Components

- Where is the knowledge created or held, tacitly or explicitly?
- What are the perceptual or behavioural factors affecting knowledge management strategies and customer relationships?
- Who owns the knowledge?
- Where should the enterprise begin to organize all this?

Repositories – Capturing Knowledge

- Inventory of external explicit mechanisms such as stored knowledge about customers or customers' perception of the enterprise.
- Inventories of internal explicit mechanisms such as stored knowledge about the firm's processes, strengths and weaknesses.
- How do we build structured documents with links, interpretations, filters, pruning and archiving mechanisms like those created by, for example, Hewlett Packard's electronic sales planner?
- Where is tacit knowledge held, such as information about good practice, socialization or organization culture?
- What data management systems do we have such as GroupWare like Lotus Notes?

Accessing Knowledge

- Can we build knowledge maps or directories? Do we actually know who knows what? For example, we know which person has a certificate in using, say, DB2, Oracle or SQL Server but do we know who is our best negotiator? No one has a negotiating certificate.
- Do we have formal knowledge sharing sessions? How do they work?
- What processes are best for building models such as models of customer behaviour?
- How can we share knowledge with customers?
- What is the best process for routinization of competences?

Encouraging New Knowledge

- How do we design a reward scheme for creating or capturing knowledge?
- What is the customer's assessment of firm's knowledge?
- Are we aware of biases in our knowledge or assumptions that we automatically make when solving problems?

Table 9.1 continued

Costs and Benefits of Knowledge

- How do we calculate the value of intellectual capital?
- What is the best way to record knowledge inputs? How can the effect of knowledge on winning tenders or generating new business be measured?
- What is the return on intellectual capital, eg patents?
- What are the costs of knowledge?

Case example: transparent knowledge and the marketing of fork-lift trucks

BT Products, is a subsidiary of BT Industries Group based in Sweden. It is a worldwide producer of warehouse trucks for inventory handling. In 1993, the company created a computer package called BT Compass, a logistics planning system, to help its customers improve their profitability by lowering the total costs of inventory handling. The system provides full analysis of the customer's operational requirements, fast comparison of different pallet-handling and order-picking solutions, optimum warehouse layout designs, accurate calculations of handling capacities and a complete analysis of projected life cycle costs.

The BT Compass system works in seven languages. It displays different layout options by using high quality colour graphics and all plans can be printed quickly using a printer or plotter. When a customer is contemplating a change in materials handling or is adding a new facility, the system helps to calculate, for example, optimal aisle width to accommodate a fork-lift truck or calculate the layout and equipment requirements to meet peak-hour needs.

BT Products measures the performance of its competitors' equipment, often buying the equipment to test it. Thus it knows the critical performance measures that customers use to judge fork-lift trucks. It also records information about customers' individual systems. Thus knowledge about customers and competitors is formally acquired and stored. The data that customers must enter into Compass requires some competence on their part. To help customers gather the required data, BT Products has developed a one page worksheet that pulls the necessary data together. Senior sales people work with the customer in doing the analysis. They even provide hands-on data collection as needed at the customer's facility.

One of the advantages of using Compass is that it combines warehouse planning with an analysis of the kind and number of trucks needed to optimize warehouse performance. In 1998, Birkenstock, a German shoe manufacturer, decided to build a new warehouse at Asbach. The in-house consultant responsible for the procurement process for the new warehouse proposed a layout that required three fork-lift trucks to handle the pallet movements. By using Compass, BT Products was able to demonstrate how an alternative layout in conjunction with its high performance trucks required only two trucks, one less track and one less operator. According to BT Products' managers, without Compass, they would not have been able to find this new solution and provide the detailed performance results for their trucks. In addition, they believed that they would not have been able to convince Birkenstock management that their solution was correct.

Source: Anderson and Narus (1998)

TACIT KNOWLEDGE, EXPLICIT KNOWLEDGE AND PRODUCTS

When managers think about teams, they traditionally perceive of them as consisting of discrete individuals, each performing a specified function. Thus the team outcome is considered to depend on the skill and reliability with which individual functions are performed. Therefore, the majority of team studies have focused on the influence of social team processes and co-ordination. However, new product development teams are engaged in a knowledge-producing activity that implies that a cognitive perspective is also needed. Cognitive psychologists have recently proposed a perception of cognition as distributed across the members of the team (Patel, Kaufman and Arocha, 1995). Each individual brings to the innovation process a repertoire of skills, knowledge and strategies that interact dynamically within the situation and with the other members of a group. The notion of distributed cognition implies that teams should function more as a single unit engaged in a single process of expertise rather than as a well co-ordinated group of individual contributors.

This raises some interesting questions for the management of teams (groups of workers) that are addressed by Madhavan and Grover

(1998). They examine how teams should be created and managed, to effectively create knowledge, by combining disparate bodies of knowledge.

THE CREATION OF NEW KNOWLEDGE

The creation of new knowledge is increasingly concerned with the role of tacit knowledge. This is knowledge that cannot be explained fully even by an expert and can be transferred from one person to another only through a long process of apprenticeship. For example, learning to whip cream to exactly the right consistency is best learnt by practice. Polanyi's (1967) famous saying, 'We know more than we can tell', highlights the point that many human skills remain unarticulated, known only to the person who has that skill. The golf player Tiger Woods knows how to hit a drive further than most other people do. . . somehow. By contrast, explicit knowledge is relatively easy to articulate and communicate. It is therefore easier to transfer between individuals and organizations. Explicit knowledge resides in formulae, textbooks, manuals or technical documents. Zuboff (1988) makes a useful distinction between embodied, or action-centred, skills and intellective skills. Action-centred skills are developed through actual performance (learning by doing). In contrast, intellective skills combine abstraction, explicit reference and procedural reasoning. This means that they can be represented as symbols and therefore easily transferred. Some customer contact staff know exactly how a customer wants to be handled in a wide range of situations. This expert knowledge is hard to capture and share. On the other hand, the script provided for call centre agents on their VDU screen makes available explicit knowledge about how a dialogue should be sustained.

Initially, tacit knowledge was conceived of at the individual level. However, it is now recognized that tacit knowledge exists in the organization as well. For example, Nelson and Winter (1982) point out that much organizational knowledge remains tacit because it is impossible to describe all the aspects necessary for successful performance. They argue that creating an effective organization is not just a matter of implementing a set of 'blueprints' because much of the crucial knowhow resides only in the minds of the organization's members. In a similar vein, Kogut and Zander (1992) differentiate between information such as facts and know-how, such as how to organize factories. The listing of ingredients in a recipe consists of information but the description of action steps is, at best, an imperfect representation of the know-how required to cook a good meal.

As soon as members of a team get together, there is the potential to create new knowledge. This new knowledge is the result of a combination of both explicit and tacit knowledge. Combining explicit knowledge is rather easy. However, the degree to which the potential new knowledge, due to the integration of tacit knowledge, is realized depends on several variables. Madhavan and Grover (1998) use the term 'embedded knowledge' to describe the potential knowledge resulting from the combination of individual team members' stores of tacit knowledge. A cross functional team is brought together because its members have collective knowledge that cannot be held efficiently by any of its individual members. However, this collective knowledge is not present when the team is assembled; it is only potentially present. In enterprise terms, a team or group of workers brings to a task knowledge that is embedded in its members and their interactions as a team. They argue that the potential for new knowledge is embedded in the team and its interactions. The team possesses embedded knowledge. New products and services, innovative ideas, represent embodied knowledge (realized knowledge). Therefore, the marketing manager's task is to manage the transition from embedded to embodied knowledge in order to improve the way in which customer relationships are handled at different points of contact.

HOW TO ENCOURAGE A GROUP OR TEAM TO CREATE CUSTOMER KNOWLEDGE

In a sense, knowledge creation is a metaphor for relationship marketing. Enterprise members are more likely to create new knowledge based on two factors. The first of these is trust and the second is the type of interactions they share.

Trust can be defined as reciprocal faith in others' intentions and behaviour (Kreitner and Kinicki, 1992). It has been identified as integral not only to the performance of small teams but also to many current organizational arrangements, such as strategic alliances or just-in-time delivery systems. Two types of trust are important. The first of these is 'trust in team' orientation. This is defined as team members having reciprocal faith in each other's intentions. It refers to a belief that members of the enterprise will work towards team goals rather than towards narrow, individual or functional goals or agendas. We referred to this in Chapter 3 as buy-in. An atmosphere lacking in such trust leads to the withholding of information and to attempts to influence decision making towards narrow interests. Trust in team is therefore a process concept and is critical in cross functional situations. Withholding information due to a lack of trust can be especially harmful to the processes of knowledge articulation, internalization and reflection (Hedlund and Nonaka, 1993).

The second element is 'trust in team members' technical competence'. This might be considered in terms of morale or *esprit de corps*. It is a measure of the extent to which team members consider each other competent to handle the complex and as yet undetermined challenges that might appear. Such competence may reside in a capacity to solve problems on their own or to get others to solve it for them, ie to syndicate a solution. Making the underlying model for dealing with a situation explicit can help here and this is why it is useful for everyone to share a clear understanding of where different customers are located within the relationship cycle. Prior technical performance can form an 'objective' basis for trust in competence, such as publications or a track record with successful projects but it also requires a subjective projection of that perceived competence into an uncertain future.

If trust is present then it seems reasonable to assume that team members will work together. Therefore, the next element of knowledge creation is to facilitate direct interaction, ie face-to-face interaction, so team members will be more effective and efficient at creating new knowledge. Successful interaction depends on a number of things, not least of which is frequency. If interaction is direct but occasional, it is unlikely that team members will get sufficient opportunity for articulation and internalization. Physical proximity alone may not be sufficient to ensure interaction, it may be necessary to offer facilities such as videoconferencing or electronic communication. Given the nature of communication required for the combination of tacit and explicit knowledge about customers, team members might need to interact on an almost continuous basis. Sociologist George Homans (1951) recognized that frequent interaction not only helps the spread of ideas but it also builds liking (personal relationships) that, in turn, facilitates group formation. The use and creation of knowledge within the group or team depends on these processes. The conditions for effective interaction are affected by the social and technical environment of the individual, as illustrated in Figure 9.1.

A third aspect of interaction is, therefore, informality. In contrast to traditional models of information processing in organizations, which

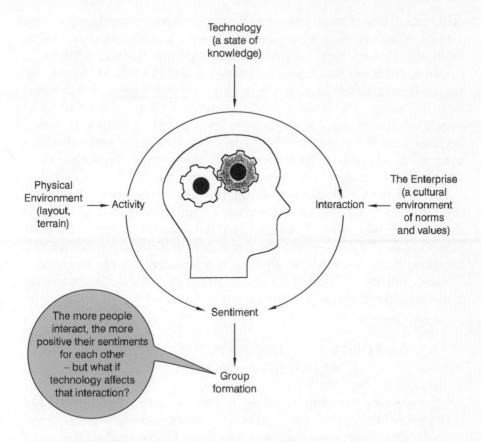

Figure 9.1 Homan's relationship triangle and the sharing of customer knowledge

imply that formal procedures and designated roles determine information flows, current research confirms the intuition that social ties among people affects information flows. For example, Stevenson and Gilly (1991) found that managers often avoid dealing with formally designated problem solvers and use personal ties to pass on information. Since patterns of information flow can determine who gets what kind of information and when they get it, and because such information is the basis for managerial decisions, social arrangements can have a major influence on the effectiveness of the organization. Meyers and Wilemon (1989) discovered that informal networks (informal discussions, knowledge transferred with team members to other projects and friendship ties) were much more significant than formal channels in transferring learning. This goes back to Drucker's observation that chance and serendipity play a part in creative problem solving. Some authors have actually described innovation as arising from the 'interaction between necessity and chance, order and disorder, continuity and discontinuity' (Nonaka, 1990). However, the successful enterprise cannot rely on luck for innovation and competitive advantage. Somehow, it has to organize itself to be lucky. In some organizations, technology can help keep people a long way apart. Imagine a small design team based on three continents or the distance between a call centre in New Mexico and a sales person in Seattle. How will they share crucial customer information?

Bringing trust and interaction together produces a final condition: information redundancy. Information redundancy, the sharing of information over and above the minimal amount required by each person to do the job, seems to be significant in influencing knowledge creation. Since information sharing is associated closely with trust, Nonaka points out that it increases the possibility of trust among organization members.

SOME ORGANIZATIONAL PROBLEMS FOR PRACTICAL KNOWLEDGE MANAGEMENT

As these ideas are put together, it will be seen that knowledge management rather confronts traditional ways of running large organizations. It depends on encouraging people to use both formal and informal knowledge, to trust each other and to share best practice. It is not especially bothered by notions of 'efficiency'. If it makes sense to replicate a function or a process in different parts of the enterprise to foster trust and customer responsiveness then that is fine, as long as the revenues associated with the duplication outweigh the costs of extra provision.

However, it is also apparent that some of these ideas confront popular notions about 'virtual office' practices and their effect on the efficiency and effectiveness of knowledge creation. A knowledge management perspective raises significant issues about the optimal way of organizing an enterprise. During the past few years, there has been a trend toward creating virtual teams that are distributed across several offices, buildings, cities or even continents. Driving this trend have been strategic factors, such as the creation of competency centres (which might need to work together on specific projects), as well as more tactical goals, such as taking advantage of time differences in team members' locations. However, as Madhavan and Grover point out, virtual teams may not be the best vehicles for knowledge creation. A team's efficiency in knowledge creation is influenced by the artefacts and other physical resources in the team's surroundings. Being in the same, information rich location enhances interaction and thereby knowledge creation. Similarly, the currently popular practice of 'hot desking' (*Wall Street Journal*, 1996), in which people do not have fixed work spaces but are assigned temporary work areas for the hours they are in the office, does not take into account some of the needs for effective knowledge creation about customers.

If these difficulties are to be overcome, managers must be trained about effective ways of managing knowledge. They must be sensitized to the issues involved and find ways to apply solutions fruitfully.

IMPLEMENTING KNOWLEDGE MANAGEMENT – CRITICAL SUCCESS FACTORS

Managers must recognize that if knowledge management and transparent marketing are to be exploited, change will be required in many areas:

- **Jobs** – employees and other enterprise members must enter into new styles of customer communication. New workflows will eliminate many traditional roles. Telephone agents may need to be rewarded through incentive schemes that focus on capturing or enhancing knowledge about customers.
- **The organization** – new functions will be created within the organization. For example, departments and teams will need to develop their own style of leadership and management. Traditional field sales people or branch outlets will develop new ways of interacting with direct sales colleagues. Territories may be redefined and customers may be managed across different departments depending on the stage of their relationship with the company. Trust and interaction will be encouraged and this will lead to a redefinition of roles and responsibilities, along with retraining and revised conditions of employment. New standards of leadership and management will emerge. Measurements of performance will include knowledge inventories and innovation measures.
- **Business processes** – service and sales will be delivered on a different timescale and to new standards. This inevitably means the construction of new business processes. The organization will need

to learn to revise and adapt these processes continually so as to ensure alignment with business goals as new markets emerge. As customers themselves develop new expectations, both through their new relationships and through their developing experience with rival competitive organizations, workflow systems will transform the company's ability to react speedily. These will then be instrumental in delivering the main components of process change. In such an environment, trust will be paramount.

- **Technology** – the new model of transparent marketing will be heavily dependent on a range of new technologies. IT departments will have to learn new techniques for application development and new, sophisticated network infrastructures that support unstructured information access for knowledge management tools. Application development departments may draw more heavily on the deployment of packaged solutions rather than in-house development. Business users will need to gain a more detailed understanding of these new technologies and their successful application. Operations staff will be required to develop new standards for system availability and resilience to provide flawless functionality, 365 days a year and 24 hours per day.

All these changes will take place at an ever-increasing pace as rival and innovative technologies are introduced into the marketplace. The changes will inevitably be accompanied by attendant disruption to conventional operations. Managers must not become complacent that new technologies on their own will solve knowledge management problems. It is vital to recognize that leadership must originate in business departments and should be held there. This in no way diminishes the role and influence of the IT and operations staff. Rather it should enhance the involvement of these departments with the development of the enterprise as a whole. It will, however, sharpen the definition of the role and responsibilities of these functions in terms of knowledge management.

MAKING KNOWLEDGE MANAGEMENT A REALITY – SEVEN STEPS TO SUCCESS

Organizations usually run into three major cultural problems when adopting a knowledge management initiative. First, people do not like to share their best ideas. They believe that doing so dilutes their standing in the organization and can impede their ability to get ahead. Most people are used to an environment that is highly competitive and have never learnt to share. To some extent, in today's highly political corporate environment, knowledge equals power. Getting people to understand that knowledge sharing is for the greater good of all requires significant culture change. Second, people do not like to use other people's ideas for fear it makes them look less knowledgeable. Third, people like to consider themselves experts at their own job and prefer not to collaborate with others. Changing this mindset is not easy because most people have operated within a knowledge-hoarding environment for so long. Once people begin to see the value of sharing knowledge, barriers begin to break down and a transformation in thinking and action can start. Greengard (1998) suggests seven steps for achieving this cultural shift.

Provide leadership

It is essential to ensure that senior management understands the value of knowledge management and supports the development of programmes and policies to make them a reality. High-level support is essential. Senior executives must understand what knowledge management offers and play an active role in the decision-making process. Executive input is essential because knowledge management touches almost everyone in the organization. Many of the processes in knowledge management involve human interaction so the support of top human resource executives is important.

Establish cross functional teams

The job of these teams is to map customer knowledge and plan initiatives. Not only is it crucial to capture the right knowledge, it is essential that people can find exactly what they are looking for. For most companies, this underscores the importance of creating a cross functional team comprising technologists and non-technologists from various departments. Without the team there is a risk of developing a system that is not relevant to end-users. It is often an enormous challenge to manage a cross functional team comprising people who are not accustomed to working together. Collaboration, trust and interaction are vital. It is important to ensure that everyone's needs are met. Above all else, stay focused on key knowledge that will work best when shared, think about what will make the biggest impact.

Ensure a knowledge management process is in place

Mapping customer knowledge through the organization is part of the battle. It is also critical to develop a system for gathering and disseminating information once it has been created. That typically involves people who can organize, analyse and verify the integrity of the knowledge that has been fed into the system. At Arthur Andersen, specialists scrutinize every bit of knowledge that enters the system so they can provide a 'value' rating. Submissions of questionable value are weeded out. All this is necessary to avoid swimming in a sea of useless information or drowning in poorly organized knowledge.

Develop or implement the technology

The scale of the technology depends on the size and scope of the enterprise but technology is essential if customer knowledge management is to flourish. There is no hard and fast rule about the appropriate technology to ensure that a knowledge management initiative succeeds but it is clear that an Intranet is one of the most powerful tools for achieving results within this arena. It allows point-to-point communication on a just in time basis and offers a way to update knowledge instantaneously. With integrated links to other systems within the organization, including human resources, finance, sales automation, logistics and supply, it is possible to break down the walls and let the knowledge flow.

Nurture a sharing culture

No customer knowledge management system can work without an organization undergoing a significant cultural change. Such change is typically required on several levels. Incentives must exist, usually in the form of compensation and rewards, to promote the sharing of knowledge. Those who contribute to the knowledge base and post the most useful or frequently used information might receive a cash bonus, a plaque or a trip to Paris. However, knowledge management is not just about rewards. It is about creating a climate in which sharing knowledge is encouraged or even demanded. It is an environment in which there is a social obligation to share. Ultimately, managers must educate their staff and help them to undergo the essential change in mindset.

Demonstrate the value of customer knowledge management

This will encourage buy-in. People must understand why the organization has turned to knowledge management and what payoff exists. Many managers and employees do not believe in sharing. They have actually built their careers around proprietary ideas, information and knowledge. Education can go only so far in breaking down the barriers. People must see exactly how sharing knowledge makes their job easier or better. It is therefore useful to start with a knowledge management capability that benefits a large number of employees and fits the needs of the entire organization. In this way it is possible to gain a greater buy-in up front.

View the exercise as a work in progress

Knowledge management always creeps into uncharted territory, even in organizations that have realized enormous gains using it. Part of the problem is that every organization is different and there is no 'one size fits all' approach. What works at one company does not necessarily work at another. What is more, the level of sophistication and expertise surrounding knowledge management tends to change quickly once an initiative is put in place. As a result, it is best to experiment, stay flexible and make changes on the fly. It might become necessary to pull the plug on a particular programme, or completely redesign it, at a moment's notice. Just because a knowledge management process works does not mean it cannot be improved.

CUSTOMER KNOWLEDGE MANAGEMENT AND ORGANIZATIONAL ALIGNMENT

Advances in information technology have produced an explosion of data storage capability. Whereas data capacities were once measured in megabytes (millions), then gigabytes (billions), they are now measured in terabytes (millions of millions). The extent, depth and accessibility of data is evolving at a rapid rate as the technology becomes steadily more sophisticated. With this greater ability to store huge amounts of data comes new problems. It is not so much a question of being unable to capture and store data, we now have to deal with the problems of how to select, prioritize and process the most relevant data from the mass available to us. This requires an ability to utilize research muscles that managers did not formerly have to use; indeed, in many cases they did not even know they were there. We are living in an age of information overload. The feelgood factor of having a lot of data has left many companies information-poor. An ability to design, define and develop a data mart, or a data warehouse (depending on the size of the enterprise) is a key survival trait.

In business, therefore, the focus is on database management. Indeed, to some extent, for a large organization, database marketing and relationship marketing are closely linked. The ability to manage a database effectively is a key tool in decision making. Managers who use software tools that trawl databases to find patterns or subsets of data at the point of need will generally find these to be too slow and inefficient. Data mining and data warehouse techniques rely on the continuous selection of pertinent, relevant data that are reorganized in databases that are parallel to those used by the enterprise for its daily transactions. Data can then be made available rapidly in the form of decision making information. This demands the ability to identify and access essential nuggets of data from the copious quantities of apparently worthless material. Knowledge management is about prompting, gathering, assessing, selecting and acting on acquired data in a way that is most productive for the organization. The way in which this is aligned with business mission and context is illustrated in Figure 9.2.

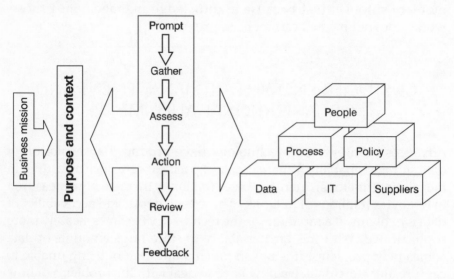

Figure 9.2 Customer knowledge and organizational alignment

PRACTICAL APPROACHES TO KNOWLEDGE MANAGEMENT

Broadly, enterprises appear to adopt two possible approaches to the management of knowledge (Hansen, Nohria and Tierney, 1999) and each of these has its place for the management of customer knowledge. The first is based on a codification strategy which, as the name implies, seeks to categorize and codify knowledge that is stored in databases where it can be accessed easily and quickly by anyone in the company. The case examples of BP and Chevron given below show how very large companies use this approach in practice. The second approach, personalization strategy, seeks to recognize that knowledge is very closely tied to the person who developed it. As a result, the role of the technology in this case is to facilitate the communication of knowledge, not to store it. Some combination of these approaches is possible but the choice of the principle method depends on how the enterprise serves its customers and the economics of its business. In turn this affects a number of other issues. These are summarized in Table 9.2.

Table 9.2 Knowledge management strategies

Codification		Personalization
High quality, reliable and fast implementation of information systems by reusing codified knowledge.	**Competitive Strategy**	Creative, analytically rigorous approach to problems based on individual expertise.
REUSE ECONOMICS Invest once in a knowledge asset and reuse it many times. Focus on accessibility and reuse with big economies of scale in relation to high volumes.	**Economic Model**	EXPERT ECONOMICS Produce highly customized, individual solutions to problems based on small teams. Focus on value added and high margins.
PEOPLE TO KNOWLEDGE BASE Develop an electronic document system with standard methods of codifying and reusing knowledge. Powerful indexing and search facilities are important.	**Knowledge Management**	PEOPLE TO PEOPLE Encourage and facilitate the development of networks for information sharing. Mentoring and asking for help are encouraged so as to share best practice. Culture fit is important.

Table 9.2 continued

Knowledge Management Strategies

Codification		Personalization
INFORMATION STORAGE, RETRIEVAL AND DISSEMINATION Big investment in IT so as to enable the management of large databases. Big investment in cross-indexing and data cleaning.	**Information Technology**	COMMUNICATIONS FOCUS Moderate investment in IT so as to produce an efficient network and easy exchange of ideas.
TECHNICAL ORIENTATION, TEAM PLAYERS Employ university graduates with first-class degrees. Train in groups, possibly using distance learning but with a strong emphasis on standard methods and team orientation. Reward people for using and contributing to the database.	**Human Resources**	CREATIVE PROBLEM SOLVERS Employ university graduates with advanced degrees, preferably MBAs. Seek out people who are creative problem solvers with a high tolerance for ambiguity. Training through one-to-one or one-to-few mentoring. Reward people for sharing knowledge directly with others.

After: Hansen, Nohria and Tierney (1999)

The codification strategy produces significant efficiencies. For example, firms such as Ernst and Young that used the codification strategy, enjoyed growth rates of 20 per cent each year in the latter part of the 1990s by pricing out their consultants at around $600 each day. These companies can hire new graduates and train them rapidly in the use of standardized methods of information search and retrieval. By contrast, BCG, Bain and McKinsey Consulting recruit much more selectively, often after several interviews with senior partners and consultants. Cultural fit is taken very seriously and subsequent training is based on a system of personal mentoring. The personalization strategy requires knowledge to be passed along on a one-to-one basis so as to create a different kind of individual value for customers. These firms offer highly customized solutions billed at an average of just over $2,000 each day during that time.

THE KEY PRINCIPLES OF KNOWLEDGE MANAGEMENT

Information capture must be focused

Unfocused information capture is not only wasteful but also damaging to an enterprise. It is very important not to confuse quantity with quality. Curiously, managers sometimes fail to carry the lessons of everyday life into business decision making. A bigger problem space simply makes choices harder. For example, given a choice of strawberry ice cream or no ice cream, most children will decide very quickly! However, given the entire resources of an ice cream store, choice can be an agonizing and protracted process with much post-purchase uncertainty. By the same token, massive amounts of poorly structured data about a customer do not really help a manager assess their situation. When managers are uncertain about the factors that influence a problem, they often seek to hide this uncertainty under huge quantities of data and communication. Indeed, they sometimes engage in this behaviour deliberately to reduce the apparent risk of making a poor choice. It is significant that expert decision makers often appear to use fewer information cues than beginners, since their very expertise resides in knowing what is relevant to a problem (and what is not).

Acquiring information in an unstructured way is at best a waste of one person's time and at worst a waste of everyone else's. For example, every e-mail should be judged in terms of context, relevance and the potential need to take action. A person generating, say, 50 e-mails or more each day is creating a massive overhead that adds to the pressure on managers as they seek to organize and share knowledge.

One of the problems of today's information environment is that we have too many inputs and not enough time to process them. This produces a curious paradox. In an information rich environment it becomes harder to learn. Network technology enables information throughout the enterprise to be brought together to create enhanced added-value information. The real problem is how to organize, disseminate and make accessible that information in the form of knowledge (about customers).

> ## Case example: BP Oil, Europe
>
> In 1998, BP completed a project for an ad hoc query tool that mapped the chart of accounts dynamically. This tool enabled any level of who, why or what code to be queried consistently across the whole of Europe. It also consolidated the data as they were brought together. This enabled the oil giant to gain significant insights into its European business that had previously been impossible to glean.

Therefore, unfocused information capture results in:

- Wasted resources as technology is deployed to no effect. Data has to be filtered and organized for relevance.
- Information overload as managers struggle to make sense of data volumes. Knowledge collection takes forethought, skill and effort if it is to be valuable.
- E-mail fatigue decreases productivity. Data must have integrity to be valuable. Managers need to understand the age, source and context of data to be confident about its integrity.
- Reduced added value as network links between information sources become harder to identify.

Knowledge frameworks are the basis of knowledge creation

New information will only create new knowledge if it is attached to an existing knowledge framework. Two frameworks are apparent:

Explicit knowledge

Formal knowledge captured in manuals, training guides and instruction sheets is explicit. Formal knowledge can even include beliefs or guidelines to behaviour if these are written down as formal policies. It can be captured on databases and shared over the network. If required, it can be made readily available. For example, tailored, personal information can be made accessible to every laptop computer using the same infrastructure that is already present in large companies. This information can therefore present a combination of hard and soft knowledge within a knowledge framework as required by the user. Each person can choose what subjects, products or customers they want to monitor and use the technology to consolidate the format from internal and external sources in a consistent way. This aligns knowledge with organizational purpose or mission, while allowing individuals to define context alongside their personal knowledge framework. It thus allows users to define what information is 'pushed' to them.

Tacit knowledge

Tacit knowledge comprises 'soft' data about markets, customers, processes, and activities. It is a valuable enterprise resource but is normally implicit, rarely stated and is not usually captured. An example might be found in the repertoire of skills, such as use of words and body language that facilitates customer acceptance in a foreign country. Making tacit knowledge explicit is one of the hardest challenges for any enterprise. There is a danger that, as attempts are made to formalize or capture tacit knowledge, it will lose its value. Consider the problem of driving a car. Initially, this involves explicit knowledge such as reading a manual or listening to formal instruction. Gradually, however, the knowledge becomes tacit as the driver learns to 'feel' for the right combination of gears, acceleration and braking. Someone driving down a fast road with the car manual in one hand and the *Highway Code* in the other would not have long to live. Nevertheless, we need to capture soft data about markets and customers somehow and add it to our database so that it can inform any point of customer contact.

Developing a knowledge framework requires a series of well-defined procedures. Data may be captured through a range of customer contacts such as field sales teams, telephone operators and even delivery drivers. Each of these contacts may pick up snippets of information in the course of conversation that may be useful to the business in terms of one specific customer or in terms of a trend associated with the capture of similar data from other customers. Data may also be captured in text form (sometimes with limited coding) in a working group or on an Intranet. It will also be collected by specific information gathering activities such as feedback from resellers, telephone research on competitor pricing, text tools that search the Internet or even newspaper clippings.

It is therefore important to recognize that:

- Knowledge about customers can only be created by relating new information to an existing framework. Frameworks are shaped not just by personal experience but also by mindset (so we are back to buy-in). The mindset needs to be right if managers are to make the appropriate connections between different sorts of knowledge.

- A piece of information is usually ignored unless it has a context and relevance to the individual receiver. Such beliefs are often time- and value-dependent. For example, information about the current needs of a high value customer with a clear indication about what must be done to develop the relationship can lead to action.
- Knowledge is contextual and resides in individuals. It comprises a set of attitudes (feelings) and cognitions (facts) that each person individually understands and holds to be true. It is not possible to relate these to objective fact in every case. Thus each individual has their own personal knowledge framework based on their own particular experiences and learning. Even with identical experiences, each person's knowledge framework is different. We recognize this intuitively in everyday speech when we say, 'I'll send you the information'. We do not tend to say, 'I'll send you the knowledge,' since turning information into knowledge is a personal thing. To learn, we need to understand the context and relevance of the new knowledge to our set of beliefs and then be able to draw new conclusions.

Organizational frameworks include beliefs and assumptions

The framework is the sum total of what the enterprise knows and assumes about its environment when making promises to its shareholders. A simple analysis would deduce that organizations possess all the knowledge of all the individuals that work for them on the basis that the value of the whole is the sum of its parts. Unfortunately, for most organizations, this simply is not true. Many enterprises do not organize their information resources so that they can be shared easily. The flow of information is usually channelled and generally directed upward. At the same time, for personal and political reasons, individuals withhold knowledge on the basis that this secures their position. The culture of the organization can have an influence here because an open, supportive culture can encourage knowledge dissemination.

Case example: Chevron Oil

Chevron Oil, now part of Chevron Texaco Corp, founded in 1879, employs about 34,000 people worldwide and is the eleventh largest oil company with a net income of about US$33 billion in 2001. Senior managers in Chevron observed a 3 to 1 difference in performance between the best and worst performers in their multi-site manufacturing operations. The managers say that the ratio is typical for most activities in the company. If a way could be found to share best practice amongst operating managers so that the worst were brought up to the level of the current average, the performance gains would be enormous. This has led Chevron to talk about the 'Billion-Dollar Prize' of a learning organization.

Between 1991 and 1997, Chevron cut its annual operating expenses by $1.1 billion in an industry that had seen a steady decline in the price of its basic commodity. Indeed, over the decade of the 1990s, crude oil prices fell from around $15 a barrel to $10 a barrel by 1999 and prices as low as $5 a barrel were envisaged. Only one region in the world has extraction prices lower than $5 a barrel – the Middle East at $2. In Malaysia, Mexico and Nigeria, costs were around $7 and elsewhere $10 to $14 (The Economist, 6/3/99, p 29).

The oil industry is very capital intensive. Typically, Chevron invests around $5 billion each year on capital projects and any way to reduce investment costs will impact fast on the company's bottom line. Accordingly, Chevron introduced a scheme known as the Chevron Project Development and Execution Process, better known within the company as 'chip-dip', which is estimated to have resulted in a 15 per cent improvement in capital efficiency.

Chip-dip is based on a network of 30,000 HP desktop computers, Windows NT, Microsoft Office, Lotus Notes and the Fulcrum search tool. The approach focuses on a continuous improvement in performance based on a steady cultural change towards shared knowledge. In this example, buy-in is more important than the technology. The key factor in technological terms is that the tools were standardized. This cuts system administration costs but also facilitates learning. More crucially, the system encourages employees not only to search the company's knowledge base for existing solutions to current problems but also to use the Lotus Notes GroupWare to discuss innovative ideas and approaches.

Even if the right cultural dimensions exist, pertinent knowledge like best practice is sometimes not shared. This is very dangerous because combustible, 'big bang' type change is easy for all to see. A knowledge management strategy is not going to help with that. However, it is the slow change in markets and customers, over a period of time, that slowly undermines existing assumptions. Most organizations are perfectly designed to be what they are. They are adapted to their environment and have many mechanisms to adjust to small incremental changes. Gradually, however, such change can reduce the relevance of the current knowledge framework rendering it useless. Marketers have known about this phenomenon for many years. A good example is offered by Levi Strauss. With a variety of clever marketing techniques, it remained at the forefront of the blue jeans market for many years. It hung on to its customer base very effectively, rather too well in fact. By 1999, many of its customers were middle aged and blue jeans were no longer so fashionable – even President Clinton was wearing them! The company was too strongly associated with this product to switch quickly into chinos and khakis and it had to downsize. On the other hand, it was still selling 1 million pairs of jeans every day (far more than any other brand) with annual revenues of $6 billion. Its 'Personal Pair' programme launched for women in 1995 had resulted in repeat purchase levels of 38 per cent, more than triple that of any other Levi's product. So Levi's had recognized the need for change and even its own forecasts predicted that 25 per cent of sales would be based on customized clothing in the next five years. What it did not realize quickly enough was that its traditional, slick, mass marketing would not sell so well to a generation raised in an interactive age. This is what we call the 'cohort effect', which refers to waves of technology being accepted by successive generations. Nor did it reposition itself substantially enough so as to respond to the success of its own relationship-based product (personalized clothing).

So, are relationship marketing managers smarter than frogs? As a reptile, the frog adjusts its body temperature gradually to its environment. If you place a frog in a pot of hot water, it will immediately try to scramble out. The change is sudden and discontinuous. If you gently place the frog in room temperature water he'll stay put. Now heat the water gradually. Somewhere around 40^0 the frog will pass into a coma and somewhere around 80^0 it will cook. Though there is nothing restraining it, the frog will sit there and boil. The challenge for managers, therefore, is: are you smarter than a frog? Can you organize a knowledge framework that will allow for recognition of the effects of small, continuous changes?

Organizational frameworks must include beliefs and assumptions:

- Promises are made to shareholders based on stated and unstated assumptions.
- The whole organization has a role to ensure these assumptions hold true, which requires an open culture of information sharing.

- Organizational knowledge is not the sum of the parts because this is hard to achieve and the knowledge vested in members of the organization must be valued and recognized.
- Small, incremental changes are more difficult to recognize than sudden discontinuous change.

Strategic and operational planning processes must be aligned

If the enterprise is clear about this, market signals and behaviours can be more easily put into context and used productively. This is especially true if knowledge management is integrated as part of the strategic and operational business planning process. Many organizations write a beautiful strategy document, which ends up feeding the promises made to shareholders. To have a chance of succeeding these need to be cascaded down through the divisions and operating units to the lowest individual activity level. The key performance indicator hierarchy described in Chapter 4 helps to achieve transparency and alignment with overall objectives. The KPIs flag areas of under-performance quickly, so the overall plan can be protected through corrective action or early communication.

It is possible to envisage a knowledge framework built around these plans. The key assumptions in the knowledge framework can then cascade in the same way as the performance indicators. Both the KPIs and knowledge will then have a clear context and purpose that is aligned with the overall objectives of the organization. These would be linked to personal performance contracts at the individual activity level to identify the activities needed to support the plan.

The main point, therefore, is to link knowledge management to the planning process:

- The potential weakness in many organizations is that strategic planning is often disconnected from operational planning.
- This results in a lack of alignment, so the lowest level of activity (which is often customer contact) is disconnected from higher level objectives. This is why organizations that have struggled to rid themselves of a bad customer sometimes re-recruit them in another part of the company.
- A linked knowledge and KPI hierarchy can help to overcome this problem.
- Purpose and context is given to each activity, which enables greater accountability.

The need for an open and receptive organization culture

Of course, a receptive organization also needs people with the skills and willingness to learn. Openness and diversity are key issues for effective learning in organizations. Confidence and trust are important, too, if existing personal or corporate beliefs are to be challenged openly and changed.

Advocacy for the here and now, coupled with an ability to put a personal view persuasively are often rewarded more than an ability to enquire into complex problems. It is usually true that people at the top of an enterprise have more turf to protect than anybody else; after all, in many cases, they were the people who shaped the enterprise in its present form as they rose through the ranks. It needs a mature team and a supportive culture before most people will admit in public they do not understand or, indeed, change their beliefs or say they are willing to change.

To deal with this, the enterprise may set up best practice networks. These are initiatives to promote the sharing of knowledge. In organizations like Bank One in the United States, such initiatives have proved to be very effective. Each month, important customer metrics such as satisfaction levels, retention rates, cross-selling and referrals are published in a ranked list with the best performers at the bottom. (There is a logic to this since these branches are generating revenues and profits that help support the rest.) Managers at the top of the list are encouraged to call nearby branches further down, to discuss what their neighbours did to achieve a better performance. In Bank One, a 'cry for help' of this sort is encouraged as a positive search for improvement.

When these sorts of initiatives fail, it is usually due to one of a number of reasons. Sometimes they are under resourced or even have no budget. They may be unrecognized as part of the personnel appraisal procedure or they may be seen as threatening, non-core activities that cut across organizational structures. In these circumstances, best practice sharing is the first thing to be dropped when something important needs doing that is on the boss's performance contract. In short, the 'Billion Dollar Prize' is abandoned.

The key points, therefore, are as follows:

- Increasing knowledge infers changing sets of beliefs. The higher the level of management, quite often the more ingrained the beliefs.
- Learning involves both personal and team skills. It cannot happen without resources such as time, money, leadership and rewards.

- Engender a culture that encourages the capture of tacit data.
- Provide an easy vehicle for data capture such as an Intranet. GroupWare such as Lotus Notes, Microsoft Sharepoint Portal Server and Autonomy are good tools for this purpose. Back up the material technology with social technology (training, coaching and appraisal) and with reward and recognition systems.
- Enable the tacit knowledge to be analysed and distributed to the people who can best use the information through intelligent software and a knowledge management unit. The unit seeks to capture tacit knowledge by undertaking some form of key insight or trend analysis into the notes. These are then published to individuals who can use the information in the form of a report, an e-mail, a file or even a revolving message banner on operational telemarketing screens. The process overview is shown in Figure 9.3.

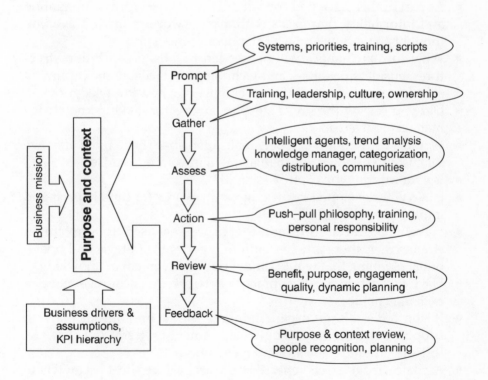

Figure 9.3 Process overview of customer knowledge management

SUMMARY

- Does your organization have an agreed approach to managing knowledge, especially knowledge about customers? For example, do you have a written policy? Do you ever have meetings where customer knowledge management is discussed as an agenda item?
- Can customers review the information that you are holding about them? What are your policy guidelines in this area?
- Have you run through all the points in the 'issues in knowledge management' checklist?
- What proportion of your current products and services were developed in the last 12 months? If less than, say, 10 per cent of your revenue was generated by this new stuff, have you reviewed the transformation of embedded knowledge to embodied knowledge with your relationship marketing managers? In other words, do you have an innovation problem?
- As part of this, have you considered the degree of trust, integration and informality that exists within your work groups? Have you thought about how you would influence these factors?
- What formal changes will be needed to jobs, organization structures, business processes and technology to facilitate the capture of existing knowledge and the development of new knowledge?
- Did you review the seven steps to success for making knowledge management a reality?
- Would a codification or a personalization strategy be more effective for customer knowledge management in your enterprise?
- Is your information capture focused?
- Have you developed knowledge frameworks for both explicit and implicit knowledge?
- Have you traced through the processes used to implement strategies? Is there any discontinuity between strategic and operational planning that would hinder the management of knowledge?
- Have you set up any best practice networks to encourage an open exchange of ideas?
- If you have a large organization, is the technology in place to support customer knowledge management, in terms of hardware, software, training, reward and recognition?
- Are knowledge assets reflected on your balance sheet or anywhere else in your accounts?

10

Integrating the technology of customer management systems

INTRODUCTION

One of the major problems in implementing customer management systems is that the process rarely starts with a clean sheet of paper. It is therefore important to consider system design carefully at the outset in order to handle the problems of integrating different customer management systems. The various CRM systems need to be integrated both to support business processes properly and to maximize return on investment.

A chief information officer (CIO) has two good ways of getting fired in this exercise. The first is by taking a tactical approach to customer relationship marketing projects. The second is by taking a strategic development and delivery approach!

A tactical approach can deliver short-term but isolated business results in each priority area. It is then often difficult to build on this early success to create an integrated capability. Each project tends to be budgeted, designed and delivered in isolation, with no business case for the bigger picture.

The strategic approach lays down a future framework (which may or may not be flexible enough to survive the test of time) but delivers no benefit in the short term. Invariably, such major projects run over time and budget. Due to the long timescale, deliverables often fail to meet the changing needs of the business over the delivery period. The inability of either marketing or IT to design an appropriate system up front often means that the delivered solution is no longer appropriate when it arrives. It does not incorporate what is learnt through early experiences of managing relationships. Many beliefs about customers, their behaviour, and the systems and data support required to manage them, get disproved along the way.

The best way ahead seems to be a combination of strategic and tactical designs. It is imperative that early project stages deliver benefits. Early victories attract further support. It is therefore important that the new systems capabilities enable the business to manage at least some customers more effectively in the short term. These short-term gains will help to preserve the top-level business sponsorship vital for securing budgetary support at later project stages.

Later stages will need to demonstrate how these early capabilities can provide an even broader benefit if they are replicated across the organization. For example, can they be extended to other customer types or groups, geographies, products or channels?

Thus, a combined tactical and strategic approach requires an IT vision and strategy. The strategy is based on a vision for the management of customer information. A set of goals then emerges, by which the vision is achieved.

Earl *et al* (1993) provide a good discussion of various strategic business systems planning approaches. To avoid reinventing the wheel and incurring additional cost and time it is important to use a comprehensive, proven, industry model. Such a model helps to achieve goals by encouraging the formation of a detailed plan covering every relevant aspect of IT across the enterprise. This plan is the overall systems architecture. The main elements of an IT architecture are described in Table 10.1.

Table 10.1 Components of an IT architecture

Component	Description
Context	A plan that conveys basic requirements, guidelines and constraints. It may itself be an output of a higher level architecture, such as a business plan, so there is an input here from the business vision statement.
Frameworks	A multi-layered approach to developing the architecture in stages. Typical frameworks consist of a series of elements and

Table 10.1 continued

Component	Description
Frameworks (cont.)	levels, which can be envisaged as a grid. Elements include computing systems, communications systems, data management and applications software. These are then specified with increasing degrees of precision as initial parameters are translated into policies, models, plans and procedures. This is how integration is achieved by ensuring that each part of this 'grid' fits to the next part. For example, the area of data management might proceed from defining data assets, through to requirements for use, access control and storage. It would not be possible to use, say, data warehousing or data mining without thinking through the implications for other elements.
Components	Commonly accepted objects that make up building blocks. The purpose of architecture is to define and arrange these. In a town, there are areas for restaurants, commerce, industry, education, residences, recreation and so on. Each has a structure, a physical location area and expected numbers of occupants. At the next level the architect designs buildings. In IT, objects will be processes, systems, procedures and rules. Within these, the architect will define hardware, software, people and decisions processes.
Interrelationships	Relationships between objects are based on some sort of modelling. The purpose is to evaluate the effect of varying relationships between components so as to maximize synergy and interaction. In a town, we would be looking at transport access and utilities. In IT, we look at customer-to-customer links (processes), the flow of decisions, the proximity of functions, data dictionaries and indexing (of databases).
Models	There is a need for standard components or interfaces, such as that provided by Windows, to act as guidelines for developers and for aesthetics. Again, town planners put restrictions on appearance, road widths, building heights, colours etc. They hide utilities like power lines from view. The aim is to ensure access and diversity. Aesthetics are important because this is where you get the emotional response to a system. If people do not like the look of a house, they might not buy it. If they do not like the look and feel of software, they might not use it.
Architects	The people who turn visions into reality and provide the link between concept and implementation. They must identify and meet the needs of users so as to produce executable plans. Users are often not directly involved in systems development so architects must link information services (IS) with business managers. A data warehouse is an expensive waste of money if nobody wants to use it because it is too complicated, slow or unwieldy. In this example, the architect would be the relationship marketing project manager.

THE OVERALL APPROACH

THE NEED FOR AN ACTIVE PROJECT CHAMPION

An involved project champion is critical for the successful deployment of IT support, rather than a detached sponsor. Without continual involvement, such a challenging and pervasive programme will lose direction. It may get hijacked by some departments or managers for their own benefit, or it may simply fail through lack of a shared vision. An active, top-level steering group is usually required, which must buy-in to a consolidated business and IT systems approach. This implies the development of an integrated plan, rather than piecemeal decision making. Experience shows that a complete systems and data vision must underpin the project. Systems and procedures must then be built in stages, implemented in phases and measured for payback at each level so that knowledge of both processes and customers is acquired systematically. In other words, learning is continuous.

THE NEED FOR GOOD PROJECT MANAGEMENT

Studies of system projects suggest that local, stand-alone or 'point' solutions offer limited benefit compared with replicated or integrated solutions. Tactical projects, whether they bring initial benefits or not, are usually not replicated. They are also difficult to scale up within the company and are rarely integrated with other capabilities. As a result, it is not usually possible to leverage higher business benefits. The absence of data linkages and feedback mechanisms from such isolated solutions creates discontinuities in the systems and data flows meant to support business processes. This is usually associated with a corresponding breakdown of the business process itself. In consequence, it is harder to measure the effect of the project, and real learning or new knowledge that could otherwise have been gained is lost.

Many early marketing projects failed to deliver much benefit because they were implemented as stand-alone solutions in this way. The sales or customer service departments were thus unable to follow up with data mining projects to identify new ways of targeting company resources towards retaining customers. Early stand-alone marketing databases often fell into disrepute, as the quality and consistency of data could not survive the most basic of 'sanity checks' by product managers and sales channels.

We can consider a customer relationship marketing venture at four levels:

- **A technology:** the lowest, most basic and to some extent simplest level. A piece of technology or a procedure is introduced in a specific and limited way to solve a specific problem. This might be a piece of software designed to capture customer names and addresses more accurately at the point of sale, or a training exercise designed to ensure that each customer who chooses not to renew a subscription is contacted to discover the reason. A technology can be introduced in a few weeks.
- **A project:** which involves technology, people and processes in a complete but discrete area of activity. It might address customer welcoming or it might encompass the whole customer relationship marketing cycle in one department or unit. It is still bounded but it involves a complete range of soft and hard technologies. A project might last 9 to 18 months.
- **A programme:** which involves the integration of several projects and is a significant change in the level of difficulty and complexity. Timescales are in the order of at least 24 to 36 months.
- **An enterprise:** enterprise-wide CRM is based on continuing progress towards a strategic vision involving customers, employees, the supply chain and business partners. It takes many years.

It is evident that successful implementation at any level depends on good management and the careful integration of all aspects of relationship management, from employee buy-in, through good customer skills, right down to simply making sure that the technology does its job. As the scale of the venture increases, the demands on project management abilities increase dramatically. The most common failings are weaknesses in the project processes and failings in the project manager, rather than IT-specific or technical issues.

Based on research carried out with 900 managers by Coverdale Research and the British newspaper *Computer Weekly* in early 2002, 75 per cent of all respondents said that unrealistic estimates of time and resources were the major contributor to project failure. This was closely followed by unclear objectives (where are we going?), poor communication, poor change management skills and poor leadership.

When it comes to finding a project leader, communication and leadership skills tend to be more important than technical knowledge, formal project management training or even previous experience with similar projects.

Problems with suppliers or third parties did not even figure in the top 10 major contributors to IT project failure, whereas failings concerning stakeholders and the project team rated higher as potential project killers. Involvement and the support of top management were seen as vital to IT project success.

For the project team itself, defining clear roles and establishing teamwork and motivation are more important than technical competence or formal training. The top five leadership skills were an ability to communicate (58 per cent), good/strong leadership (28 per cent), technical knowledge/experience (21 per cent), previous knowledge/training (14 per cent) and a clear understanding of project objectives (11 per cent).

Most unsuccessful projects suffer from management, rather than IT, failures. If there are no strong sponsorship, a lack of cultural readiness, insufficient supporting budgets and an absence of complementary customer management skills, the prospects for success are small. The venture must be driven by business managers, especially those in the customer relations department. If technical managers are left to define a solution for themselves, the resulting IT solution often supports business issues poorly or not at all. Examples of customer-unfriendly systems are easily recognized when, for example, customers are asked to repeat the same information to several employees as they are handed off from process to process. Poor initial design tends to be associated with much redesign, many false starts and a general feeling that 'we'll never get this right'.

THE CRM ECOSYSTEM

The leading customer loyalty analysts – including Meta, Datamonitor and Bloor – refer to CRM ecosystems. They apply the analogy of a closed ecological loop (such as the Amazon rainforest or the Pacific Ocean) to CRM. As prerequisites to achieving a 'closed-loop' CRM ecosystem, these analysts have identified three forms of integration:

- **Collaborative CRM**, where channels or touch points share and use information about customers.

- **Operational CRM**, where each channel or touch point directly accesses the organization's back-office systems for straight-through processing.
- **Analytical CRM**, where the integration of customer, financial and marketing information allows more focused, effective and profitable information analysis and directed activity across the organization.

The result of applying and integrating collaborative, operational and analytical CRM is 'closed-loop CRM'. This is when a continuing learning loop – a virtuous circle – is created that delivers increasingly effective activity in each area. Additional customer information is acquired and stored at every interaction, while the organization's customer knowledge is deployed and redeployed to optimize the value of each relationship. The common enabling factor in all these forms of CRM is integration – which we deal with later in this chapter.

A key element in systems models for CRM is whether the data can be traced from business requirements to source and to other uses of the same data. Systems models should therefore provide for easy integration of best practice, one-off applications into an integrated systems approach. For example, a new profitability reporting application can identify and share data from earlier projects, requiring only previously unused data to be incorporated. Even project change costs can be reduced as additional databases are modelled and mapped with overall consistency.

The complete full-cycle architecture produces an operational business system. In the past, decision support systems were considered as non-operational IT. Only transaction systems were seen as operational. The production of reports for decision making was regarded as having only a loose connection with day to day business operations. The feedback loop through decision, action and measurement was not fully implemented. Current systems provide for timely, one-to-one campaign management, rapid product customization, and for yield management (product repricing based on demand management). These features depend on constant market intelligence and rapid decision making affecting both operational and non-operational systems.

BUILDING A 'FULL-CYCLE' SYSTEM

The complete data cycle is complex. If the start point is considered to be sources of data mostly from customer interactions, we then need to manipulate these data in various ways. They have to be combined from different originating points, transformed and analysed before using them for business decisions. Once implemented, decisions produce further customer interactions which have to be measured. The cycle is illustrated in Figure 10.1.

In the diagram:

- Data are sourced from customer or partner contacts, legacy systems and external data sources.
- A common data store such as a data warehouse or data mart is designed and built for all selected, cleaned and structured data.
- Customer data are then analysed using online analytical processing (OLAP) and data mining tools. These produce customer scores which forecast the probability of responsiveness to different kinds of marketing campaigns and likely profitability within actionable customer segments.
- Planned customer dialogues and contacts are then optimized for maximum return.
- Marketing campaigns are designed and executed based on these plans, with contact follow-up activities.
- The campaigns are evaluated individually, against each other and against plan.
- Learning and new knowledge is internalized into processes and campaign improvements.

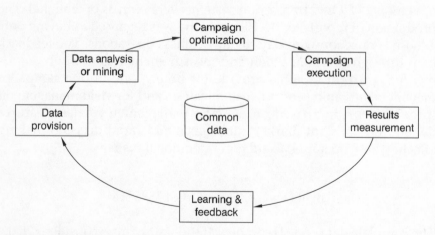

Figure 10.1 The learning development cycle

This implies neither that the systems solution should be defined in detail at the start, nor that the whole system must be built before benefits are obtained. It is designed and built in stages. Focus on the development of a specific capability usually provides a basic definition of systems and data needs. With this focused approach, the IT implications of the early stages are often much smaller than expected. For example, not all legacy system data need to be extracted, cleansed, structured and analysed. A narrow focus on business requirements will normally delimit quite a small subset of data, which reduces timescales, effort, cost and risk. As an example, a cross-selling project may only require details of current product holdings, specific buying indicators, potential profitability and risk. Quite often a subsequent project phase will then need only small additions to the data already available and in use. Much customer data will prove to be common to many new capabilities. In this example the same data are likely to be common to retention or target acquisition projects. In the worst case, only limited additional data will be required. It is not necessary to build the complete cycle systems and data, with all feedback mechanisms, to create the first learning loop. Interim feedback mechanisms can be created to enable rapid learning capability.

At a high level the architecture and approach looks very similar, even for different industries. At a more detailed level, experience shows that there are many variations in the type of customer data required, where they are collected, the volume, type and frequency of customer interactions, the relative need for rapid decision making, the type of action that results and the improvements gained. These differences must be reflected in industry data models and applications, and by using sound and experience-based decision-making techniques during implementation. Consulting and delivery methods are available to assist here which take into account the systems available to speed implementation while reducing costs and risk. A good CRM systems architecture and approach will draw on many years of previous implementation experience, while retaining the flexibility to customize the approach in each project.

The planning approach or architecture should not determine pre-set business or data cycle times. Rather it should enable incremental improvements in cycle times as customer management capabilities develop. In this fashion, an initial campaign management capability may begin with well-planned bi-monthly promotions to large customer groups. Through the learning process, an understanding of actionable segments and key customer buying or lapsing events can be derived. As experience and understanding of managing customers improves, it becomes more practical to make just-in-time marketing responses to individual customers, which should result in an improved return from each project.

For example, a home improvement retailer in the UK realized (unsurprisingly) that customers tended to make multiple and repeat purchases when a house move, building extension or major redecoration project was under way. Using loyalty discount cards to encourage customers to identify themselves ('hand raising') at each store visit, they were able to rapidly recognize the likely project type from what was bought. They were then able to offer customers incentives to spend more of their project budget in the store through targeted promotions. New customer servicing activities were also introduced to support the marketing scheme in an integrated manner.

The systems solution will evolve continually, and different data items will be identified as key at different stages. Responsiveness, cycle speed and personalization are likely to increase dramatically, although cycle volumes may change as the most appropriate data are identified. One financial services provider aiming to cross-sell additional products initiated a data mining exercise to identify the attributes and needs of previous cross-buyers. Additional customer information was obtained through research, before this knowledge was used in the call centre to customize the conversation (or script) flow during a dialogue. Using simple decision tree logic, and rules derived from data mining, it was possible to identify the most appropriate product offers by intelligent questioning of callers. Specific additional data captured during the telephone conversation and supplemented by follow-up calls to selected customers helped complete an understanding of key buying indicators.

Significant differences may be identified either within small customer segments or across large customer groups. While the systems and data architecture should be able to support the management of differences across many small segments, it is not usually advisable to implement this feature. The basic architecture should however enable planned, continual systems changes in response to both trials and operational use.

For a successful system, the key requirements that should be considered are:

- Carefully thought-through systems architecture for the complete solution. This includes development and management of linkages and feedback loops to ensure a seamless transition between business processes.

- The use of an existing industry data model. This can save substantial time and cost in both the short and long term. A fairly complete, well-tried model will have been applied many times in different projects, gaining content and rigour from each application. Such a model can underpin the 'build in stages, use in stages' systems approach, as the required data for each stage have an integrated structure. Even when additional data items are identified, such as new customer attributes, there is normally an obvious place for them to be added within a proven model.

Although the data supporting customer contact management are very similar across industries (after all, these are usually the same customers), data supporting the management of profitability (of customers and products) are usually unique to each company. For example, in an industry like financial services, the management of good and bad customer risk plays a larger role than in, say, retail.

The data model often introduces a common, agreed business language for the first time. For example, the terms 'lapsed customer', 'product' or even 'customer profitability' may well have been in general usage previously, but they will need to be defined exactly if they are to be employed by a computer-based system. While these definitions may appear 'obvious' to different managers, big differences often emerge between and within business departments, between business managers and IT managers, and between merged or international companies. A common language is important to successful CRM, as this requires the business to act in a consistent manner. There may also be legal or cultural implications for the use of terms in the data model. These are important to a company when implementing a global programme. It is easy to underestimate the eventual in-house build cost of such a model, and standard models can often be purchased for much less.

It is crucial to be able to view all data by customer; this is after all a customer database. In many cases, the customer will be not an individual but a household or other buying group. Such groups are the basis of what the financial services industry calls a party database. A party database seeks to capture and represent data about all relationships relevant to the contact life cycle. It is equally important to retain views of data by product, channel or intermediary. This is sometimes forgotten in the rush for a 'customer' database. A practical system will enable any or all of these views to be exploited as required. A great deal of learning and expertise of this sort can be imported through a bought-in system.

When models are designed and built in-house, a step at a time, there is often a need to restructure periodically. For example, in one project it was very unclear at the early stages where profit data should reside within the database. Using an established system helps avoid the costs associated with unnecessary data complexity introduced insidiously as a result of what might be called 'mission creep' – adding a little bit here and a little bit there. In another project the importance of the household buying group was not documented in the initial systems requirements. It was identified and added to the model much later. Due to this late, major change the database survived only a few years before yet more unexpected changes required a fresh start to control unnecessary complexity and cost. The impact on the business project timescale, delayed development of customer management capability and eventual ROI was substantial.

LEARNING THROUGH EXPERIENCE

The final IT solution cannot necessarily be specified completely at first. Due to questions of ownership, measurement and knowledge, business sponsors may not yet be fully committed or even in a position to offer advice at the level of detail required. Many top managers seem to wear an 'I am customer focused' T-shirt but are unable to translate this into practical management direction!

Business users or even IT managers have been known to raise a purchase order for a one-off application such as a mailing package and expect the software alone to deliver a complete business capability. This cavalier approach ignores issues of management championship, budgetary needs, cultural change, skills development, definitions of customer data, knowledge acquisition and risk management. It is from this sort of starting place that letters addressed to 'Dear Deceased' originate, or even (as has been known) 'Dear Annoying Git'.

Relationship marketing IT projects are very invasive and can encompass almost every system within a company over time. Such projects are inevitably large, and may appear overwhelming. Deciding where to start and having a plan are all-important. Each phase of the plan must be significant enough to demonstrate that real progress is being made towards the objective, but too much at once can cause overload.

Many successful projects have been started with a new, practical approach. Using techniques that have much in common with knowledge management, kick-off workshops are held to bring together prior research and relationship marketing expertise. These draw on participants both internal and external to the company. Traditional strategic plans developed over long periods are sometimes abandoned when the complete strategy proves impractical. Valuable time and money can be lost through this approach, whereas the rapid initiation of early projects can generate actions and enthusiasm that provide a practical additional input to strategy development. The aim must be to combine strategic thinking with a practical understanding of current capabilities, so as to build a system that can be implemented successfully over time.

There are two common failings of isolated strategic project planning. First, while existing business and systems situations can be mapped and a future vision defined, it may be unclear what steps are needed to achieve the final goal from the current starting point. Second, while different elements of the systems and data solution can be identified, such as customer profitability analysis, data warehousing, call centres and e-business, it is often unclear how these can be built in stages, so as to provide an integrated systems solution.

The important thing to recognize is that the strategy required must be 'fit for purpose' and may therefore be unique to your company. Strategies that are appropriate for multi-nationals will be very different to those for niche players. For example, the financial services company Virgin Direct trades on its brand strength with young people, encouraging early investment in pensions through a direct telephone operation. Major banks such as Deutsche Bank, HSBC, BNP Paribas or Bank One, with many branches and a large existing customer base, have different objectives. They will need different relationship marketing capabilities from Virgin Direct, and these respective needs must be emphasized and exploited through the strategy. Companies with fast-developing customer bases can act differently from those with established bases. Companies with existing capabilities can act differently from those in the early stages of development.

To achieve these unique solutions, business and IT managers must co-operate and learn together, in a mixed team, with shared responsibility for the achievement of objectives. Neither side may know at first exactly how to proceed or be able to define future developments in any detail. The guidelines for building a co-operative learning team include:

- Form a single, multi-skilled programme team for a set period.
- Through kick-off workshops, share previous company and customer experiences of what works and what doesn't.

- Complement this with external knowledge from key suppliers and from research into best practice.
- Look for business and IT achievements elsewhere – across all industries.
- Use the best publications and selected extracts as part of the education programme for relationship marketing managers.
- Join a working forum with other companies, if learning experiences can be shared without threat.

The focus of starter projects must be to achieve worthwhile business results. At the same time they should be developing a practical and valuable capability for the future. The starter project should be small enough to achieve initial results in a timeframe of, say, three to nine months depending on scope, but must be significant enough to be recognized as a major step towards the relationship marketing goal.

CHOOSING THE FIRST PROJECT

The first projects may well be investigative, for example linking existing customer databases for better analysis or collecting more data through market research. Customer segments derived from data mining can be used to make the market research more specific. These early metrics, providing an improved understanding of the past and anticipating future benefits, are normally required to support the first systems and data investments.

Typical first projects benefit from demonstrating new capabilities. Examples include:

- managing a large number of customers in a new way;
- managing customers successfully across divisions or marketing channels;
- managing customers across critical handover points between divisions or channels;
- applying a new systems capability throughout some or all of the relationship stages for a selected customer group.

There is a danger that any single project could be considered too trivial to provide a convincing demonstration that a broad and integrated capability is being built in stages. To avoid this, aim to select early projects that demonstrate breadth and/or depth, as illustrated in Table 10.2.

Table 10.2 Scope of initial relationship marketing projects

Relationship Stage	Breadth Projects	Depth Projects
	Demonstrate the development and use of a broad capability.	Demonstrate the development and use of a follow-through capability.
One Stage	Manage all customers safely through the welcoming process, ensuring new business contacts are not lost.	Manage an identified, high net worth customer group safely through all relationship stages, from targeted acquisition to full development.
Multi-stage	Provide a consistent servicing process for a variable product mix across multiple contact channels (eg call centre, e-mail and Web).	Manage identified groups of customers safely through critical relationship stages, for example to include planned hand-offs of customers between channels from acquisition through development.

The experiences from a carefully selected set of early projects enables the programme to be scaled up more rapidly with the confidence and continued backing of the business champion. Projects might initially be within a single business unit. They should address the most immediate needs for fast payback and rapid development: for example, retention in one unit, acquisition in another. Early projects that span or link divisions are selected based on their capacity to generate business by managing customers safely across relationship cycle stages. For example, they can steer the customer through from acquisition to account management (up-selling or cross-selling).

These new capabilities can then be transferred elsewhere. The IT implications and developments of these early project stages become very obvious, making it possible to specify rapidly early systems and data requirements. Most initial steps do not require large IT developments, but those that do can be prioritized and funded accordingly.

Rapid project initiation does not replace strategy work; rather it creates another input. Knowledge of the customer base and of what works is critical to developing a strategy which drives real competitive advantage. Whether the strategic or initiation work is started first, they both gain from each other. The inevitable result is that consultants and integrators can work more closely to deliver benefit and achieve learning. In this world consulting does not precede delivery; rather it is an intrinsic part of delivery.

BUILDING A 'FULL CYCLE' SYSTEM

The complete data cycle is complex. If the start point is considered to be sources of data mostly from customer interactions, we then need to manipulate these data in various ways. They have to be combined from different originating points, transformed and analysed before they are used for business decisions. Once implemented, decisions produce further customer interactions which have to be measured – generating yet more data – and are then analysed again as the basis of learning and further improvement.

UPDATING CURRENT IT SYSTEMS

EXTENDING THE ROLE OF TRANSACTION DATABASES

During the 1980s, when many companies focused on efficiency of operations, most IT investment was in transaction systems. The major purpose of transaction systems was to provide clerical support. Their aims are to reduce costs, improve consistency of performance and provide management control. In the 1990s these transaction systems came to be asked to do a quite different job, and this trend has continued into the 21st century. Newer transaction systems provide a wider range of support. The new-breed direct sellers in areas such as financial services pioneered them. The systems are now required to support swift product innovation and flexible product construction and billing. For example, in the automotive industry they support the sale of customized, mass-produced cars and individualized financial packages.

The move from a product to a product and customer focus has usually led to the development of a common customer database in front of or alongside legacy transaction systems. This customer (or party) database is transactional, as it supports contact with the customer in daily business operations, for example in the call centre or behind the Web site. The implementation of a separate front-end customer database enables new contact management capabilities to be implemented without replacing other administrative systems in the short term.

Some early implementations of this sort of front-end database are little more than indexes, pointing to customer data held within multiple legacy systems. With only a customer index and a unique customer reference such as a credit card number, name or date of birth, it is usually possible to identify whether the customer has an existing relationship with a company. The product holdings of that customer can then be found, even though the details may be spread across a number of legacy transaction systems. This is not a perfect method and does lead to some duplication when new records are created. Mr J Smith may describe himself as Mr J T Smith next time he calls, and this necessitates periodic de-duplication. Customer data reconciliation of this sort is very difficult, if not impossible, to carry out in real time while handling the customer.

Over time, developments of the transaction database allow for consolidation of common customer data so that each record is held only once. Common data can then be removed from the legacy systems or updated as a shadow or copy of the single customer view database. Other data relevant to the management of the customer may then be added, for example customer value or potential value indicators. A contact log is especially important, as this is required to manage the customer across multiple contacts. Otherwise, each contact is made without reference to the others. Both customer and company expect all relevant contacts to be taken into account in the relationship, whichever channels they take place through.

The customer database is designed for rapid access from a number of different channels or channel applications to support individual customer contact. For example, immediate and simultaneous access may be required for Internet and call centre enquiries, as a transaction may start in one channel and move to another.

It would not normally be appropriate, therefore, to use the same database for analysis. The data structures here would be designed for performance, rather than for ease of use for report production. For technical reasons, the performance of this type of database is likely to be poor when used for analysis. Performing an analysis would degrade daily operational response rates. In addition there is a need for more historic and supplementary data for analysis. Consequently it makes sense to have some separation of data structures, storage and use between the transaction and information systems.

Enormous improvements can, however, be made to customer contact systems such as those in call centres, sales agent support systems and retail point of sale systems, without major changes to the underlying legacy systems. Once a transaction customer database is in place, legacy systems can be replaced over time, as illustrated by Figure 10.2.

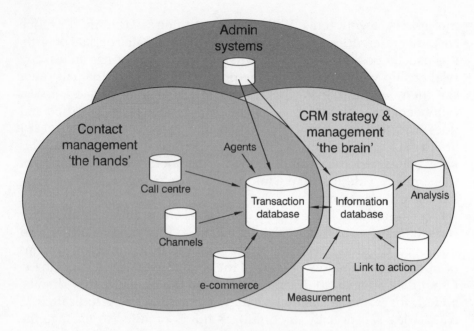

Figure 10.2 Relationship between transaction and information database

The 'hands' represent integrated contact systems and required support data. Channels might include any or all direct or indirect contact methods based on different technologies. The transaction database is used directly or indirectly to support and co-ordinate all customer contacts dynamically. The 'brain' represents integrated decision and learning systems, sometimes called business intelligence systems. It draws on both current and historical data. Analysis might include segmentation management, campaign planning, contact management, profitability management, knowledge management and other applications. The link to action may include direct customer contact, agent or dealer management, or product development. Administration represents product support, administration and legacy systems.

In the CRM ecosystem the hands provide collaborative CRM, the brain is analytical CRM. Integrating these together with the administrative and transactional systems creates the closed loop that completes the ecosystem.

This architectural approach is becoming common to CRM systems in many industries. Consumer and market pressures are driving most if not all industries to enable multiple contact channels where previously a few major channels existed. For example, in the automobile industry, previous dependency on a tied dealer channel is opening up to allow multi-franchise dealers and direct customer contact through e-business or call centres. At the same time a much broader product mix is becoming available across those channels, with the addition of many new financial and physical services aimed at the development of the same customer base.

SUPPORTING HYBRID CHANNEL MANAGEMENT

Many projects now aim to utilize channels co-operatively (or in collaboration) to achieve greater revenues through a hybrid sales and marketing approach. New business can be pre-qualified by mail or through a call centre, before the sales team gets involved. Customers can review or amend their business arrangements electronically as they decide. However, although products like mortgages can be arranged over the Internet, personal contact is often required by the client during the process, for assistance or even just for reassurance. This hybrid channel approach requires a common service centre to co-ordinate prescriptive (outbound to customer) and responsive (inbound initiated by customer) contacts.

The customers may deal with the company through any mixture of channels that they prefer. Typically, they would visit a local car dealership to inspect vehicles or get information but purchase the car direct over the Internet. In this environment, it is important that a common database is available behind these different channels to ensure consistency. This will support the same basic actions, identify customers, understand their current arrangements, and customize responses to what we know of them from the contact log.

The contact log provides a record of all outbound and inbound customer contacts, through any contact method including Internet, e-mail, mail, phone and others. It can be considered as part of the transaction database or can be held alongside it. It will also be duplicated within the information database or data warehouse, when required for mining or analysis.

The costs and complexity of such systems are usually significant because of the many links with multiple product administration systems and customer contact channels. The business case is only likely to succeed if customer service managers have substantial budgets and power. The financial benefit of improved customer service is not usually easy to justify, unless it is provided as part of a full-cycle project. Financial benefits are usually couched in terms of revenue increases from cross-selling opportunities. It is usually not easy to establish the value of these revenues in the short term, so a focus on retention efforts can be a stronger base for development and learning. As a result projects usually start with stand-alone systems in campaign management or in the call centre. Inevitably these need to be integrated with other systems eventually. The transaction database then becomes a key component in that integration. If it is overlooked, dramatic consequences may arise in contact co-ordination which are only too evident to the customer.

These systems investments concentrate on the ability to act. They are developing the hands, arms and legs of the organization. However, we cannot manage customers effectively without a brain. The brain in the IT systems process is the other major investment area. The integration of these capabilities is key.

BUILDING THE BRAIN

Until the mid-1990s, decision support systems had something of the second-class citizen about them. Often there was no obvious link between data analysis, decision making and operational actions. Nor was there a link between action and measurement. More recently the importance of customer management strategies has become apparent, and there is increasing focus on the use of information to understand customers and build relationships.

This capability goes under a variety of labels including decision support system (DSS), market intelligence system (MIS) and the more recent business intelligence (BI) or analytical systems. These systems support the organizational decision making and learning. The enormous quantity of business information produced by transaction systems has to be interpreted by business managers in some way to direct future efforts towards CRM goals. Without effective intelligence, the business's capacity to act is greatly reduced or wasted. For example, effort may be made trying to cross-sell unprofitable products to unprofitable customers, or to acquire and retain bad customers. Transaction systems with the capability to implement new products rapidly, or to customize existing products, cannot be exploited without understanding what customers will respond to. This understanding emerges from BI.

THE ROLE OF THE DATA WAREHOUSE

The brain is built around another customer database, the data warehouse. This database is the partner of the transaction database and exchanges data with it. A data warehouse is generally structured for performance, in terms of ease of access, fast analysis of large data sets and efficient report generation.

Prodigious amounts of data are required for the statistical and operations research routines used by a data warehouse. Comprehensive historic data is important so that the past can be used to predict the future (which is not always possible if sudden changes in trend occur or where customer behaviour is very erratic). Nevertheless, past responses to marketing campaigns are often used as an indicator of future behaviour. How much historic data needs to be held becomes clearer over time, and depends on the nature of the data and the volatility of the market. Detailed transaction data are usually required to gain insight into buying events. Storage systems can now hold enormous data sets which ever faster processors are able to analyse in a cost-effective manner. The costs of storage and processing power continue to drop rapidly, improving the economics of this sort of exercise. Historic data can usually be removed from transaction systems once a data warehouse is in place, which saves duplication of these data.

Accurate data timing in the transaction database is central to the reliability of the data warehouse, as this forms the basis of sales and other time-based reports in previous periods. One UK bank predicted that existing account holders would be more likely to take loans if they had a large account balance from a recent credit transaction. In fact the bank was only recognizing borrowers after the loan had been paid into their accounts, subsequent to loan approval! In a similar case, a property insurer predicted that claimants were likely to have had a recent survey. Of course this turned out to be a post-claim survey. Careful interpretation of timed data is obviously vital.

Generally the data warehouse will hold much more data than any other, even more than the transaction database. It will hold not only historic data but supplemental data such as geo-demographic, lifestyle, risk data and the developing contact log. It may even hold potential prospects, and will grow over time as relationship priorities develop. Many large companies are building and using these strategic data warehouses to provide the BI to drive marketing strategies. While smaller versions of these, known as data marts, were (and are) being built as experimental or development tools, they were often incompatible with other enterprise systems. While a data mart provides some tactical benefit, there is often no way to proceed towards an integrated capability without replacing it completely.

One example of a component now understood to be a specific data mart is commonly referred to as the MCIF (marketing customer information file). During the 1980s many companies in the United States started to create MCIFs, in isolation from other system components, in order to build a basic campaign management tool. Sometimes they were developed without even the involvement of the IT department. Effective system performance, however, requires the full-cycle architecture to achieve the right level of integration and interoperation.

As customer information is acquired and the data warehouse develops, it makes no sense to hide this valuable information away within a few internal departments. New PC-based tools and other technologies are making ready exploitation of this data more viable. Most PCs now have standard Web browsers readily available as the primary user interface. These tools enable easy database access from almost any PC. Appropriate data can then be made available from the data warehouse to branches, business partners and even customers. Regular reports, for example by sales territory, can be distributed automatically, enabling security-protected 'drill down' by authorized users so they can better understand the reason for out-of-line business indicators. It is this technology that underpins the use of key performance indicators (KPIs).

Reporting tools can then work on an exception basis, identifying and broadcasting reports only when KPIs are out of line. This push technology enables broadcast data to be sent to almost any device, including a Web site, an e-mail address, a fax machine, a laptop computer, a mobile phone, a pager or a personal digital assistant (PDA). Such data services are becoming recognized for their value in managing business relationships.

COMBINING ANALYSIS AND ACTION

There are major differences in the way operational or transaction data and information, and decision support data, are managed. If these differences are ignored in the basic architecture and in feedback mechanisms, then major problems occur for large-scale usage. For example, in a marketing campaign the pre and post analysis of data is informational, while campaign execution and response management are considered operational. Yet only together do they form a complete closed-loop process.

More recently systems-automated or direct linkages are being created from information to transaction systems (from the brain to the hands). For example, the actual mailing of targeted leads derived from scoring by the data warehouse can be distributed over the Internet to sales agents and to the call centre, which is then ready to handle customized campaign responses. Batch data movement processes or common messaging hubs can provide this integration function.

It is not only data such as scores and offers that can be passed in this way. Knowledge in the form of algorithms can be passed too. This knowledge can be used to make the call centre scripts dynamic, varying both questions and answers to callers according to their enquiry, thus supporting call handlers 'intelligently'. Response management, product customization and pricing can then be driven more effectively. Algorithms and customer information can be used in real time to respond to customer needs and likely profitability. This enables the sales agent or call centre to act in real time, making better decisions about how to manage the relationship with the customer. It becomes especially valuable for decision making, as the customer starts to initiate the higher contact levels associated with transparent marketing.

Meanwhile, the contact and transaction systems add more information to the data warehouse about customer responses and purchases, in turn improving the knowledge-handling algorithm even further. In other words, more iterations yield more data which improves relationship handling which produces more interactions, and so on, exploiting the closed loop as a learning loop.

The importance of feedback from transaction to information systems to measure the effect of previous decisions is now recognized, at least as an objective. However, there is much less understanding of the need for feedback at the modular level. For example, scoring customer data is a reusable systems module that can prepare for marketing campaigns or personalization support through several different channels. If customer scoring is to be used as an independent, modular activity this must be considered at the design stage, so that scored data can be passed to, say, contact optimizers or campaign execution tools. In the same way, mail contacts need to be passed to the active contact log, responses and purchases need to be made available to the campaign evaluation process, and so on. The importance of a well thought-out architecture, with sound informational and operational feedback loops, quickly becomes apparent.

The difficulty of integrating these feedback links into a complete system design should not be underestimated. Even with a proven architectural approach, this is a major implementation problem. Systems complexity quickly escalates, and this is not only expensive but can become a major constraint on further development work. While a number of companies have now developed integrated CRM system strategies, there are very few examples of companies that have achieved more than the first few stages of implementation successfully. The race is therefore very open, and the winner may well reap substantial reward in the form of competitive differentiation.

Route maps or IT cook books are just beginning to emerge that encapsulate the growing years of experience from both successful and failed projects. From these, the crucial importance of pilot projects, prototypes, staged build and outsourcing are increasingly recognized. As more fast-start assets of this sort become available, the cost, timescales and risk of large CRM project implementation will reduce. Experienced CRM skills are in short supply in every industry. The use of an agreed architecture and project method can therefore help ensure that available skills are used to best effect. In addition it then becomes practical to utilize other, less experienced developers as part of the project. A broad mix of many different technical skills will be required, but there is a tendency at the moment to specialize on one topic such as change management, data quality, or call centre operations. As there are few hybrid skills available, architecture and method assume greater importance in terms of leveraging and co-ordinating expertise to best effect.

THE IMPACT OF MERGERS AND ACQUISITIONS

Companies recently merged, or with merger strategies, may encounter special systems and data challenges, not just in creating a strong strategy but in ensuring practical implementation. Mergers within a country or market can often delay evolving CRM programmes by two to three years. This is due to the increased complexity of integrating marketing postures, differences in the operational management of units such as call centers, and the added complexity of integrating IT systems and databases. From many perspectives, the most valuable assets of a modern enterprise are the knowledge (in the form of expertise) and the information (in the form of databases) that it owns. If this is to be recognized, the 'predator' company's first steps when considering a merger or acquisition should be to devise ways of retaining key personnel in the target company, and ensuring that the information services of the two enterprises can be combined at reasonable cost.

The merger objective is often market share and cost reduction, so that immediately after the fusion of the two companies, there is a flurry of cost reductions. Product rationalization is often the basis of the cost reduction exercise, so as to enable processes and systems to be simplified. However, this can quickly backfire. Indeed, it has been known to result in almost the complete loss of customers from the target company, as products and services that attracted and retained them are removed.

An alternative approach is to analyse the two sets of databases for common customers and for differences. Building a strategy for the management, retention and growth of the merged customer base provides a better starting point for positive rationalization. In practice, there are very few examples of mergers being tackled in this manner. Many companies miss this one-time opportunity, and they can take years to recover. They may even claim that merger activities have made them too busy to consider CRM issues.

Global or cross-market mergers are usually carried out to gain additional market access. This is still the most usual approach to becoming a more global player. In this scenario the challenge is to gain benefit in other ways from the merged company. For example, a global financial services company may intend to replicate its CRM projects between markets, so as to leverage its marketing capabilities through parallel learning. Alternatively or additionally, central resources may be shared to reduce operating costs. If financial responsibilities are then delegated to country or market level, the CRM programmes will only be able to benefit where there is a co-operative management structure and a strong project champion at the highest level. In short, while the rewards of integration may be very high for merged companies, the execution of strategy is considerably more difficult to achieve than at first appears.

INTEGRATING CUSTOMER MANAGEMENT SYSTEMS

The potential benefits – to companies and customers – of customer management are fairly clear in most industries, particularly when customer management strategy is based on a well thought-out model of customer management and when the implementation programme is carefully planned and managed. However, few companies anywhere have overcome the technical barriers to achieving the full potential of customer management.

From a systems point of view, the key is integration of the many systems that a company uses to manage different aspects of its relationship with customers (and increasingly that customers use to manage their relationships with the company). Integration allows data arising and used in many different types of interaction, in many channels, and for different products and services, to be brought together and transformed into valuable and accessible customer information.

The reason for this is that many companies develop their IT infrastructures organically over decades, adding systems to meet particular business needs as they arise. This means that many companies have systems that were conceived during the 1980s or even earlier, running alongside ones implemented in the 21st century. The older ones are usually referred to as 'legacy systems', although in many cases they are critical operational systems without which the business would collapse. The technologies and computer languages that these use are completely different, and there are formidable obstacles that make it very difficult for these systems to communicate with each other. In many cases, because companies have over the last few years introduced several CRM systems to meet the needs of different channels or products, even these systems cannot share data easily.

To improve the consistency, productivity and benefit of customer management, data must be derived from many incompatible systems and turned into useful information that can be used to build a complete picture of each customer. It requires specialist knowledge, combined with experience of previous projects, to transform data resident in many systems into actionable information that can be used when managing a particular customer. The information is used to ensure that:

- The right product is offered to the right customer at the right time.
- Where the product can be customized in any way (such as in features or pricing), it is done in such as way as to optimize the customer's lifetime value and profitability to the company.
- The business has the resources, at that moment, to close and fulfil all the deals that will flow from the offer.
- Customers are managed in a way that optimizes the cost-effectiveness of each channel.

- Senior and middle managers always have what they need to make the best informed strategic decisions more quickly than their competitors.
- In its most advanced form, customer knowledge is used by every layer of management, from the CEO for strategy development, across sales, marketing, operations and financial management. The aim is to provide an integrated approach to CRM from the CEO right through to the database administrators.
- Collaborative working takes place across departments and channels, especially in areas such as customer retention and new product development.

INFORMATION WHERE IT'S NEEDED... WHEN IT'S NEEDED

Integration involves more than unlocking data that is imprisoned in many legacy systems. Just as important is the ability to move current data around the business. Particularly now, with customers being offered and choosing to use a variety of touch points, it is important that some forms of data are updated instantly.

Of course, not all areas of business are time-critical, requiring immediate access to up to the minute information. For example, much data can be batch processed using traditional ETL (extract, transform and load) techniques. Where customer management requires a customer view that is correct and up to the minute, it is important to make sure that – say – the branch, the call centre, the Web site and the interactive television service all show the same information at any given moment.

There are two methods of transporting and transforming those data, and most companies use different combinations of each. In the first, a traditional ETL model is used. Data are moved in batches, often in overnight or in even less frequent runs. This is appropriate where there is no penalty if users access out of date information, for example for budgets or end-of-month figures. The alternative approach is to update in – effectively – real time, and is the preferred model where customers or customer-facing staff use the information, or where data is being employed in time-sensitive activities.

If the latter approach is used, a company can use advanced middleware (for example, messaging software such as IBMs MQ series) to interchange data immediately between many different systems and then make it available to all channels, in real time. This software acts as a hub, accepting messages from one system and employing XML (extensible mark-up language) technology to make these messages intelligible to all the others. This approach has several additional benefits:

- It can greatly reduce time to market, allowing new functionality and products to be integrated into the business and launched very quickly.
- It provides a company with a single, comprehensive view of each customer.
- It facilitates superior workflow practice when a prolonged interaction with an individual customer is required.

WHEN THEORY MEETS PRACTICE

Closed-loop CRM may not be readily achievable by every company – or even desirable. Companies seem to have a number of requirements in this area. Those that are confident about their customer management strategy, perhaps already having deployed a number of CRM systems, may only need to customize and implement a further component. A package from an established vendor may well be sufficient here. The software package market in 2002 was heavily dominated by Siebel with over a 20 per cent share in terms of global customer relationship marketing revenues according to Hewson Group Market Research. The vendor market is itself very volatile, with many mergers and acquisitions, but database suppliers such as SAP, Peoplesoft, Oracle and Vignette are all making inroads into the CRM field, with shares of somewhere between 7 per cent to 4 per cent. However, more than 30 companies are currently active in this market.

Companies less confident of their customer management strategy, and those with no customer management infrastructure at all, may require a complete solution from a single source. Most companies fall between the two extremes. They have deployed some customer management systems, but now require objective analysis and advice to feed into the continuing process of evaluating and re-evaluating their customer loyalty strategy. The first step in any such process is to make a realistic appraisal of the current position and align this with their strategy. The C-View 02 tool supplied with this book illustrates the sort of initial approach that is needed.

SIMPLIFYING DATA MIGRATION AND INTEGRATION

The process of migrating, integrating and consolidating data is littered with obstacles. It often causes serious slippage in project timetables, and equally harmful budget overspend. Frequently, projects fail to deliver the anticipated business benefits, simply because the data they produce is too suspect to be useful. Worse, some projects are never completed at all. The reason for much of this is the unpredictability of the integration process. Until recently, the investment in time and money required to assess the issues involved has been so great that it has not been feasible to gain a full understanding of a project's scope and scale until the migration and integration team is well into its work. Even then, there is no guarantee that unwelcome difficulties will be avoided. What is certain is that often up to 50 per cent of a project's cost and time can be taken up by the data migration and integration effort.

WHEN YOU CAN'T START FROM SCRATCH

A primary objective of a customer loyalty initiative is to build as clear a picture as possible of each customer, through a continuing process of acquiring and using information. For most projects, the richest source of start-up information is the historical data stored in the company's legacy systems. These databases may contain transaction histories for different sorts of products or services (including ones for which the customer is no longer active), responses to various direct marketing offers, customer service queries (complaints, requests for information), core customer data, product subscription records, and so forth. Generally speaking, all of the different sources of data are likely to have been constructed at different times, for different purposes, and often using different technologies. The challenges of transforming such varied data into usable and valuable information are formidable. Conflicts can be as basic as having the same data presented in different length fields in different databases, for example, allowing for 30-character names in one database and only 25-character names in another. More seriously, data with the same meaning may be recorded differently in various systems, resulting in varying degrees of reliability. Some data may not even match their original document description: 'age' may refer not to customer age but to length of time with the company. When this 'semantic drift' and 'data mutation' arise, assessing the value to be placed on each source takes on a central significance.

As the business issues that drive customer management initiatives become more acute, the ability to migrate and integrate data quickly and cost-effectively delivers an increasingly critical competitive edge. Below, we describe the methodology used by IBM, just to give the reader a sense of the technical complexity involved.

DATA INTEGRATION METHODOLOGY

Here is a suggested methodology:

1. Use specialist tools to analyse and profile the content, structure and quality of the source data, and to produce a normalized data model. The process is carried out three-dimensionally (down columns, across rows and between tables) and permits the selection – in consultation with the customer – of the data model that the new application will use.
2. Use the source data model created to design the new target data model. This target data model is designed and customized to address precisely the business requirements of the new CRM project, and may be based on one of several commercial database models. From this mapping, batch data transformation and load routines can be generated using ETL techniques to pre-load, batch or synchronize regular changes between the databases. It is also at this point that issues regarding the quality of data can be identified, and the data cleansing criteria defined.
3. For interactive updating, specialist messaging software can allow an immediate interchange of information. Here data transformations may be undertaken by adapter programs that carry data between the source system and the messaging software's hub. XML (extensible mark-up language) formats are loaded into the target mapping function created in step 1, so that a specialist tool can map between the source model and the XML format to generate a data transformation design. This design can then be encoded to facilitate data interchange.

These new tools and methodologies work equally well for data migration (when the source data are being merged with or moved to an existing database in a one-time operation) and for data integration (when the target application or data warehouse is being freshly constructed and then continuously synchronized).

Using traditional manual analysis techniques, 50 per cent of an average migration and integration project's labour costs are typically expended on data analysis, while 30 per cent go into development, and the remaining 20 per cent into the actual movement of data. When specialist data integration tools are used, the data analysis element is typically slashed to 15 per cent of the original labour budget, saving up to 35 per cent overall. Equally important, a similar reduction can be expected on the time required to execute the project. None of these figures takes into account the cost of aborting analysis and integration work that cannot be brought to fruition owing to complications that remain unforeseen well into a project timetable – an all too common experience when using traditional techniques. When the Standish Group published its *Migrate Headaches* report in 1999, it suggested that only 17 per cent of e-business initiatives requiring corporate systems integration were wholly successful. Forty-nine per cent overran, and a full 34 per cent failed, meaning that projects were twice as likely to fail than succeed. It is in order to contain and manage these risks better that many experts advocate treating data migration and integration – along with data cleansing – as a discrete sub-project within a CRM implementation.

Using specialist software tools continues to provide savings well after the data migration and integration project has been completed. Because the analysis has been done on an end-to-end basis, a good base of metadata (higher-level data, derived from original data, usually by combining different data elements) can be defined. This, together with the actual process, can then be reused for subsequent projects. For example, if the initial project is to build an operational customer file, the metadata and process can be reused during the development of the informational customer data to go into a data warehouse or mart.

There will be very few occasions when a data migration and integration project results in a closed database containing only historical records. There is almost always a need to refresh the data on a continuing basis. The mapping and profiling carried out as part of the original work will allow new data to be synchronized continuously between the source and target databases.

SUMMARY

Integrated systems are required to support business capabilities for customer management. New capabilities can be added alongside existing systems and integrated to improve the company's ability to gain a return on investments. These developments can be prioritized and carried out in stages if a consistent approach is deployed which reuses skills, methods and tools against a common architecture and roadmap. A closed-loop operation can be developed in one business area or for one customer management objective and extended to others. Over time the CRM ecosystem is developed by combining collaborative (multi-channel) and analytical capabilities through operational integration.

- Do you have strong leadership and commitment at board level? Gaining strong business sponsorship and an active business champion is essential.
- Have you thought about your CRM project in terms of a change exercise? Careful change management planning is essential from the outset. Does the organization structure need to be redesigned? What new skills and abilities will employees need? Have you designed new incentive and reward schemes to reflect this new focus?
- Customer input must be obtained at a fairly high level. After all, this is a relationship management project! How is customer value to be changed? In what way will this influence loyalty?
- Does your board understand clearly the difference between a technology and a project? The belief that a software package will create a relationship management platform is mistaken. Architecture and integration issues are much more important.
- How is the customer base to be made into an asset? Where and how will it deliver added value to both parties? It is of limited value to better understand customer profitability if nothing is done to influence the future value of customers by applying the knowledge where customers are touched by the company.
- Has the project been planned to ensure that findings can be implemented and the results measured so that, for example, the subsequent purchase rate associated with a particular marketing initiative can be traced?
- Is the project linked into operational systems and business approaches? For example, can the insights gained from data mining be used by day-to-day business processes?
- Is there good communication and close co-ordination between departments? (How do you know?)
- It is very useful to have good KPIs from the outset. Do you have good KPIs right now based on a long term set of clean data? These can then act as the basis of measurement and evaluation as the venture progresses.

11

Managing good and bad customers

THE MORAL MAZE

We all tend to make regular decisions about the worth of other people. On the whole, the majority of people make these decisions in a responsible way. Christians refer to this as the so-called Golden Rule, which is based on the advice in the Bible (Matthew 7:12) to 'do unto others as you would be done by'. In other words, treat others as you want to be treated. Actually, the sentiment can be traced back much further. In the Jewish tradition Rabbi Hillel said much the same thing and, even earlier, Confucius used a similar rule to summarize his teachings. Since most of the world's major religions and many non-religious thinkers teach this rule as being of central importance, it seems reasonable to assume that this is a general moral truth that influences people from many diverse cultures (see, for example, Hertzler, 1934).

Somehow or other, this rule seems harder to apply when people are acting in their capacity as managers. Bureaucracies not only rationalize work, they rationalize behaviour and attitudes also. They do this with policies, rules and procedures and they create an ethical environment of their own. People who do not conform to this environment are often punished, either formally or informally. For example, the boss might regard a debt collector, who tries to be kind by giving concessions to debtors, as untrustworthy. The concession might be rationalized in the sense that if the debtor is well treated, they will not only try harder to repay their debt but, also, their relationship with the supplier might be expected to improve. Nevertheless, the 'kind' debt collector may not get promoted as rapidly as a colleague who recovers debts at any cost and who, therefore, has a better collection record.

Part of the problem here is that bureaucracies actually separate people from the consequences of their decisions. Managers rarely visit the families of sacked workers or the businesses of customers whose credit rating has been reduced. 'Tough' decisions are often admired and tough managers have a way of out running their mistakes. They get promoted more rapidly and leave the blame for those left behind. Indeed, ethical issues often get translated into issues of public relations so that the interests of individual customers appear to be offset against the welfare and employment offered by the organization (Bensman, 1983).

As a result, well educated, professionally trained managers in companies with international reputations have been known to take decisions that ran the risk of provoking public censure. They seem especially inclined to do so in cross-border or cross cultural transactions (Newman, 1980). The Bhopal accident in India during the early 1990's might be an example of such activity. Here, a chemical plant, owned by Union Carbide of the United States, leaked a highly toxic substance called dioxin. Their response to the resulting deaths and injuries was very different to what they would have been required to do had the plant been located in, say, Wisconsin.

Loyalty is certainly a factor in these sorts of decisions. Loyalty infers a willingness to sacrifice. Perhaps managers making questionable decisions are sacrificing their personal beliefs in what they consider to be the interests of the organization. Of course, this raises questions of its own, especially in terms of the Golden Rule. If customers are expected to be loyal then maybe, in turn, they deserve loyalty from their suppliers. Managers justify their questionable behaviours in several ways. They argue that organizations cannot be expected to have the same morality as individuals and, in any case, all their competitors are doing it. They claim that their responsibility is to shareholders and owners. They also suggest that it is not the responsibility of organizations to take care of consumers either in their own country or, even less so, in others, this is the province of government. Basically, these are all profit maximization arguments (Smith, 1990).

Some governments have taken action to try to protect their citizens. In the early 1960's, the US government passed the Consumer Bill of Rights. This identified four basic rights: the right to safety, the right to be informed, the right to choose and the right to be heard (that is, to have the consumers' interests fully considered). Obviously, there are groups of consumers who are in special need of protection such as children, the poor, the mentally impaired and the illiterate. However, with complex products, such as electronics or financial services, even well educated consumers in high socio-economic groups may not fully understand the implications of a choice. Subsequently, other countries have introduced similar legislation though few have gone so far as the United States.

Customer relationship marketing requires managers to make decisions about the goodness and badness of their customers. An undifferentiated strategy that seeks to treat all customers as if they were the same, and seeks to retain all customers, will surely be less successful in many marketing situations than one that seeks to recognize variety. The technology described in Chapter 10 makes it possible for enterprises of all sizes to differentiate between 'good' and 'bad' individuals and groups. Here, 'good' and 'bad' are defined according to the organization's objectives and are reified in sets of rules that allow good and bad customers to be isolated within a customer database. This is not new; traders have been making judgements about their customers since trade began. What is new is the scale on which it can be done and the sophistication with which it can be executed. In a digital world, information from many sources can quickly be brought together to paint a comprehensive picture of a person and their life. In consequence, data protection legislation has been introduced in many countries to try to ensure respect for notions of privacy, though very often governments exempt themselves from this legislation. This, in turn, has to be balanced against laws designed to ensure freedom of information.

Even within this legal framework, developments in information systems make it easier to find predictors of 'goodness' or 'badness' using a range of statistical indicators. Where legislation prevents direct use of certain indicators, such as gender, race or religion, this initiates a search for surrogates. For example, it is possible to infer membership of certain ethnic or racial groups from their names or by the pattern of nouns and vowels in their names.

WHAT IS A GOOD CUSTOMER?

Customer relationship marketing requires an enterprise to define what it means by a good or bad customer. It is up to individual managers to resolve the ethics of these decisions and they must keep them under continuous review, not just from a moral and legal standpoint but also from a marketing standpoint. In the commercial arena, we can identify some of the characteristics we might expect from good customers:

- **Valuable** – clearly a good customer is a valuable asset. They yield a positive net value to the supplier after taking into account all servicing costs, including relationship costs. Let us illustrate the point with retail banking. Customer A keeps a reasonable current account balance, never uses an overdraft without permission, rarely goes into a branch and makes most transactions through an ATM. Customer B keeps the same average account balance as A. He constantly moves into overdraft and uses branch services frequently. Even though customer B pays higher bank charges, these do not fully compensate for the extra administrative costs of servicing the account. A is therefore of higher net value than B.
- **Moral** – they are honest and stay on the right side of the law in all their dealings with the company.
- **Prudent** – they live within the resources available to them and do not overextend their financial position.
- **Punctual** – they pay bills on time, keep appointments and follow servicing and maintenance procedures carefully.
- **Responsive** – to marketing communications that are relevant to them. In other words, if they respond, there is a chance that this will lead these customers to evaluate seriously the possibility of buying the product or service. They do not respond in a casual or eclectic manner. This is known as the 'schoolboy brochure collection' or 'tyre kickers' phenomenon and can be observed at most major exhibitions. Interestingly, the World Wide Web has proved to be a very cost-effective way of handling brochure collectors. One of the major problems faced by companies is to manage cost effectively communications that have a low probability of leading to retention or development of revenue. Even if the communication is solicited, the customer may respond in ways other than those anticipated by the company.

- **Open** – happy to give relevant and truthful information to the enterprise and to update information previously given. This allows the customer database to be updated regularly even if the customer is not a current user. For example, the purchase cycle for furniture is several years. The enterprise needs to keep in touch with the customer in between purchases to monitor life style changes. This improves targeting and conserves resources since inappropriate promotions are reduced.
- **Healthy** – in habits and perhaps even in genes. Heavy drinkers, smokers and risk takers do not stay in the customer pool as long as healthy customers.
- **Safe** – to use the product or service as intended.
- **Responsible** – by observing their rights and responsibilities good customers learn how to work with the company to achieve most mutual benefit. They check warranties, read documents, follow agreed procedures and assume a joint role in making the relationship effective.
- **Reasonable** – a good customer complains only when justified. This feedback is important; after all, disloyal customers do not care, they just buy elsewhere. A sensible company recognizes this and channels such feedback to areas where it can be dealt with quickly.
- **Loyal** – hopefully with good reason. Part of the value in a good customer lies in the fact that the company is as important to them as they are to the company.
- **Advocates** – a good customer is prepared to recommend the service or product to others.
- **Stable** – and predictable. Predictability is very important. Some customers can be good in one domain and bad in another. The stability of this pattern, and perhaps even the stability of groups, allows the organization to trade with them profitably. Although in theory all risks can be dealt with by insurance, when it comes to the balance of risk and value, stability is the key. For example, a high-street retailer setting up a new store may reckon on a particular level of abuse in the form of credit default, shop theft and staff fraud. This is based on its experience with similar stores. As long as each new store displays a similar pattern, standard control procedures can be deployed. If a new store displays very different characteristics of risk and value, new approaches to customer management may need to be adopted.

WHAT IS A BAD CUSTOMER?

It is, of course, possible to make a reasonable living out of customers who cannot be described as good. After all, there are insurance companies that specialize in high risks, finance houses that lend to the imprudent and 'pile 'em high, sell 'em cheap' retailers that sell to the erratic. On the whole, however, bad customers are largely possessed of characteristics that are opposite to those listed above. They also include debtors, switchers, liars and convicted thieves.

Telling black from white is usually quite straightforward. Separating shades of grey is a different matter. For example, a large customer who pushes discounts and service limits outside the policy envelope can be a bad customer, especially for a small and medium-sized supplier. If a company has decided to offer a 48-hour response yet has a customer who regularly demands faster service, extra pressure is put on staff, the normal scheduling of tasks is upset and the company incurs exceptional costs. Similarly, a loyal customer who makes frequent small purchases, with regular demands for service, is also not very desirable.

Bad customers learn to be bad very quickly because the incentive in terms of potential gain is so large. In some cases they also transfer their learning to other individuals or groups. For example, they learn how long they can delay payment by querying statements and invoices and share this information with others. Sometimes, such ripple effects can be predicted. Government benefit frauds are often organized within families and tampering with utility meters often spreads geographically in a local area. In other cases it is harder to anticipate.

PREDICTING GOODNESS AND BADNESS

Being able to predict whether a customer is going to be a bad customer can save a great deal of trouble and expenditure. Rapidly identifying a potentially good customer makes it worthwhile to use all the opportunities for relationship building and maximizes the profit potential. Organizations are therefore increasingly keen to use their customer databases to develop profiles of good and bad customers so that they can categorize new or potential customers before entering into a relationship. This allows the organization to price the relationship in areas such as insurance or banking, change its terms by asking for prepayment like utility companies or simply refuse to go any further. Once the relationship has started, most of these actions are much more difficult. Even the customer may be trapped into continuing the relationship simply because knowledge of their higher level of risk means that no other company will accept them. Customers who make frequent insurance claims, incur bad debts, have criminal records or, less controversially, make several sales enquiries without buying are not popular anywhere.

The problem is that identifying bad customers is not easy. Seriously bad customers are adept at copying good customer behaviour. An easy example is provided from the automotive industry. A fraudster will buy, say, three cars for cash from a dealer to create the appearance of a good buyer. They will then purchase a fourth car on credit and vanish. In the utility sector, similar behaviour is known as 'debt hopping', where customers move from one supplier to another, leaving a string of unpaid accounts. In the UK, the government's regulatory body has proposed licence modifications that protect a regional electricity company's right to block supply switching if the customer has unpaid debts. However, if the customer switches to a second tier supplier (one who is supplying energy through another company's distribution system) they are harder to identify and block. This can create a big debt if the customer is a business. Even a small factory can use a lot of power. In the UK, a debt ageing exercise by a water utility on small businesses in 1998 resulted in over 80 per cent of bills being settled on gold credit cards. The bad news is that the converse can also happen. A really good customer runs into trouble and is immediately treated with suspicion. It might even be because they have a genuine complaint or dispute but they will exhibit many of the signs of a bad customer.

Demarketing refers to the technique of reducing prospective market potential. Energy companies such as those in Germany are sometimes pressured by governments to demarket their products so as to conserve energy. Demarketing is also used to try to prevent contacts with bad customers by, for example, excluding them from marketing campaigns. Customers who are likely to be of low or negative value can be avoided in advance by not soliciting their business in the first place. The UK Claims and Underwriting Exchange (CUE) run by Experian is an example of a database that helps identify bad insurance customers who make fraudulent motor claims. In CUE, nearly 30 companies enter claims data for household buildings, household contents and motor policies.

Insurance fraud in the UK is estimated to cost £650 million a year. It is far from being a victimless crime, as the losses made through fraudulent claims are passed on to everyone else in higher premiums. According to the Association of British Insurers (ABI), 3.7 per cent of every premium paid is the direct result of fraud.

CUE is a massive data warehouse project that aims to spot multiple claims for the same incident. It also allows insurers to check accurately, within seconds, the claims history of anyone applying for a new insurance policy, giving the insurer the option of declining the business or setting a premium that correctly reflects the applicant's history.

Before CUE was established, fraudsters were able to play insurance companies off against each other by either claiming under multiple policies for the same loss or even staging a series of incidents to make multiple claims for the same injury or car crash. They also attempted to fool insurers by using variations on their names, such as reversing first and family names. The record for multiple claims is 75 in one year by a single individual. Personal injury claims have also been received for the loss of three or more legs by the same individual! The CUE database holds the records of 25 million household claims, representing 85 per cent of the total in the UK, and 10 million motor insurance claims, representing 65 per cent of all motor claims. New companies are being added to the database every week, and the aim is to get as close as possible to 100 per cent participation. The database will also be expanded to include travel insurance claims.

Insurance companies send details of every claim they receive to the CUE database over a fixed electronic link, on disks or via dial-up connections. The industry has agreed a set of standards for presentation of data to the database, which is done in batches according to the claims processing procedures of the participating insurer. Other data sources are used, including postal addresses supplied by the Post Office, which help validate the claims data. CUE is based on a large IBM mainframe, but the software that makes it work has been developed especially for the project by Experian, rather than using an off-the-shelf product. This software tries to match as many claims as it can by name, address or vehicle, and any matches are returned to the insurer for further investigation. The Data Protection Act rules mean that only the matching information can be returned to the insurer, so the data returned may only be that there have been multiple claims at a particular address or relating to a particular vehicle. It is up to claims assessors to decide if this information has an impact on the validity of a claim.

USING DATA FOR PREDICTING CUSTOMER RISKS

One of the greatest areas of success for the use of statistics in management is credit scoring. This allows all kinds of financial institutions to assess the creditworthiness of individuals. The assessment is based on an analysis of individual data that is then compared to profiles from within a large, similar data set, to determine whether an individual should be granted credit. Credit scoring can be used to identify individuals whose profiles match those who have failed to make payments on time or who have defaulted on debts (Crook, 1997). Table 11.1 shows how this sort of customer profiling is employed.

None of these strategies can be regarded as especially 'anti-customer'. They are all normal marketing objectives and strategies. However, it is possible to consider the profiling activity as intrusive and unfair. An individual who struggles to cope with difficult circumstances may acquire a bad credit rating, which is then very difficult to redress. A small business whose major customer makes a late payment or a person whose alimony payments are not met may default on debts despite their very best intentions.

The most sophisticated organizations develop predictive models to identify not only whether a previously unknown individual is good or bad and to predict future states but also to predict state changes. Thus the aim is to identify the debt hoppers in advance. This approach is applied not only to individuals but also to the millions of small businesses that account for the majority of economic activity. Notice that sometimes there is a crossover between the business and the individual.

Table 11.1 Applying customer profiling

Objective	Strategies
Increase revenue by increasing the size of the customer base.	Increase the number of good customers recruited. Reduce the number of customers lost or not buying again.
Improve revenue by increasing the lifetime value of each customer.	Keep good customers for longer. Get customers to buy more each time they buy. Get customers to buy more often.
Cut fixed and variable costs.	Cut the direct variable costs by better targeting, cheaper collection efforts. Reduce fixed costs and overheads through reduced debt collection and smaller credit control functions.

After: Saxton (1996)

In many instances both may appear as customers, for example in tax gathering, the utility sector or in the automotive industry.

Of course, this is what small businesses and private traders have always done. A doctor knows which patients will pay, a local shop knows its customers personally and a small manufacturing business knows both its suppliers and customers. Pattern matching and prediction are not new. In some ways recent trends are simply techniques that allow large organizations to recover from the disadvantage of being large. They are now able to do what a small organization can do but on a bigger scale altogether.

Figure 11.1 illustrates how large organizations can use these data for an escalated response to different customers based on growing trust. The table in the figure illustrates their targeting force. The key question is how many customers there are in each segment. The more customers in the cells to the lower-right side of the table, the greater the chance that volume targets can be achieved and entry overheads covered for out of territory operations.

Ethical issues

We are therefore back in the moral maze. In the past, discrimination between individual customers took two main forms: creating different offers so that customers can select different treatment according to their desire to spend money; and vetting for creditworthiness, fraud and previous payment history so as to exclude certain customers because of their predicted likely costs.

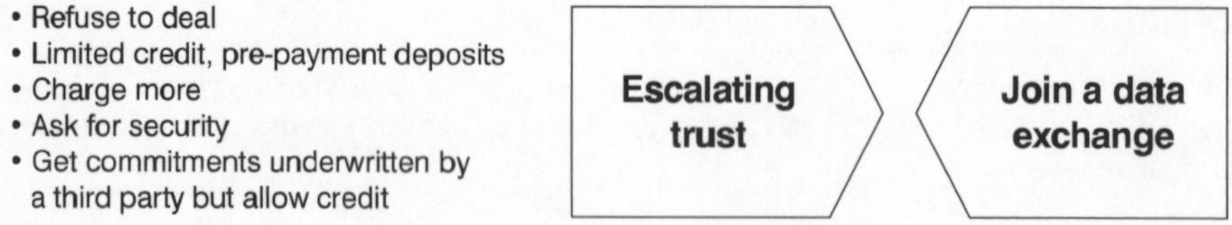

• Refuse to deal
• Limited credit, pre-payment deposits
• Charge more
• Ask for security
• Get commitments underwritten by a third party but allow credit

Escalating trust / **Join a data exchange**

		'Moral' Risk				
		High	Quite High	Medium	Quite Low	Low
Usage	Low	✗✗	✗	✓	✓✓✓	✓✓✓
	Medium	✗✗✗	✗✗	✗	✓✓	✓✓✓
	High	✗✗✗✗	✗✗✗	✗✗	✓	✓✓✓✓

Figure 11.1 Strategies for managing bad customers

Relationship marketing purports to take discrimination between customers to the ultimate extreme, according to *forecast* individual customer profitability. Some managers believe that one of the principles of their business is to limit what they see as discrimination, while others are frightened of using politically sensitive indicators such as genetic, ethnic or racial. There is no doubt that this is a legal minefield. In some cultures, late payment of debts is considered normal but when immigrant groups display these characteristics elsewhere and suffer debtor exclusion, they sometimes associate this with unfair racial discrimination.

For purely business reasons, companies cannot afford to ignore any available data. Otherwise they will be subject to cherry picking of their 'good' customers by the competition, while bad customers stay with companies where data and processes are weak at spotting them early enough. This is known as adverse selection. Moreover, some suppliers are unable to choose customers. For example, public utilities and retailers must normally do business with any customer, no matter how problematic or litigious. The issue is not simply one of what customers can do in principle. Rather, it is a question of which customers are most encouraged to buy. By branding, marketing communications, store layout, pricing, product range and all the other elements of the marketing mix, customers can be encouraged to choose themselves. For example, retail customers requiring a very close relationship may understand from the layout and staffing of a self-service store, along with the absence of any loyalty or storecard scheme, that the company does not encourage close customer relationships. A store with valet parking, a concierge and name-badged personnel is clearly at the opposite extreme.

Case example: Johnson & Johnson

Probably the company best known for its ethical stance is the giant US pharmaceutical company, Johnson & Johnson. The company's credo, which dates back to 1943, was based on the philosophy of one of its founders, General Robert Wood Johnson, who guided the company from a small, family owned firm to a worldwide enterprise. Regarded as an inspirational and far-sighted document when it was first published, it has guided the company's actions ever since and has been sorely tested on more than one occasion. However, the company has never wavered in seeking to adhere to its credo of putting customers first, then employees before the community and stockholders and it has never been seen to put commercial considerations ahead of its corporate philosophy. Over the years, the language of the credo has been updated and new areas recognizing the environment and the balance between work and family have been added. In the context of data ethics, it is worth citing this section of the company's philosophy:

> We are responsible to the communities in which we live and work and to the world community as well. We must be good citizens – support good works and charities and bear our fair share of taxes. We must encourage civic improvements and better health and education. We must maintain in good order the property we are privileged to use, protecting the environment and natural resources.

A useful 10-point guide to developing a privacy policy can be found in Peppers and Rogers (1999).

Social and political issues

It is not surprising that the data usage practices of large organizations have attracted the attention of governments, social scientists, moral philosophers and others concerned with the ethics of organizational behaviour. They raise three main questions. How can the organization achieve its objectives by using customer data? What are the consequences of doing this? Are there any public policy issues which should cause governments to constrain the use of such data?

Some inconsistency is emerging in practice. For example, genetic data may not be used in the health insurance industry on the grounds that certain adverse medical conditions that are genetically correlated are also ethnically correlated. An ethnic bias is politically unacceptable. However, this runs counter to accepted practice in other parts of the financial services industry such as motor insurance, small business operation and individual banking. A person prone to blackouts may find it more difficult to get motor insurance. In these areas it is also common practice to note the bias in certain areas of risk. These are then used to determine customer recruitment policies, individual customer pricing and risk management. While it may be politically incorrect to say so, single parent families in general (at the statistical level) have a harder time of meeting their financial commitments than two-income households.

Legal issues

One of the major problems that companies have to contend with is lack of clarity in the law. This is partly because the laws on data protection are, like most laws, subject to interpretation. This has led to a need for clarification through legal advice. In the UK, Gaskill (1996) noted that the Data Protection Registrar attempted to extend the reach of the Data Protection Act to include the duty of fairness beyond the collector of the data to anyone who uses it. This was based on guidance notes to industries such as financial services, credit referencing and mail order. It should also be noted that in some countries such data protection laws refer to any form of data holding, on paper or electronically. Nowhere are these sensitivities more easily illustrated than by the storm that erupted with the release of Intel's Pentium III processor in 1999.

Case example: the Pentium III Processor and privacy

In order to foster electronic commerce by facilitating the recognition of a unique electronic signature, Intel burned an identification number into each of its new Pentium III processors released in 1999. The ID number could be turned off, but left on it would identify each computer in a secure way. Connected to the Internet, or indeed to any other network, the computer containing the processor could be instantly identified. While this would enable the computer (if not the user of the PC) to be recognized and located, not least to reduce a great deal of computer theft, it caused the kind of furore usually associated with thought police.

Strangely enough, the unique identification of computers had been possible for several years. Each Network Interface Card (NIC) on a PC has a unique address (a hexadecimal number) which can be read by software. As the debate acquired more heat (and less light) it emerged that Microsoft had been reading this number and including it in their Office 97 files. Indeed, any Word, Excel or PowerPoint document would reveal the number. All that had to be done was to load any of these files into a text editor such as Notepad and search for the text _PID_GUID. Shortly after, between curly brackets { } the unique identifier would be displayed. Thus each time the computer was attached to a network, either within a company or on the Internet, that particular machine, its use and behaviour, could be tracked.

Until the release of the Pentium III, most people were unaware of this fact and, while Microsoft subsequently offered to release a software patch to prevent the number being read, no one really knows how much software from other companies was also using that number.

In some industries, the collection of data from customers via electronic communication is becoming more common. This has led to the need for clarification of the legal position. Many Data Protection Acts have separate principles concerning how data is obtained and used, a separation that is hard to maintain in many situations. For example, decisions are sometimes made almost instantly in call centres where the customer might be connected using IP (Internet Protocol) telephony.

During e-commerce transactions, personal consumer information may be harvested and referred immediately to third parties without the consumer being aware of the implications of clicking on certain buttons. This is of particular concern to the data protection authorities. Many Internet sites and call centre software use an 'opt-in' button to ensure compliance with data protection legislation although consumers are often unaware of what will happen when they click this button (Chang, 1998). Extensive data is often gathered with no clear indication as to how it will be used. Similar issues have been raised in the context of smart cards, where there is a debate about who should own the smart card and the data on it. The smart card reveals the customer's purchasing habits.

Part of the problem is that the United States, unlike Europe, does not have a data privacy law. You might think that Internet entrepreneurs would therefore adopt sound policies on data privacy and promote this fact on their sites. You would be wrong.

There are, of course, honourable exceptions. Firefly Network has defined an approach to data privacy that is consciously based on European principles. For instance, it precludes disclosure without informed consent. Indeed, the Firefly Open Passport requires specific consents from the data subjects. Since Microsoft acquired Firefly, this approach is likely to become standard. By mid-1999, IBM had thrown its weight behind improved privacy standards to encourage confidence in e-commerce. It implemented a privacy policy that holds to the view that customers visiting a Web site should have easy access to that company's privacy policy, should be told clearly what information is being collected and how it will be used, and should have a choice whether to provide any information.

There are also a number of consortia, such as TRUSTe, BBBOnline and the Online Privacy Alliance, which have defined codes of practice for data privacy. Sites complying with these codes (and paying a modest registration fee) display a distinctive symbol and are subject to independent audit. However, by the end of 1998, only about 75 firms had committed to TRUSTe, for example, and it would seem that relying on the benefits of privacy to encourage registration will produce no more than 5 per cent compliance. Clearly, then, the United States needs a privacy law. Good regulation can be a benefit to business. Credit cards did not become really popular until the government limited the financial forfeiture following loss of a card to $50. Rapid growth followed but the need for similar legislation for e-commerce is not accepted by the US government, which has asked the IT industry to develop a system of self-regulation.

Economic issues

Being able to use individual customer data clearly provides great benefits for companies. These include lower risk, increased ability to target higher value customers and a reduction in certain communication costs. It is also clear that data works as both a barrier to entry and a facilitator of entry. Companies that have better data about customers can define offers that are more suitable for these customers and target them more cost effectively. The growth of the data provision industry has been a big factor here. A company that rents lists wisely, and has sound mechanisms for determining which lists have produced good results, can break into markets more easily than if they had to use techniques that encouraged customers to identify themselves ('hand raising'). The Internet and Digital Interactive TV may reduce the advantages of rented lists by making hand raising easier.

Data sharing can also be used as a barrier to entry such as in airline alliances or as a way of reducing barriers to competition. Thus retailers may open their loyalty card databases to providers of financial services, energy and telecommunications. Knowing who the good and bad customers are means that companies whose processes are designed to handle these kinds of data can cross industry frontiers more easily.

Their skills are in customer management. All they need to make money in a new sector is a brand and some customer data.

The end result can be a redesigned value chain, as companies desert conventional distribution channels and choose distribution partners because of their customer knowledge. Other effects include the confident outsourcing of a variety of customer facing activities. The widespread availability of customer data enables the identity and status of individuals to be checked more easily, so some parts of the process of customer recruitment, retention and development can be outsourced. A worrying aspect of this is that information on 'bad' customers can also be easily shared in this way. While this facilitates bad customer avoidance more securely, a customer in legitimate dispute with one supplier might well be avoided by other suppliers without good cause.

There are also international effects. Companies wishing to enter new overseas markets are as interested in acquiring customer databases as they are the physical assets and skills of business. The international ramifications of this kind of data exchange are very significant. Some rather poor data protection legislation was hurried into existence in the UK in 1984 when it was realized that without such legislation, the UK could be excluded from certain kinds of cross border data transfers, a major competitive disadvantage. This was strengthened and extended by the Data Protection Act of 1998, which incidentally also provided for government rights of access to privately held personal data (Section 29).

MANAGING THE RISK

One of the principal issues at play is the balance between risk and customer value. Companies are increasingly focusing on the idea of a customer portfolio rather than just seeing their markets as a set of revenues deriving from product sales. This, in turn, has increased the importance of relationship marketing since issues of customer recruitment and retention come to the fore. The ideal is to develop a portfolio of customers of good value and minimal risk. Unfortunately, the two criteria are sometimes inversely related. The insurance industry is aware that customers with large houses are more likely to be burgled. Indeed, those with more at risk may even be more tempted to make fraudulent declarations in order to obtain insurance coverage at lower prices.

THE PORTFOLIO APPROACH

In the commercial sector, high value customers are not simply those who make large purchases. High value is a net outcome over perhaps several years of buying behaviour and management costs. Going back to our example of banking, the customer who keeps a small positive balance, uses branch services frequently, complains periodically and never buys any additional services may be of net negative value. However, that person can be transformed if they can be persuaded to use plastic rather than the branch and to pay some charges. Goodness is therefore partly a function of what the organization does and is not entirely in the hands of the individual. More broadly, the policy framework, within which the relationship with the customer is managed, and the terms of the offer supplied by the organization, influence customer quality.

SHARING DATA

According to the proverb, a problem shared is supposed to be a problem halved. In marketing, the sharing of data has always been a little problematic. Sharing data about market strengths can be of major benefit to all suppliers. Sharing data about customers is usually somewhat fraught, especially where it is unwelcome. In the early 1990s, Virgin Atlantic brought a successful action against British Airways when they discovered that BA were 'sharing' data about passengers through access to their joint reservation system.

The insurance industry is keen to share data about bad customers but less certain to share data about good customers. Yet financial and other profiling techniques produce common results both in this and other markets. This form of sharing is indirect and merely confirms that a particular profiling technique or set of data was useful in a targeting exercise. Has the insurance industry made an arbitrary decision in refusing to share customer data? If market survey data were made available about loyal (non-switching) customers, would the original supplier of such data be trampled in the rush or quickly made bankrupt? Customers who are known switchers might be avoided by some companies but targeted by others, confident that they had the price/service combination to make the customer loyal. Loyal customers might be avoided because there would be little perceived chance of switching them. CUE, mentioned earlier, is a good example of a data exchange.

The earliest writer to consider the behaviour of firms and customers in competitive markets was probably Antoine Augustin Cournot. A French mathematician, Cournot wrote a book in 1838 entitled *Recherches sur les Principes Mathématiques de la Théorie de Richesses* (Research into the Mathematical Principles of the Theory of Wealth). The book was concerned with the problem of a fixed number of firms trying to choose output levels in order to maximize profit. Cournot's work has inspired several researchers in modern times, where the general theoretical approach is known as game theory. For those interested in the mathematics of these models, a good start might be made by consulting Harsanyi (1967) or for those with less confidence in their mathematics, Rasmusen (1990).

This question of data sharing raises all the issues characteristic of game theory. In such a game, we have a situation characterized by non-co-operation (suppliers are not interested in maximizing their joint profits), incomplete information (about the payoffs sought by other players) and the potential to modify strategy between moves. A very complex game environment to which we cannot hope to do justice here. However, Table 11.2 seeks to represent this game in a simplified form. The table describes a situation in which companies pool data based on a propensity for customers to be loyal or to switch.

It appears that the balance of advantage lies in sharing unless one company is confident that its data set is better than that of the sharing group. This company would still have an advantage to go it alone.

Table 11.2 A game theoretic approach to sharing customer data

		THE COMPETITION		
		All Share Data	Some Share Data	None Share Data
YOUR COMPANY	Share Data	The advantage goes to the company that is best at using information for customer management. Other companies suffer.	The advantage of sharing goes only to a few companies.	The advantage goes to the company that is best at using the classic marketing mix.
	Not Share Data	Competitors have two options: avoid the cost of targeting difficult customers; or develop services that suit these customers best and may even change these customers' behaviour.	Only a few competitors gain an advantage.	All suppliers suffer from customers with a high switching propensity.

However, it seems that the key element of the decision is not to do with the principle of sharing but to do with an assessment of competitive strengths. There are also other factors, such as marketing strategy, which need to be taken into account but the table provides an initial basis for decision making. Interestingly, the essence of a successful application of game theory is to repeat games. In this particular game, there is no killer solution or end-game that can be created by breaking trust.

The nature of shared data

It is not just current data that must be shared. The history of customer behaviour is important too. Suppliers with larger numbers of customers, more complete data sets or a longer data history have an advantage here and therefore may not be prepared to share. The National House Building Council (NHBC) in the UK illustrates the point. NHBC is an insurer of major building repairs. They only cover costs for the first few years, usually 10. However, a need for substantial repairs could arise many years after buildings are first constructed. NHBC can eventually inspect and match all claim types to changes in building techniques over a very long period. In these circumstances, a new entrant, with no access to historical data, would find it hard to compete successfully. Price matching is only possible if competitive quotes are visible or where price structures are simple. This is not true in most insurance situations, where price quotations are usually individual and offered direct to the customer. Without a substantial data set, a new company could find its claims pattern to be much higher than expected, especially if its risk portfolio is very different from its competitors'. A similar situation arises in motor insurance, where personal injury claims sometimes occur a long time after an incident.

If those who benefit from openness get together, does this force those who benefit from isolation to join? Of course, the answer depends partly on their initial market share and the economics of information. On balance, sharing information and techniques about customers may help them to cut marketing costs.

MANAGING THE RISK/VALUE PORTFOLIO

Perfect predictions of risk and value are beyond the state of the art. This is one reason why companies balance their approach by accepting customers of varying risk and value. The other reason is that in most markets there are simply not enough 'good' customers for every supplier, if economies of scale are to be maintained. Companies need to be of a certain minimum size to balance risk and value. Too small a customer base reduces the possibility of understanding patterns, of absorbing risks, of obtaining reasonable terms for laying off risk (on third parties) and of supplying value economically.

The customer portfolio management approach aims to acquire and retain particular numbers of customers with different risk and value characteristics. However, the correlation between risk and value is not random. As we have observed, a risky customer, who is undetected by a company, has a strong incentive to develop a high gross value relationship with that company. They can then turn this to their advantage by, for example, demanding further products or services against the implicit threat of defaulting on a large debt if they do not receive additional supplies.

This places an extra burden upon companies to identify the characteristics of customers who set out to defeat the risk/value selection criteria. The phenomenon is most easily illustrated by the example of social security frauds. Here, the fraudulent customer would nominate apparently 'respectable' people to develop a high value relationship. The leaders of the conspiracy keep well in the background and hire plausible cases to register for a variety of benefits in ways that are hard to detect.

On the other hand, valuable customers may help recruit further valuable customers who have otherwise been unidentifiable to companies. Member-get-member programmes are among the most successful direct marketing techniques, implying that companies find it harder than existing members to find similar high value members. The reasons for this may include:

- The recruited customers do not share the normal characteristics of valuable customers.
- The normal characteristics of valuable customers are of the type that cannot be detected using available data, ie the customers are well hidden.
- The recruited customers share the characteristics of existing valuable customers but are unresponsive to the current recruitment techniques.

DEALING WITH COMPLAINTS

We have already noted that making a complaint does not turn someone into a bad customer. On the contrary, the response mechanisms for handling complaints are of great importance for nurturing good customers. Too often, complaints are regarded as a negative aspect of a relationship. Many employees view the job of fielding customer complaints as arduous. They are also aware that there is a tendency in many companies to shoot the bearer of bad news. If this happens, they will keep complaints to themselves. Customers will also stop complaining because nothing happens and they will just take their business elsewhere. What needs to be remembered is that it is more likely to be loyal customers who complain. There are also delays between a decline in service levels and customer desertions and between service improvements and the following new recruitment. Effective complaint handling is therefore an important aspect of managing good customers. Michelsen (1999) offers five main guidelines for effective complaint management to build customer loyalty.

1. Do not think of customer contacts in one dimension

One of the least understood realities about customers is that they generally do not complain when there is a problem with product or service. In most cases, if a customer is dissatisfied with a product or service, they simply do not purchase again. Very high proportions of dissatisfied customers do not complain. Figures as high as 96 per cent have been cited. However, although they may not complain, over 60 per cent of these silent dissatisfied customers will not buy again. Around 15 per cent of all customers who switch brands do so because a complaint was not handled to their satisfaction. Sometimes a complaint can be interpreted as a demand for an extended product or service. This might be because the terms of the original offer were not made clear but a complaint might also be another selling opportunity. Try to encourage feedback from customers to discover exactly what they are thinking. Encourage feedback and be positive. Be specific without making the customer uncomfortable. Ensure that the customer understands the company's intention to fix the problem rather than assign blame.

2. Is the complaint justified?

After receiving a complaint, the first thing to discover is whether the complaint is justified. If the complaint is justified, offer to solve the problem. Within reasonable bounds, solving a problem, even at a loss, will pay valuable rewards if a good customer is retained. If the basis of the complaint is a misunderstanding of what was expected then a useful insight into the marketing communications and contact management has been obtained.

3. Consider the context

It is important to consider who and when. While you can please all of the people some of the time, and some of the people all of the time, you cannot please all of the people all of the time. 'Who' is also relevant in terms of the power position of the complainant. Can they affect this or future sales? Some care is needed here. Just because a complainer is not responsible for purchasing, they may well influence future purchases. Drivers of company-owned cars do not place the order but they do influence model choice.

The timing of the complaint may be critical in relation to the purchasing cycle. Contesting a warranty claim at the end of a three year purchase agreement when a replacement choice is expected is not smart. On the other hand, determine priorities. If the complainer is a relative nobody (a potentially bad customer) then delegate handling or reschedule for a less busy time.

4. Address the problem immediately

Once the nature of a complaint is understood, look into it immediately. Nobody likes to feel that his or her problem is being ignored. On the other hand, if a complaint is going to take time to solve, let the customer know when they can expect a resolution. Complaints should be viewed as invitations for more business. This means that complaints should be channelled quickly to parts of the enterprise that can offer a rapid response.

5. Observe and report

A complaint is a crucial opportunity to build and strengthen the customer relationship. Everyone knows that it takes skill and understanding to solve a problem. Even if the resolution is not in the customer's favour, their attitude to the company will be improved if someone has clearly invested time in solving a problem and letting them know that they did their best.

When a customer takes the time and trouble to complain, it should be considered as a platform for relationship building. When a customer extends that invitation, the company that recognizes an opportunity to extend good service is likely to maintain the customer relationship for a longer period.

THE CUSTOMER PERSPECTIVE

There have been several studies of how consumers react to database marketing. In a study of 500 UK consumers, Evans *et al* (1996) showed that direct mail was fairly successful in that many consumers respond to it. However, a high proportion of customers view the extent to which they receive targeted direct mail as excessive. Around half or more of the respondents felt that direct mail invaded privacy. It also created worries about how the sender knew about them and who else might get their details. Over 40 per cent did not agree that direct mail was ethical, while over 70 per cent did not believe that it was ethical for companies to sell lists. All these proportions increased with age. The survey showed that women were slightly more worried than men about data issues. Concern is also class related with those in lower SEGs being more worried than those of higher social class. Evans also cites US studies by Schroeder (1992) and European studies by Woudhuysen (1994), which show similar results. The major contributors to perceptions of privacy invasion seem to be:

- perception of excessive mailings;
- concern about how 'they' know about me;
- lack of informative value;
- age;
- the ethics of direct mail;
- the amount of direct mail.

To balance these concerns is a demonstrable willingness on the part of consumers to buy from direct channels, particularly in financial services. Paradoxically, it is in these very transactions that the customer is required to share the largest amount of personal data.

Perhaps this is at the root of the problem. Consumers provide more personal data that is then used in cross-selling and retention activity by financial services companies. The concerns being expressed may therefore be the other side of the coin of increased receptiveness to direct approaches. The industry forces at work are illustrated by the utility sector. These effects are echoed in the airline, automotive, insurance and telecommunications industries.

Case example: the strange world of sewage

What is the largest area of economic activity in the United States, or, for that matter, most large economies outside the former Soviet Bloc? If pressed to provide an answer, perhaps you might offer suggestions along the lines of automotive manufacture, pharmaceuticals, financial services or healthcare. At over $320 billion in 1998, the answer would actually be the utility industries, electricity, gas and water (including sewage disposal!).

Utility industries worldwide moved through a period of enormous transition at the end of the twentieth century. Providers of commodity products with limited differentiation, weak branding and restricted added value, utility companies in many countries faced the prospect of competition for the first time in decades, the first time ever in some cases, as deregulation or privatization were introduced. Taking the lead in this structural change were the UK, the Nordic countries, California and the New England States in north-eastern United States. However, some 30 or so other countries were preparing to transform their utility markets at this time.

In the short term, political and organizational change issues tended to occupy a great deal of senior management resource. Nevertheless, some significant strategic issues emerged. The forces to which the utility industries were responding also affected many other industries. Essentially, these can be categorized in four ways.

Structural change

In monopoly or regulated conditions, one company often did everything from generation to supply. In order to create a market, governments created conditions in which generation, transmission, distribution and final supply were the province of separate companies. Sometimes, several companies in different regions of the country handled each of these areas.

Unbundling

Unbundling refers to the separation of a product or service into its component parts, principally to isolate the core product or service from value added elements. This has been referred to as the 'McDonaldization' of an industry and basically is a response to the demand for increasing consumer choice. The reference to McDonald's is based on the choice represented by the ability to take a low service, no-frills meal as opposed to the value added service offering in a conventional table-service restaurant. In the case of utilities, unbundling is based on the separation of the commodity from commodity services. The implications of this in terms of consumer choice are profound.

Imagine the effect of a 'smart' domestic utility system. This system will pick up weather forecast information from a radio signal and automatically adjust the house's climate control system accordingly. In addition, since the system will use a smart controller, it will shop around for the cheapest source of energy to power the system at the time it is needed. This energy may have been generated in another country, it may have been purchased on the spot market by a trader and sold on by a second tier distributor. Quite a long way from a situation where the whole of the value chain was controlled and regulated by a monopoly (state) supplier.

Convergence

Convergence may sound like the opposite of unbundling but it refers to a much more complex set of forces and processes. It includes issues such as virtuality, e-commerce, knowledge management, supply chain management, enterprise resource planning and business intelligence. Conceivably, the Internet phenomenon behind all these factors was still at a very early stage at the beginning of the twenty-first century. For example, if it were assumed that 250 million of the world's population were currently connected to the Internet then that actually represents only 0.04 per cent of the world's total population, or 0 per cent rounded to the nearest integer. Growth potential is therefore substantial. Real telephony has yet to come on stream (that is, at the same quality as its counterpart device). Real (high-quality) video is still some distance away, despite the use of techniques such as video streaming.

The hardest mile for the Internet to travel is the last mile, into people's homes. At the moment, people take their Internet connections through a PC but it seems plausible to imagine that in the future this will become a minority Internet device. People will want their Internet connections in the most convenient format for the current application. They might want it through their digital TV, their mobile phone, telephone, work pad, information kiosk, laptop or even their radio. The information display will be automatically reformatted according to the reception device. How will it get there? It does not seem very convenient to have dozens of alternative cable and communication links into each and every home. Even satellite dishes don't look too pretty. In fact, the communication options are considerable. There are several ways of getting data and information into and out of your home: satellite broadcast, telephone cable, TV cable, radio broadcast, TV broadcast and, of course, the power grid.

Your utility provider might therefore become your Internet Service Provider (ISP). Indeed, they might also provide a number of value added services through this connection so that, for example, real time appliance monitoring or continuous usage assessment are available, along with an electronic bill.

Affiliation

This refers to activities such as customer management, field sales force management, billing, outsourcing, partnering, networking and strategic alliances. In the same way that British Airways outsourced more or less everything except customer management and the logistics of aircraft movement, there is no particular reason why neighbourhood utility companies should struggle with, for example, their own call centre. Indeed, as utilities such as Scottish Power, RWE and Electricité de France become more international in scope, they may well outsource their customer helplines to, say, Edesa in Spain, where labour costs are currently lower.

The new world of competition in the utility industries

Once the problem of avoiding bad debtors is sorted out, utilities have four other major targeting needs.

The *prospect pool*, in which a utility identifies clearly what criteria define a good target customer – usually on another utility's territory – and then contracts to an outside agency to supply it with good prospects. In some markets, customers will be relatively likely to switch in the early years of deregulation and then the market will settle down. This means that it will be very important to catch as many customers in the first year as possible. Hence the desire of all the utilities to go flat out for volume in that first year, though it is worth noting that the easiest customers to attract are those who are least loyal and possibly 'bad'.

Using the customer database, the next priority is the *retention pool*. This aims to identify customers who are likely to leave, using profiling and data mining techniques then signalling what sort of actions would be appropriate to help retention. For example, some customers might be retained by a simple telephone call or letter just to remind them that they have been 'remembered'.

The third group is the *'lock-in' pool*. This refers to customers who would be prepared to lock themselves into a supply contract above the statutory period customers. It represents a form of commitment marketing and may involve some contribution in exchange for benefit, in other words a lower price for a longer contract. Regulatory authorities, of course, discourage such moves immediately before deregulation.

Finally, there is the *business-to-residential crossover pool*. Utilities have many small and medium sized businesses on their database where the directors are also higher domestic consumers. The crossover is normally in both directions for smaller businesses, in the sense that a customer at risk for the business use might be about the same value as the customer at risk as a residential user. In medium sized businesses, the key need is to identify the director at home and work on acquisition or retention strategies for the business account.

Even though they are in fierce competition, the new utility companies probably need to exchange information on bad debtors as a top priority simply because of the extent of financial exposure. This needs to be followed quickly by processes to ensure that any debt transfers work properly.

ORGANIZATIONAL AND BUSINESS CUSTOMER MANAGEMENT STRATEGIES

DATA STRATEGY – ACQUISITION, DEVELOPMENT AND MAINTENANCE

With the ever increasing power of information technology, it is easy to overestimate the ability of companies to target or avoid individual customers or groups of customers based on their data characteristics. For example, Fletcher, Wright and Desai (1996) found that:

> Computing resources are limited and controls placed on resources are likely to be high. Further, current information is poor and the use to which it is put is limited. Many opportunities for enhancing information are being lost. Information held is limited and its potential value for enhancing customer profiling, cross-selling and decision-making overlooked.

They ascribe this mainly to the operations focus adopted by financial services companies, as opposed to a customer focus. There is no shortage of advice purporting to guide companies wishing to design their customer marketing databases. However, these sometimes fail to take into account three key factors:

- the costs of creating high quality databases weighed against the benefits;
- the systems and organizational issues involved in sourcing data from many different internal databases;
- the procedures required to maintain data once it has been added to the database.

Long, Angold and Hogg (1998) carried out a study using the framework of the British Data Protection Act to investigate the use of consumer data for relationship marketing purposes. They focused on service and retailing companies, asking them for copies of details held about themselves. Surprisingly, the number of companies claiming they held no data rose considerably in comparison with a study the authors carried out five years previously. However, they also found that the number of registrations of customer information had risen in many cases. This clearly adds to the costs incurred by companies in disclosing information to consumers. It may account for a rise in the number of companies charging for data transcripts (as they are entitled to do), as well as in the number of companies failing to reply within the prescribed 40 days.

Companies are increasingly adding data from a variety of sources to their databases. For example, in the UK, the major data providers use information gathered from a variety of sources such as household shopping questionnaires, product guarantees and direct marketing responses. This is supplemented by data from the Electoral Roll, credit referencing data such as County Court Judgements and area based information from the census. Industry specific profiling systems have also been constructed, often using data from specially commissioned surveys, to help companies estimate with even greater accuracy the likelihood that a customer will buy a product (Berry and Leventhal, 1996). Advanced data mining methods can then be used to look for new patterns of behaviour among consumers.

Discussing what companies and governments should do with all this 'factual' information implies that the collection and analysis is a straightforward task. In fact, the experience of most companies (and governments) is that customer data strategy and management is a very difficult area. It often consumes enormous resources yet produces poor results in terms of actionable information at the point of decision. Many organizations actually have no clear customer data strategy. Indeed, most do not have a clear customer management strategy. Nor do they have stable processes to manage customer recruitment, retention and development.

This means that the information they need to manage good and bad customers grows organically. It is spread over many different databases that are often incompatible with each other and therefore requires significant efforts in the form of data warehousing to integrate them into one analysable data set. Making this work at the point of contact with the customer, or the point of decision about how to manage the customer, is a significant extra task. Few businesses have the luxury of defining their customer data requirements from the beginning. Even then, fine intentions in terms of a clear data strategy are eroded as they move into new markets or new products. To support new operations, additional databases are set up and before long they are in the same position as established businesses with large legacy systems.

Acquiring and storing data is one thing, developing it is another. As customers' needs and behaviour change and marketing strategies respond, new data sets are required. This merely allows the enterprise to manage customers as well as they were being managed before. Each data set collected will therefore need to be developed dynamically. Some data will cease to be relevant, other data will need to be added. This may sometimes mean going back over old ground with customers. For example, a company holding householder data may need to collect names of children if it decides to extend its services on a family-wide basis. Quite possibly, such data were not collected when the customer was first recruited or equally possibly it needs to be refreshed (checked).

Refreshing data is also a major task for a data set of any size. Customers do not stand still, they change. Data about them needs to be maintained. Not only do their addresses and family composition change but so does their risk level, health and creditworthiness. Data management strategies are therefore crucial to policies in relation to good and bad customers.

ACCEPTABLE EXPOSURE VERSUS MISSED OPPORTUNITIES

Theoretically, the more customer information a company has, the more accurately it can assess goodness or badness and the more accurately it can predict future values. The decisions to be made range from simple binary choice, such as whether or not to offer a specific product to a specific customer, through to more complex decisions. These include which product to offer to different customers and the terms of the offer. However, it is clear that data is subject to the law of diminishing returns, both for collection and maintenance.

In some cases, the customer risk for each is high, relative to the profit. This applies in consumer markets like general insurance, credit cards and the distribution of power supplies. In business-to-business markets, it also applies in any area where customers are given extended credit or where the costs of managing the customer are incurred some way ahead of the customer's response in terms of real revenue. In these cases, the returns from more accurate information are high so that companies can set very tight exposure limits. More can therefore be invested in data collection and maintenance.

Similarly, if valuable customers are relatively rare, the returns associated with good predictive data that indicates likely future value are also high. However, to establish how much data needs to be collected and maintained, companies need to have some estimate of the link between the costs and the benefits not only overall but also for each data item. Established direct marketing companies with long histories of customer management can usually estimate the return from using particular sets of data. Most other companies simply do not have a stable enough data set and analytical framework to make this decision sensibly.

In many cases, a company's knowledge about the customer will only become apparent after customer acquisition. This is the 'getting to know' stage. At this point the customer's pattern of transactions, payments, complaints and queries becomes clear. Ideally, systems need to be established to relate the cost of information to the benefits of being able to manage good and bad customers at the first point of contact.

SUMMARY

- Do you have a working definition of good and bad customers, recognizing that most customers are a mix of good and bad attributes?
- Are your definitions based on hard evidence, not simple prejudice?
- Are these definitions reviewed regularly?
- Do your operating procedures help 'train' your customers, rewarding good behaviour and discouraging bad?
- Have you analysed your customer database to determine any predictive characteristics for good and bad customers?
- Do you have a risk scoring system? For example, can your staff easily identify good customers from within your customer database and understand what makes them 'good'?
- Are your definitions available to staff at the moment of truth (the point of first customer contact)? Remember that the cost of demarketing is higher once you have entered into a relationship.
- Are you confident that your demarketing policies will deter only potentially bad customers?
- Are your strategies for dealing with bad customers clearly communicated?
- Does your company have a declared ethical stance that managers can use as a guide in their dealings with customers, employees, the environment and stockholders?
- Do you have a data privacy policy that is easily accessible to customers?
- Do you have procedures to ensure compliance with any national or trans-national data protection legislation (such as the EU Data Privacy Directive)?

- Have you assessed formally the possible financial and relationship benefits from participating in a data exchange?
- The decision on how much to spend on data management must be made in relation to the risk of exposure to bad customers. Have you assessed the costs of risk management in relation to possible revenue gains?
- Do you have a clearly communicated policy for dealing with negative feedback? What criteria are used to distinguish a justified complaint from an attempt to avoid payment?
- Is customer feedback taken to a rapid action point within the company? Are complaint responses monitored for sales opportunities and consequent satisfaction and loyalty changes?
- Do you know how your customers feel about the nature and frequency of contacts from your company?
- To what extent are you confident that you have the systems in place to analyse and action all the customer data you are holding? Is data complexity kept under constant review?
- Can you relate the cost of information held to the benefits of being able to manage good and bad customers?

12

Justifying the CRM investment

DELIVERING CUSTOMER VALUE THROUGH RELATIONSHIP MARKETING

During the late 1990s American Airlines ran a striking advertising campaign. The advert pictured a 747 in front of which was a huge crowd of people. The uniforms in the photo showed more or less everyone who could have contact with the plane: flight crew, cabin crew, maintenance people, caterers, baggage handlers, loaders, drivers, cleaners, tarmac crew, reservations and so on. The caption read, "Who pictured can pull the plane?"; in other words, who could stop it from flying? The answer given was, "Anyone can." The message to customers stressed the importance placed by the airline on a shared commitment to quality. The image is striking. Any missing ingredient can cause what a computer will describe blandly as a 'fatal error'. A missing pinch of salt can spoil a great dish.

Unfortunately, the message still has some way to go. In 1999, a survey by consultants KPMG (Strategy, 1999) revealed that only 16 per cent of companies in their sample used customer information fully. Forty-three per cent of companies admitted that they did not understand the causes of customer defection, and of those who claimed they did, 22 per cent were unable to say how they knew! Yet 83 per cent of companies

323

put customer retention as their primary marketing objective. In another survey at around the same time by the Chartered Institute of Bankers in the UK (Gandy, 1999), a similar, confirmatory picture emerges. Eighty-four per cent of bankers recognized customer relationship marketing technologies as key competitive differentiators, but 94 per cent thought that their investment in past technologies such as simple customer databases had not created the customer focus required. Huge problems were recognized across the sector in terms of functional integration, acquisition, retention, winback and contact management, all seen as key determinants of future organic growth.

Just having a customer database does not deliver a relationship marketing approach. Just having an e-mail system does not mean you are wired for e-commerce. Count up your e-mails. How many originate from *inside* the company? If the proportion comes to more than 50 per cent, ask yourself where the emphasis of your effort is being spent: is it internally focused or externally focused? CRM initiatives are expensive, in terms of the time, money and sheer organizational effort that has to go into producing results. It is therefore essential that they deliver value in return for this huge investment.

Value is defined here in its broadest sense of stakeholder or owner value. For companies owned by stockholders, value is represented by share value. For companies owned by customers (mutual companies or co-operatives), value is usually represented by customer dividends or bonuses. For companies owned by employees (co-operatives), value is usually represented by bonuses paid on earnings. For publicly owned organizations, value is usually represented by a mixture of cost of provision and quality of service. For charities, value is represented by a similar mixture, with the services received by beneficiaries of charities being important.

Behind some of these forms of value lies value to customers. Value to customers is usually measured in terms of the appropriateness of what they receive (benefits) relative to what they have to pay – either directly or indirectly (eg user costs, taxation). In most cases, stakeholder value and customer value are closely related, though the relationship between the two can diverge in the short run for all sorts of reasons, such as government intervention, lack of competition, or customer inertia. However, in the long run the two tend to go in the same direction. Companies that deliver value to their customers tend to prosper, produce reasonable returns for their stakeholders, and in consequence provide secure and rewarding places for people to work. This means that enhancing customer value is critical for most organizations. This is not done solely by relationship management – simply producing excellent products at low cost is another feasible route – but it is the relationship approach which is of interest here.

Good customer relationship marketing practices can improve value at different points in the value chain.

- **Value for customers**: is the fundamental driver of shareholder value. Customer value is created through the development and effective delivery of the right proposition to the right customers.
- **Value for employees and partners**: creating value for employees and partners is an important focus of the activity. Much business research and many academic studies over the years have demonstrated a relationship between business performance, the employment environment (organization culture) and attitudes to work.
- **Value for shareholders**: share value is not just based on profit but is determined by the stock market using a number of factors. If a company is perceived to be managing customers well, the share price may go up. Putting the customer at the forefront of management thinking is certainly more likely to improve perceptions of a company even with analysts. Certainly there is no direct and immediate relationship between corporate performance in terms of profitability, corporate image and overall economic performance, or at least not one that is well understood. If there were then no one would lose money on the stock market! Nevertheless, share value can be influenced by the way decisions on improvements to customer management capabilities are announced and subsequently managed.

Value is created at each stage of the relationship management cycle.

- **Analysis and Planning:** value is created through insight, knowledge and effective planning, which means understanding which customers you want to manage, understanding how much you can afford to spend in acquiring and retaining them; putting the appropriate plans in place to acquire the right ones; retaining those who are worth retaining; and efficiently developing those with potential. Planning is also used to match resources to gross value, so that not too much is spent on attracting, retaining and trying to develop customers who are unlikely to deliver value.

- **Creating a focused proposition (the offer):** the proposition should help you find, keep and develop those customers you want to manage. The aim is to develop a proposition that attracts selected customer segments, retains them and develops their value. The proposition needs to be developed in close collaboration with all your supply chain providers (to ensure that it can actually be delivered). It is also vital to communicate your proposition continuously to the staff who actually manage customers and to their immediate managers, so that they can manage customers in a manner consistent with the proposition. They will do this better if you support the delivery of the proposition with incentives, rewards, competency development, process standards, measures, IT content and accessibility.
- **People and organization:** you create value through effective people and partners and this depends on clear visible leadership for relationship management. This means that internal communication works smoothly, especially among customer-facing staff and between them and the rest of the organization. You also need slick decision-making structures and the right competencies. Thus motivation and supplier management must be employed as key enablers of good customer management.
- **Processes:** need to be defined with the customer proposition in mind, based on an in-depth understanding of how they will affect customers. This is what is meant by being customer centric.
- **Information and technology (including data):** create value through efficiency, service and intelligence. Customer and transactional data must be acquired and managed professionally at each stage. These data should also be made available to customers, partners and employees where and when it is required.
- **Measurement:** is essential at each stage of the process. One of the most difficult aspects of justifying customer relationship marketing investments is that very few companies have a clear idea of the costs and benefits of their present relationship management programme. That's right: all companies have relationship management programmes, even if they do not label them as such and measure their effects. Value is created through understanding the relationship between resources, activities and performance. Good measurement enables CRM resources to be managed effectively.
- **The customer experience:** value is created when there is an understanding of how satisfied and committed the customer is. The

customer experiences the different aspects of the proposition, and it is essential to monitor whether the proposition is being received as it was intended.

- **Customer management activities:** create value through excellent acquisition, retention, development and recovery activities. Thus the company puts plans into action: targets the right customers efficiently, makes the most of all enquiries received, ensures new customers understand and enjoys its products and services, retains and develops new customers, and services them well. It allows customers to easily configure what the company offers to meet their needs through a variety of channels. It also manages well customers who are dissatisfied.

Case example: event-driven customer relationship marketing

Using a value-driven approach, the aim is to develop a business strategy that identifies areas of the CRM value chain that could represent competitive advantage for the company. Sometimes, these will be existing 'pain and pressure' points. These are the weakest areas of the value chain. Once these areas have been identified, the company can better consider the relationship management actions that will enhance value creation and delivery.

Let us take an example. Many companies collect life stage and demographic data. These can be used as a basis for understanding what is happening in the life of the customer. Many companies are also building links between different operational systems to develop a complete view of the customer relationship. This is necessary to understand the implications of a change in customer behaviour toward the enterprise. Yet relatively few companies effectively integrate their potential understanding of external events with a positive response to changing customer needs. Table 12.1 illustrates some life events that might be detected within a customer base, and the sort of responses that could be made.

A good example of event-driven relationship management is provided by US Airways. The airline monitors weather reports for key airports around the United States. When a storm looks likely to close an airport, it identifies all affected platinum status frequent flyers, books them overnight hotel rooms, rebooks their flights and tries to ensure they experience minimum inconvenience.

Table 12.1 Responding to customer events

Event	Detection	Reaction
Event in customer's life:	Change of:	
Moving house	address;	X sell relocation services
Birth of Child	spend pattern;	Send link to child site
Retirement	age/income trigger.	Offer 'last chance' deals
Changing relationship		
First time purchase	Warranty card received	Send accessories brochure
Request for service	Systems integrated with	Satisfaction survey
Declining spend	call centre	follow up
	Systems integrated with	Refine service proposition
	billing	
Changing environment		
Market deregulation	New competition	Escalate loyalty benefits
Falling stock market	Web monitoring	Automatic notification
Fulfilment problems	Integrate supply chain	Offer alternative service

Putting relationship management ideas into effect means that you should have processes in place to detect significant external issues that might impact on the customer relationship and ensure that procedures are in place to respond to them.

SOME MARKETING PARADIGMS

We have tried to avoid wherever possible the notion that there is 'one best way' to implement a marketing strategy. There are numerous marketing paradigms. Customer preferences, the nature of the product and service offer and developments in technology do not always lead to simple conclusions about which approach is best.

PASSIVE MARKETING

Classic marketing

There are several classic marketing models where the nature of customer management is not specified explicitly but where there is a very strong implicit model. Classic marketing is used primarily in retailing but it can also be seen at work in areas like sales force management, where customer relationship marketing was born in business-to-business markets, and in mail order. Sales force management introduces ideas like key account management, industrial buying centres, quality and customer service. Mail order, the source of the earliest and in some ways still the most professional ideas about mass relationship marketing, draws heavily on notions of customer value, customer retention and customer dismissal (losing bad customers). Generally, the approach is prescriptive and, from the customer's point of view, passive. Basically, you research the market, design a product or service and tell people when and where they can buy it.

Spot buying

Spot buying is also customer passive. The idea here is that customers aim to get best deals, either from a roster of suppliers or by using an agent like a travel agent or a financial services adviser. It can operate in several ways. Pure spot buying rejects all relationships and buys solely on the basis of current perceived value. This, in turn, is strongly influenced by classic marketing mix variables such as availability, perceived product quality, product and brand management, terms of sale (including promotional discounts) and distribution. There are two principal variations of this theme, either by using a roster of suppliers or by using an agent.

- **Roster spot buying** – Some customers prefer to get the best deal in terms of value for money, not necessarily lowest price, at the time of purchase. They do this from a selected roster of suppliers. This is characteristic of heavy users of fast moving consumer goods and also of many industrial purchases. The roster is used to ensure optimal variety, product quality and service. In such situations, attempts to develop behavioural loyalty (so that a customer buys more than their normal proportion from one supplier) usually require a promotional incentive. Branding and presence are often critical factors. These determine whether you get included on the roster and what share you get. Presence (in the mall) is important in retail markets.
- **Agent spot buying** – In some cases, drawing up the roster can be a complex task so customers engage the help of an agent. This may

also happen when the customer has to register as might happen when buying over the telephone or over the Internet. The customer may prefer to register with an independent agent rather than with the original product or service supplier. Examples of this kind of behaviour include financial services, travel and deregulated energy purchases.

ACTIVE MARKETING

One to one

One to one is the seminal position advocated by Peppers and Rogers. In terms of relationship levels, it is at the other extreme from classic marketing, though most of the fundamentals of classic marketing still apply. You have to get the product or service right. In this ideal position, most aspects of the marketing mix are actively adjusted to the (changing) individual, based on information given by the customer during contacts. Some but not all customers will be very receptive to one-to-one marketing. Customers have different propensities to respond and to enter into the necessary dialogue. To make this approach successful on any scale requires a huge investment in technical (IT) and social (culture, training, commitment) systems. Due to the scale of the investment required, the returns on these enormous investments are not always clearly attributable to the efforts that are being made in the relationship marketing area. Nevertheless, Peppers and Rogers cite several case studies of successful applications. The relationship between major suppliers such as Procter and Gamble and Unilever, and the giant supermarkets such as WalMart, Tesco and Carrefour, is a good example. Although the products supplied are standard, the rest of the offer (payment terms, delivery, packaging, information) is usually heavily customized.

Transparent marketing

Transparent marketing moves slightly away from one to one. It is based on the premise that the customer owns the relationship with the supplier, a position enabled by advances in technology. After all, your competitor on the Internet is only one mouse click away. The customer is therefore in the driving seat. The idea is that many customers like to manage their relationship with companies rather than the other way round. They would like to control who solicits information and the type of information and how any offers are customized in terms of content and timing but are usually not allowed to do so. Where this is possible via advanced call centres or the Internet, some customers are very responsive to it. In the automobile industry some companies allow customers online access to product specification systems. This may be provided via authorized dealers or over the Web. However, most companies still do not offer anything like this to their customers and often waste a lot of money trying to guess what customers want, based on inadequate information as the Institute of Bankers survey demonstrates.

Relationship marketing through segmentation

This is a popular aspiration for many companies. In reality, it is harder to put into practice than it appears and most companies make much slower progress than they would like. However, it is possible to implement the approach with reasonable effect by prioritizing those areas of the relationship where the current offer is most at variance with the need. Adjustments are then made that are most probably going to influence high-value customers in a positive way. The technique recognizes that the relationship is only one part of the marketing mix and that there are often situations where classic elements of the market mix are more critical for marketing success. For example, leadership through product, price, brand or retail location.

Mass customization

Mass customization seeks to combine the economies of scale from mass production with the marketing advantages of individualized products and services. The most easily observed examples occur in areas like automotive, personal computers or, as in one well-known Japanese example, bicycle sales. The product is purchased from a dealer or over the Internet on the basis of a wide variety of options. These are communicated electronically to the factory that makes the customized product to order. Personalized communication along with targeting for packaging and selection purposes of the personalized offer are a feature of the approach.

The method has become very widespread and has been extended by good practice in direct mail and telemarketing. It makes good use of available data, including that previously given by customers, and depends on careful data quality management. It can lead to substantial uplifts in response and conversion rates along with significant savings in communication costs, particularly outbound. The segmentation method may involve hundreds or even thousands of cells in a large outbound mail campaign, the offer made to each customer being selected from one of many, often modular, products or services. These are each determined by the customer's profile and are presented to the customer using personalization. In its most advanced form, data received at the point of contact is used to create or modify the customer profile and the offer is then modified dynamically.

Top vanilla

We described this in Chapter 5. It relies on excellent customer management before, during and after the sale, probably based on segmentation. The 'as good as the best' offer is made to everyone in the target market. On this basis, some 80 per cent to 90 per cent of the market takes care of itself. However, high-value customers are identified separately and managed intensively on an individual basis.

WAY TO GO?

Obviously, these paradigms overlap. They may need to be combined in different ways for managing different customers and for different products. The choice of method is likely to be influenced by all sorts of contextual factors:

- The state and rate of technology change can encourage customers to seek reductions in uncertainty. Relationship marketing or spot buying through agents can achieve this but it can also create big differences in spot value.
- Industry characteristics can also make a big difference. For example, underlying production and distribution techniques, costs of variety and benefits of economies of scale. Market structure fundamentals such as patterns of competition or regulation and the degree and type of intermediation along with the amount of perceived value added by intermediaries will have an effect. An international reservation service depends on a huge investment in technology that is difficult for competing suppliers to match. On the other hand, the marginal costs of each sale are tiny and it is easily possible for intermediaries to add value. In this case, transparent marketing may work best.

- Customer characteristics may also influence choice. The transfer of learning and expectations between different experiences will affect how customers respond. In areas such as financial services, banking and insurance, comparisons are quickly and easily made. Customer behaviour and psychographics, what they think and feel, how they buy, their needs for personal control and associated lifestyle issues are also important factors in these industries. For segmentation or mass customization approaches, timing issues are more critical. Thus, the speed with which customers' needs can be identified, how quickly a response can be made, the rate of entry of 'new to category' customers and customer expertise – whether customers are good at identifying their own needs – all help determine whether these methods will be viable.
- Culture and values are also clearly important for both customers and suppliers. Enterprise and systems cultures are one part of this. The legal environment and ethical issues are another. Understanding the basis of customer value and being able to assess the importance of risk for both customer and supplier will also influence the decision. In industries such as utilities, luxury, high-cost products (aerospace) or telecommunications, understanding good and bad customer characteristics as the basis of a top vanilla approach might be crucial.

SATISFYING THE BOARD

Customer relationship management generally requires a large investment proportionate to the size of the enterprise. For a large company it can cost from $30 million to $90 million during a three-year period, even assuming a co-operative and open approach from each affected domain such as sales, marketing, logistics, production, customer service and support. Due to such evidently high costs, both large and small businesses increasingly require financial justification. Thus project teams should include financial analysts along with business and technology analysts.

It has to be acknowledged that developing return on investment (ROI) calculations for CRM is not easy. The more extensive the venture, the more difficult the calculations, since the activity will touch on an increasingly wide area of the enterprise. At the technology level (defined in Chapter 10), in a closed and bounded planning environment, it should be possible to set up good, reliable and accurate measures. At the enterprise level, such an achievement is very difficult, not least because it is more or less impossible to normalize and take account of all the many extraneous events that affect every company over long (or even medium-term) timescales. Changes in business performance could be attributable to normal economic cycles, the workings of government or regulatory bodies, changes in exchange rates, alterations in levels of consumer confidence, changes in personnel and so on. Not least, there is often a difficulty in calculating the total costs of ownership (TCO) of CRM technologies. These are rarely related to a straightforward purchase price. Very often system changes are required elsewhere in the current IT, procedure changes are needed to work with the new software, there are increasingly complex software licensing and maintenance provisions, there is a need for substantial employee training and personnel development, and there are of course a number of employee and customer benefits that are hard to quantify.

There is therefore a 'terrible' temptation not to make the attempt. After all, if it has been decided to throw money at the venture, why not ride the wave? In any case, there is rarely a baseline figure or set of existing relationship management metrics that can be used to determine the effect of the new systems. Other than vendor case studies, which must be read with a pinch of salt since they tend to address selected subsets of the activity and tend to assume ideal or greenfield conditions, there are few published studies. Certainly, any sensible manager will consider very carefully cases cited by leading suppliers, since these are clearly going to be designed to heighten expectations and encourage, perhaps falsely, the idea that paybacks can be achieved in a relatively short span of time such as six or nine months. A moment's consideration will show that such short payback periods are highly implausible, not least because real, lasting changes in customer behaviour are hard to identify and detect in such a short period. Nevertheless, a relationship management initiative is a major business decision which requires justification in the same way as any other.

THE BASIC METHOD OF APPROACH FOR DETERMINING AN ROI

Although there may well be some immediate and very short-term benefits from a new CRM venture, the project itself is likely to be multi-phased and to deliver a change in posture and performance over time, hopefully in a progressive way. Some of these are illustrated in Table 12.2.

Table 12.2 Expected benefits from a CRM initiative

Company benefits	Customer benefits
Increased revenue	Increased convenience
Increased margins and reduced costs – we get more things right first time	Increased savings or at least much better value for money
Increased productivity through better up- and cross-selling	More information when and where it is wanted
Increased lifetime value	Increased confidence in the supplier, plus the potential for better enjoyment and benefits from products and services
Bigger share of customer's wallet	Increased emotional loyalty – the customer 'feel good factor' is increased
Improved customer loyalty	The effort to seek out suppliers is reduced. Customers do not have the feeling that their preferred supplier will attempt to retain the sale at all costs. Based on higher trust, they are more inclined to use their preferred supplier portal as the first port of call
Ability to acquire and retain valuable customers is improved	Ease of trying out new products and services
Enabling customer management of the company, reduces total cost to serve	Reduced costs of information gathering, especially for comparison shopping
The competitive position is strengthened as other companies have greater difficulty in recognizing and challenging the basis of customer value	Greater brand awareness
Flexibility and responsiveness to market conditions is improved, making the company more agile and therefore more robust	Much improved communications and the feeling that a real dialogue is taking place
Better supply chain integration	Cheaper product design – customers can tailor products and services to their needs more easily
Greater employee satisfaction. This reduces levels of stress, increases buy-in and employee retention, underpins productivity growth and reduces recruitment costs	Increased reliability and greater confidence in the supplier

Clearly, measuring – or at least quantifying the benefits – is an important step. However, it is immediately apparent from Table 12.2 how difficult that can be. The task of identifying TCO is no easier, as suggested by Table 12.3.

Table 12.3 Elements of the total cost of ownership of CRM systems

The investment	The 'non-investments'
Hardware	List/name acquisition costs
Software licences	Enhancement costs
Consulting	Outsourcing costs
Deployment including systems integration	Development, logistics and delivery costs
Marketing resources	E-mail support costs
Document management and archiving	Training and HR development
Data warehousing	Account servicing
Content management	Call and contact centre costs
Knowledge management	Your reputation!
Portal development for Web personalization	
What is the investment supporting?	**Inter-company factors**
Volumes	Supply chain collaboration, including customer control
Complexity	
Speed	Market management
Efficiency	Mergers and acquisitions
Quality	
Transparency/trackability	
Measurability	
Risk control/reduction	
Business transformation	
Where is the investment visible?	**Critical requirements for determining ROI**
Enterprise resource planning	
Systems integration	Getting the basic ROI technology in place
CRM, including customer contact management	Analyse and data mine for insights
Data warehousing	Tracking all contacts by customer
Content management	Ensuring data accuracy
e-business and e-markets	Establishing LTV
Knowledge management	Producing decision support reports
Document management and archiving	Identify holes – how do we know what we don't know?

Once the benefits and costs can be identified properly, probably following a series of workshops involving the affected departments and managers, the process of assessing the benefits can proceed. This will follow the normal procedure for any new project:

- Establish the list of key performance indicators (KPIs) that is to act as the basis of tracking.
- Measure the current value of these KPIs.
- Produce a momentum forecast. This is a projection of the business position if you were to maintain and continue all activities at their present level. These include current relationship management measures. If therefore it is current practice to increase the customer relationship marketing training budget by 3 per cent per year, this is included within the momentum forecast.
- Make assumptions of the effect of the new relationship management project on the KPIs.
- Set up measures to detect and record changes.
- Compare actual performance with momentum performance as a basis for calculating ROI.

This is an exercise of some substance. For example, producing the momentum forecast will require a categorization of basic factors such as tax levels in different areas of activity and for different strategies on capital expenditure; net operating margins in different parts of the business; an assessment of the cost of capital based on different acquisition strategies; an assessment of interest rates for borrowing; a policy on the depreciation of hardware (over what period), amortization of software (in years), planned total annual revenue growth, current customer retention rates and so on. At the same time, estimating the benefits to revenue through improved lead effectiveness, improved lead routing, decreased sales cycle times and increased customer satisfaction also require some assumptions. In many cases, very specific KPIs will need to be tracked, such as increases in the average revenue per sale, customer retention rates, average sales cycle times, decreases in the cycle time, and the number of new deals that new sales representatives close in their first year compared with earlier years.

EXAMPLES OF REVENUE CALCULATIONS

From these data it is now possible to undertake the necessary calculations. Let us assume that the average amount per sale is $20,000 and that at the moment some 5,000 sale opportunities are lost through insufficient systems support. Imagine that we can reduce the lost opportunity figure by say 10 per cent as a result of the CRM initiative. A revenue benefit of $1 million could then be assumed (500 times $20,000).

Another example might be based on increased productivity of the field sales force. Let us assume that the company currently has 50 sales representatives working for 45 weeks, or 225 days per year. Of this time, 50 per cent is actual selling time. Each sales person has a target of $200,000 per year, or $22.5 million for the whole team. Now assume that the CRM initiative will increase productive sales time by 10 per cent. The revenue benefit in this case would be $2.25 million.

SUMMARY OF KEY POINTS

- There is little doubt that ROI calculations for CRM are hard.
- The more complete and complex the CRM programme, the more difficult the calculations.
- It is difficult to get good internal data, especially over a time series.
- It is important not to overlook the customer benefits, which may be 'soft'.
- A phased rollout with benefit calculations at each point is probably better and easier.
- However, there is also no doubt that CRM is an expensive undertaking for an enterprise.
- To encourage stakeholders (especially board-level stakeholders), some form of ROI must be done.
- The downside of not undertaking better CRM massively outweighs the additional costs and difficulties. The danger is that the programme loses credibility through lack of a good, continuing business case.

HOW ROI WORKS OUT IN PRACTICE

A fundamental proposition of the American Consumer Satisfaction Index (ACSI) is that satisfied customers represent a real, albeit intangible, asset for a company. However, the ACSI recognizes the pressures on organizations to show measurements for even intangible assets, and has worked with the faculty of the University of Michigan Business

School (UMich) to allow managers and investors to relate satisfaction to future streams of income. The ACSI measures stretch back to 1994 and provide an interesting insight into satisfaction levels within the American economy, in terms of general trends and on the basis of comparisons between different industries.

Two measures are of interest to us here. The first is a link between customer satisfaction scores and corporate earnings. UMich can show that satisfaction scores in one period of time are predictive of earnings in the following period (in other words there is a lagged correlation). They suggest (reasonably) that a satisfied customer is more profitable than a dissatisfied one. If satisfaction declines, customers are more reluctant to buy unless prices are cut. If satisfaction increases, not only are customers more inclined to buy, but they are less sensitive to price changes. This is illustrated in Figure 12.1.

The second and perhaps more potent measure from the perspective of ROI is a link that has been established between satisfaction and shareholder value. UMich suggest that the difference between market value and invested capital is likely to be greater for the firm that manages its customer asset well. Market value added (MVA) measures the difference between what investors put in to a company and what

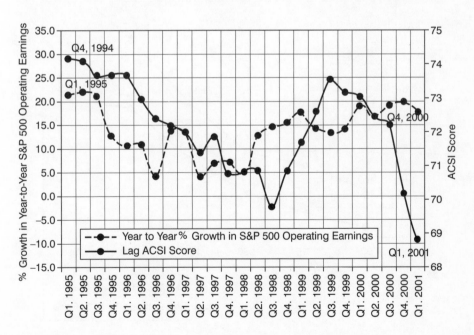

Figure 12.1 ACSI and annual percentage growth in S&P 500 earnings

they can take out. As such it provides a useful cumulative measure of corporate performance. The UMich studies based on ACSI scores show that high ACSI firms produce significantly more MVA than those at the lower end of the scale. This is shown in Figure 12.2.

Data from different sources seem to offer a consistent picture on which approximate targets for the return from a CRM venture might be based. Few companies that track business benefits from relationship management projects find a direct relationship between the level of benefits before and after the project as a percentage of turnover. It is very difficult to assign benefits in this way. This is because there are rarely baseline data before a system is implemented; there are many other independent variables at work; and many benefits are soft and therefore hard to quantify. However, data from the British consulting firm QCi, obtained in 2000, suggested that turnover increases of between 2 per cent and 58 per cent are possible. The Insight Technology Group produced similar figures for CRM projects followed through to

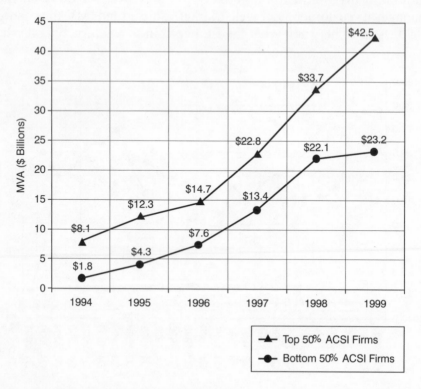

Figure 12.2 Top and bottom 50% of ACSI firms

completion over a three-year period. Insight Technology determined that companies achieved benefits (actual results) in five key areas. The upper limits of the benefits they described were as shown in Table 12.4.

Table 12.4 Insight Technology's estimation of benefits from CRM projects

Revenue increases	+42%
Sales cost decreases	–35%
Sell cycle reductions	–25%
Margin improvements	+2%
Customer satisfaction	+20%

To determine the potential benefit, you must take into account the following:

- **The turnover of the company,** which influences the scale and variety of potential benefits.
- **The size of the investment made**; a ratio for Return on Investment (ROI) that is remarkably similar for a number of different companies appears possible.
- **The maturity and competence of the organization in customer management,** this affects:
  - the size of the investment needed;
  - the potential prize; and
  - the expected timing of benefit.

These in turn determine the project risk.

BENEFITS AS A PERCENTAGE OF TURNOVER

There is some evidence to suggest that smaller companies or business units may achieve greater benefits than larger companies but, for the time being, it is interesting to consider QCi findings based on four large companies.

The size of the investment: the 4:1 rule

The data from four business cases from different international companies tracked over three years showed the remarkable similarity in ROI across three very different businesses. See Table 12.5.

341

Table 12.5 The size of the investment: the 4: 1 rule

Company	Overall size of company (turnover)	CM investments as a percentage of turnover	Benefit as a percentage of turnover	Size of benefit	Return on investment (ROI)
Company 1	€735 million	2%	8.5%	62.8m	4.3
Company 2	€7.8 million	15.5%	52.6%	4.1m	3.4
Company 3	€11.7 billion	0.5%	2.1%	240m	4.1
Company 4	€610 million	1%	8.3%	50.4m	4.2

Source: QCi (2000)

In the example:

- Size is turnover at the start of the period, and all benefits are calculated in Net Present Value terms.
- Customer relationship marketing investment as percentage of turnover is exactly as stated.
- Benefit as percentage of turnover is the total net benefit across the three-year forecast period.
- Return on Investment is defined as the total increase in revenue relative to the total additional investment applied.

Table 12.5 appears to show a relationship between the level of investment and the benefits from improved acquisition, retention and development. There are no general rules for efficiency gains, as these depend so much on how efficient the company was before the investment. In general, increased revenue is around four times the original investment. Though this is a small sample it seems to be consistent with other data from a variety of sources.

The organization's maturity and competence in relationship management

The data in Table 12.6 illustrate the planned ROI achieved from the companies in this study at different stages of customer management maturity. As might be expected, how the investment pays back varies by the company's relationship management maturity. Companies that manage their customers especially badly are likely to see a much greater benefit but from a higher level of investment, over a longer period of time. They have more to invest and more to gain.

Table 12.6 Indicative returns on investment

Customer management performance	Likely level of investment required	Primary investment areas likely	Likely ROI year 1	Likely ROI year 2	Likely ROI year 3	Overall ROI (simple average over 3 years)
Lower quartile performer	High	Whole CRM cycle	1	3	7	3.7
Third quartile	Medium–high	Whole CRM cycle	2	3	7	4.0
Second quartile	Low–medium	Measurement, activity, proposition, IT	3	4	5	4.0
Highest quartile performer	Tactical	People, activity, customer experience	4.5	5	5.5	5.0

Companies at the lower end of the maturity scale will have to invest heavily in infrastructure and programmes. Careful project planning is vital to allow quick wins to help contribute to this investment, but *net benefits* will be more apparent towards the latter stages of, say, a three-year programme. Higher performers will be those with well-developed relationship management positions. They will already have a well-developed people and systems infrastructure and a mature, customer-centric culture. These companies 'know who they are', what they offer and which customers they are managing. They are flexible in their planning, and their decision-making ability allows them to react to market changes quickly. Their IT systems and culture will be customer-focused, so that, for example, their databases will contain the full customer 'context' across any channel and transaction. Data capture will be consistent across channels, and a common set of business rules will apply, for example offering prompts as to how an individual contact or transaction should be handled, irrespective of medium (on the web, in the call centre or sales force, in partner intermediaries or in retail outlets). The business rules will help identify issues and opportunities, and rather than being given to uninterested agents, will be used by empowered service staff as the context demands. The benefit for these companies from further investment in CM is likely to be lower overall, because they have already achieved a great deal.

Note that these data are indicative only, as they are based on a very small number of detailed tracking studies.

Expected timing of benefit

Table 12.6 also indicates how the cumulative ROI is likely to change, year on year. Once again, the broad pattern is of interest, rather than the detail. Consistent with the maturity position, companies that have poorly developed relationship management platforms will tend to need high initial investment, followed by slow initial gains and major gains after two to three years. Those that are already performing well will show quicker initial gains, since the infrastructure to capitalize on gains is already in place, but the level of investment will not change much year on year. Benefits will then tend to follow a steady rate, rather than leap up dramatically at any point in time. The major overall implication identified across numerous forecasts is that it is likely to take time for the full effects of a relationship management venture to be delivered.

KEYS TO ACHIEVING THE MOST FROM YOUR CUSTOMER RELATIONSHIP MARKETING INVESTMENTS

- Provide relationship management leadership with authority. The best performing companies have leaders with clear responsibility, authority, understanding and determination to make good customer management a reality in their companies.
- Ensure your organization encourages analysis of the customer dimension and uses a decision-making process focused on improving customer management. Improved techniques for analysis, measurement and knowledge management allow companies to achieve higher quality decision making in relation to CM. Though not many organizations are able to use these techniques, the ones that can tend to perform best.
- Align objectives relevant to customer management throughout the organization. If plans identify retention, efficiency, acquisition and penetration (REAP) objectives, these should be communicated to the groups and individuals who can put these ideas to work.

Mismatches may occur when customer management planning is cross-functional but objectives are set functionally.

- Recruit and develop the right people. The customer management competencies of all the people who affect the customer experience (this may include people in product development, marketing, sales, service, finance, administration, operations and technical support) need to be defined. The right people need to be recruited, their competency gaps identified and their competencies developed. In customer-facing roles, some top-performing companies recruit staff based on their *attitude* to customer management, believing that it is easier to develop an individual's knowledge and skills, than to modify his or her attitude. It is worth remembering here the formula proposed by the Reverend Jesse Jackson in his civil rights campaigns. *Altitude = Attitude + Aptitude.*
- Provide the incentives and reward required to encourage desired customer management behaviours. In best-performing companies, employees believe that their salary and incentives match their customer management objectives and those of the company. This is a difficult area to get right, and employee groups can help determine it.
- Understand employee satisfaction and commitment. Try to understand whether employees feel that the organization listens to them and reacts appropriately to their issues. There is a relationship between staff satisfaction, customer satisfaction and long-term company value.
- Manage partners and alliances well. High-performing companies score more highly in the area of supplier management.

E-BUSINESS AND GLOBALIZATION

The first interesting paradox is identified by Michael Porter and concerns the nature of globalization (Gibson, Toffler and Toffler, 1999). Porter notes that a global perspective is now assumed for even quite small enterprises. An independent graphic designer can undertake work for a publisher in Hong Kong as easily as for a publisher in Buenos Aires through electronic links. This affects the structure of enterprises. It makes sense to source inputs from the lowest-cost location. No longer need all processes be owned by the same company or located in the same building; they can be outsourced in whatever way is most cost-effective. While knowledge workers in particular may be located anywhere, even inputs such as capital and labour can be sourced nationally or internationally. Thus it might make sense to locate your UK call centre in, say, India.

As a result, the presence of so many global markets and companies has essentially nullified the advantage of globalness of itself. Anything a company can access from a distance is no longer a competitive advantage because now everybody can access it. Paradoxically, this puts an increasing premium on what Porter calls the 'home base'. The home base refers to that unique critical mass of skill, expertise, suppliers and local institutions that makes certain locations important centres of innovation in a particular business. There are numerous examples of industry clusters that have become the innovation centres in their fields. By this argument, the chances of being successful in any given field can be dramatically improved by location. The odds of becoming a world-class software company are much higher if you are located in the United States. In electronics, there are around the world a variety of silicon valleys, villages, parks, glens and whadis. You would find it harder to become a top-level fashion house outside a small number of the world's capital cities. To market wine, clothing or even submarines, the home base is still important.

Whereas the scale of the firm was critical, now increasingly it is the scale of the cluster, network or infrastructure that is important. Each individual enterprise can be smaller if there are a lot of good supporting companies around. This evolution in globalization is putting a greater and greater premium on specialization, on doing those particular things that you can do best in a particular location, rather than doing everything in one location.

These 'home bases' are at the heart of future competition between nations, according to Porter, because they are the sources of wealth and high wages. Fundamental shifts in technology can have an incredible impact on the importance of geographical location. As changes in technology diminish the importance of certain aspects of location due to electronic communication, these aspects become nullified as competitive advantages. New technology thus sweeps away potential advantages that it created itself. Access to domestic capital is no longer an advantage because technology and market developments allow companies outside of the country to get access to that capital. Similarly, employees working at home will no longer be an advantage, because companies anywhere in the world can use them through the same technology.

The key to the future, therefore, lies in learning. Companies that are going to become and remain successful will be the ones that can learn fast, can assimilate knowledge and can develop new insights. They must create an environment where people expect change, where their own products and services are under constant revision based on the dialogue they are holding with their customers. Companies must regard their relationships with both internal and external customers as their most valuable asset. Asset value does not lie in buildings, employees or even customers as such. It lies in the network of links that enables companies to compete effectively in various national clusters.

THE PARADOX OF PROGRESS

An improved ability to capture, manage and use customer information and to interact with customers means that managing relationships over many transactions becomes a realistic strategy. In effect, it enables relationship marketing on a large scale. On the other hand, this very ability to engage in transparent marketing and spot buying may also reduce customer loyalty.

Utilities – the case of the disloyal environmentalist

In newly deregulated markets, such as that in the UK or in California, the marketing model is based on the notion that the individual will have a relationship with the electricity or gas supply company. The customer signs a contract and agrees to buy power from that company. The company, in turn, proceeds to buy electricity or gas at the best price. This can lead to an extensive relationship. Cross-selling of different power sources along with associated services such as domestic security or even financial services is possible based on personalized marketing.

However, IBM has demonstrated simulations of a Web agent that offers the customer a choice of energy sources generated from different fuels, such as natural gas, wind, hydro, fossil or nuclear from a particular geographical source. In this situation, the customer logs in and can switch power sources according to, say, price fluctuations or personal preferences. A consumer might, for example, be basically green but set an upper price limit to greenness, switching into fossil if green electricity becomes too expensive. This would be agent-managed spot buying. In its extreme form, of course, the consumer could set the computer to do the task, setting control parameters so that the source could be switched without human intervention. The loyalty of the computer in these circumstances is zero.

Telecommunications – the case of the disloyal mobile user

The days when a telephone represented an expensive business or domestic asset, rooted physically in one geographic location, are long gone. Today, some families might have three or four telephony providers such as a long-haul carrier like BT or Sprint, a cable company, a low cost local supplier and one or more mobile providers. In theory, customers can make each call by choosing the supplier with the best rate. Indeed, this can be done automatically by software, as is routinely done in business situations. The difference might be that the software is built into a multipurpose handset; indeed, consumers may come to expect this. Thus, roster spot buying would be in operation. Customers may be slowed down by the price-confusion strategies deliberately employed by the telecom companies but it seems likely that various regulatory authorities will intervene eventually to reduce their effects. However, even in the short term, some customers will be motivated to do the comparison themselves for specific types of call. For example, to friends and family overseas or to often-called numbers, especially those on long-distance. Here again, there will be no loyalty other than to price.

The enormous take-up of pre-paid mobiles indicates that many customers are happy with the classic marketing model, with no relationship. In Italy, for example, over 50 per cent of mobile phones are pre-pay. On the other hand, some customers may be influenced to buy their pre-pay top ups from particular stores by using relationship marketing techniques. For example, the store might offer double points on the store loyalty card if the margin is there to allow this. High value customers may accept a relationship marketing approach with the network provider if their company is paying the bill and they get a free, personal incentive. For example, a business phone user might get free air miles for personal use.

Case example: Orange

British mobile phone network operator Orange faced a profitability problem when it was building market share. The problem focused on handsets. Customers kept changing them. Indeed, they seemed to want to upgrade them regularly as part of the service. The problem was that the operator was subsidizing the costs of the handsets and it took between 12 and 20 months to recover that cost. Yet after about 12 months, customers were calling to ask for a new, improved handset for the same price as the old one. In a highly competitive market, if they did not get it they would switch.

The problem was presented to the relationship manager, who faced two options. The first was to try to develop a predictive model about why people were switching and test it hypothetically. He could then take this model to his company analysts who would spend a few days to determine whether the model had merit. This might yield about half the information needed by the marketing manager. The manager would then devise a campaign and take it back to the analysts to see whether it might work. The whole process took about four weeks and was in any case based on data that might be outdated by the time the campaign started.

Instead, Orange came up with an idea that not only aimed to please the customer but would also generate new revenue. Following a day's training, customer representatives were instructed to offer a new handset based on two alternative deals. The first offered a discount on a new handset if they kept the old one in use (the 'old' handsets were perfectly serviceable and were generally just being thrown away). The second offered the customer free batteries and extra talk time in return for an extra six months' usage. Fifty per cent of customers responded to the deal. The net effect was customer acquisition, customer retention and higher revenues.

(Martin, 1999)

Financial services – the case of the disloyal investor

In the UK, the invasion of supermarkets, such as Safeway or Tesco, and insurers, such as Standard Life Bank or Prudential, has caused very large numbers of customers to switch their savings away from retail banks. Using direct marketing techniques based largely on call centres and the Internet, new financial services providers have encouraged people to switch their savings more rapidly into accounts yielding higher rates of interest. Effectively, consumers line up one or more companies on their roster, based on stepped interest rates or family group interest rates. They then switch money according to the amount of cash they have to spare. In doing so, they will have a very specific objective. This is one of the few areas where value for money is completely transparent and loyalty is simply a function of the service being offered.

In financial services, the level of cross-buying is generally low. Few mortgage holders seem to buy their pension from their mortgage company. One of the reasons for these low cross-selling ratios, particularly in life and pensions, is that the higher the value of the customer, the more likely the use of an independent adviser. The independent adviser acts as an intermediary who will spot recommend, based partly upon benefit to the customer and partly on the commission paid to the adviser. Very few companies seem to offer incentives to existing product holders or to ask questions about other relationships. They seem to work on the assumption that commission-based competition for the adviser's loyalty will see them through. Many financial services companies were shocked to discover how low their ratio of cross-selling was as they established their first data warehouses.

SO WHAT NEXT?

Lou Gerstner, former Chairman and CEO of IBM is reported as saying:

> I believe we're at the threshold of a very important change in the evolution of the information technology industry. This young industry is about to play out its most important dimension. That's because the technology has become so powerful and so pervasive that its future impact on people, businesses and governments will dwarf all that has happened to date.
>
> (Edouard and White, 1999)

It is easy to see that the technology has made, is making and will be making more and more data available. Whether this will enable managers to manage their customer relationships more effectively depends on a number of factors. We started this book by reporting that in the United States (the only country from which such a data series is available), customer satisfaction ratings in several major industries have been reducing, based on trends dating back to 1994. The same may well be happening in other countries. Why should this be, in the era of relationship marketing? Perhaps people's service expectations have been steadily rising faster than actual service levels have risen. Perhaps some industries genuinely have taken their eye off the ball and have allowed the technology to distance themselves from their customers. Certainly the telephone technology likely to provoke the most hostile anecdotes is those automated responses that put people in queues yet tell them to hold the line because 'your call is important to us'. If it's really important, why don't they hire more agents to deal with us? Perhaps the pressures and stresses of modern life are increasing.

The consultancy QCi reported in 2001 that despite the continual investment in CRM technology, performance in this area overall is declining noticeably. The evidence from their relationship management assessment tool showed that the overall scores for information and technology dropped from 40 per cent to 35 per cent, the biggest drop in any section. Organizations are *acquiring* increasing quantities of data, from internal and external sources, without being sure what they are going to do with it and how they are going to maintain it. This results in a level of 'data chaos' that may eventually have legal consequences (Stone *et al*, 2001).

Customer trust and loyalty are undoubtedly being eroded through the collection of too much customer information (much of it irrelevant) and poor use of the data. Organizations are also investing heavily in technology without enough investment in managing data. They appear to be struggling to understand the impact and implications of data protection and privacy legislation. A 2001 survey of CRM systems (www.crmguru.com) shows that overall, customer satisfaction ratings for CRM vendors are very low. The survey claims that world-class products and services routinely achieve Customer Satisfaction Index (CSI) scores in the mid 80s and low 90s. Good, but not outstanding performers typically generate CSI scores in the high 70s. However, the average CRM software package CSI score in this survey was 63.1. The survey suggests that, 'Scores in the 60s or below are usually "panic-level" scores'. This average does not disguise some high-scoring products. The overall CSI range for all products reviewed was from 58 to 66. Ease of implementation was the most cited problematic issue with CRM software. Most companies appear to be buying blind.

Nevertheless, on the positive side, it is apparent that companies are increasingly making CRM systems available to customer-facing staff and to customers. These systems are generally highly functional and increasingly relevant to the people that use them. Global CRM spend continues to rise steadily, and most analysts predict that it will actually increase dramatically in the period to 2007. At the same time, consumers are becoming steadily less loyal, or at least happier to switch suppliers.

Direct mail, telemarketing, face-to-face selling and television are still the media of choice for most companies, with the largest share of marketing expenditure and steady growth forecast. Call centres will also undergo a great change in the next few years, and evolve towards fully functional contact centres. This will place yet more demands on technology and corporate training, as the move to a more service-oriented culture makes itself felt. So what should the customer relationship marketing manager be expecting in the next three to five years?

SUPPLY SIDE COMPLEXITY

Companies are faced with many choices in customer management. The larger the company, the more complex the choices. The choices include:

- **Product and product variations** (although products are becoming more similar). Product marketers have done a good job of providing subtle variations to differentiate their products from those of competitors. The difficulty with this is maintaining the product line with the increased cost of development and brochure ware.
- **Channels**: which channels to use to access which customers – retail, outbound/inbound call centre, kiosk, intermediary, direct sales force, Web, wireless (eg SMS), and mail.
- **Segment targeting:** which customers to target for which products.
- **Choice of partners**: which partners to choose for which products, segments and channels, and at what level of the supply chain.

This increased complexity is confusing to both marketers and the consumer. It may well be one reason IT vendors have had such an easy time selling to companies who are desperate for a solution to sort out this complexity. In reality, it rarely does.

DEMAND-SIDE PROMISCUITY (AND CONTROL BY CUSTOMERS)

Customers are reacting faster and becoming more comfortable about switching between suppliers. They are more *positive* about changing suppliers – they embrace it, often seek it, and are confident about it. They are more demanding of their existing products and suppliers and less accepting of error (although very loyal customers can be very forgiving). Globalization, deregulation and easy access to the Web enable consumers to seek the products they want. They can seek, source and purchase the product, then leave without ever talking to a sales-person. Individuals are more confident about making their own choices, partly because they have access to many more information sources than previous generations. They demonstrate their new confidence by:

- accessing the company how, when and where they want to;
- controlling the relationship and not wanting to feel controlled;
- asking to be valued and treated specially, particularly if they are valuable customers;
- switching suppliers if they feel aggrieved, or if they receive unful-filled or disappointing service 'promises'.

MULTI-CHANNEL MARKETING

Figure 12.3 illustrates a series of interactions for a customer buying a financial services product, in this case car insurance, using a variety of marketing channels. The scenario is highly plausible and is certainly within the realms of most current IT. Whether it is within the realms of

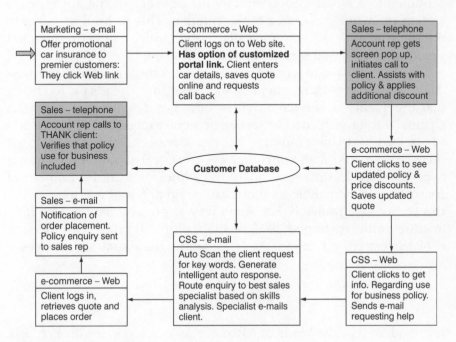

Figure 12.3 Integrated contact: financial services

most customer service and support (CSS) functions is another question! Notice that the transactions switch seamlessly between different forms of contact – the Web portal, e-mail, telephone and personal contact – and between several people – the CSS, general sales, specialist sales. A moment's thought will reveal that a company would have to be in an advanced customer relationship management position to support such a process.

UNIVERSAL QUEUE SERVERS

When transactions move between different media, as they commonly do, good customer service allows a company to pick up information from one contact point and feed it into the next. If an e-mail enquiry is followed by a telephone call or if a phone call is followed by a letter, the customer expects the company to be able to 'remember' the basis of previous communications. This is not easy if you have several thousand or several million customers. The technology that integrates contacts from different media is known as a universal queue server.

The purpose of universal queuing is to integrate voice and data transactions into a single contact queue for delivery to the appropriate system or customer service representative. This technology aims to integrate seamlessly phone calls, e-mail, Web collaborative-chat sessions, video-based service requests and so on.

The universal queue is composed of four essential elements: business rules, workflow routing, queuing and reporting. The idea is to ensure that the quality of service provided does not depend on the contact channel through which a transaction or inquiry might arrive. It is clearly very expensive to have multiple separate service channels and try to get them to share information manually. A great deal of time and effort has been invested in universal queuing technologies, and a number of competing, incompatible solutions exist from different vendors. As yet, this technology probably has some way to go, and may not be fully 'mature' until late to end 2003. At that point, call centres will need to evolve to contact centres to take advantage of these common services.

THE SKILLS GAP

It is evident that the kinds of customer service representatives (CSR), call centre agents and even customer relations officers in post today will need to develop and hone their personal skills to keep abreast of new technologies. Indeed, if we consider for a moment just the role of call centre agents, we can see that the sort of e-CSR needed to handle the environment illustrated in Figure 12.3 will be quite different from their current counterpart. They will require a much wider repertoire of skills. Companies will not be able to countenance the same sort of HR approaches that are currently adopted for call centre agents. High labour turnovers, high stress levels and no evident career progression just will not do. After all, an e-CSR will be a much more valuable 'property'. More will have been invested in his or her training and more time and effort will be needed to plan his or her personal development. E-CSRs will want a career path. This will put pressure on skills development. Thus we could envisage a skills gap development like that shown in Table 12.7.

Table 12.7 Skills developments for customer relationship marketing

Skills emphasis in 2002	Skills emphasis in 2005?
Management skills	Leadership skills
Call centre management skills	Technical knowledge
Training and motivation skills	Political judgement
Internal selling skills	Enterprise business knowledge
Cross-selling skills	Internal/external selling and marketing skills
E-mail handling skills	Multi function/multi channel
	Contact centre management skills

SMALL AND MEDIUM ENTERPRISES (SMEs)

Microsoft have estimated that less than 3 per cent of small and medium-sized enterprises are using any form of customer relationship management technology in 2002. In Europe, the figure is almost certainly much lower. It might be thought that small (less than 50 employees) and medium (less than 200 employees) companies do not need technology to support their relationship efforts. Anyone who has had contact with a business that only employs perhaps half a dozen people will know that is not usually the case. You quickly run out of situations when a number of yellow 'post-it' slips stuck to a desk or a VDU will be sufficient to share and communicate details of a customer case, especially if it is complex, involves more than one person, or continues over more than a few days.

As a result, Microsoft are planning to introduce a special CRM product for up to 100 users in the early part of 2003. This is a highly targeted product as it will deliberately exclude businesses requiring advanced sales and service models, sophisticated content management, very high levels of personalization, close call centre integration and so on. It is aimed directly at the bulk of companies which form the backbone of most developed economies yet which still have a way to go in improving their CRM platforms.

Of course, such companies could deploy a number of existing technologies to meet their RM needs. What is significant about this development is that, one, it is a specific product designed to integrate with existing Microsoft Office tools (which most SMEs already use) and two, it will have the reputation and support of the Microsoft organization behind it. This may well encourage small businesses, notably reluctant to engage in training and management development, especially in Europe, to proceed.

INTERNET TIME

We have outlined only a few of the current developments that are taking place in CRM technologies. There are a number of others. However, one additional factor that needs to be taken into account with all of these issues is that the pace of change is, if anything, increasing. Today, almost all projects are on 'Internet time', and CRM is no exception. Take the example of contact centres. In 1990, call centre managers faced fewer, less-complex projects – perhaps an ACD installation or implementing a tracking application. While these projects were difficult, there was more time allowed for their completion. Today, projects are more complex, involving more technologies, more channels and more integration. Managers are expected not only to understand this complexity but also to integrate each element of the contact centre and then integrate contact centre as a whole to the company, at a faster pace than previously. In short, managers are being asked to do more with less. This puts even more pressure on the need for hybrid managers, technologically literate, politically knowledgeable and with a good knowledge of the business.

SUMMARY

Other speculative effects consequent upon these changes might be imagined. As companies master the technology and implement effective relationship marketing strategies on a global scale, the dissemination of best practice might spread, along with some interesting effects on current trade barriers such as taxation levels, trading standards and even the use of language. There is no Rosetta Stone for marketers which allows us to map a known past onto a probable future. Certain fundamental principles of marketing will continue to be true but some will not. We are still at the beginning of a transformation of markets in which the very basis of competition will change. Developing an enterprise-wide commitment to customer relationship marketing and being able to implement that philosophy effectively may well be crucial to success and survival.

Appendix 1

A complete relationship marketing planning recipe

Technique/ Area	Detailed Description, Comment and Typical Problems or Failings	Leader	Team
1. Strategy Development and Analysis	**Developing the overall approach to managing the business**		
Corporate mission, objectives and strategy development	Development of corporate mission, objectives and strategy. Take into account the requirements of customers and the need for the company to build and maintain profitable relationships. This allows other functions eg operations, finance, personnel to take these requirements into account when they develop their own functional strategy.	Senior management	Senior and middle management
Customer relationship strategy development	Once the corporate level has been dealt with, it is possible to set out the company's strategy for managing customers. This will determine numbers of customers to be recruited and retained, typical volumes and values of business from each customer, how this business is going to be achieved, organizational, policy and process changes. It will also consider which channels of communication and distribution are to be used.	Senior manager with relationship marketing manager	Middle management, customer facing personnel, external consultants

Technique/ Area	Detailed Description, Comment and Typical Problems or Failings	Leader	Team
	Too often, this is left until marketing strategy development has been completed. A customer relationship strategy is then 'patched' together.		
Marketing strategy development	The marketing functional 'view', in which the acquisition and retention of customers is broken down into the classic elements of the marketing mix: product, price, distribution, marketing communications. It is not advisable to do this in isolation from customer relationship strategy development: ideally the company will develop these two approaches in parallel. The key here is to ensure that the sales, marketing and service strategies are developed with the customer relationship strategy as the integrator. This also applies to the rest of the tasks in this section.	Senior management (see problems)	Marketing team and customer relationship marketing manager
Sales channel strategy	This determines how your customers will be managed through your sales channels. Sales channels may include: • direct sales team; • third party sales team; • agents; • telemarketing / sales operators; • retail channels.	Senior manager and the sales director	Sales managers and customer relationship marketing manager
Customer service strategy	This should include all customer interfacing systems and people eg billing, service engineers, complaint handlers, technical support.	Senior manager, service director	Service team and customer relationship marketing manager
Research relationship needs	A key element of the research must examine who the best and worst customers are. It must also look at customer value, what the customer likes most or dislikes most about the way they are managed by you and/or by the 'best in class' competitors or *comparators*. A comparator refers to companies in parallel industries which are not competitors but whose key customer management processes can be compared with yours. The key here is to ensure that the research is *policy* driven.	Marketing manager	Marketing, sales, service representatives

Technique/ Area	Detailed Description, Comment and Typical Problems or Failings	Leader	Team
Analysis and interpretation	The data available from both customer research, competitor research and internal systems must be analysed and the relationship management elements fed into the strategy development. Data samples used in analysis must be truly random, statistically valid.	Relationship marketing manager	Senior manager, marketing personnel, service and sales personnel, external agency
Development of clusters or segments	This takes place at a high level, to help you with strategy development. It may be taken to a more detailed level if there are large numbers of customer groupings who behave or respond very differently.	Marketing manager	Customer relationship marketing manager, consultants, marketing analysts
Developing profiling approaches based on segments	This allows you to identify prospects with the same characteristics as your (best) existing customers.	Marketing manager	Customer relationship marketing manager, consultants, marketing analysts
Modelling of relationships between customer data, own and competitive policies against economic, social and demographic data	This shows the relationship between good customer management and returns to the business and provides the basis for forecasting. This is required for many purposes, from business case development to planning individual communications.	Marketing manager	Customer relationship marketing manager, consultants, marketing analysts
2. Customer Information Strategy and Management	**Resolving All The Information Needed To Build The Customer Database And Manage Relationships With Customers**	**Leader**	**Team**
Contact audit	Audit of all points of contact between the company and its customers. Possible content and outcomes of these contacts, resulting information flows and possible opportunities for enhanced relationship or revenue building.	Relationship marketing manager	Marketing, sales, service representatives
Content analysis of in-house database	A formal analysis of the marketing database, examining the content, definitions, population, age, relevancy and assumed accuracy of the data.	Relationship marketing manager	Systems personnel, marketing representative

Technique/ Area	Detailed Description, Comment and Typical Problems or Failings	Leader	Team
Customer data audit – quantity and quality	This will examine the data available within your systems, relating to the contact audit and to data that are currently used in the dialogue between the customer/company but not captured.	Relationship marketing manager	Systems personnel, marketing representative
Data enhancement	The work carried out above may indicate a need to enhance the data held by internal systems. For instance, it may be that some (older) customer groups need to be tested, researched or may be archived. It may be that some key data fields have appeared incomplete or inaccurate but still relevant such as product purchase information, promotion information. Data can be enhanced from internal or external data sources or from specific research and data gathering exercises.	Relationship marketing manager	Systems personnel, marketing representative
Data strategy development	A strategy for the ongoing maintenance of key data must be developed showing who is responsible, what they have to do, how often and how it will be measured.	Relationship marketing manager	Marketing staff
External data overlays including geographic, social, demographic and lifestyle data sets	External data sources may be researched and obtained. These will be overlaid on current customer data (eg company financials, credit reference data for consumers) or new names may be added to the customer base.	Marketing manager	Customer relationship marketing manager, marketing personnel
Other internal sources of data which can be matched back to customers	Examples include responses to earlier promotions, customer service records and surveys.	Relationship marketing manager, then implemented by systems personnel	Systems personnel
Merging of database with those of joint venture partners, suppliers (such as suppliers of financial services), distributors etc	This has become increasingly common as companies identify non-competitive partners with whom they can jointly develop a market. Sometimes, data is pooled with competitors to identify problematic customers (eg in the insurance and credit industries).	Systems manager, once joint venture partners have been identified by the marketing department	Systems personnel

Technique/ Area	Detailed Description, Comment and Typical Problems or Failings	Leader	Team
Forecasting	Likely evolution of customer base, taking into account attrition and recruitment trends, own policies and likely competitive initiatives.	Marketing manager	Customer relationship marketing manager, consultants, marketing analysts

3. Planning and Internal Marketing	Preparing the Company for the Move to Relationship Marketing	Leader	Team
Business case development and project planning	Draws together all analyses to produce a case for changing how customers are managed. Associated investment and profit implications are assessed. A project plan to manage and monitor progress towards improved customer relationship marketing is developed.	Relationship marketing manager	Senior marketing, sales, service and financial managers, external consultants
Business case brief, development and approval	Developing the business case. It is helpful to 'quantify benefits in three classes: very likely, likely and difficult to quantify but very possible	Relationship marketing manager	Team from marketing, IT and finance usually
Budgeting worksheet development	Showing how money will be spent, on what and identification of interim benefits.	Relationship marketing manager	Team from marketing, IT and finance usually
Lobbying programmes (internal)	Internal lobbying of senior managers for business case sign off is a key task in large organizations. There are specialist techniques to be used to do this.	Relationship marketing manager	Marketing staff and external consultant
Culture development, general education and training programme development and delivery	A key task and in some companies a very long exercise. The key is in planning the programme to be a continuous series of philosophy and process reinforcement.	Training	Relationship marketing manager and delivery specialists
Paper based, video, electronic or multimedia communication development	The media selected for internal lobbying needs to be developed.	Relationship marketing manager	Marketing staff, external agencies, training dept.
Development of prototype 'system' to demonstrate key aspects of the 'new capability'	This may be necessary to convince people new to this approach, of the systems support required to manage relationships with customers.	Relationship marketing manager	Input from marketing, sales and service staff

Technique/ Area	Detailed Description, Comment and Typical Problems or Failings	Leader	Team
4. Capability Development	**Putting the Infrastructure for Relationship Management in Place**	**Leader**	**Team**
Organizational development	The relationship marketing strategy may require a very different approach to organizational structure. . . .	Senior manager	External consultants
Human resource development – recruitment and training	. . . and to recruitment and training.	Personnel manager	
Process development	Also called business or customer process re-engineering, this involves recreating the customer management process around the objectives and ideas of relationship marketing.	Relationship marketing manager, supported by IT and personnel management	Other marketing staff, supported by IT and personnel management
Development of systems strategy (eg telemarketing, database, MIS, EPOS and planning)	Arises from the strategy and data work above. The key is in planning the programme to be a continuous series of philosophy and process reinforcements. This should be developed from the relationship marketing strategy and with the customer interface at the front of your mind.	Systems manager	Relationship marketing manager, external consultants, systems analysts
Telemarketing strategy / telebusiness	May be necessary, depending on the customer relationship marketing strategy.	Senior manager	Sales, marketing, service, system and external consultant input
Database specification (eg customer, MIS, telemarketing, EPOS, campaign management)	Specification of the systems requirements will come out of the systems strategy. Note that the system for telemarketing and campaign management may be manual to start with.	Systems manager	Business input, external consultants
Pilot database development	A pilot operation for one or two key programmes may be advantageous in some organizations.	IT manager	IT manager plus relationship marketing manager
Application software, computer telephone integration (CTI) telephony package evaluation, selection and installation	Software packages may provide the best route to early delivery of all or part of the system solution. Too hasty a choice here is normally extremely expensive, so it is essential to define requirements very clearly to stand any chance of getting this right.	Relationship marketing manager	Relationship marketing manager, IT, marketing and sales personnel, external consultant

Technique/ Area	Detailed Description, Comment and Typical Problems or Failings	Leader	Team
Main database development	A very systems intensive task, although this may be contracted to a bureau.	IT manager	IT, bureaux
Database operation	Given the high volumes of data, some of it of poor quality, this task should be left to skilled professionals.	Senior IT manager	IT or bureaux
Monitoring of database activity and data quality	Ensuring that data quality standards are being met. The responsible manager must have the authority to tell managers what is happening. The IT people cannot be responsible for data quality, they just monitor it and report anomalies.	IT manager	Marketing and sales managers
Data processing (eg merge, purge, de-dupe)	Ensuring that duplicate or incorrect records are deleted or corrected.	Marketing manager	Bureaux
Training (customer service, telemarketing strategy, direct marketing)	Ensuring that all customer interface staff are trained to handle the customers and the systems and processes that have been put into place to help them do so.	Training manager	Marketing, sales, service and relationship marketing manager
Selecting suppliers (eg agencies, bureaux)	In most cases, companies – particularly those who are new to relationship marketing – will require considerable external support. Eventually, they will be able to do much more themselves as they learn from their suppliers.	Relationship marketing, advertising, direct marketing and IT managers	Various, external consultants
Change management	The process of moving towards the new way of working needs to be managed properly at the human and technical level.	Senior manager	All functions affected
5. Programme Development	**Development of Particular Programmes for Managing or Contacting Customers**	**Leader**	**Team**
Media planning and use	Nearly all marketing communications media are used in relationship marketing, including direct mail, telephone and the direct sales team. Many different marketing communication disciplines are also involved, eg point of sale, PR, advertising and so on. The key is to ensure an integrated approach.	Advertising and direct marketing management	Agencies
Customer targeting	Detailed analysis of database to identify which groups of customers are appropriate targets for particular initiatives.	Relationship marketing manager	

Technique/ Area	Detailed Description, Comment and Typical Problems or Failings	Leader	Team
Campaign planning, co-ordination and scheduling	Campaign objectives, strategies and timings need to be set to maximize effectiveness and minimize overlap.	Relationship marketing manager	All managers responsible for particular media, groups of customers etc
Test matrix development	Where testable media are used, given the cost of communicating with large numbers of customers, campaigns should be evaluated wherever possible.	Direct marketing management	IT staff, agencies
Creative strategy development	This applies particularly to print and broadcast media but also to the telephone. It is heavily influenced by the brand.	Agencies, marketing director	Relationship marketing, advertising and direct marketing managers provide feedback

6. Imple- mentation	Implementing Programmes for Managing or Contacting Customers	Leader	Team
Project/ campaign management of programmes	Checking that campaigns are running to schedule and, if not, chasing.	Relationship marketing manager	Advertising and direct marketing managers
Briefing suppliers (eg agencies, bureaux, mail houses)	Suppliers need to be properly briefed about their role in each campaign, in time.	Advertising and direct marketing management	Relationship marketing manager, agencies
Telemarketing script development	Given the high costs of contact, it is critical that the script be optimized to get the highest quality, right information in the shortest time that is consistent with customer service objectives.	Relationship marketing manager	Telemarketing agency
Actually managing marketing campaigns	For example coding, sending packs out, making calls, handling responses.	Relationship marketing manager	
Lead management	Ensuring that the right transactions and information flows are taking place at the point of contact with the customer. Lead data and feedback is chased and updated on the system.	Relationship marketing manager	Agencies, customer-facing staff and their managers
Account management of suppliers	Ensuring suppliers' part of the programme is running smoothly, properly communicated to the client and any problems resolved.	Suppliers	

Technique/ Area	Detailed Description, Comment and Typical Problems or Failings	Leader	Team
Interpretation and analysis of programmes	Identifying what has worked and not worked and any process/ people/ policy programmes.	Relationship marketing manager	All marketing management

Appendix 2

C-View 02©: Your customer relationship marketing audit tool

C-VIEW 02 ©:NATURE OF THE PROGRAM

C-View 02 © is an introductory audit tool for organizations contemplating the purchase and implementation of a customer relationship marketing exercise or for organizations wishing to assess their current relationship management position.

An initial audit or assessment is an essential start point for any exercise of this kind. It performs the following roles:

- identifies 'pressure points' in existing relationship platforms;
- acts as a basis for a requirements specification;
- forms the basis of return on investment (ROI) and benefit calculations;
- provides a continuous measure of progress as the exercise is implemented;
- offers a possible benchmarking tool against selected enterprises (where these are also running this software):
  - by industry sector;
  - by region;
  - by business unit (department or division).

THE C-VIEW 02 © SOFTWARE:
STRUCTURE OF THE PROGRAM

LEVELS

The software is available at three levels.

Level I   Supplied with this book. The program looks at eight areas with about 100 questions

Level II   Considers 15 areas with about 162 questions. A level II assessment and above may also be used as part of the ViewConsult Europe database for benchmarking purposes. It may be used by managers directly or with consulting support.

Level III   A fully comprehensive assessment over some 30 areas of activity and about 270 questions. Usually undertaken with consultancy support for report writing and interpretation.

Areas

Area	Abbreviation	Area	Abbreviation
Business definition	Bd	Client management	Cm
Planning & strategy	Ps	Technology	
Customer knowledge	Ck	management	Tm
Organization	Og	Project management	Pm
Channels &			
intermediaries	Ci		

OUTPUTS

There are two forms of output. The first is a detailed written report that records your answers to the questions in the program, with a record of the evidence or support that you have provided to justify your answer. This also provides detailed scores. The written report:

- Provides a detailed report by area of activity and section.
- Is based on *evidence*. You are not supposed to make the answers up! Be as honest as you can about your own position. Use the evidence

box in the answers section as a way of 'proving' your answer. Managers tend to overestimate their corporate capabilities. If you believe that you have a clearly developed retention strategy, describing fully which customers you seek to retain and which you do not, your evidence would take the form of a policy document, a procedure or a report from the marketing department. Staff should understand and be able to describe this policy if asked.

- Includes importance and effectiveness measures. You decide what is important to your company. This is not a one size fits all exercise. Different areas are of varying importance to different organizations.
- Acts as the basis of a guide for action. It will tell you how effective you are at the things which you, the manager, consider to be important.

Leadership and management focus can then be concentrated on the right areas.

The second output is a graphic report which allows you to assess tactically and strategically what your management response should be. An output from the graphic report is illustrated in Figure A2.1.

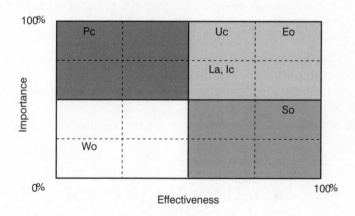

Figure A2.1 Customer management positioning

HOW IT WORKS

The graphic report illustrates four quadrants which we like to call, attain, sustain, maintain and restrain. They are illustrated in the table overleaf.

Attain	Sustain
These are important areas at which you are currently not very effective. Resources and attention need to be increased here to move them into the sustain box.	These are important areas for your company and you are good at them.
Maintain	**Restrain**
Not very important and areas where you are not particularly strong. Just keep an eye on these.	These are not important areas but you are very good at them. You should think about reducing resource levels here and transferring them to activities in the top-left quadrant.

SUMMARY OF MAIN FEATURES

- It is an internal assessment.
- Based on management's own views.
- Relates performance to the individual focus of your business.
- You use your own assessments of importance and effectiveness.
- Requires *evidence* of each stage.
- Can be updated and rerun as a progress monitor.
- Takes about four to six hours.
- Does not require a consultancy presence.
- Allows internal benchmarking capabilities, even between business units in the same enterprise.
- Requires minimal training, for a manager who understands CRM principles.

INSTALLATION AND USAGE

Copy the software onto your own computer into a directory of your own choosing and double-click the C-View 02 icon. The software will autorun. After the splash screen you may enter details of yourself and your company. These fields are all compulsory. The software will not proceed if you leave a blank section here.

On the main data collection screen, the areas of interest are displayed in the left-hand window. Question abbreviations are shown in the right-hand window. Double-click an area on the left to answer that section. For each question, double-click a response choice and type details of your evidence into the note box.

You may go back and alter any entry in the program at any time. You may also run reports as often as you like.

DISCLAIMER

The C-View 02 software provided with this book is intended for the sole, personal use of the owner of this book only. The authors make no claims or representations for the software. If you choose to install it on any computer you do so entirely at your own risk. The authors offer no warranty or guarantee in respect of the software or the media on which it is supplied and disclaim any responsibility for its use or the effects of its use on any computing device. It is expected that in line with normal good practice, users of this software will protect their computers with up to date virus checking tools.

COPYRIGHT NOTICE

The C-View 02 software engine is the copyright of ViewConsult Europe Ltd and Paul R Gamble. The questions are the copyright of Paul R Gamble and Merlin Stone. This software and its contents may not be reproduced in any form, sold or given to any person or organization without the prior permission of the copyright holders. The owner of this book may make personal use of one copy of this software on one computer that he or she owns. If it is desired to transfer the software to another machine owned by the owner of this book, any other copy of this software must be completely deleted from the first machine on which it was installed.

TECHNICAL NOTE

The C-View 02 software provided with this book is designed to run under Windows XP in the presence of Microsoft® Office XP™. The database program Microsoft ® Access 2002 must be present on your computer as part of your Office XP suite if the software is to run. An alternative version for Windows 2000 is provided but it must be noted that the ideal environment is intended to be XP.

References

Anderson, J C and Narus, J A (1998) Business marketing: understand what customers value, *Harvard Business Review*, **76** (6), Nov/Dec, pp 53–65

Assael, H (1987) *Consumer Behaviour and Marketing Action*, Kent, Boston

Bartlett, C and Ghoshal, S (1995) Changing the role of top management: beyond systems to people, *Harvard Business Review*, May/June, pp 132–142

Bensman, J (1983) *Dollars and Sense: Ideology, ethics and the meaning of work in profit and non-profit organisations*, Schocken Books, New York

Berry, J and Leventhal, B (1996) The development of a market-wide segmentation system for the UK consumer financial services industry, *Journal of Targeting, Measurement and Analysis for Marketing*, **3** (2), pp 111–124

Berry, L L (1983) Relationship marketing, in *Emerging Perspectives on Services Marketing*, eds L L Berry *et al*, pp 25–28, American Marketing Association, Chicago

Berry, S and Britney, K (1996) Market segmentation: key to growth in small business banking, *Bank Management*, **72** (1), pp 36–41

Braganza, A and Myers, A (1996) Issues and dilemmas facing organisations in the effective implementation of BPR, *Business Change and Re-engineering*, **3** (2), pp 38–51

Butscher, S (1998) *Managing Customer Clubs*, Gower, Aldershot

Chang, S (1998) Cutting-edge Internet database marketing to the Pacific Rim region, *Journal of Database Marketing*, **5** (3), pp 255–266

Clark, M and Payne, A (1994) Achieving long-term customer loyalty: a strategic approach, *Marketing: Unity in Diversity*, (MEG Conference Proceedings), pp 169–178

Computer Weekly (1996) Dataview, *Computer Weekly*, 18 April, p 1

Copulsky, J R and Wolf, M J (1990) Relationship marketing: positioning for the future, *Journal of Business Strategy*, July/August, pp 16–20

Craig, S (1990) How to enhance customer connections, *Journal of Business Strategy*, July/August, pp 22–26

Crook, J (1997) Application credit scoring: an overview, *Journal of Financial Services Marketing*, **2** (2), pp 152–174

Darby, I (1997) Banking on a sure thing: the Virgin Direct case study, *Marketing Direct*, June, pp 30–31

Davenport, T H and Prusak, L (1998) *Working Knowledge: How organisations manage what they know*, Harvard Business School Press, Boston

Day, J, Dean, A and Reynolds, P (1998) Relationship marketing: its key role in entrepreneurship, *Long Range Planning*, **31** (6), pp 828–837

de Chernatony, L and MacDonald, M H (1992) *Creating Powerful Brands*, Butterworth Heinemann, Oxford

Dichter, S S, Gagnon, C and Alexander, A (1993) Memo to a CEO subject: 'Leading organisational transformations', *McKinsey Quarterly Review*, Spring, New York

Drucker, P (1998) The discipline of innovation, *Harvard Business Review*, **76** (6), Nov/Dec, pp 149–157

Earl, M, Cross, J and Sampler, J (1993) Experiences in strategic information systems planning, *MIS Quarterly*, **17** (1), pp 1–25

Edouard, N and White, W (1999) *The Development of the Internet and the Growth of e-Commerce*, MCA, London

Evans, M *et al* (1998) Consumer reactions to database-based supermarket loyalty schemes, *Journal of Database Marketing*, **4** (4), pp 307–320

Evans, M, O'Malley, L and Patterson, M (1996) Direct mail and consumer response: an empirical study of consumer experiences of direct mail, *Journal of Database Marketing*, **3** (3), pp 250–262

Fay, C J (1994) Royalties from loyalties, *Journal of Business Strategy*, **3** (3), pp 47–51

Fletcher, K, Wright, G and Desai, C (1996) Customer information files: database marketing in the financial services industry, *Journal of Database Marketing*, **3** (3), pp 223–236

Fournier, S, Dobscha, S and Mick, D G (1998) Preventing the premature death of relationship marketing, *Harvard Business Review*, **76** (1), Jan/Feb, pp 42–50

Gandy, A (1999) *Understanding Customer Relationship Marketing: Special report*, Chartered Institute of Bankers, London

Gaskill, S (1996) A review of the data protection registrar guidance note for direct marketers, *Journal of Database Marketing*, **3** (3), pp 263–267

Gibson, R, Toffler, A and Toffler, H (1999) *Rethinking the Future*, Nicholas Brealey, London

Gofton, K and Cobb, R (1996) *Marketing*, Supplement on Direct Marketing Association/Royal Mail Direct Marketing Awards, December, p 14

Gofton, K (1996a) IPA advertising effectiveness awards, *Marketing*, p 18

Gofton, K (1996b) In pursuit of mutuality, *Marketing*, 26/9/96, Sales Promotion Supplement, p III

Goodstein, L D, Butz, H E (1998) Customer value: the linchpin of organisational change, *Organisational Dynamics*, **27** (1), pp 21–38

Greengard, S (1998) How to make knowledge management a reality, *Workforce*, **77** (10), pp 90–92

Grönroos, C (1985) Internal marketing: theory and practice, in *Services Marketing in a Changing Environment*, eds T M Bloch *et al*, American Marketing Association, Chicago

Grönroos, C (1990) Relationship approach to marketing in service contexts: the marketing and organisational behaviour interface, *Journal of Business Research*, **20**, Jan, pp 3–11

Grönroos, C (1993) From marketing mix to relationship marketing: towards a paradigm shift in marketing, *Management Decision*, **32** (2), pp 4–20

Hagel, J and Armstrong, A G (1997) *Net Gain: Expanding markets through virtual communities*, Harvard Business School Press, Boston

Hamel, G and Prahalad, C K (1994) *Competing for the Future*, Harvard Business School Press, Boston

Hammer, M and Champy, J (1993) *Reengineering the Corporation: A manifesto for business revolution*, Brealey, London

Hansen, M T, Nohria, N and Tierney, T (1999) What's your strategy for managing knowledge, *Harvard Business Review*, **77** (2), March/April, pp 106–116

Harsanyi, J (1967) Games with incomplete information played by Bayesian players, parts I, II and III, *Management Science*, **14**, pp 159–182, 320–334, 486–502

Hedlund, G and Nonaka, I (1993) Models of knowledge management in the West and Japan, in *Implementing Strategic Processes: Change, learning and co-operation*, eds P Lorange *et al*, pp 117–144, Blackwell, Oxford

Henley Centre (1994), The loyalty paradox, *Research Report*, Henley Centre, UK

Hertzler, J O (1934) On golden rule, *Ethics*, **44**, pp 418–436

Homans, G C (1951) *The Human Group*, Kegan Paul, London

IBM (1998) *Web Site Survey: Consumer packaged goods*, IBM Distribution Industry Solution Unit (EMEA), March

Johnson, C A (1994) Winning back customers through database marketing, *Direct Marketing*, **57** (7), November, pp 36–37

Jones, G (1997) Breaking up the market, *Post Magazine and Insurance Week*, 12 June, p 27

Kapferer, J N (1992) *Strategic Brand Management*, Kogan Page, London

Kaplan, R and Norton, D P (1996) *The Balanced Scorecard*, Harvard School Press, Boston, MA

Kogut, B and Zander, U (1992) Knowledge of the firm, combinative capabilities, and the replication of technology, *Organisation Science*, **3** (3), pp 383–397

Kotler, P (1997) *Marketing Management: Analysis, planning and control*, 9th edn, Prentice-Hall, London

Kotler, P (2003) *Marketing Management*, 11th edn, Prentice-Hall, London

Kreitner, R and Kinicki, A (1992) *Organisational Behaviour*, Irwin, Homewood, IL

Lavinsky, D (1997) Customer segmentation key to utility success, *Electric Light and Power*, **75** (12), p 13

Lewis, D (1998) Information overload, in *Forward to Reuters 1998*, Reuters Inc

Long, G, Angold, S and Hogg, M (1998) Data, privacy and relationship marketing: a conundrum, *Journal of Database Marketing*, **5** (3), pp 231–244

Madhavan, R and Grover, R (1998) From embedded knowledge to embodied knowledge: new product development as knowledge management, *Journal of Marketing*, **62** (4), pp 1–12

Martin, C (1999) *net future*, McGraw-Hill, New York

Matthyssens, P and Van den Bulte, C (1994) Getting closer and nicer: partnerships in the supply chain, *Long Range Planning*, **27** (1), February, pp 72–83

McCann, D (1999) The customer continuum, *Management Accounting* (Jan), pp 38–39

McChesney, M (1998) New kids put net banking on the block, *Computer Weekly*, 16 November, p 6

Meyers P W and Wilemon D L (1989) Learning in New Technology Development Teams *Journal of Product Innovation*, **6** (2) pp 79–88

Michelsen, M W (1999) Turning complaints into cash, *American Salesman*, **44** (3), pp 6–10

Miller, D (1986) Configurations of strategy and structure: towards a synthesis, *Strategic Management Journal*, **7**, pp 233–249

Miller, D (1990) *The Icarus Paradox: How excellent organizations can bring about their own downfall*, Harper, New York

Mintzberg, H, Raisinghani, D and Théoret, A (1976) The structure of unstructured decision processes, *Administrative Science Quarterly*, **21**, pp 246–275

Murphy, J and Suntook, F (1998) The relationship between customer loyalty and customer satisfaction, *FT Mastering Management Series*, April

Narver, J C and Slater, S F (1990) The effect of a market orientation on business profitability, *Journal of Marketing*, October

Nelson, R R and Winter, S G (1982) *An Evolutionary Theory of Economic Change*, Beiknap, Cambridge, MA

Newman, B (1980) Consumer Protection is Underdeveloped in the Third World, *Wall St Journal* 8 April p 1/23

Nonaka, I (1990) Redundant, overlapping organisation: a Japanese approach to managing the innovation process, *California Management Review*, **32** (3), pp 27–38

Palmer, A (1994) *Principles in Service Marketing*, McGraw-Hill, London

Patel, V L, Kaufman, D R and Arocha, J F (1995) Steering through the murky waters of a scientific conflict: situated and symbolic models of clinical cognition, *Artificial Intelligence in Medicine*, **7** (5), pp 413–38

Peppers, D and Rogers, M (1998) A reply to Fournier, Dobscha and Mick (readers' reaction), *Harvard Business Review*, **76** (3), May/June, p 178

Peppers, D and Rogers, M (1997) *Enterprise One to One: Tools for competing in the interactive age*, Doubleday, New York

Peppers, D and Rogers, M (1994) The only business to be in is the business of keeping customers, *Marketing News*, **28** (3), p 6

Peppers, D and Rogers, M (1999) *The One to One Fieldbook: The complete toolkit for implementing a 1to 1 marketing program*, Bantam Doubleday Dell, New York

Polanyi, M (1967) *The Tacit Dimension*, Doubleday, New York

Rasmusen, E (1990) *Games and Information: An introduction to game theory*, Blackwell, Cambridge, MA

Rayport, J F and Sviolka, J J (1995) Exploiting the virtual value chain, *Harvard Business Review*, Nov/Dec, pp 75–85

Reichheld, F F and Kenny, D W (1990) The hidden advantages of customer retention, *Journal of Retail Banking*, **XII** (4)

Reichheld, F F and Sasser, W E (1990) Zero defections quality comes to services, *Harvard Business Review*, Sept/Oct, pp 301–307

Robinson, P J, Faris, C W and Wind, Y (1967) *Industrial Buying and Creative Marketing*, Allyn and Bacon, Boston

Saunders, J (1997) Distribution, innovation and the consumer, in Financial Services: Motivating Consumers, *Admap*, May, pp 22–25

Saxton, J (1996) A model for strategic decision making in database marketing, *Journal of Database Marketing*, **3** (3), pp 237–249

Schroeder, D (1992) Life, liberty and the pursuit of privacy, *American Demographics*, June, p 20

Schlesinger, L A and Heskett, J L (1991) Breaking the cycle of failures in services management, *Sloan Management Review*, **32** (3), pp 17–18

Slater, S F and Narver, J C (1998) Customer led and market oriented: let's not confuse the two, *Strategic Management Journal*, **19** (10), pp 1001–1006

Smith, N C (1990) *Morality and the Market: Consumer pressure for corporate accountability*, Routledge, New York

Stevenson, W B and Gilly, M C (1991) Information processing and problem solving: the migration of problems through formal positions and networks of ties, *Academy of Management Journal*, **34** (4), pp 918–928

Stone, M, Findlay, G, Evans, M and Leonard, M (2001) Data chaos: a court case waiting to happen, *International Journal of Customer Relationship Management* **4** (2), pp 169–84

Stone, M, Woodcock, N and Wilson, M (1996) Managing the change from marketing planning to relationship management, *Long Range Planning*, **29** (5), pp 675–683

Strategy (1999) Keeping your customers, *The Strategic Planning Society*, March, p 3

Sweeney, D M (1998) Global market trends in the networked era, *Long Range Planning*, **31** (5), pp 672–683

Tabrizi, B and Walleigh, R (1997) Defining next generation products: an inside look, *Harvard Business Review*, Nov/Dec, pp 116–124

Thompson, H and Stone, M (1997) Customer value management, *Close to the Customer Briefing*, **1**, Policy Publications, London

Wall Street Journal (1996), Road warrior, 18 November, R27

Waterman, R H, Peters, T J and Phillips, J R (1980) Structure is not organisation, *Business Horizons*, June

Woudhuysen, J (1994) Tailoring IT to the needs of customers, *Long Range Planning*, **27** (3) pp 33–42

Ziethaml, V A, Berry, L L and Parasuranam, A (1988) Communication and control processes in the delivery of service quality, *Journal of Marketing*, **52**, April, pp 35–48

Index

More Essential CRM titles from Kogan Page

the
CUSTOMER
MANAGEMENT
scorecard
MANAGING CRM FOR PROFIT

neil woodcock · merlin stone · bryan foss

IBM®   QCi   OgilvyOne

THE CUSTOMER MANAGEMENT SCORECARD
MANAGING CRM FOR PROFIT

NEIL WOODCOCK, MERLIN STONE & BRYAN FOSS

'This is the book that tells organizations in every sector, all over the world,
what they need to do to measure how well they manage their customers,
and then improve it. It is the only book of its kind that is based on truly
global, independent, research.'

Gareth James, President, Sales & Marketing Europe, Cable & Wireless

The Customer Management Assessment Tool (CMAT) is a unique diagnostic tool developed by QCi which forms the global standard for
assessing how well organizations manage their customers. This book
draws on the results of research that applied CMAT to over 300 leading
companies around the world and across a variety of sectors. In so doing
the authors are able to demonstrate how to make CRM initiatives profitable, achieve a 50 per cent increase in turnover and a 400 per cent return
on investment from well-managed CRM.

£39.95   hardback   448 pages   246 × 189mm   0 7494 3895 9

CRM IN FINANCIAL SERVICES
A PRACTICAL GUIDE TO MAKING CUSTOMER RELATIONSHIP
MANAGEMENT WORK

BRYAN FOSS AND MERLIN STONE

'Merlin [Stone] gets under the skin of CRM issues in financial services, drawing together strong examples of best practice. Essential reading for companies who want to get it right, this book dispels the CRM myth that one size fits all. If you think you know it all, read on, think again.'

Ray Perry, Chief Executive, E Centre, and Director of Corporate Marketing, Chartered Institute of Marketing

The first book devoted exclusively to showing how organizations in this sector can improve their CRM and achieve their desired return on investment. Based on extensive global consulting and research, and packed with illuminating international case studies and examples, the book analyses the state current state of CRM and e-business in the financial sector and then provides comprehensive and practical guidance on both strategy and implementation.

£60.00   hardback   720 pages   246 × 189mm   0 7494 3696 4

THE CRM PROJECT MANAGEMENT HANDBOOK
BUILDING REALISTIC EXPECTATIONS AND MANAGING RISK

MICHAEL GENTLE

'This book is not a glossy tome that prescribes a dry, off-the-shelf formula through CRM rose-tinted glasses. It is a guide to the CRM jungle – giving advice based on experience – read this before your next CRM steering committee meeting!'

Howard Hughes, Senior Consultant, Ciberion CRM Solutions, London

CRM project failure rates run as high as 80 per cent, so how do you plan and implement a project that delivers tangible results? This groundbreaking book emphasises a back-to-basics approach that stresses measurable goals and tactical, rather than strategic, uses of CRM. It identifies the common stumbling blocks that face every project, and proposes practical solutions to get round them. An experienced CRM project manager, Michael Gentle outlines critical success and risk factors, and features a range of case studies (both successes and failures) and a 40-question risk analysis.

£22.50   paperback   240 pages   234 × 153mm   0 7494 3898 3

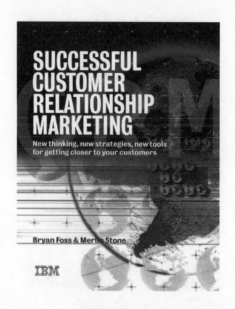

SUCCESSFUL CUSTOMER RELATIONSHIP MARKETING
NEW THINKING, NEW STRATEGIES, NEW TOOLS FOR GETTING CLOSER TO YOUR CUSTOMERS

BRYAN FOSS AND MERLIN STONE

'This book provides a practical guide to gaining return-on-investment from CRM, highlighting the requirements to develop from prescriptive marketing to a real understanding and development of the customer experience.'

Nigel Howlett, Chairman, OgilvyOne

Successful Customer Relationship Marketing is probably the most in-depth and detailed book ever published on the subject of CRM. It is based on an extensive global research programme, led by Merlin Stone, into the CRM activities of organizations from a range of sectors such as travel, utilities, retail and telecommunications. The results tell you everything you need to know about how to profitably integrate a CRM policy into your overall business strategy.

£35.00   hardback   544 pages   246 × 189mm   0 7494 3579 8

CUSTOMER RELATIONSHIP MARKETING
GET TO KNOW YOUR CUSTOMERS AND WIN THEIR LOYALTY

MERLIN STONE, NEIL WOODCOCK AND LIZ MACHTYNGER

In a world where best practice in e-business is beginning to emerge, this book can now be considered the best practical introduction to customer relationship marketing.

Most companies are still having problems getting to grips with implementing the more classic methods of relationship marketing, such as using the mail and telephone, as well as other methods of managing customers. Stone, Woodcock and Machtynger offer solid, practical and accessible advice on how to move on and make the most of the technology and methodology now available to businesses large and small.

Taking into account new global research and practice that has been carried out by QCi, IBM and Mummert + Partner in the area of e-commerce, the following areas are examined:

- the role of market research;
- customer retention and loyalty;
- integrating CRM strategies;
- people and performance;
- the future of e-CRM.

£14.99   paperback   240 pages   234 × 153mm   0 7494 2700 0

All titles are available from good bookshops

For further information, please contact the publisher at the following address:

Kogan Page Limited
120 Pentonville Road
London N1 9JN

Tel: (020) 7278 0433
Fax: (020) 7837 6348

www.kogan-page.co.uk

**KOGAN
PAGE**